AF530211

DIGITAL LIBRARIES AND DIGITIZATION

DIGITAL LIBRARIES AND DIGITIZATION

Gurdev Singh
M.A. (Economics); MLISc; Ph.D. (DU)
Librarian, Sri Guru Gobind Singh College of Commerce
University of Delhi, Pitampura, Delhi-34

Ess Ess Publications
New Delhi

Digital Libraries and Digitization

ISBN: 978-81-7000-650-3

Rs.1800/-

First Published 2011

Published by:
Ess Ess Publications
4837/24, Ansari Road,
Darya Ganj,
New Delhi-110 002.
INDIA
Phones: 23260807, 41563444
Fax: 41563334
E-mail: info@essessreference.com
www.essessreference.com

Cover Design by *Patch Creative Unit*

Printed and bound in India at Salasar Imaging Systems.

Contents

Preface

Digital technology is contributing to almost every area such as information, entertainment and education. With the advent of new technologies in the field of information technology and telecommunication, considerable changes have also taken place in the field of library and Information Science. The recent development in communication technology, networking, use of internet and electronic resources has brought revolutionary changes in the dissemination of information process.

Information and communication technologies have transformed the way information is generated, preserved, archived and made accessible. With the development of modern information technology, the concept of library has changed. Now more and more libraries are being transferred into digital libraries. One of the most important developments in the field of Library and Information Science is digitization of library material. There is paradigm shift from hard copy to soft copy, print to digital, ownership of documents to access of information, traditional to digital libraries. The development in information technology has changed the concept of traditional library.

Digital library is nothing but the computing terminals which have linkage to various sources of information in electronic or digital form. Digital libraries are organized collection of information stored on digital media such as CD-ROMs, online and networked database. Digital library is a library which has numbers of machine readable publications such as e-journals, e-books, etc. Digital resources have now become an important part of library resources.

These developments have led to the creation of digital and virtual libraries. A digital library is one which collect, store and disseminates digital information.

User demand is ever increasing and changing at the rapid pace. To satisfy the information needs of the users are the main objective of a modern library. It cannot be achieved without adopting the modern tools and techniques. Therefore, there is an urgent need of modernization of libraries. Modern libraries are not only digitized but networked also. A modern library is a group of interlinked servers and workstations, which are connected to each other through high speed networks.

The digital libraries have great advantages over traditional libraries. Digital libraries require very little space. The transition to electronic form essentially eliminates the space problem. Today, students, researchers, information professionals etc. can directly access many of the rarest information of the world with high quality images. Digital libraries have potential to store much more information. Digital libraries provide faster access to information; also help to perform searches that are manually not possible. The purpose of digital library is to provide convenient access to large amount of digital information. The users of digital libraries need not go to the library physically. One can access information anytime from anywhere, from office, home or any other location. Digital libraries provide better retrieval and faster communication. Information is available 24 hours a day and 7 days a week. Digital library can store a large volume of digital information in archival form.

Digital libraries are completely paperless system which allows remote access of its resources to other libraries by breaking down physical boundaries through national and international network. Digital libraries provide an easy mechanism for resource sharing with other libraries. Digital libraries have the ability to enable world wide access to never ending supply of distributed information. The new challenges in the field of Library and Information Science can be met by adopting the process of digitization and networking. The basic role of digital library is to provide right information to the right user at the right time. There is a need of sharing of resources globally in order to provide right information to the right user at the right time. Thus, Digital libraries provide an easy mechanism for resource sharing. Digital library plays an important role in this regard.

This book is significant in many ways. This book covered the various aspects of digital library and digitization. It gives a wide range of information on various aspects of digital library and digitization such as digital library resources and services, e-publishing etc.

It is hoped that this book would be very useful for the library professionals and for those who would like to do some work on digitization.

While writing this book I have taken some help from some learned authors. For them I am very thankful and grateful. I am also very thankful to the authors cited in the text.

At the end I am also thankful to Shri Sumit Sethi, the Publisher and owner of the Ess Ess Publications for publishing this book.

Reader's view, comments, and criticism related to the present work are most welcome.

Delhi **Dr. Gurdev Singh**
13.04.2011 (Vaishakhi)

Abbreviations

ASCII	American Standard Code For Information Interchange
CAS	Current Awareness Service
CCD	Charge Coupled Device
CD-RW	Compact Disk Rewritable
CGI	Common Gateway Interface
DC	Dublin Core
DES	Data Ercription Standard
DLF	Digital Library Federation
DLI	Digital Library Initiatives
DOI	Digital Object Identifier
DVD	Digital Versatile Disk
EAD	Encoded Archival Description
EDDS	Electronic Document Delivery Service
FTP	File Transfer Protocol
HTML	Hypertext Markup Language
HTTP	Hypertext Transfer Protocol
ILL	Inter Library Lending
IPR	Intellectual Property Right

IRC	Internet Rely Chat
ISBN	International Standard Book Number
LAN	Local Area Network
MARC	Machine Readable Cataloguing
MIT	Massachusetts Institute of Technology
OCLC	Online Computer Library System
OCR	Optical Character Recognition
ODA	Online Data Access
OPAC	Online Public Access Catalogue
OSS	Open Source Software
RAP	Repository Access Protocol
RDF	Resource Description Framework
TCP/IP	Transmission Control Protocol/ Internet Protocol
TEI	Text Encoding Initiative
TIFF	Tagged Image File Formet
TIFF	Tag Image File Format
URI	Uniform Resources Indicator
URL	Uniform Resource Locator
WAN	Wide Area Network
WSC	Word Wide Web Consortium
XLC	Extensible Style Language
XML	Extensible Markup Language

1

Introduction to Digital Libraries

INTRODUCTION

The recent development in information technology has changed the concept of library. One of the most important developments in the library field is digitization of library material. Digital libraries have received wide attention in the recent years allowing access to digital information from anywhere across the world. The dramatic innovation in information and communication technology has emerged which have created a truly global environment for information exchange. The development has imposed certain responsibilities and challenges to library and information professionals. This dramatic revolution in IT especially in digital storage media, the user community is getting more advantages through the electronic media/electronic resources better than conventional method of information system. The concept has brought a phenomenal change in the information collection, preservation and dissemination of information.

We use the term digital library to describe the situation

where the documents are stored in an electronic form rather than on paper. The term digital library is being used to characterize a large storehouse of digital information accessible through computer because it can be stored in many forms. It may be text, sound, graphics, images, etc. Digital libraries are electronic libraries in which large number of geographically distributed users can access the contents of large and diverse repositories of electronic objects, networked text, images, maps, sounds, videos, catalogs of merchandise, scientific, business and government data sets and they also include hypertext, hypermedia and multimedia components.

The digital resources are the information existing in the form, which the computer can store, organize, transmit and display without any intervening conversion process. A digital library is understood to have the information stored predominantly in an electronic or digital medium. We can say digital library basically store materials in electronic format. The digital library consisting of information in digital, analog and digitize form. The analog materials are information in any format (print, microfilm, video, sound recording etc.), which requires an intervening conversion process before a computer can store, organized, transmit, or display the information. Information in digital libraries is electronically stored and accessed. Access to the digital library is, therefore, not bound by space or time. The digital libraries have the ability to enable worldwide access to a never-ending supply of distributed information, which is constantly and conveniently available and updateable.

Digital libraries are organized collections of information stored in digital media whose structure resembles to a traditional library which provide a large set of materials and services. In the recent years, the use of the digital libraries has tremendously increased as an advantageous alternative to specialized sites on the web.

Digital libraries are appearing all around the world. Universities, publishers, government agencies, and public libraries manage digital libraries. Some of the companies are shifting to use them for records and reports as well as for customer access. The digital revolution has affected nearly every aspect of library services, from automation of library activities to digitization of physical collection. Digital technology connects more people to the resources and services those only libraries and information centers can provide.

The knowledge dissemination is an integral part of success story of popularity of creating digital libraries. The aim is to provide universal access to human knowledge and given the advancement of digital storage and communications this goal is now achievable.

Digital libraries were evolved through a cycle of fast technological developments in order to cater to the information needs of the users efficiently.

The digital information collection may include digital books, digital scanned images, graphics, textual and numeric data, digitized films to be the most useful one. A digital library maintains all, or a substantial/part, of its collection in computer form as an alternative, supplement, or compliment to the conventional printed and microfilmed materials that currently dominate library collection.

A digital library is an electronic collection of real or virtual resources, which may also be available elsewhere. These resources must be whole work, with which human can have a complete cognitive or affective engagement. A digital may allow either online or offline access to the elements it organizes and houses, and may multimedia as well as multilingual data.

Digital library is a system, which has various service and information object to support users who need the information object. The digital libraries basically store materials in electronic format and manipulate large collection of those reading materials effectively. The key technological issues are how to search and display desired selections from and across large collections.

The information object can still be a book or paper, but the metadata is formatted electronically which can be accessed through digital devices. Digital library feature is integration of LONTAR digital library into e-learning system, SCELE. By using this feature, users can search documents in the library.

Sun Microsystems defines a digital library as the electronic extension of functions users typically perform and the resources they access in a traditional library. These information resources can be translated into digital form, stored in multimedia repositories, and made available through web-based services. There are many different kinds of digital libraries creating, delivering and preserving digital objects that derive from many different formats of underlying data, and it is very difficult to formulate a definition that encapsulates all these.

WHAT IS A DIGITAL LIBRARY?

Definitions of Digital Library

The term digital library is being used to characterize a large storehouse of digital information accessible through computer because it can be stored in many forms. It may be sound, text, graphics etc. Digital library has received wide attention in the recent years.

In digital library, information is digitized, collected, operated by electronic computers, transmitted by the computer network, and freely shared. In this way, required information can be easily and efficiently retrieved and disseminated.

Some of the definitions given by different authors are given below:

There is no universally accepted definition of digital library. Different authors define it differently. The term digital library, electronic library and virtual library are used synonymously to denote the same concept. All these are being used to communicate same connotation and concept.

1. **Larson** defines digital libraries a "global virtual library -the library of thousands of networked electronic libraries."

   He defined digital libraries as "no single stand-alone, repositories of digital data. Instead they are a heterogeneous collection of network based repositories using a variety of protocols for users (and repository) interaction, data encoding and transmission."

2. **Association of Research Libraries (ARL)** define digital libraries as "not a single entity, requires technology to link the recourses of many, linkages transparent to the user, permit universal access, not limited to document surrogates but extend to the digital artifact."

3. Digital library is a logical extension of the networked environment and the development triggered thereof and provides users with coherent access to a very rare, organized repository of information and knowledge. In a sense it is a global virtual library-The library of thousands of networked electronic libraries/ databases.

4. The **American Digital Library Federation** has defined the digital library as" Digital libraries are organization that provide the recourses, including the specialized staff, to select, structure, offer intellectual access to, interpret, distribute, preserve the integrity of, and ensure the persistence over time of collection of

digital works so that they are readily and economically available for use by a defined community or set of communities."

On the basis of the above definition Cleveland (1998) gave some of its chrematistics. One of the characteristic is "Digital libraries are and include electronic (digital) as well as print and other (e.g. Film, sound) materials."

This is full and a good working definition because it is broad enough to comprehend other use of the term.

5. According to **Lesk** a digital library is "a collection of information that is both digitized and organized and which offers capability beyond those of the traditional library."

   Digital libraries are the digital face of traditional libraries that includes both digital collections and traditional, fixed media collection. So they consist of both digital and paper material.

6. **Sharma and Vishvanathan (2001)** says that "growth of digital libraries involves digitization of existing library material: connectivity to the users in the world online and offline; integration with networking: and availability on the World Wide Web."

7. According to **William Arms** "An informal definition of a digital library is a managed collection of information, with associated services, where the information is stored in digital formats and accessible over a network. A crucial part of this definition is that the information is managed. A stream of data send to earth from a satellite is not a library. The same data, when organized systematically, becomes a digital library collection"

8. According to **Gladden HM, et. al.(1994)**

   "A digital library service is an assemblage of digital

computing, storage and communications machinery together with the software needed to reproduce, emulate, and extend the services provided by conventional libraries based on paper and other material means of collecting, storing, cataloging, finding, and disseminating information."

This definition is considered to be the most comprehensive definition of digital library.

9. **Bawden and Rowlands (1999)** defined digital library as:

   "...a library/information space, located in either a physical or virtual space, or a combination of both, in which a significant proportion of the resources, or a combination of both, in which a significant proportion of the resources available to users of that service exist only in digital form."

10. The definition, which came up in the course of the 1994 Institute of Electrical and Electronics Engineers Conference on Artificial Intelligence Applications (IEEE CAIA), emphasizes both the technical and service oriented aspects of digital libraries.

    It states as follows:

"A digital library is an assemblage of digital computing, storage and communication machinery together with the content and software needed to reproduce, emulate and extend the services provided by conventional libraries based on paper and other material means of collecting, cataloguing, finding and dissemination of information. A full service digital library must accomplish all essential services of traditional libraries and also exploit the well known advantages of digital storage, searching and communication."

Digital libraries are networked collections of digital texts, documents, images, sound, data, software, and many more that are the core of today's Internet and tomorrow's universally accessible digital repositories of all human knowledge.

On the basis of the above definitions the following features of digital library can be drawn:

- A digital library is a collection of services
- A collection of information objects
- Organization and presentation of these objects
- Available directly or indirectly
- Electronic/digital availability
- A supporting users with information objects
- **Collection**: Digital libraries can hold any information that can be encoded as sequence of bits. Sometimes these are digitized versions of conventional media, such a text, images, music, sound recordings, specifications and designs and many more.
- Digital libraries are being perused because they allow for a wide distribution of a vast amount of data and because they provide new ways of interacting with information and manipulating data.

11. Edward Fox has defined the digital library as "the new way of carrying out the functions of libraries encompassing new types of information resources, new approaches to acquit ion, new methods of storage and preservation, new approaches to classification and cataloging, intensive use of electronic systems and networks and dramatic shift in intellectual, organizational and electronic processes."

Summarizing from workshops conducted in 1991 and 1992, this definition states that a National Electronic Library is:

1. A service
2. Architecture

3. A set of information resources, databases of text, numbers, graphics, sound, video, etc.
4. A set of tools and capabilities to locate, retrieve and utilize the information resources available. The users of national electronic library would include students, teachers/professors, researchers, , librarians, authors, publishers, information providers and practitioners.

The above definition remains among the most comprehensive by including services, architecture, content, enabling technologies, users and content.

12. Online Dictionary of Library and Information defined digital library as "A library in which a significant proportion of the resources are available in Machine-readable format, as opposed to print or microform.

The digital library is the collection of services and the collection of information objects that support users in dealing with information objects available directly or indirectly via electronic/digital means (Lieiner, 1998)

According to **Seadle 2006**, "A digital library" is fundamentally a resource that reconstructs the intellectual substance and services of a traditional library in digital form. Digital libraries consist of digital contents (which are sometimes but not necessary text based), interconnections (which may be simple links or complex metadata or query based relationships), and software (which may be simple pages in HTML or complex database management system). A single, simple, standalone web page is probably not a digital library in any meaningful sense, any more than a single page or a single book is a traditional library. A mass of raw data such as comes from the Hubble telescope is probably also not a digital library, though its contents arguably belongs in one digital libraries are not replacements for traditional libraries. They are rather the future of traditional libraries, much as medieval manuscript libraries simply become a specialized and much revered part of the larger print-based libraries that we have today.

According to this definition it is hard to determine whether a particular resource was a genuine digital library.

A digital library is not a single entity; The digital library requires technology to link the resources of many services that are transparent to the end users; Universal access to digital libraries and information services is a goal; Digital library collections are not limited to document surrogates; they extend to digital artifacts that can not be represented or distributed in printed format. (ARL, 1995).

A managed collection of information, with associated services where the information is stored in digital format and accessible over a network (**Arms, 2000**).

Cleveland (1998) gave some of the basic characteristics of digital libraries. One of the characteristics is "digital libraries are the digital face of traditional libraries and include both electronic (digital) as well as print and other (e.g. films, sound) materials."

According to **Don Waters**, former Director of the Digital Federation (1998).

Digital libraries are organizations that provide the resources, including the specialized staff, to select, structure, offer intellectual access to, interpret, distribute, preserve the integrity of, and ensure the persistence over time of collection of digital works so that they are readily and economically available for use by a defined community or set of communities.

Some definitions require that digital libraries contain the full content of information resources in computer readable form and often assume that they contain more than text alone(Fox etal, 1995, Levy and Marshall, 1995), Lesk (1997), in a book on "practical digital libraries' defines a DL simply as " a collection of information which is both digitized organized" The Digital Library Foundation(DLF) has defined the digital library as organization that provide the resources including the specialized and qualified library staff to select, structure, offer intellectuals access, to interpret, distribute, preserve the integrity of and ensure the persistence over time of collections of digital works so that they are readily and economically available for use by a defined community or set of communities.

Adam and Ayesha (1996) defines 'A digital library is a distributed electronic collection that covers virtually all fields of human endeavor including art, music, medicine, science, movies, videos, books, products, literature, news papers, brochures and catalogues."

CSTR Electronic Library Project Group California, Berkley, 1994 Larson defines it as "Digital library is a global virtual library the library of thousands of networked electronic libraries" These are similar to networked libraries.

From the above definitions the following statement can be drawn:

A digital library is based on documents in digital form that are handled like traditional library documents in standard processes (collecting, cataloging, and providing access) and that are made available online for users via catalog records.

A digital library is an electronic product of software that contains both primary data and manually created or manually proofed metadata. The primary data can be either thematic or collections based and must constantly be maintained. A digital library also includes the three main functions of a traditional library: cataloging, long term archiving, and access.

A digital library is an electronics provision of digital documents in connection with online services, building on the tasks of a traditional library, which enables worldwide access to its collection via Internet. Digital libraries are in fact probably too young to define in any permanent way.

Digital library therefore is a combination of:

- Collection of Services
- An architecture
- A set of information resources, databases of text, numbers, graphics, sound, video, etc.
- A set of tools and capabilities to locate, retrieve and utilize the information resources available (Borgman, 2000).

Most of the technology for digital libraries exists and is in active use on the internet and the World Wide Web. Most of the library holdings would no longer be printed text, but would incorporate large amounts of multimedia information as well.

However, "digital library" remains a contested term, meaning different things to different peoples.

The two part definition by Borgman et. al , 1996 is a useful definition which is as follows:

1. Digital libraries are a set of electronic resources and associated ethnical capabilities for creating, searching and using information. In this sense they are an extension and enhancement of information storage and retrieval systems that manipulate digital data in any medium (text, images, sounds; static and dynamic images) and exist in distributed networks. The contents of digital libraries include data, metadata that describe various aspects of the data (e.g. representation, creator, owner, reproduction rights) and metadata that consists of links or relationships to other data or metadata, whether internal or external to the digital library.
2. Digital libraries are constructed, collected and

organized, by (and for) a community of users and their functional capabilities support the information needs and uses of that community. They are a component of communities in which individuals and groups interact with each other, using data, information and knowledge resources and systems. In this sense they are an extension, enhancement and integration of a variety of information institutions as physical places where resources are selected, collected, organized, preserved and accessed in support of a user community. These information institutions include, among others, libraries, museums, archives and schools, but digital libraries also extend and serve other community settings, including classrooms, offices, laboratories, homes and public spaces.

3. A digital library is a machine readable representation of materials, which might be found in a university library together with organized information, intended to help users find specific information.
4. A digital library is a distributed technology environment, which dramatically reduces barriers to the creation, dissemination, manipulation, storage, integration, and reuse of information by individuals and groups.
5. A digital library service is an assemblage of digital computing, storage, and communicates machinery together with the software needed to reprise, emulate, and extend the services provided by conventional libraries based on paper and other material means of collecting, storage, cataloguing, finding, and disseminating information.

According to **Borgman** definitions shows the following three combinations:

1. Library= library + archive + museum

2. Distributed information system + organization + effective interfaces
3. User community+ collection (content)+services.

Thus, digital libraries are complex system that:

1. Help satisfy information needs of users (societies)
2. Provide information services (scenarios),
3. Locate and present information in usable way (spaces)
4. Organize information in usable ways (structure), and
5. Communicate information with users and computers (streams)

We find that the term "digital library" is used in two distinct senses. In general, researchers view digital libraries as content collected on behalf of the user communities, while practicing librarians' views digital libraries as institutions or services. As is evident from the above definitions, librarians tend to take a broad view of the concept of a "library". They see libraries as organizations that select, collect, organize, conserve, preserve and provide access to information on behalf of a community user. Upon closer examination, we find that the term "digital library" has multiple meanings. These definitions cluster around two themes. From a research perspective, digital libraries are content collected and organized on behalf of user communities. From a library perspective, digital libraries are institutions or organizations that provide information services in digital form.

We need digital library technology to manage large amount of digital contents

Thus, digital library is a library that holds a collection of resources in digital or electronic format and that is made accessible to the users through the electronic system and network. Digital libraries are electronic libraries in which large number of geographically distributed users can accessed the contents of large and diverse repositories of electronic objects, networked text, images, maps, sounds, videos, etc. It also includes hypertext, hypermedia and multimedia components. Although accessible online, a digital library is not identical to a website or a portal. However, while portals, specialized websites and search engines covers a wide range of subject areas, digital libraries are more narrowly focused around one or specific group of disciplines. Digital libraries, moreover, attach content specific and highly descriptive metadata such as, descriptors or keywords to describe each item in the collection. Therefore, searches in a digital library can produce more useful results, save time and effort in searching, and in the best of case browsers may directly accessed the text or multimedia content for which they executed their search.

CHARACTERSTICS OF DIGITAL LIBRARY

The digital library is not merely a collection of electronic information. It is an organized system of digital information that can serve as a rich resource for its users community. A digital library emphasise the equitable and timely access to a vast amount of diverse resources in a shared mode in a given specialty, lifting traditional barriers of time and space.

One definition given by Cleveland (1998) gave some of the characteristics of digital library. One of the characteristic is "Digital libraries are the digital face of traditional libraries and include electronic (digital) as well as print and other (e.g. film, sound) material."

1. Storage of information is in digital form.
2. Digital libraries enable managing very large amount of data, preserve unique collection, and provide faster access to information.
3. Facilitate dealing with data from more than one locations.

4. They also help to perform searches that are manually not possible.

The following are some of the important characteristics of digital libraries:

1. Digital libraries are the digital face of traditional libraries that include both digital collections as well as print and other (e.g. audio, video, graphics animation, etc.) materials. So they encompass both electronic (digital) and paper material.
2. A digital library owns and controls the information. It provides access to information, not just pointer to it.
    1. A digital library will also include digital materials that exist outside the physical and administrative bounds of any one digital library.
    2. A digital library ideally provides a coherent view of all of the information contain within a library, no matter its form or format.
    3. A digital library has a unified organizational structure with consistent points for accessing the data.
    4. Digital libraries will serve particular communities, as traditional libraries do now, though those communities may be widely dispersed throughout the network.
    5. Digital libraries will require both the skills of librarians as well as those of computer scientists to be viable.
    6. A digital library is not a single entity; it may also provide access to digital material and resources from outside the actual confines of any one digital library.
    7. A digital library support quick and efficient access to a large number of distributed but interlinked

information sources that are seamlessly integrated.

8. Digital libraries have collection that:
    1. Are large and persists overtime.
    2. Are well organized and managed.
    3. Contain many formats
    4. Contain objects and not just their representation
    5. Contain objects that may be otherwise unobtainable.
9. Digital libraries include all the processes and services offered by traditional libraries, though these processes will have to be revised and enhance to accommodate differences between new digital and traditional paper media.

FEATURES OF DIGITAL LIBRARIES

Some of the features of digital libraries are:

1. Support multimedia component.
2. Provides access to very large information collections, primary , secondary etc.
3. Supports and provides search and retrieval interface.
4. Ease of handling, searching and managing.
5. Digital library is expected to overcome the distance barrier through remote accessing of rare and expensive material.
6. Provides a powerful user-friedly interface effective search and retrieval.

SOME RELATED TERMS

Virtual Library vs Digital Library vs Electronic Library vs Hybrid Library vs Automated Library vs Traditional Library

The terms such as "digital library", "electronic library"

and "virtual library" are often used synonymously and therefore used interchangeable. However, the former term, namely 'digital library' currently represents the more modern approach.

Digital Library vs Virtual Library

The term "virtual Library" or "Library without walls" usually refers to the meta resources, subject portals that extend virtual accessibility of digital collection from several diverse resources without the users even knowing where the resource actually resides. A virtual library could potentially be enormous, linking huge collections from all around the globe, or it could be very small, consisting of few hundred links to digital resources maintain by an individual. Moreover, another term, namely, 'hybrid library' is taken to be cognizant of a continuum between the concept of the conventional library and that of digital library, where electronic and paper based information services are alongside each other. The aim of hybrid library is to encourage end-user resource discovery and information use in a variety of formats and forms a number of local and remote sources in a seamlessly integrated way. Digitized libraries collect, store, organize and use globally distributed knowledge resources of diverse information type and contents stored in a variety of electronic forms, and finally disseminate the same via communication network.

There is confusion in the use of terminologies like' virtual', 'digital; and electronic' libraries. One person's digital library is often an other's virtual library. Some differences can be made. Electronic library is a library that has collection in digital forms such as CD-ROMs, online etc. and provide services over cables and telecommunication lines.

A modern digital library is a group of interlinked servers and workstations, which are connected to each other through high-speed networks. Unlike traditional libraries, digital libraries do not reside in the building. The three main characteristics of digital libraries are the storage of information in digital forms, usage of communication networks to access and retrieve information, and 'copying' by either downloading or online/offline printing from a master file. Preservation, search and access, content creation, and delivery are its essential components.

In recent past the term like "virtual library" had also got into attention of the library professionals and information scientists. The shift of the term 'Electronic library' to 'Digital Library' is perhaps because of the growing interest in digital network, digital audio and video relative to electronic publishing. The concept of ' virtual library' has emerged simultaneously perhaps because all the information at present we are enjoying through networked libraries at the desktop quite virtually without the physical existence of the books on the shelves. These terms can also be taken equivalent to digital library provided the information is completely digitized. The concept of virtual library also emerged simultaneously with electronic library and digital library. This emergence is perhaps because all the information uses are at present through networked libraries at the desktop, which is quite virtual (practical) without the physical existence of books on shelves.

In the recent years, the new terms like virtual library, electronic library and digital library are emerging. Though the libraries witnessed the application of computers in 1960s, yet the concept of 'virtual library in infancy.' The concept of virtual library has developed with the growth in the telecommunication networks, especially the Internet. The term "virtual" library, the 'digital library,' and the 'electronic library' are interchangeable. 'Virtual library' is companion term to 'digital 'library. A digital library possesses the same functions and goals of the traditional print-base library. The difference lies in the 'digital' part of the term. It indicates merely that the material is stored and accessed digitally. The virtual library environment encompasses the concept of the digital library but is more than a collection of digital resources. The virtual library provides access to an integrated collection of print, electronic and multimedia resources delivered seamlessly and transparently to users regardless either of their physical location and ownership of the information.

Virtual library is a library without walls, spread across the globe from where one is able to retrieve the whole world of information through a properly networked workstation.

Though the library does not physically exist, yet the user is able to retrieve the information required by users. Virtual library is a library with little or no physical collection of books, periodicals reading space or support staff, but one that disseminates selective information directly to distributed library, usually electronically. It is companion term to digital library, brought forth by the National Science Foundation. Each virtual library is designed to provide users with online access to an extensive array of fultext documents on a topic of current high interest or critical concern. The virtual library usually takes the form of a web page containing a series of hyperlinks arranged in heirchical manner for easy searching. A virtual library provides a hyperlink to the documents it catalogs e.g. the main page of the WWW virtual library is maintained at the Stanford University.

The virtual library is a web-based archive used to provide access to resources. It helps you to:

1. Organized your books with subject indexing
2. Track where your books are
3. Share books with your friends

The information is stored in digital form in all these

types of libraries. The form of information storage is indicated, in real term, by the term 'digital library' only. May be because of this simple reason, this term has come to stay in usage. Therefore, the current usage of the term 'digital' appears to include both electronic and virtual libraries.

The application of computers and information technology in libraries has given impetus to the networking of libraries and information centers for sharing of information. Networking of libraries implies putting together sub-sets of library and information centers in order to act in a cooperative and coordinated manner with a predetermined obligation. Digital library networking concept is a cooperative venture of all the participating libraries with the provision to transmit data on short and long distance lines from one library to another. No library can satisfy all the information needs of its users.

Therefore, resource sharing through networking is required. It is also due to the acute financial, space problems, and continuing increases in the prices of reading material are some the problems faced by the libraries and information centers. Large library networking programmes such as INFLIBNET have been announced. The libraries that participate in such programmes will be better placed to derive the benefits of the applications of information technology to the libraries and information centers.

Hybrid Library

It was designed to bring a range of technologies from different sources together in the context of the working library and to explore integrated systems and services in electronic and printed environments. It reflects the transitional state of the library which today can neither be fully print nor fully digital.

Automated Library

Can automated library be regarded as digital library?

Why an automated library may not be called digital library?

"An automated library may not be digital library but a digital library is an automated library" because an automated library consisting entirely of conventional physical material such as printed books may be automated. This automation does not make it "digital". The digital library includes the collection of digital services, a set of information resources etc. However, it is true that a digital library must be automated in some of its essential functions. Because the material is in digital (or computer readable form).

CATEGORIES/TYPES OF DIGITAL LIBRARIES

Digital libraries may be categorized as:

1. Stand alone digital libraries
2. SDLs networked as a Digital Library system.
3. Web based paralyzed Digital Library system.

COLLECTION OF DIGITAL LIBRARIES

A collection of digital objects including text, video and audio along with methods of access and retrieval. Its managed collection of information with associated services with the information is stored in digital formats and accessible over a network. Digital libraries can hold any information that can be encoded as sequences of bits. Sometimes these are digitized version of conventional media, such as text, images, music, sound recordings, specifications and designs, and many, more. As digital libraries expend, the contents are less often the digital equivalent of physical items and more often items that have no equivalent, such as data from scientific instruments, video games and databases. A stream of data sent to earth from a satellite is not a library. The same data, when organized systematically, becomes a digital library collection. The digital library includes text, audio, video, photographs, images, drawings, computer programmes, numeric data, sound, graphics, etc.

Thus, digital library is a library of digital documents, artifacts and records.

The term digital library is being used to describe any of the following:

- Collection of electronic journals and books
- On-line education portals
- Repositories of multimedia files
- Archive information created from local knowledge
- Electronic version of libraries
- The entire internet

CONTENTS OF DIGITAL LIBRARY

All types of content will be available through digital libraries. They will become the high end of the information systems world, not only including bibliographic and full text content but also images, music, and video. Included will be medical image, images of scanned pages, engineering drawings, educational videos, courseware, oral histories, 3D renderings of museums objects, musical performances, etc. Thus digital library is interpreted simply as a collection of digital objects such as sound, video, electronic documents, digital picture. That people can access from their desktop personal computers.

The contents of digital libraries include data, metadata that describe various aspects of data (e.g. representation, creator, owner, reproduction rights), and metadata that consist of link or relationships to other data or metadata whether internal or external to digital library.

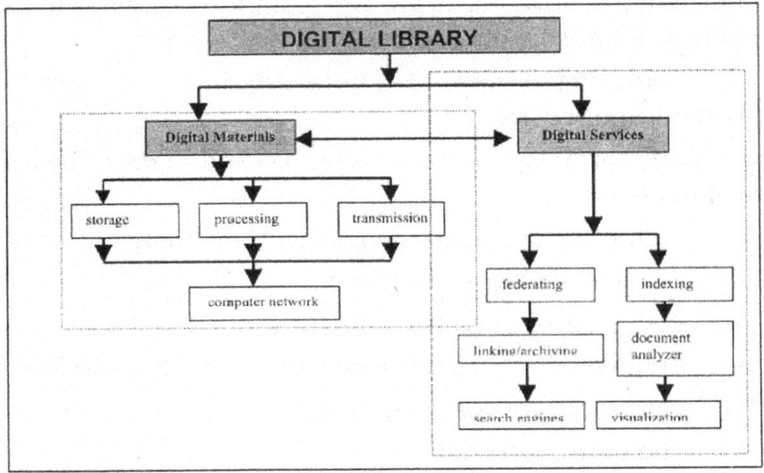

Fig. 1. Conceptual view of Digital library

OBJECTIVES OF DIGITAL LIBRARY

Some of the important objectives of digital library are:

- To expedite the systematic development of the means to collect, store, and organize information and knowledge in digital form. To convert the existing print documents into digital form with the help of new information technology.
- To promote the economical and efficient delivery of information to all sectors of the society
- To encourage co-operative efforts which leverage the considerable investment into research resources, computing and communication network.
- To strengthen communication and collaboration between and among the research, business, government, and educational communities.
- To capture, store manipulate and distribute information
- To introduce and provide new services.
- To provide efficient information retrieval.

- To create digitized collection.
- To create electronic databases.
- To identify all relevant sources quickly.
- To maintain cost effectiveness of library operations.
- To capture, store, manipulate and distribute the information.
- To provide fast and efficient access, with multiple access mode.
- To provide need based and retrospective search services to the user.
- To provide rapid access to bibliographic as well as full text information.
- To have large number of database in CDs.
- To subscribe and access the electronic journal across the world.
- To avoid routine and redundant activities.
- To digitize documents for preservation and for space saving.
- To provide facility for networking and resource sharing.
- To manage all the activities pertaining to acquisition, processing, shelving, circulation and control of entire digital library.
- To digitize the document for preservation and for space saving.
- To support library functions such as circulation, serial control, acquisition, stock checking and other routine jobs.
- To save the time of library staff as well of the users.
- To minimize the massive storage and space problems in libraries.
- To provide effective and efficient digital information services.

Digital libraries acts as global, multilingual repositories of data, knowledge, sound and images .In digital libraries knowledge is recorded and stored in many forms, often using different languages and symbol systems.

FUNCTIONS OF DIGITAL LIBRARY

The main functions of digital library are similar to that of traditional library such as identify, select, process, organize, provide access, preserve and manage the collection. Digital library deals with the documents in digital form and in digital environment by using the modern information communication technologies in managements of digital collection.

Some of the functions are:

1. **Storage management**: process of organizing and management digital contents to ensure that it is available to user whether they want access to it providing stable reliable storage and management of data in an open environment across abroad spectrum of platform.
2. **Search and access**: to be able to access what the user need quickly.
3. **Distribution**: to enable information owns to distribute the material in numerous ways; though existing networks clients/server business solution or the Internet.
4. **Right management**: providing extensive access control capabilities enabling content owner to capitalize on their protected assets.

MAINTENANCE OF DIGITAL LIBRARY

Creation, maintenance and provision of services using digital library collections require several resources.

Two major resources required for setting up and operating digital library collections are:

1. Technology infrastructure and
2. Personnel.

Technology infrastructure includes computing and other equipments, software and networking connectivity. Personnel will require for handling various tasks associated with the creation and maintenance of the collection.

The maintenance of digital library is a costly affair. The cost of maintenance includes:

1. System hardware.
2. Software upgrades.
3. New equipments.
4. Improved or alternative network solutions (ISDN,ATM, etc)
5. Technical personals.
6. Copying digital holdings periodically on different media tapes and plays back devices.
7. Maintaining various activities in digital environment, upgrading, deleting the links to obsolete objects.
8. Digital content change.
9. Tools for indexing.
10. Tools for acquiring.
11. Link management requirement as hypertext links are created among distinct documents.

2

Historical Development of Digital Libraries

INTRODUCTION

The history of library is as old as the recorded knowledge. The libraries were in the form of archival collection, which consists of collection of historical records, which includes letters, photographs etc. These records have been accumulated during the course of time and gradually developed into a library. The collection was by the individuals regardless of media or format. In ancient times, small tablets made out of clay were used as a written medium. Collection of these clay documents made up the very first archives.

They were at the root of first library.

Assyria : The Kingdom of existed as the same time as Babylonia. The Assyrian King Asurbanipal (668-626 B.C.) is regarded as the earliest commentator on the work of the librarian. He established a library of more than 20,000 clay tablets. In this library the tablets were tagged for identification.

Cuneiform Script : This is one of the earliest known

forms of written expression. The form of the Egyptians book was the papyrus roll, and the instruments for writing were a brush like pen and ink. The papyrus rolls were usually kept in clay jars or in metal cylinders with identifying marks outside the container, which were usually stacked on shelves.

Rome : The Romans used Papyrus etc as writing material. The forms of books in ancient Rome were the roll and covered various subjects such as philosophy, law, politics, religion etc. More than 25 public libraries flourished in Rome in the second century. The libraries in Rome could be used by any person, who could read. Libraries were actually open to the public. The era of scholarship, learning and libraries listed about 500 years.

Papyrus : was used in ancient Egypt for recording knowledge. Papyrus is a thick paper like material produced from the pith of the papyrus plant found in Egypt around third million BC. By the AD 800 the parchment and vellum had replaced papyrus used in Egypt and was introduced by Arabs. The reason for this switch over includes the significantly higher durability particularly in moist climate.

Greece : The Greeks adopted 22 letters alphabets of the Phoenicians. The introduction of the alphabetic script in the 8th century may be regarded as representing a new birth of literacy in Greece. Aristotle (383B.C-322B.C.) is said to be have been the first person to collect, preserve and use the culture of the past. The most important libraries of Ancient Greece were established during the Hellenistic Age. These libraries were located at the new city of Alexandria in Egypt, founded in the third century B.C. by the time of Julius Ceaser. The Alexandria library contained 700,000 volumes/ rolls. The holdings were classified and organized.

DEVELOPMENT OF LIBRARIES IN VEDIC AGE IN INDIA

Establishment of libraries is not a new concept. The oldest library dates to around 2700 years.

In 400 AD there came into being one of the biggest known universities, the Nalanda University, which by 450 A.D. became a renowned seat of learning, its fame spread beyond the boundaries of India. Nalanda near Patna grew to be the foremost Buddhist Monastery and an educational center. The library of Nalanda had a rich collection of manuscripts on philosophy and religion and text related to grammar, logic, literature, Astrology, medicine etc. The University of Nalanda and its library flourished down to the 12th century A.D. The University at Sompuri, like that of Vikramshila, occupied a significant position since the days of Dharampala 769-867 A.D. Like Nalanda, this library also had an own library.

It has been stated that Nalanda authorities could feel that a monastry without library was like castle without an armoury. Nalanda University as such, maintained a very big library of considerable importance to cater to the needs of the teachers and students. The books for in this library was mainly palm leave manuscripts carefully preserved with a cloth cover and a cord, stored mainly on built-in stone or brick shelves in the library hall.

Besides Nalanda, there were other equally large educational institutions with well equipped libraries .Some of these are Taxila, Vikramshila, Mithila, Nadia and Banaras.

Early Middle Age

Of the Medieval period, 500 to 1000 A.D. have traditionally be called as dark ages.This period, however, had witnessed the preservation and transmission of learning. The collection in the libraries, attached to the temples, churches and monasteries, were more or less secret.

The libraries of middle age is characterized by the use of parchment codex for the physical form of books. The materials used for writing were plain or dyed parchment or vellum, quill pens and kinds of colored inks.

It may be stated that the idea about libraries

developed in India during the middle period. Besides public and state libraries, private collection of rare manuscripts on different subjects were also in existence both in the South and North of India.Mohammad of Ghazni is said to have maintained a larger library, which had more than 30,000 volumes. During this period no separate building was allotted to the library. It was part of the palace and sometimes it was attached to religious places. As the paper was scare and costly, the books were rare and generally not available for private use. The benefit was limited to only a few scholars.

Late Middle Ages

During this period, only royalty, nobility, the church and the universities could afford books. The libraries become for the first time, an independent centers of study. With the growth of readers, range and variety of reading material also grew. The demand for books could no longer be satisfied by handwritten copies. The need for a new and faster medium for transmission of thought and knowledge become immediate and urgent.

Towards the second half of 15th century printing with movable types was invented. The forty two lines Bible, commonly called the Gutenberg Bible (printed by Johann Guttenberg of Maize, Germany in 1454) is regarded as the first printed book in Europe. About one half of the books printed in the 15th century were religious books. The most important library of this period was the Vatican Library. Libraries increased in numbers and size.

During the late medieval age, India being ruled by the Mughals. The Mughals emperors from Babar to Aurangzeb patronized learning and scholarship and also maintained their palace libraries. Of the early Mughals, Akbar was more intend on establishing the libraries. He enriched the libraries with valuable material collected from various sources. He created a separate department for libraries to look after not only state library but also the public libraries located in the capital. In addition to the regular librarian, there was other staff such as book binders, calligraphers etc.

The collection in the library were generally arranged by subjects.Of the later Mughals, Jahangir, Shahjahan and Aurangzeb took great care of the Imperial Library.

Library buildings of the Mughals period reflected architectural style. Libraries were spacious, well ventilated halls and rows of almirahs. Palm leaves and parchment manuscripts comprised the main stock.

In the Vedic age instructions were imparted "orally", without the medium of books.

Before the invention of paper and printing, people used to communicate mainly through oral communication. There was oral communication among the users. They met at specified places to exchange their views on various fields. This verbal communication was the major medium for the transfer of information. But oral communication as a source has serious limitations. The amount of information transmitted in this way is less. Unless information is recorded, the information transmission is difficult. In earlier days people recorded the information in stones, palm leaf manuscripts, metal etc. and transfer such piece of information to other places.

MODERN LIBRARY

Modern time begin from 17th century and during this century the idea of 'Bibliotheca Universalis' was first initiated. This idea advocated more liberal policies of book provision in libraries. The seventeenth century saw the first publication of periodicals, in the late 17th century newspaper made their appearance, and the first modern encyclopedia was published in Switzerland in 1630. With the French revolution in 1789, Church libraries became national properties. The French Royal Library become national property and was renamed as La Bibliotheque Nationale with about 300000 books and many valuable manuscripts. The Library of Congress (USA) was authorized in 1800.

In addition to establishment of national libraries throughout the Europe, many private libraries were also established during both in the 18th and 19th centuries. To meet all the new demands for books from the people who were unable to buy them, a new kind of library was developed. By the end of 18th century lending libraries had become a common feature of every town in Europe In 1850. The British Parliament passed the first Public Library Act. During the first 20 years of the Public Library Act, thirty five libraries were established.

The second quarter of the 19th century was a period of scholarly and literary activities and time of industrial and commercial development in America. In this climate of literary scholarships, educational progress, wealth and prosperity, the free public libraries came into being.

The Bombay Government put up for the first time in 1808 a proposal to registered libraries and gave funds for the 'encouragement of libraries'. It was in the year 1835 that the first Public Library-Calcutta, Public Library with a stock of about 15,000 volumes was established through the initiatives and resources of private individuals. In 1902 this library was designated as the 'Imperial Library'.

CURRENT TRENDS

The demand on modern library service has increased in the modern period and large libraries with millions of volumes are being set up throughout the world. In addition to the largeness, variety of libraries are organized - the public, national, government, academic, research, special as well as children.

The early decades of the 20th century were characterized by the expansion of library services in United

States, Great Britain, the Scandinavian countries and India. There has been growth of all established libraries specially public and academic.

Alexander Graham Bell invented the telephone, Charles Babbage invented a machine that eventually developed into today's computer and William Burt invented the typewriter. Bell, Babbage and Burt invented indigenous machine to improve the management of information. During the medieval period, paper and printing were invented. This has given a boost to the development of communication system. Up-to 20th century, paper medium dominated the world of information sources.

The present century has witnessed a big change in the information transfer process.

In our current technological society, changes are occurring at a rapid pace. One of the most evident changes that affect our lives is in the area of communications. Not only we rely heavily on traditional print media as a source of information, but we are also becoming increasingly aware of and dependent on non-print communication form.

Universities were equipped with regular libraries not of printed materials but of materials of manuscripts of different varieties and on different subjects for the use of students and teachers.

DEVELOPMENT OF DIGITAL LIBRARY

Though the concept of digital library is growing very fast, yet its progress is nearly 30 years old. Way back to early 1970, the digital libraries started functioning using computers and communication technology available at that time. In 1967, Air Force Development in US Govt. Started digitizing their legal documents followed by scientific communication. Several character coded software package were released during mid 1970 and late 1970 for storage, indexing and retrieval of documents. By the end of 1980 many mainframe, microcomputers and Local Area Network (LAN) were available for storage and retrieval of text. During this period several sophisticated information storage and retrieval system were built. Online host like DIALOG and STN came forward and started providing not only online data based services but also the fultext online journals. However, their fields did not contain pictures and graphics.

The use of CD-ROMs started in 1980s with heavy storage capacity, long lasting, easy in transportation and requiring minimum storage space. Digital library includes both digital collection and traditional fixed media collection, so they encompass both electronic and paper materials. Digital libraries also include digital material that exists outside the physical and administrative bonds of any one digital library. Digital library will also include all the processes and services that are the backbone and nervous system of libraries. However, such traditional processes though forming the basic digital library work will have to be revised and enhanced to accommodate the difference between the new digital media and traditional fixed media.

Libraries have always adopted newer technologies for fulfilling their basic commitments, and the adoption of digital technology in libraries is a part of this historical process.

Digital libraries provide comparable or better services to traditional libraries at relatively low cost over existing networks and tools like those used for WWW. They are built in most cases upon prior technologies, such as library automation packages or records management systems. Research systems like **MARIAN and Dienst** may become more widely deployed. Certainly, lightweight software such as that used for open Archives will be commonly used. Connecting an URN scheme, a repository mechanism, search engine(s), and a WWW interface can lead to a relatively simple system in short order.

Traditional libraries are limited by storage space; digital libraries have the potential to store much more information, simply because digital information requires very little physical space to contain it. Unlike electronic documents, paper documents are localized. Only one person can consult the document at a time in different places. While the electronic documents can easily be accessible by different persons at different places at the same time. The paper documents at the same time, suffer from its own limitations of wear and tear due to physical handling, particularly owning to environmental hazards as well as the ageing. The material such as maps, charts and such materials are fading rapidly.

In the 1970s, digital libraries were based on microcomputers and used to provide basic services for remote access and online search and retrieval. In the 1980s, sophisticated information storage and retrieval systems came into light. The invention of CD-ROM in the 1980s was a turning point in the digitization of information. Digital libraries used different techniques to share bibliographical record and link different remote systems. The 1990s marked a progressive move towards digitization due to networking, electronic document delivery service, online services, and electronic journals, etc.

The field of digital libraries is still young, digital library collections have been built around the world and are being deployed on numerous public web sites.

Digital libraries began to appear in the early 1990s as research and development projects. Centered within computer science departments of universities sometimes funded by Government grants. As these projects matured then Information Technology (IT) groups began to partner with the library to develop campus-wide standards for the operation of digital libraries as a part of the education enterprise.

With the introduction of Internet and networking technology users may able access to information, from any location, at any time. Digital libraries are fulfilling the same objective.

This has brought a revolutionary change in the way libraries adopt and function shifting from print to electronic information dissemination. These libraries are addressed as electronic or virtual or digital information resource centers/ library.

Three related tasks for library involvement in the 1990s are:

i. To upgrade existing services by making use of technology.

ii. To plan and develop new services and products which make use of technology; and

iii. To study library users, anticipating and meeting their changing information needs. It is necessary to consider the goals of the library and its users and then assess the utility of technology for achieving those goals. Many libraries are in transit from the traditional towards the digital library.

The notion of the library has long expanded beyond the physical building. Forced by decreasing budgets, many libraries have redefined their acquisition policy from purchasing documents "just in case" to "just in time", since no library can afford to purchase every item that might be needed. Through collaboration and reciprocal services among libraries, one can provide a much larger range of resources to all users and fulfill their information needs quicker, cheaper and more completely than one library alone would be able to do. Therefore, the digital library is a must for sharing the resources over a network. In order to share the resources the concept of resource sharing and networking has emerged. This is important to satisfy the information needs of the users effectively and efficiently.

The era of digital libraries perhaps began with emergence of electronic journals. They are now becoming popular, especially because of the fast emerging networks. The networks help us to access such electronic journals from different services. Electronic journals are easy to distribute, less expensive and easy to search. It occupies less space, possibly of instant access, availability of information in the multimedia environment. It can stay for many years. There are now many electronic journals available on-line on various subjects.

In the context of digital libraries, electronic publications refer to publications of primary or documents in machine readable form. In the early days of electronic libraries even the machine-readable databases were referred to as electronic publications. The first electronic book was published in 1985 in Germany.

Technology has made it possible for digital libraries integrate different formats such as texts, images, audios, and videos. Now a days, visual information systems are getting more popular compared to text based information systems. Therefore, digital libraries are becoming more graphical in nature. Also the concept of hypertext has been introduced in digital libraries.

THE ROLE OF TRADITIONAL LIBRARIAN

The traditional role of librarian was to act as a mediator between the reader and the book. The main duties were associated with acquiring and making the resources available in the library. The task was to acquire, purchase, organize, store, and display the reading material.

TRADITIONAL LIBRARY AND DIGITAL LIBRARY

As such, the cost of maintaining a digital library is much lower than that of a traditional library. A traditional library must spend large sum of money paying for staff, book maintenance, rent, and additional books. Digital libraries do away with these fees. The libraries have changed with time from mere static storehouse of interested collection of documents to dynamic centers serving all professional and nonprofessional utilizing useful and need base information storage has changed from clay table to papers and now to electronic and optical media of CD-ROMs.

The traditional library is different from digital library in the following way:

Libraries of yesterday	Libraries of Today
1. Repository, a ware house or store	Resource, responding to need with the right material
2. **Collection**: concern primarily with gathering and protecting material	**Connection**: putting you in touch with digitize resources, local or remote on the web.
3. Isolated, operating alone	**Networked**: linked to global resources and working with partners.
4. **Regulated**: preoccupied with rules that become barrier	**Accessibility**: easy to use, offered help and support.
5. **Static**: unchanging, uninspiring encouraging	**Dynamic**: a catalyst, inspiring enjoyment and discovery.
6. **Historic**: old, maybe unique legacy	**current**: reflecting today's communities

Library Evolution

The following development has taken place during the course of time:

1. Paper Library with card catalogue.
2. Automated library with computerized catalogue
3. Computerized library with digital collection/ information
4. Electronic library with the above three types

5. Hybrid library with the above four types

Traditional libraries → Automated Libraries→ Electronic Libraries → Digital Libraries → Virtual Libraries → Net or E-Libraries → Interactive E-Libraries

Collection

Self important but undistinguished through reinterpreting historic collections.

The print on paper is slowly shifting to electronic publishing due to advance in information technology. Setting of digitized knowledge services is actually a development trend of libraries in the 21st century.

Electronic contents have several advantages like economy in providing multiple pointers (access point) location independence, easy manipulations of contents, breaking the boundary between metadata secondary information and primary information, capability to handle dynamic content and possibility of collaborative working even though, web captured information, taxonomies topic maps and categorization/classification of web captured information are significant areas for LIS professionals

WHY THE NEED ARISES FOR DIGITAL LIBRARY?

Libraries collect the material in order to cater to the information needs of the users. Most of the rare materials housed in various libraries of the world are require preserving the same for future use. Library professionals are looking forward for digitization of documents as a possible solution. In this process they not only doing the job of preservation and conservation, but also providing the users easy and remote access to knowledge sources with the help of powerful retrieval tools. Through Internet it has now become possible to a part of "global village" and exchange the information instantly. World Wide Web is the most advanced browsing and searching system. Digitized media is a supportive tool for searching, locating the information faster to the targeted users. The basic concepts behind the digital libraries are the sharing of resources globally. The basic purpose is to provide right information to the right user at the right time.

In an electronic environment libraries must reach out more towards the sources of information. Libraries must also perform more of the functions that rationally have been carried out like packaging, transmission, and the provision of manipulating tools. Print and electronic publications will co-exists, in parallel, for the immediate future.

Information technology that will shape the future information world is the fusion of computers and telecommunications technologies. Computer process information and disseminate it. Development of more powerful computers with new methods of information processing, computer networks, and integrated communication system are of great relevance to the 21st century as these are basic and important information technologies responsible to bring drastic changes in information society of tomorrow. If we look back in the history we find the roots of today's information technology.

A digital library comprises from the digitization of the collections and information to the electronic text publication. It is not only a digital collection but also a unit of collection, services and human resources that participate in the complete vital cycle of creation, dissuasion, use, preservation of data, information and knowledge. Library operations will be affected in a fundamental ways by the revolution to electronic form.

The libraries have changed with time from mere static storehouse of interested collection of documents to dynamic service centers.

The digital library is nothing but the computing terminals which are linked to various sources of information in digital form.

With the utilization of computers and their application in many areas, the libraries today have equipped themselves with the latest information and communication technology to provide efficient service. Electronic information otherwise called as digital information, in the new era is changing the duties and services in all fields from traditional to digital form. Libraries also facing changes in new form and library professionals also doing their best to meet new challenges.

Digital library technology plays an important role in promoting the use of information. Digital libraries give solutions to the main challenges of traditional libraries such as storage of space, economic survival and management of materials; it has its own limitations. End users who are exposed to information technology will have difficulty to access the information, which is stored inside the computer in digital format. So it may not be an underestimation so that digital library serves as a supplement to traditional library and one cannot so easily jump to a conclusion that digital library is going to replace all the traditional concepts including paper.

Information available through the Internet and accessible via home or office workstation, fulfilling the promise to provide information at any time, to any place and for any user. In electronic publishing, the traditional steps between content owners and users are changing in scope and nature. Technological convergence between tele-communications, cable and other media is an example of how traditional role changes and how business sectors now are in competition with each other. Digital libraries are cost effective because these libraries required less manpower to manage and less storage space.

With the advent of information society, libraries, being

part of the society, are gradually bringing in the speculated changes in their structure, function and services. Traditional libraries are shifting their budgets to digital services, CD-ROMs etc.

The digital era started between late 1980s and early 1990 with the beginning of full text online databases. Use of scanner and camera for digitizing documents was a step ahead in the formation of digital libraries. At present several document-imaging softwares packages are available. The work of digitization started with the help of using client systems such as MS Window, MS-DOS, Apple and UNIX. These system in those days had several problems mainly the maintenance and up keeping. After one or two years they needs upgradation of creating new facilities invented during that period. The development of WWW brought a revolution in true sense and offered several facilities, which include Graphics Web Browser and other ready to use technologies.

Digital libraries evolved along with the Internet. Since 1960 these libraries are growing individually in the different organizations throughout the world, i.e. entire globe itself is an electronic library. In and after 1970s the private and public libraries were initiated to introduce long-term projects to facilitate the access of their databases.

These projects integrated the emerging information technologies with traditional printed materials. Among the materials of printed and non printed materials, such as microfiche, microfilms, tapes, sound recordings, and electronic files gave the birth to digital library .Earlier technology with regard to digital library had focused on the creation of card catalogues known as OPACs (Online Public Access Catalogues).These led the traditional as well as a new libraries to crate electronic databases that evolved the digital library system.

MODERN DIGITAL LIBRARY

The vision of digital library is not new. It was started with the development of computers. The first serious attempts to store library information on computer, in late 1960s, which face serious problems including the high cost.

Digital libraries began to appear in the early 1990s as a research and development projects.

The term library is generally related to storehouse of information in the form of paper publication like books, periodicals, conference proceedings, reports, etc. and also documents in other forms such as films, CDs, etc.. Digital libraries basically store materials in electronic format. Electronic information is available in the form of CD-ROMs, DVDs, etc.

The development of information technology has effects all aspects of human life including libraries. Huge amount of information is being generated in every moment with the application of new information technology. The present day is characterized by reducing distances, digitized storage and retrieval system.

The method of information seeking is changing from print to digital search. The means of information acquiring is changing. Therefore, the libraries are adopting new technologies and provide access to information beyond the wall of traditional libraries.

Advances in computer technology have brought the information closer to them. The information is not only confined to books and documents only. In the present days computer based facilities are available such as e-mail, CD-ROMs and Internet are available in the libraries.

Modern age is rightly known as the Post Internet Age in which information is considered as the foremost need for the successful living. The present day information society is looking for a major breakthrough in the accessing of information globally because in the present information era, the success and failure at national or international level depends significantly on users and exchange of useful, scientific and technical information.

With the changing needs of the society, library is also changing its concepts, status and role in the society and it is charged to have the latest mode of information storage and retrieval.

Application of computer was primarily introduced into library operations to performs routine functions such as circulation, cataloging, serial control, etc. However, technology continue to improve rapidly and introduction of CD-ROMs as a data storage media, the development of networking hardware and software for linking multiple personnel computers, GUI(Graphical User Interface), FTP(File Transfer Protocol) to transfer file on networked computers, and the new generation of web browsers like Netscape Navigator, Microsoft Internet Explorer, etc. have revolutionaries the information dissemination and access of information.

Thus, technology advances have replaced traditional services with digital services. Now the libraries are offering enhanced search capabilities to access the local collection as well as to access the holdings of the area.

Libraries are now providing a web interface to their LICs with web interface directly linked to electronic journals, electronic books and other Internet resources.

The electronic publishing has led to new era of communication and information sharing at a comparatively faster rate. Over the last few years there has been a rapid rise in both the number of journals on the web and services offering access to them. The E-journals has undergone a dramatic transformation in style and format since their initial appearance in the early 1990s.

The impact of information technology is due to the following reasons:

1. Due to the growth of literature.
2. Communication revolution.
3. Globalisation.
4. Computer revolution.
5. Emergence of new disciplines.

The main purpose of a library is to acquire, storage, retrieval and dissemination of information. Information technologies provides a wide range of tools and services for the developments of libraries and educational institutions. Therefore, different electronic and digital media have been playing significant role in the dissemination of information to the users.

During the past decade steep declines in the cost of commodity components, combined with the availability of high bandwidth networks, have made sophisticated digital and internet based services and rapidly expanding global digital contents have made possible a "Virtual Learning Environment" that delivers the capability to enhance the classroom experience or conduct learning apart from a physical campus. The digital library is a core component of this VLE.

According to Clifford Lynch, a noted authority on digital libraries "these developments are extended the role of the library, and changing the relationships between the library and other parts of academic enterprises"

The emergence of the World Wide Web in 1993 and its rapid development therefore, has allowed developers to provide universal access to digital libraries.

Previously, access to digital collection was supported by proprietary/networks or by local or campus wide network.

3

Traditional/Conventional Library Vs Digital Library

INTRODUCTION

The collection of a traditional library consists of books, periodicals, maps, atlases, standards and specifications, trade catalogs, reprints etc. mainly in printed format. In traditional libraries, development of collection, library services, library activities such as acquisition, cataloguing, etc. information storage and retrieval were mainly manual in nature. All these operations are time consuming and required more space and needed sizable number of library staff to perform their duties in this environment. On the other hand, digital libraries use information technologies, communication technologies, online databases, CD-ROMs, multimedia, databases, e-mail services to meet the information needs of users. Information in digital libraries is digitally stored and accessed. Access to digital library is, therefore, not bound by space or time. These libraries provide access to information via electronic gateway to remote digital and digitized documents.

The term digital refers to representation of

information on electronic media. Digital libraries are electronic libraries in which large number of geographical distributed users can accessed the contents of large and diverse repositories of digital objects such as images, maps, video, networked text etc. That also includes hypertext, hypermedia and multimedia composites. Digital libraries (DLs) act as collection of electronic resources and render service for the delivery of materials in a variety of formats. Digital libraries include personnel, distributed, centralized collection such as Online Public Access Catalogues (OPACs) and bibliographic databases, electronic journals, other online databases, etc.

A digital library is an assemblage of digital computing, storage, and communication machinery together with the content and software needed to reproduce, emulate and extend the services provided by conventional libraries based on paper and other material means of collecting, cataloging, finding and disseminating information. A full service digital library must accomplish all essential services of traditional libraries and also exploit the well-known advantage of digital storage, searching and communication. It provides access to part of or all its collections, such as plan text, images, graphs, audio, video materials and other library items that have been electronically converted, via the Internet and WWW.

The new digital libraries can tries to go beyond being paperless versions of traditional libraries in at least in three ways:

1. Free of the need to store copies of (sometimes rare) documents, they can focus more on services that will help students and faculty find and organize information in vast virtual collections.
2. Freed of the need to maintain collections in locations physically near their communities of readers, they can

plan to aggregate virtual holdings into more encompassing, complete and up-to-date collection.

3. Freed of the dominance of static print (audio and visual can be digitized as readily as can typed text), digital libraries can grappled with the complexities of representing and cataloguing new multimedia documents.

Digital libraries combine communication technology and information source, which allow remote access of its resources to other libraries by breaking down the physical barriers through national and international networks.

Digital library is an analog or metaphor of traditional library. However, digital libraries differ from their counterparts in significant ways; storage is digital, remote access is quick and easy, and materials are copied from a master version. Further more keeping extra copies on hand is easy and hampered by budget and storage restrictions, which are major problem in traditional libraries. Thus, digital libraries overcome many of the physical and economic limitations of traditional libraries. The content of digital libraries includes data, metadata that describes various aspects of data, and metadata that consists of link or relationships to other data or metadata whether internal or external to digital library.

The digital collection is differentiated from traditional collection on the bases of following factors:

Cost : The purchase cost of the electronic version is much lower than their printed version.

Space : In conventional library, physical space such as land area, shelves, racks are required for managing the collection where as in digital form eliminates the space problem.

Preservation : The subscription of e-journals is more cost effective, but preservation required some extra care.

The purchase of archival collection in digital version is much more costly than the binding and traditional way of preservation of old journals.

The information in digital form provides different formats such as video and film, text graphics, sound number and data. The users have an interactive experience with a multidimensional interaction of reading, viewing, listening, and interacting through activities such as exploring, searching, manipulating, etc.

Time : The digital library support the forth law of library science "save the time of the reader". One of the major advantage of digital library is time saving. It is available 24 hours a day, 7 days a week. Access to the contents will not be constraint by time. The information can be accessed any time anywhere in the world.

Service : Digital libraries have facilities for the users to identify document on internet, to access the relevance of an article before reading and retrieving the full text. It creates a customized document retrieval, which includes combination of bibliographic and other elements, to access specific piece of information such as equation a fact or a diagram and also to access information movies, sound and simulations of scientific experiments.

It can be said that quality service can be achieved through digital libraries. The time of the users can be saved. What can Digital libraries do, that traditional library cannot?

- They provide a time and place independent information service to the users.
- They are more than just a collection of hyperlinks on a web site. They form a comprehensive storehouse of data that can be indexed and searched, all in one place.
- Corporate organizations and public bodies possess knowledge that cab be refused for in-house training.

DLs have emerged as a powerful knowledge management tool in such scenarios.

- Useful in distance education where issuing books is a challenge.
- Digital libraries are able to integrate freely available information on the web..
- Preservation and archive digital works or scanned documents, manuscripts, printings etc. over a long time.

ADVANTAGES OF DIGITAL MATERIAL OVER PRINTED MATERIAL

Digital materials have several advantages over printed material, which are as under:

1. May be available to users anywhere and at any time.
2. May be used simultaneously by more than one person.
3. Can revise and reformatted easily.
4. Make feasible on demand.
5. Result in saving in tern around time.
6. Can integrate sound and motion with text.
7. Can be linked with other text through hypertext linkage.
8. Can be made interactive and responsive.
9. Can be copied and safeguard from loss, damage or catastrophe.
10. Can be searched fully using Boolean operations.
11. Material can be delivered directly to the user's computer.
12. Information search is easy, and
13. Any number of documents can be given to users. Not only is that, multiple distributions of copies at any time, anywhere possible.

14. Maintenance is easy.
15. Multiple usage and easy access are the prime factors behind the advantages of the digital library over traditional library. But it is possible only when the information is in digital form.

Advantages of electronic information over non-electronic information

- Supporting multimedia content
- Networking accessibility
- User-friendly interfaces
- Unique referencing of digital objects
- Multi-user and refer various area in same time
- Current information services
- Advanced search and retrieval
- Supporting both formal and informal learning
- Remote access
- Online discussions and commands
- Accessibility from anyone anywhere, any time, during travel, etc., supporting, opportunity to publishing, annotation and integration of new information.

Differentiation in electronic information from other resources

1. Organization in terms of digital files/objects
2. Contain material in digitized form
3. Key metadata
4. The only services are those performed by computer software
5. There is no librarian
6. Objects can disappear anytime and mutate anytime
7. There is no defined user group

8. Use of services mostly required payment
9. No concept of author
10. Objects are not located in a physical or logical place
11. No authority control
12. Objects are searchable.

From the viewpoint of contents, a digital product is nowhere different from a printed publication. Yet in usage, the variation can be observed. A book can be used anywhere, where as a digital product requires specific equipment such as computer and other equipments. Of course, after the matter has been downloaded in printed format, and by putting the printed sheets in the specified sequence, to a large extend it becomes a monograph. Since, it becomes analogous to book; many users prefer such a format. However, the Copyright Act prohibits such a use. In other words, downloading the copyrighted material without the permission of the author is an offence. However, in digital environment, this has to be looked into afresh, and for archiving and preserving purpose, such restriction has to be removed.

The growth in the electronic and communication technologies has transformed the world into global village.

Electronic contents have several advantages like economy in providing multiple pointers (access points) location independence, easy manipulations of contents, breaking and boundary between metadata secondary information and primary information, capability to handle dynamic content and possibility of collaborative working even though, web captured information etc are important areas for library professionals.

To use a traditional library, the user almost invariably goes to the library. Some libraries will deliver books or photocopies to privileged users, but even those users must be near the library and known to the library staff. In contrast, users of digital library have no incentive to visit any particular location. The librarian, webmasters, and other professionals who manage the collection have offices where they work, but there is no reason why they should ever see a user. The digital library could store its collection somewhere else.

In the early days of digital libraries, a common question was whether digital libraries would replace printed books. The initial discussion concentration on question of readability. With experience, people have realized that computers and books are not directly equivalent. Computing allows powerful searching, which no manual system can provide. The human factors of a printed book are superb. It is portable, it can be annoted, it can be read anywhere, and no special equipment is needed to read it. Since digital texts and printed material serve different purposes, some publishers create print and online versions of the same materials. One advantage of digital network technology is that information can be moved rapidly from place to place. Libraries need not own material themselves so long as they or their patron can obtain it quickly from other sources.

Traditional libraries are not easy to use effectively; however, they change slowly, and over the years their users develop expertise. Digital libraries evolve so quickly that every month brings new services, new collection, new interfaces, and new problems.

ADVANTAGES OF DIGITAL LIBRARY OVER CONVENTIANAL / TRADITIONAL LIBRARY

Some of the key advantages of digital library are:

1. Digital libraries are completely of paperless systems, which contain technology and information sources and allow remote access of its resources to other libraries by breaking down the physical barriers through national and international computer networks.

2. An other advantage is that at the same time users from many locations can access simple electronic information, can copy, print and preserve at his location or wherever he desired.
3. Digital libraries provide better, retrieval and faster communications.
4. Digital storage permits libraries to expend the range of material that they can provide to its users. Digital material can also permit access to videotapes and multimedia material that are created only on computers.
5. Due to advent of digital libraries there is a significant growth in the use of internet to share information.
6. Digital library technology has made it possible to have a continuous, easy and quick flow of information from point of organization to location of its use.
7. It offers faster and easy access to a large number of users.
8. It allows greater sharing of information than ever before.
9. It allows the applications of latest research findings in remote areas in villages.
10. Internet is its chief delivery mechanism for services thus increasing the variety, efficiency and availability of improved library services.
11. Communication and data transfer or interchange can be done easily with the help of Internet, e-mail attachments and CD-net.
12. It has minimized the duplication of efforts.
13. Digital services allow better accessibility, prompt, availability and desktop availability of information for socioeconomic and cultural development.
14. It has reduced the world into a global village where

every one can adopt findings and implement new technologies thereby leading to modern techniques and improved output.

15. Digital library is a new technological development operating via internet and World Wide Web and focus on advancing the means to collect, store, organize and disseminate information to the users.
16. Access to digital information is not bound by space or time.
17. Information is available 24 hours a day and 7 days a week.
18. Important information is downloaded and printed by the end users.
19. Digital services help in protection of collection from damage.
20. It is highly durable.
21. **Space**: The transition to electronic form essentially eliminates space problem. Traditional libraries are limited by storage space. Digital libraries have the potential to store much more information, simply because digital information requires very little physical space to contain it.
22. **Preservation**: the subscription of an e-journals are most cost effective, but the preservation or the archives required an extra care. The purchase of archival collection in digital version is much more costly than the binding and traditional way of preservation of old journals. These aspects are very important for preserving the on-line journals. Skilled professionals, hardware support and software support.
23. **Quality**: The information in digital form provides different formats such as motion videos, and films, still photographs, text, graphics, animation, sound, number and data. The multidimensional interaction of

reading, viewing, listening, and interacting through activities such as exploring, searching, manipulating, working, linking etc.

A digital object is like a physical artifact in many ways. But there is an obvious shift in emphasis from the object containing information-that is the book -to the content itself. Digitized object can be linked to other objects on the World Wide Web allowing users to jump from one source to an other across the traditional boundaries of the book.

Some of the key advantages of digital library include:

1. Ability to search.
2. Ubiquity.
3. Support wide range of material.
4. Preservation.
5. Access current information.

There are several advantages of a digital library over a conventional library. While traditional libraries are limited by storage space. These include minimizes storage space and cutting down cost of library maintenance and resource distribution.

As such, the cost of maintaining a digital library is much lower than that of traditional library. A traditional library must spend large sum of money paying for staff, book maintenance, and additional books.

A digital library is also not merely an automated conventional library, where the resources are electronically cataloged and are available only for browsing purpose. Digital libraries can immediately adopt innovations in technology providing users with improvement in electronic and audio book technology as well as presenting new forms of communications such as wikis and blogs.

Although conventional libraries do preserve socio-culture ambiences within their spaces, a digital can provide intellectual artifacts that cannot be represented or distributed in printed formats, such as audio/video multimedia content. Thus, a digital library may evolve into a complex system that makes information available in hard copy, on magnetic tapes and discs, CD-ROMs and videodiscs, including those from online sources.

The barrier of space and time in the search for knowledge are also being eliminated. Today, students, researchers, informational professionals, etc. can directly access many of the rarest information of the world with high quality images. Right at the desktop or other web enabled devices, at any time and from any location. Audio recording of historic speeches, video clippings from old telecasts, etc are being delivered directly to the desk.

Sun Microsystems defines a digital library as the electronic extension of functions users typically perform and the resources they access in a traditional library. These information resources can be translated into digital form, stored in multimedia repositories, and made available through web-based services. The emergence of digital library mirrors the growth of e-learning or distance learning. As the student population increasingly turns to off-campus alternatives for life long learning. They can locate information resources from anywhere any time.

With the advent of Internet, individuals' expectations for access to information have increased dramatically.

With the development of digital library, an individual can:

1. Gain access to the holdings of libraries worldwide through automated catalogs.
2. Locate both physical and digitized version of scholarly articles and books.
3. Optimize searches; simultaneously search the

Internet, commercial databases, and library collections.

4. Save search results and conduct additional processing to narrow or qualify results.
5. From search results, click through to access the digitized content or locate additional items of interest.

All these capabilities are available from the desktop or other web-enabled devices such as personal digital assistant or cellular phones. Additionally, the users can customized his or her information request so that search results reflect individual needs and preferences.

We can say that digital libraries are not going to replace the physical existence of documents completely but no doubt to meet the present demand, to satisfy the non-local users digitization must be introduced so that at least libraries becomes of hybrid nature.

4

Need, Purpose, Use, Advantages and Disadvantages of Digital Libraries

INTRODUCTION

There are electronic tools, which enable this to be done quickly and easily by text search. Also the growing use of multimedia data has introduces new challenges in storage and communication of diverse multimedia objects like video, audio and images. The World Wide Web makes it easier to transfer such information over national/international networks. There is rapidly increasing interest in digital libraries. Academia, libraries, publishers, system developers, and diverse users' population are collaborating in existing new way to create digital library model and technologies. There are electronic tools, which enable this to be done quickly and easily by text search. Libraries and archives with unique collection are digitizing their material not only to preserve them, but also to provide extensive access to their content from multiple locations, and provide a way to enrich the teaching and learning environment, not possible otherwise with traditional printed materials. There is also rapidly increasingly interest in digital libraries.

WHY WE NEED DIGITAL LIBRARIES?

We need digital library technology to manage large amounts of digital content, such as thousands of images or hundreds of audio clips to perform searches that are impracticable manually. Also the growing use of multimedia data has introduced new challenges in storage and communication of drawings and multimedia objects like audio, video and images. The WWW makes it easier and possible to transfer such information over national and international networks.

The shrinking budget of the libraries, changing information needs of the users, remote preference increasing demand for electronic resources and services, changing learning style 24x7, to support distance and distributed learning are some of the factors which are responsible for the creation of the digital library.

Library professionals are favoring digital libraries because

- they shall be relieved from the additional responsibilities and tensions as there is no fear of loss or damage of documents;
- no need to procure multiple copies of a single title;
- no security needed;
- no storage cost needed;
- No shelving and re- shelving;
- No administration of reminders overdue fine etc.
- Traditional libraries are limited by storage space;
- Digital libraries have the potentials to store much more information, simply because digital information requires a very little physical space to contain it.

- A digital library shall also satisfy the basic laws of library science.
- A particular digital library can provide a link to any other resources of other digital libraries very easily round the clock; thus a seamlessly integrated resource sharing in a structured approach can be achieved.
- The user of a digital library need not to go to the library physically; they can view the contents at home, office or any other non-library locations.
- People from all over the world can access to the same information, as long as internet connection is available. Thus, valuable time, energy of the scholar working on the forefront of knowledge can be saved.
- Digital libraries have the ability to enable worldwide access to a never-ending supply of distributed information.

REASONS FOR BUILDING DIGITAL LIBRARY

The need of digital libraries can be summarized as follows:

a. They can help us to preserve our linguistic, literary, historical and cultural heritage.
b. They make access simpler and cheaper.
c. They lower the costs of disseminating information.
d. They help us to establish new communities around new collections that can now become available.
e. They support teaching and learning, especially in the context of distance or lifelong teaching.
f. They allow rich media types to be included and managed effectively.
g. They encourage authors to create, share, and others to collaborate and quickly build on newly discovered knowledge.

h. The fundamental reason for building digital libraries is a belief that they will provide better delivery of information than was possible in the past. Digitization actually fulfills the need for preservation and conservation.

i. Value addition through new or improved searching aids, text retrieval and links to other items through appropriate use of metadata.

j. Improved customer service through virtually instant search and retrieval of documents.

k. More efficient collection with other institutions.

l. Sharing the information internally within the organization or over World Wide Web.

Traditional libraries are a fundamental part of society, but they are not perfect in terms of services. Information once available only to the professionals is now directly available to all. From a personal computer, the user is able consult material that is stored on computers around the world.

Creation of digital libraries is advocated not only to preserve and conserve materials, but also to increase their customer base by making older and rarer or heavily used documents available to a much wider audience. In addition, the number of electronic publication is increasing rapidly in key areas encompassing journals, patents, abstracts, maps, etc. This has implications on acquisition, storage, preservation and service policies of libraries.

In digital libraries, information in a variety of formats including text, image, video, and audio is available to a much wider community of users than that was possible with print format.

Libraries collect and preserve materials in order to serve their information seekers and to satisfy their information needs. The most obvious benefit of digitization is to preserve and provide the aggregation of various recourses in digital form using digital technology. Digitization means acquiring, converting, storing and retrieving in standardized manner, with the help of modern technical gadgets.

In the period of last decade of 20th century a number of libraries and information centers in a number of courtiers and localities have developed their computer system to create electronic bibliographic databases in place of traditional card catalog for identification and physical location of documents where they are available. To find such physical location of available information, the digitized system is always used not only to serve the purpose but also for all the activities of library. Therefore, there is a need of digitized information system for each and every library of traditional nature for the time saving services to the users.

Digitization may also be taken as a visible proportion to enhance the shelf life of printed information by preservation apart from the virtual of increased and easy access. Digitization also helps reduce drowsiness and boredom to great extent. There is also close interaction between the user and the computer. Digital libraries are characterized by equitable access; reduce barriers of distance, timeliness, shared resources and content delivery. They can provide access to a large quantity of collection of primary and secondary documents. They can also support publicity and integration of new information. Additionally they offer greater opportunities to users to both deposit and use information. Digitized library can further help and organize printed work into a universal library and thus provide access to it from anywhere in the world.

In the digital form, since users can make any numbers of copies and only these copies of the material are being used, at one point of time, there exist fair chances of at least one electronic copy to be available on the network for use by posterity.

Digital libraries have the ability to enable worldwide access to never ending supply of distributed information, which is constantly and conveniently available and updateable.

Digitization supports distance learning, comparative study and training staff that needs reference. In the case of resource which is not so in digitization. Digitization helps to avoid duplication in generation and collection of data by different agencies. It enables librarian to choose the information from various agencies by quality control and standardization. It is an information repository and act as central agency. Copying and maintaining rare material can be easily done with the help of digitization and thus safeguarding the material from the loss and damage. A national digital library collection helps in preventing duplications of efforts and wastages of scare resources. Digitization enhances integration of sound and motion with text having more effect. It helps link with other text through hypertext linkage. Digitized object can be linked to other objects on the World Wide Web (WWW) allowing users to jump from one resource to other.

Digital libraries are easier to maintain since the chances of having broken links (links that refer to pages that no longer exists) is less than that of websites with standard HTML pages. This is because the links are created by the digital library software and not manually inserted.

Now the modern day librarian is experiencing the new information technology and its impact on every facet of information handling. The advent of the digital computer and advances in communication technology and digital audio-visual technologies have opened up new possibilities in dealing with problems arising from collecting, organizing and disseminating a vast amount of information in various forms and formats

There are various factors that explain the need of digital library which are as follows:

1. Information Explosion

This is an era of information explosion due to multidisciplinary and interdisciplinary research, proliferation of publication activities, and transfer of information among user community. Digital libraries can fulfill the requirement of providing high quality output to the users. Literature is growing at an exponential rate causing problems for space, storage as well as utilization of voluminous information.

There have been several inherent problems in information use and handling, because of the information explosion, inter disciplinary nature and mission oriented nature of R&D activities, geographical, language and other barriers. However, in order to overcome these barriers, there exist today a vast array of electronic tools and techniques for accumulating, storing, organizing, retrieving and interpreting information on a world wide scale, in a volume and at a speed and with accuracy that would have been impossible a few years ago.

Due to the high growth of information, changing information needs of the user and the development of new techniques in processing and dissemination of information are some of the challenges faced by the librarians/ information managers. To store such a huge amount of information physically is very difficult and time consuming and complicated. But with emergence of digital library, storage and retrieval has become easier, comprehensive and affordable.

The professionals, scientists and researchers have to spend their lot of time in searching and reading a literature for information of their subjects. The failure to locate and to find the appropriate information may lead to create duplicate work. The immediate access of information from different databases throughout the world is only possible through digital or electronic library. The latest information is accessed through digital library. Digital library plays an important role in accessing the information from outside the world.

To avoid the time consuming process and to access the current and urgent information the digital or electronic library system needs to be adopted by a number of organizations.

2. Storage of Information

Information is growing at an exponential rate causing problems for space, storage as well as utilization of voluminous information. In order to solve the space problem in libraries; many libraries are going ahead or planning to go further in order to provide electronic access of information to their clientele. Resources are preserved for future generation and simultaneously made accessible for current use.

The advantages of having library material in digital storage are:

1. The contents occupy less space and can be replicated and used electronically.
2. The content can be made available on networks.
3. The search for content can be automated.

Now the question is whether the digital libraries are going to replace traditional libraries or not.

Digital library technology plays an important role in promoting the use of information. Digital libraries give solutions to the main challenges of traditional libraries such as shortage of space, economic survival and management of materials; it has its own limitations. End users who are exposed to information technology will have difficulty to access the information, which is stored inside the computer in digitized format. Training each user will be tedious task. So it may not be an under estimation to say that digital library services as a supplement.

To traditional library and one can not so easily jump to a conclusion that digital library is going to replace all the traditional concepts including papers. In order to reduce the subscription cost of journals, we must go for electronic form of resources to reduce the subscription cost of library. Library automation has helped libraries in improving library activities. It saves the efforts, time and manpower of libraries. In an automated service the information can be altered and updated without the repetitive work involved in the manual system. The development of computer, any information can be turned into sequences. It saves the time for the users, staff, and increases productivity and reliability. Digital information can be sent in multiple copies simultaneously over information networks in a fraction of a minute or even of a second. Therefore, the librarians should initiate the digital library with the management support. Digitization in all aspects will save time, energy, manpower, space, etc.

Digital libraries have the ability to enable worldwide access to a never-ending supply of distributed information which is constantly and conveniently available and up datable. The number of people accessing digital library collection through the web is increasing rapidly.

ADVANTAGES OF DIGITAL LIBRARIES

Digital or electronic libraries are organized collection of digital or electronic information. Digital information is new technology for information handling. It improves the performance of libraries in the dissemination of information. It removes the geographical barriers. One can get information from any part of the world from his desktop computer. Digital library is not restricted to the provision of information in text format, audio, visual, and video resources. It can disseminate information across a network and user can retrieve information in the same way and shared by many at a time very easily by putting them in the network.

Digital library is an important component for capturing the explicit knowledge. This has to be supplemented with the implicit knowledge to the digital library system, which will eventually get transformed into a knowledge management system.

It will be useful to digitize and store textbooks in the library, which can be accesses by the students whenever required. This additional facility will enable easy availability of books to the students for instant reference and study through Internet and intranet access. We need to integrate the tele-education system with the digital library, so that the students can read and refer to the books suggested by the teacher from a distant location through online learning services. There are large numbers of files and records occupying valuable space in our libraries. It is essential to segregate the important files, which have to be digitized and stored in the digital library.

The following advantages can be summarizing as follows:

1. No physical boundary

The user of a digital library need not go to the library physically.

Digital libraries bring the library to the user from any part of the world. A digital library brings the information to the user's desk, either at work or at home. The user of a digital library needs not to go to the library physically. Peoples from all over the world can gain access to the same information, as long as an Internet connection is available. There is a library where there is a personal computer.

2. Round the clock availability

A major advantage of digital library is that people from all over the world can gain access to the information at any time, as long as an internet connection is available.

Service at doorstep at 7x24 hrs. A major advantage of digital libraries is that people can gain access to the information at any time, night or day. The doors of digital library never close. This does not mean that digital libraries are perfect. Computer system can fail, and networks may be slow or unreliable. But, compared with a traditional library, information is much more likely to be available when and where the user wants.

3. Structured approach

A digital library provides access to much richer contents in a more structured manner, that is, we can easily move from the catalog to the particular book, than to a particular chapter, and so on.

4. Information Retrieval

There is flexibility in the use of search term, that is, key words. A digital library can provide very user-friendly interface, giving clickable access to its resources.

5. Preservation Space

An exact copy of the original can be made any numbers of times without any degradation in quality. The library has no space for extension, digitization is the only solution.

6. Networking

A particular digital library can provide the link to any other resources of other digital libraries very easily; thus a seamlessly integrated resource sharing can be achieved.

7. Cost

In theory, the cost of maintaining a digital library is lower than that of traditional library. A traditional library must spend large sums of money paying for staff, rent, and additional books. Although, digital libraries do away with these fees, it has since been found that digital libraries can be no less expensive in their own way to operate. Digital libraries can and do incur large costs for the conversion of print materials into digital format, for the technical skills of staff, and for the cost of maintaining online access (servers, bandwidth cost etc).Also, the information in a digital library must often be migrated every few years to the latest digital media. This process can incur very large costs in hardware and skilled staff.

8. Improved access, search and browsing

An important advantage of digital conversion is increased accessibility to users. There is also availability to individuals who may not be traditional users of a library, due to geographic location or organizational affiliation. There is an ease of access through digital libraries and online access.

Support the full text searching-finding the information in paper -based material is very difficult. In most aspects, computer system is better than manual methods for finding information. Search system is improving.

9. Information can be shared more easily

Resource sharing can be done easily with the digital collection. Digital library is indicative of network collection of historical, cultural, scientific and knowledge related artifacts in various digital formats. These collections are accessible to peoples who need them. In the present era, there are no barriers in reaching the resources. Such emerging trends have produced positive impact in sharing the resources and it effectively meets the user's requirements.

10. Effective searching and retrieval

There is powerful searching and browsing possibilities.

The user is able to use any search term (word, phrase, title, name, and subject) to search the entire collection. Digital libraries can provide very user-friendly interface, giving click able access to its resources.

11. Hypertext linking is possible

Placing digital information on a network makes it available to everybody. Libraries and archives contain much information that is unique. Many digital libraries or electronic publications are maintained at a single central site, perhaps with a few duplicate copies strategically placed around the world. Sharing of digital files is much easier. Provide an easy mechanism for recourse sharing with other libraries. Sharing of digital files is much easier.

12. Easy to keep information current

Information can be updated continuously and much more easily. Keeping information current is less laborious when the definitive version is in digital format and stored on a central computer. Many libraries maintain online versions of directories, encyclopedias and other reference work. Whenever revisions are received from the publishers, they are installed on the library's computer. The Library of Congress has an on-line collection, called Thomas that contains the latest drafts of all legislation currently before Congress.

13. Wider Access

A digital library can meet simultaneous access request for the same electronic document by easily creating multiple instances (or copies) of the requested document. A digital library can thus meet requirements of much larger population of users. Digital libraries also permit libraries to expand the range of material they can provide to the users.

Digital material can also permit access to videotapes and new kinds of multi-media materials that are created only on computers and have no equivalent in any traditional format.

14. Provide user-friendly interface

The user is able to use any search term bellowing to the word or phrase of the entire collection. Digital libraries can provide very user-friendly interfaces, giving click able access to its resources.

15. Multiple accesses

The same recourses can be used at the same time by a number of users. The same resources can be used simultaneously by a numbers of institutions and users. This may not be the case of copyrighted material: a library may have license for "lending out" only one copy at a time; this is achieved with a system of digital right management where a resource can become inaccessible after expiration of the lending period or after the lender choose to make it inaccessible (equivalent to returning the resource).

16. Improved Preservation

It is easy to copy digital information, without errors-no fear of maintaining one physical object permanently. So rare publications and artifacts may be preserved better by providing access to their digital versions. An exact copy of the original can be made by any number of times without degradation in quality.

17. Networking

A particular digital library can provide a link to any other recourse of other digital libraries very easily. Thus a seamlessly integrated recourse sharing can be achieved. Sharing the information internally within the organization or over WWW.

18. Bring together the people with formal, informal and professional learning missions.

19. Digital libraries may save money

A traditional library must spend large sums of money paying for staff, book maintenance, rent, and additional books.

The cost of maintaining a digital library is lower than that of a traditional library. The traditional library occupies expensive buildings on prime sites. Big libraries employ hundreds of peoples -well educated, though poorly paid. A traditional library must spend large sum of money paying for the staff, books maintenance, rent and additional books. Libraries never have enough money to acquire and process all the material they desire. Publishing is also expensive. Today's digital libraries are also expensive—initially more expensive than conventional one.

Digital libraries can and do incur large costs for the conversion of print materials into digital format, for the technical skills of the staff to maintain them, and the costs of maintaining online access (i.e. server, bandwidth cost, etc.). However, given the declining costs of technology, if a library can understand how it will be fund the first refresh cycle in five to ten years, it can expect that the next refresh cycle will be so cheap as to be insignificant. In, particular the cost of distributing and of storing digital information decline. The reduction in cost may not be uniform. Other costs will not decline at the same rate and may even increase. Overall, however, there is a great opportunity to lower the cost of publishing and libraries.

20. Allow collaboration and exchange of idea

Technology of the digital libraries is closely related to e-mail and teleconferencing.

21. Saves the space, which is required for physical documents

Where as traditional libraries are limited by storage space, digital libraries have the potential to store much more information, simply because digital information requires very little physical space to contain them and media storage technologies are more affordable than ever before. When the library has no space for extension digitization is the only solution.

22. Support multimedia content.

23. Access current information:

For researchers, digital libraries provide access to up to date current information and there by help them to be aware of current trends.

24. Computers have become portable

Although digital libraries use networks, their utility has been greatly enhanced by the development of portable "laptop" computers. By attaching a laptop computer to network connection, a user combines the digital library resources of the Internet with the personal work that is stored on the computer. When the user disconnects the computer, copies of selected library material can be retain for personal use.

25. Reduced manpower

Lesser manpower is required in a digitized library.

Some of the other benefits are:

- Increased speed of access
- Connects users with authors instantly
- Promote paperless office environment
- Promote e-learning
- Ensure increased productivity
- On-line user education
- Instant downloading of information
- Faster addition and gap reduction.
- Promote universal accessibility.

- Provide access to more information than physically acquired information.
- Protects rare books that are rapidly deteriorating due to over use and poor storage condition.
- Provides facility for the downloading and printing.
- Saves the cost and manpower required for publishing and bringing out new editions.
- **Added value**: Certain characteristics of objects, primarily the quality of images, may be improved. Digitization can enhance legibility and remove visible flaws such as stains and discoloration.
- Support both formal and informal learning.
- Unlimited data span.
- Wide availability to public.

Digital technology has revolutionized the ability to create electronic replica of print materials, and institutions around the world are moving ahed with project to digitized books, manuscripts, photographs, maps, architectural drawings, films, sound recordings in their collection.

DISADVANTAGES OF DIGITAL LIBRARY

Though it is too early to comment on its advantages and disadvantages. However, one can visualize that by this conversion from paper to electronic document .The old report will be easily searchable and accessible by different persons at different places at the same time. It will enable resource sharing among different libraries all over the country and database can be accessed through LAN, WAN etc. It will save the intellectual resources of the library / institution which have immense potential for further research and economic benefits for the country as a whole in addition to its archival value also. Documents stored electronically are very flexible. They are easy to revise, rearrange, reformat and combine with other documents.

Digitization of information does help us to great extent. However, there are problems for handling and using these large volume of digitized information.

Digital libraries are not without their limitations, at least for the time being. Some of the limitations are as follows:

1. Hardware

The major risk to digital object is not physical deterioration, but technological obsolescence of the devices to read them. While the lifetime of optical and magneto-optical cartridges are expected to be in decades, those of reading devices are only about one decade.

2. Software

A more serious problem is software obsolescence. It has been pointed out that the variety of software formats for exceeds the number of hardware devices manufactured, and these programmes come and go more quickly than the hardware does.

3. Copyright problem

It is very easy to copy, replicate, message and distribute digital information. Enforcing copyright in digital environment is a major issue. However, other digital libraries (more specially, digital collections, which may be acquired by the libraries) accommodate copyright concern by licensing content and distributing it on a commercial basis, which allows for better management of the content's reproduction and the payment (if required) of royalties.

Access to digital libraries and their collection is depending on a stable information technology infrastructure (power, computers, communications link etc.). Hence, despite the egalitarian potential of the digital library, many of those who could most benefit from its global reach (for instance in the third world) are not able to do so.

An other key issue is that of interlocking of different digital libraries. Given the distribution of library resources around the world, no one can expect that there would be a single digital resource. This means that we need methods of finding either individual items or collection in different places, and assembling virtual collections that users can search or browse.

4. Network bandwidth

With the exploding numbers of users, multi-media contents, web sites and applications (e.g. chat, games), bandwidth available for accessing digital libraries is going to be a serious issue. Even a single speed CD-ROM drive @ 150 KBPS) provides faster access time than a 56 KBPS modem. As another example, over a 64 KBPS ISDN, line an ASCII text page arrives in less than half a second while an image page takes 4 seconds which is a definite lag.

Some of the other limitations are as follows:

1. Compatibility and standardization problems are likely to be faced due to the use of variety of software, hardware, information collection, and storage and retrieval methods.
2. There is shortage of library skilled professionals having knowledge of information technology.
3. A problem frequently encountered and difficult to overcome will be the one of copyright and intellectual property issue.
4. The unrelenting invasion of the viruses will pose an other ethical problem.
5. Browsing of digitized form is difficult when compared to printed form.
6. Remote accesses to documents are uncomfortable as compared to spot access.
7. Problems in the scholarly publishing.

8. Some documents are used only when they are seen.
9. Locating and searching the information on the Internet requires good skills.
10. Problems of intellectual property rights of the author and publisher, etc.
11. There is a problem of health hazard associated with the use of computers e.g. eye and back problems as well as the exposure of radiation from monitor. It has bad effect on eyes.
12. There will be a necessity to be proficient in computer usage. One should have sufficient knowledge of computer applications.
13. With the growing use of networked system, security will become a key issue. Protecting valuable databank from infiltrations by the disgruntled users will require special effort. In fact, security is one of the most complex challenges facing information providers on the Internet today.
14. It is also difficult for the users to locate and access the information because information is not usually structured and no rules or codes are followed and besides no one controls the information that is made available. Here, the information or data may be of different types.

Some people criticizes that copyright law hampers digital libraries because works cannot be shared over different periods of time in the manner of a traditional library. The contents are in many cases, public domain or self generated only. Some digital libraries, work to digitized out of copyright works and make them freely available to the public.

Digital libraries cannot reproduce the environment of a traditional library. Many people also find reading printed material on a computer screen, although this depends heavily on presentation as well as personnel preference. Also, due to technological developments, a digital library can see some of its content become out of date and its data may become inaccessible.

A digital library is not less expensive because large costs incurred for the conversion of print materials into digital format, for the technical skills of staff, and for the cost of maintaining online access (i.e. servers, bandwidth cost, etc.).Copyright law hampers it, because works cannot be shared over different periods of time in the manner of a traditional library. It has been observed that some users prefer reading printed material to the material on a computer screen.

Digital libraries are wholly dependent on cheap, abundant sources of electricity, a secondary form of energy, which is produced primarily from fossils fuel and to a lesser extent from nuclear and "Green" sources. Without electricity, the contents cannot be accessed. Hence, any threat to the energy security of a society will threaten the very existence of the digital library. The traditional library after serving the society for sanctuaries together shall diminished. Moreover, man working with machines may become a machine by himself without a human heart. There is health hazards attached to the latest technology although economic factors are taken care of.

5

Components of Digital Libraries

INTRODUCTION

The digital library components must also be tailor made to capture, encode, and deliver information according to the standard practice adopted by the libraries. Because of the rapid pace of technological change, some standards are concrete and others are emerging. These components might not all be part of a discrete digital library system, but could be provided by other related or multi-purpose systems or environments. To interoperate with the existing library infrastructure, the digital library must be designed to work with existing library catalogs and incorporate industry standards, formats, and protocols.

A fully developed digital library environment involves the following elements/components:

1. Digital documents (both digital or by conversion of content to digital form)
2. The extraction or creation of metadata or indexing information describing the content to facilitate searching as well administrative and structural

metadata to assist in object viewing, management and preservation;

3. Storage of digital contents and metadata in an appropriate multimedia repository. This will meet the requirement of Intellectual Property Rights;
4. Client services for the browser, including repository querying and workflow;
5. Content delivery via file transfer or streaming media;
6. User access through a browser or dedicated client; and
7. A private or public computer network.

Digital library consists of following main components:

1. User interfaces or user.
2. Storage media or (repository) and
3. Identifiers.

User Interfaces or User

A standard Internet browser is used for the actual interactions with the user. This can be Netscape Navigator or Microsoft Internet explorer. Through the browser, user connects to client server (repository) URL with TCP technology.

Storage media (Repository) and Identifiers

A repository is any computer system whose primary function is to store digital material for use in a library. Currently, the most common form of repository is the web server. Stores and manage digital objects and other information. The interface for this is called Repository Access Protocol (RAP). These repository will have identifier with the help of identifier users can identify Internet resources such as digital objects.

In other words identifier of the repository where the objects are stored.

Repository consists of

1. Data
2. Meta Data
3. Meta-objects

Data

Data is a general term used to describe information that is encoded in digital form. The things, which are digitized from the data. The materials selected may include image, text, audio and video. The material need to be acquired and process is called data acquisition. Scanner and digital cameras can do this. The place where all the digitized objects are stored is called repository. The information stored in a digital library can be divided into data and metadata.

The data consists of books, journals and articles stored in digital form in a hard disc of computer. The storage of digitized information is completed through two methods. The one method is to make the photographs and scanning of images through electronic devices and an other method is to store the text by its each and every character by ASCII code. Less spaced storage software are available in ASCII coded from to scan the printed matters by using scanner, and converted those scanned characters into coded form.

Numerical Data

Numerical data consists of tables of different types, i.e. data of physical property, data of astronomy. Such stored digitized information can be used by the curve setting programs and spared sheet programs in a required format.

Graphical

This type of data consists of the photographs, maps, drawings etc. The storage of data is done through the scanning of images. These scanned images are stored in codes that contain in the abstract information. Maps are stored by using latitudes and longitudes, and also with the coordinate issue of cities and roads.

Photographs

Colour and monochrome are stored in bit mapped from using compression algorithms to reduce storage space.

Audio

Audio data are digitized and compressed by using a common accepted standard compression algorithms and stored systematically. The musical stores may also be coded and stored along with the audio data.

Video Data

This data required a lot of storage space, in compression with other data, due to the need of repeating the frames at least 30 times per second. The data are compressed in such a way that help to decompress the data and displayed it in original form.

Indexing

The indexing and interlinking multimedia data are most important for easy retrieval of stored data. The key words from the textual documents are selected and linked with related words to link logically with software and data. This is called hypertext. Data in other media (audio/video) are also selected and linked to retrieve the stored data is known as hypermedia. Such links allow the users to navigate the data through multimedia material.

Linking

The information collected and stored in digital library is not normally stored in one computer. It is stored and distributed in many computers known as servers. All these servers are linked by high-speed communication links. In fact the stored and distributed digitized information need not be kept at the knowledge of users. Only the access of data is to be known to users by taking a care that the users would not make any change in digital information stored so far.

Users

Users are the most important components of the digital library. Users can access the information through digital library from any corner of the world. The users use the different terminals to acquire the needed information.

DEVICES/EQUIPMENTS

The digital library requires the different devices to collect, store, and retrieve and to send the information of digitized nature. The devices are the computers, electric equipments, microfilms and microfiche readers, scanners and other auxiliary equipments. All these devices can do the work of storage and display of information in digitized form.

The basic components of a digital library include necessary hardware and software and skilled and well-trained manpower.

HARDWARE COMPONENTS

1. Server with high capacity hard disk and clients in the LAN, Web Servers and FTTP server etc.
2. Latest PCs.
3. Capture devices such as scanners, digital cameras, OCR, data compression devices.
4. Storage devices for backup etc.
5. Printers.
6. High power UPS.
7. Secondary storage: CD-ROM (R and RW).
8. High speed LAN and WAN.
9. Internet connectivity.
10. network

SOFTWARE COMPONENTS

Software comprises of:

- Operating software; LINUX
- Optical Character Recognition (OCR)
- Scanning software.
- Adobe Acrobat Reader.
- CD-read Write software.
- Windows -NT Networking software.
- Web designing software such as JAWA.
- Storage softwares

Full text search engines to index and provide access to digital resources.

MANPOWER

The manpower, who are supposed to implement and manage the IT should be trained and retrained in order to keep themselves abreast of the latest technologies and tools of IT. It is one of the crucial activities of a digital library that require skilled manpower. The skilled manpower is an important component of digital library, without which the digital library cannot be developed for its certain purposes. The skilled manpower development programme has already been started by a number of institutions. These skilled persons are required to develop the digital library.

Factors affecting resource requirement

A few factors associated with the digital library determine type and extent of resources required. These include:

- Nature of digital library collection - one off/ static collection or dynamic /live collection.
- Volume of material to be digitized.
- Document formats (e.g. text images, audio, video) to

be supported and storage requirements.

- Backup and preservation requirements.
- Metadata and cataloging requirements.
- Quality requirements (document format and metadata).
- On-line and offline access.
- Internal/ external access, and
- Indexing, search and retrieval requirements.

Difference between data, Information and Knowledge

Data are facts, images or sounds that may or may not pertinent or useful for a particular task. In our daily life we get data from various sources such as from newspapers, journals, and from other sources. We receive so much data every minute that unconscious minds cannot possibly pay attention to all of it. On the other hand information is data whose forms and contents are appropriate for a particular use. Converting data into information by formatting, filtering and summarizing is a key role of librarian/information managers. So knowledge is a combination of instincts, ideas, rules and procedures that guide active network and shows way a library collects vast amount of data often fails to satisfy the user's information needs.

Metadata

The term Meta comes from the Greek word that denotes 'alongside or with or after'. More resent Latin and English usage suggests 'meta' to refer something transcendental or beyond nature. Literal meaning of metadata is data about data that describe the contents and attributes of any particular item in a digital library.

Metadata is defined as "data about data" or "information about information". This term is widely used. It is the information, which describes significant aspects of a digital resource. The extraction or creation of metadata or indexing information describing the content to facilities searching as well as administrative and structural metadata to assist in object viewing, management and preservation.

Providing access to the internally created digital resources is very important. Therefore, a suitable software and format has to be chosen and adopted in order to access the resources using various data elements. It is necessary to catalog these digital resources using suitable software, which supports Dublin Core (DC) Standard that is being adopted internationally to create metadata of digital resources. Metadata may be catalog record, or web page or digital resource. Metadata record consists of a set of attributes, which are necessary to describe a resource. It is used to describe the digital and non-digital resources located in a distributed system, in a networked environment.

The distinction between data and metadata often depends on the context. Catalog records and abstracts are usually considered to metadata because they describe other data, but in an online catalog or a database of abstracts they are the data.

One of the most challenging aspects of the digital environment is the identification of resources available on the web as well in the digital repositories. The existence of searchable data increases the chance of accessing the achieved digital object for use.

Metadata are well-organized, descriptive information about web resources, like catalogue cards in the case of printed documents. Constantly changing content and information resources on the Internet and the lack of a single format making cataloguing, search, and retrieval difficult. A universally accepted standard format for identification and organization of data elements of Internet resources is, therefore, crucial.

Metadata describes the items that are digitized.

Metadata is important for digital libraries because it is the key to resources. It is a concept familiar to librarians because it is one of the primary things that librarians do - they create cataloguing records that describe documents. Examples of metadata systems include library catalogs, archival finding aids, and museums inventory control register systems. Over the years, metadata formats have been developed for a wide range of digital objects. Within this range of formats, there is a degree of consistency across all metadata schemes that support interoperability. For example, most schemes provide for a title field, data field and identifier field.

It is the Internet term for information that librarians traditionally have put into catalogues and it most commonly refers to descriptive information about web resources. Any one who has used Alta Vista, Excite, or any of the other search engines on the Internet knows that simple full-text searches don't scale in a large network. An example of metadata is traditional card record of a book. Each digitized item will have metadata. For the creation of metadata MARC or Dublin Core Format is used. The first workshop took place at OCLC headquarters in Dublin, Ohio, hence the name "Dublin Core". The Dublin Core workshops defined a set of fifteen metadata elements—much simpler than those used in traditional library cataloguing. Some of the Dublin core elements are Title, subject, description, source, language, relation, coverage, publisher and creator. Normally metadata are created using HTML or XML.

In computerized environment, metadata may be automatically or semi-automatically extracted or derived from the original content, or the "full text" may simply be indexed and searched without involving metadata (as happens on the WWW when search engines are employed). Yet, if only metadata is available in computer form to describe a digital object, it must be used in digital libraries. Hence, metadata should be used whenever available in a digital library, and is an important aspect in many such systems.

Need of Metadata

Today metadata -related activities are a matter of concern and interest to authors, publishers, website developers, database administration, catalogers, curators, archivists and librarians.

Metadata is needed because

1. Lack of bibliographic control tools/aids for managing digital network information resources.
2. Absence of elaborate rules for managing multiple forms of digital information including text, image, video, audio, etc.
3. Demand for content analysis and organization of digital resources.
4. Failure of search mechanism, for effective information retrieval.
5. Changing in information handling methodology for information generation, distribution and access.
6. Information overload in terms of quality and quantity.
7. Electronic information communities with total ignorance/vested interest in rights management's issues.
8. A problem with preservation of contents and contexts of digitizes sources.

Applications

With the changing trends in information handling, metadata has wide applications in organizing digital collection. Metadata opens new avenues for information availability, accessibility and authority so as to meet the varying demand of different communities in information business.

More precisely the objectives are to:

1. Organize and maintain the organization's investments in data.
2. Provide information to data catalogue.
3. Provide information to aid data transfer.
4. Provide common agreement on what elements to use or what their contents should be.
5. Give information that effects the use of data, such as legal conditions on use, in size and age
6. Give history of data such as original source of data and any subsequent transformation give information about the owner or creator of the text, and
7. Give relationship with other resources such as linkages to previous and subsequent versions.

Types of Metadata

There are three types of metadata:

1. Descriptive
2. Structural and
3. Administrative

1. Descriptive metadata

Describe the intellectual content and association of a document or resource in a way that facilitates search, identification and collection of information contained within or exemplified by the resource. It is ideally meant for resource discovery and identification. Example data contained within a bibliographic record. Information about the book like title of the book, author, date of publication, publisher, ISBN, keywords, subject, language, etc.

Descriptive metadata is usually expressed as text, however, it can be used to describe information that is in formats other than text, such as images, sound recordings, maps, and computer programmes. Descriptive metadata often is stored in catalogs and indexes that are manage outside the repository. These catalogs and indexes may be held in separate repositories and may cover material in many independent digital libraries. Identifiers are used to associate the metadata with the corresponding data. A single catalog can combine records for all genres, media and formats. This enables users of digital libraries to discover materials in all media by searching textual records. Professionals usually crate descriptive metadata.

2. Structural Metadata

Information about formats and the structures. Define the physical structure of a complex entity to facilitate navigation, information retrieval and display. This metadata contains information pertains to each page, like the size of each page and whether the page is blank or has an important context attached to it—such as the beginning of the chapter, end of the chapter, index, preface, table of contents, etc. Such information enables us to improve the navigation of the book for the end users and also improves search and retrieval system.

3. Administrative Metadata

Which includes, rights, permissions, and other information used to manage access. It includes the administrative detail of the book, like the location where the book was scanned, the original source of book, scanning details, etc., may not be of interest to the end-user of the book but are useful to the operational organization. These details can be used to trace the progress of the project, generate reports and identify bottlenecks in the scanning process. For example, it would enable us to trace the scanner that was producing low quality scans. Some metadata refers to a group of objects. Administrative metadata used for access management may apply to an entire repository or to a collection within a repository. Finding aids apply to many objects.

Identifier: One item of metadata is identifier, which identifies an item to the outside world.

Meta-object: The repository may have plenty of digital objects in the form of data each of this data will be explained used metadata. The Mata-object provides references to the set of digital objects.

FUNCTIONAL COMPONENTS OF DIGITAL LIBRARY

- Conversion of print to digital and acquisition of digital media.
- Metadata creation, processing and description
- Storing of digital resources in appropriate repository in a networked environment for hosting in intranet, extranet and internet.
- Creating a single user interface and gateway for the digital resources.
- Patron access through a browser or dedicated client.

6
Digital/E- Library Resources

INTRODUCTION

The primary function of a library is to serve the users by satisfying their information needs. It is with the help of various resources available in the library. Recourses form the important component of library. Library and information centers are providing numerous types of information resources and services. Electronic resources have now become an important part of the library resources today. Information contents and services are changing with the passage of time. Microfilms, microfiche, micro card, etc. were popular library resources a few years ago. These microforms are now becoming replaced gradually by electronic media namely electronic books (E-books), E-journals, Electronic thesis, etc.

Digital library resources are like other library materials in many ways. They are selected, acquired, cataloged, managed, explained and promoted to users, evaluated, preserved, withdrawn, and cancelled. Digital information resources include journals, government documents, electronic images etc. Digital information exists in a format (numeric digits) that computer can store, organized transmit, and display without any intervening conversion process. Some digital information is created in that format, often described as "born digital". Digitized information has been transformed from an analog source. The printed page analog.

In early 70s most of the electronic resources were available on magnetic tapes and other magnetic media. But today various types of resources are available and accessed are intranet online (locally produced e-resources) and internet on line (remotely stored e-resources) and physical media (stored data on CD-ROM, audio, video cassettes etc) based. The third one is much like the traditional paper based publications with the exception that they require computer hardware and software for their utilization.

Creation of digital resources with the establishment of digital library is the need of the day. The digital information resources are going to play most vital role in the 21st century. The rapid developments in information technology have facilitated the emergence of new electronic devices, media and formats.

There is paradigm shift from hard to soft copy, print to digital, ownership of document to access of information, physical to virtual libraries. Application of information communication technology in libraries has provided enough opportunities for e-resource development and disseminate in the manner that their users preferred.

The digital resources are available on various digital medias such as CD-ROM, DVDs, floppies, on-line databases, digital archives, etc. Electronic information resources contain originally published information in digital form or information originally published in print form and then made available electronically. Among e-resources, e-journals and e-books are mostly in demand by the users.

Some information is available both in print and digital form as well.

Due to the changing demand of users for pin pointed and exhaustive information within a limited time, e-resources have become substantial part of library collection.

With the growing popularity of e-resources, the traditional libraries are gradually migrating from documents to e-resources where proving access to information is considered more important than owing it.

Digital libraries, which can be termed as virtual library in an Internet age, can be defined as a collection of information (not just books) using digital format. This digital format may vary from e-books, e-publishing, e-journals, reports, on-line databases, softwares, CD-ROMs or connected through networks across the world. Digital libraries promote the concept of free flow of information in a portable format and help in resource sharing among knowledge societies and public in general. They also help not only in storage of information but also act as information repositories.

The major function of digital libraries is to facilitate systematic and efficient access to and sharing of information on matters, considered important by the users. Not only does digital libraries promotes resource sharing, but also in the long run it can help in sharing of knowledge and resources. Some on-line libraries or information centers have started collecting a nominal fee for access to their resources, as they are well connected and networked with institutions, which provide specialized subject information.

Information is now available in various formats. It is the basic responsibility of any information center to make available all types of relevant information from different sources in different formats.

Digital resources are now available through global

networks if digital library collection created or stored at one library are to be available to others.

DIGITAL LIBRARY MATERIAL

Digital resources encompass many genre, format, and storage and delivery medium. Genre includes newspapers, reference books, journals, notification books, novels, indexes, and abstracts. Tool such as application software, and system for electronic documents delivery can be considered part of digital library

WHAT ARE DIGITAL/ELECTRONIC LIBRARY RESOURCES?

An electronic resource means the publication and dissemination of information by electronic means, especially by the use of optical disk formats such as CD-ROMs and networking. Other option can include the use of electronic databases, videotexts, e-mail, and electronic newsletter .These may be delivered on CD-ROM, on tape, via internet and so on. Over the past few years, a numbers of techniques and related standards have been allow documents to be created and distributed in electronic form. Hence to cope with the present situation, libraries are shifting towards a new media, namely e-resources for their collection developments that the demand of users is better fulfilled.

A digital library may refer only to electronic resources or means combinations of electronic resources, services that support using those resources and services that are provided via a network. In simple terms e-resources are those resources which requires computer access or any electronic product that delivers a collection of data, be it text referring to fultext databases, electronic journals, image collections, other multimedia products and numerical, graphical or time based, as a commercially available title that has been published with an aim to being marketed.

Uses of e-resources such as e-books, e-journals need

access to internet and WWW not for profit institutions may provide free access to these services. Some time these are paid services, some institutions provide free access to these services. Though the cost is coming down, but still the access to Internet and www are confined to institutions and their clients.

The e-resources on magnetic and optical media have a vast impact on the collection of libraries. These are more useful due to inherent capabilities for manipulation and searching, providing information access is cheaper to acquiring information resources, saving in storage and maintenance etc. and sometimes the electronics form is the only alternative.

Digital library resources includes

1. Collection in which complete contents documents are created or converted into machine-readable form for online access.
2. Scanned images, images of photographic or printed text etc.
3. Scientific data sets.
4. Online databases and CD-ROM information products particularly those with multimedia and interactive video components.
5. Computer storage devices such as optical disks, CD-ROMs/DVD-ROMs.
6. Databases accessible through Internet and other networks.
7. Digital audio, video clips or full length movie.

   Access outside the library's normal house of service.

WHY WE NEED DIGITAL LIBRARY RESOURCES?

Due to the increase in the information generation the task of collection, organization and retrieval of information made the task very difficult. That is why most of the libraries prefer electronic resources to print collection for optimum use. The other reasons are physical space, escalation in journals prices, digital literacy has force the libraries to opt for electronic resources in order to meet information needs of large community of users. According to Paul Glister "digital literacy is the ability to understand and use information in multiple formats from a wide range of sources when it is presented via computers." The proliferation of electronic resources has had a significant impact on the way the academic community uses, store and preserve information. Cataloguing, indexing, searching, retrieving print resources are tedious and time-consuming job, therefore expertise in creating an effective indexing and resources discovery system is required for search and retrieval services. According to Lawrence without efficient and comprehensive search services the content may not improve access greatly. Manpower is the most essential component for the library system. Professional experience and expertise make efficient use of e-resources. Digitization project can make print materials more easily accessible to users, create surrogates that are less vulnerable to theft and wear and serve as a preservation medium.

Digital library can store a large volume of digital information in archival form. A digital library may refer only to electronic resources or mean a combination of electronic resources, services that support using those resources or mean a combination of electronic resources, services that are provided via a network. It provides the users fast search tools, immediate access to the rapidly growing information in multimedia form quickly on the screen in an interactive mode. It also offers expensive and special collections of information from any remote location and multiple simultaneous users.

ADVANTAGES OF DIGITAL LIBRARY RESOURCES

Electronic resources offer libraries and their users many advantages. There are several advantages of using e-resources such as ease of usability, readability, affordability and accessibility. They can increase speed and ease of access and the amount of information available. They can save library space and staff time. They are not yet, however, the solution to all libraries' financial, space, access, and service problem. Most libraries continue to operate in a dual environment-print and electronic-resources, whether physically located within a library or accessed via a network, are part of the library's collection and should be evaluated and assessed with the same criteria and rigor applied to all collections decisions.

Some of the advantages of electronic resources can be listed as:

- Easy and effective retrieval search
- Current information
- Quick access through efficient search engines
- Teleconferencing
- Downloading the text, image, audio with the MM concept
- Teaching and learning process in a live manner
- Meet the people of the subject specialization
- Vast statistical data.

The following are the advantages of e-resources over the print media :

1. Multi Access

A network product can provide multiple points of access at multiple points in time (24x7) and to multiple simultaneous users.

2. Speed

An electronic resource is lot quicker to browse or search, to extract information from, and to integrate that information into other material and to cross search or reference between different publications.

3. Functionality

E-resources will allow the user to approach the publications to analyze its contents in new ways by click of the mouse on search mode.

4. Contents

The e-resources can contain a vast amount of information, but more importantly the material can consists of mixed media i.e. images, video, audio animation which could not be replaced in print.

Some of the potential benefits include:

- Ease of search and powerful search and retrieval capabilities.
- Remote access to the resources from outside a single physical library.
- Consolidation of many volumes and years into one searchable file.
- Inclusion of video and sound.
- Reduction in theft and mutilation.
- Contents, including formulae and graphics that can be extracted and manipulated.
- Use by several people simultaneously.
- Ease export of information to a personnel database.
- Reduced cost for binding, storage, and stack maintenance.
- Hyperlinks, which move beyond the linearity of print within documents and link citations with fultext documents.

MEDIUM OF STORAGE OF DIGITAL RESOURCES

The medium that is used to store and deliver contents sometimes called the container.

This may be a CD-ROM, magnetic tape, or server, accessed through a network. The delivery format is often different from the native format. The contents neither are nor materially altered when it is rendered from native format to the delivery format.

TYPES / CATEGORIES OF DIGITAL LIBRARY RESOURCES

Use of e-books and e-journals needs access to Internet and WWW not for profit institutions may provide free access to these sources.

Resources in digital libraries can be divided in two categories:

1. Resources, which are originally created in a digital format, such as electronic books or electronic journals and data sets.
2. Those documents such as manuscripts, printed materials and other non-digital resources are digitized subsequently. Digital libraries include non text information such as drawings, images, illustrations, photographs, animations, numeric data, digitized sound and moving visual images etc. In addition to this, machine readable data files, often with scientific and technical applications, various online databases and CD-ROM information products, computerized networked library systems, components of the emerging national information infrastructure; and computerized networked library and information system are needed.

   The digital resources include:

   E-mail, browsing with multimedia applications, OPAC, e-books, e-journals, etc.

There are two major types of e-resources:

1. On-line e-resources

Online e-resources include:

a. E-journals (full text and bibliographic)

b. E-books

c. Online databases

d. Websites

2. Other types of e-resources.

Other e-resources which are available digital media such as:

- CD-ROM
- Diskettes
- Other portable databases.

1. On-line Digital Information Resources

Over the last decade all aspects of computer technology, processing technologies, storage media and input/output devices have become faster, more compact, sophisticated and less expensive. Internet is one of the boons of information technology. Introduction of Internet and web technology has reduced the cost, time and manpower of publishing documents. As a result organizations, institutions and even individuals are publishing on the Internet. Internet provides a wealth of information such as online e-books, e-journals, e-newsletters, e-databases, etc. These vast resources can be accessed by the library and information centers and can be provided to the users.

Information resources on the Internet are all stored as computer files of IP address. Each file has a file name and a path name, which defines the directories and sub directories in which it is stored. Immediately, accuracy and currency of information are the most important factors in fulfilling users' information needs. Thus, the aim of this sub-menu is to provide information about information collection.

Electronic resources are revolutionizing the libraries. Electronic journal is a major component of electronic resources. Electronic journal means a journal for which the full end product is available on optical disc, over a network or in any other electronic form. Strictly a journal in which all aspects of preparation, refereeing, assembly and distribution are carried out electronically.

Due to emergence of information technology individuals, organizations and institutions are publishing scholarly papers, creating digital libraries using scanning technology and other software. Publishers are also publishing a huge document on the Internet. But all the libraries and information centers are not in a position to spend a huge amount to subscribe or to procure the same within their financial limit. In addition to the chargeable resources, a lot of digital resources are available free of cost. Online information sources are referred to be free when accesses to the sources are not dependent on subscription or membership in organization or a publisher.

Portal services of scholarly journal literature

J-Gate

J-Gate is an e-journal portal and access gateway. It provides means of access to a global literature in e-search journal. J-Gate aims to help users in:

- Browsing Table of Contents (TOC) of more than 8000 e-journals.
- Searching reasonably well indexed bibliographic database of journal articles from these journals.
- Locating local library in India where the articles he finds from the search could be available.
- Sending e-mail to authors for a reprint requests.
- Accessing fultext of about more than 100000 currently

published articles since 2001, which are freely available.

- Every bibliographic record in J-gate is linked to a full text article on publisher's site.
- Libraries who subscribe to e-journals will find J-Gate as a means to have seamless access to their subscribed journal content.

ELECTRONIC JOURNALS (E-JOURNALS)

Introduction

Journals are the most effective source of primary literature and are the most important source of for the researchers. Journals can be obtained in physical or electronic form. Any journal available over the internet can be called Electronic journal or e-journal. Electronic journals are those journals which are available in electronic form through an online host known as e-journals. Of course the idea of e-journals conceived in late 1970s, however, its real progress could be noticed during mid 1990s especially with the progress of internet and WWW. The major advantage is that it can be accessed from the remote places of the world. The second advantage is that it allows the readers to search the derived articles /paper without having being searched a particular volume of issue or page number.

Thus, e-journals form a major part of digital library.

Electronic journals have surely an advantage over traditional form such as speedy delivery, availability unlimited by time or geography, and searching facility to select and save relevant data. The electronic delivery of journals also results in the elimination of paper, storage and transportation cost and the ability to handle complex data, tables, moving pictures, sound images and video clips. Unlike sequential design of printed paper, web technology makes it possible for the publishers to design things never possible in print such as interactive hyperlinks to related, sources, and links to the full range of multimedia.

Definitions

Electronic journals (e-journals) are serial publications available in digital format such as on CD-ROMs etc. Serials include magazines, newspapers, annual publications, journals, proceedings, etc. Some e-journals are distributed via e-mail or on CD-ROMs; most of the journals are now available through internet. Some are free, some are available only by subscription .Increasingly, and publishers are using standards based native formats, such as XML, into the creation of products but rendering the contents in multiple formats (e.g.HTML and PDF) for delivery.

Electronic journals may be defined as "any journal existing in an electronic format that embraces all periodicals available electronically as well as in paper copy, including the text of periodicals accessible through online networks and those periodicals distributed in CD-ROM form."

Some other definitions of e-journals are:

McMillan defined it as any serial produced, published and distributed nationally or internationally via electronic networks such as Bit net and the Internet. The e-journals are different from the on-line journals. The latter are the electronic counterparts of journals in the print.

E-journals can be defined as a periodically available on-line or in CD-ROM format. Generally E-journals in fultext delivery system and differs from conventional bibliographic database available on-line.

"Any journal existing in an electronic format that embraces all periodicals available electronically as well as in paper copy, including the text of periodicals distributed on CD-ROM form."

"An electronic journal (e-journal as being a version of a traditional print on paper) which is disseminated electronically in some form directly to the end users"

E-journals are full text journals that are accessible via internet/intranet. Hypertext has made it much easier for libraries and other institutions to place their collection on the Internet for the users to access them.

In libraries electronic publishing is the publication process where the manuscripts are submitted in electronic format, edited, printed and even distributed to readers by employing computers and telecommunication.

The basic concept of 'electronic' or 'online' journal is that one where the text is read on, and /or printed by the end users computer rather than as print on paper. The data is downloaded directly from the host computer rather than via an intermediate medium such as CD-ROM. But the medium is not being over shadow the fact that most of the electronic journals we deal with at the moment are still traditional journals. And many of the procedures for dealing with them will be little different from those for print on paper. Electronic journal or e-journal means a journal for which the full end product is available on optical disc, over a network or in any other electronic form. Strictly a journal in which all aspects of preparation, referring and assembly and distribution are carried out electronically. E-Journals are often referred to interchangeably as "electronic periodicals" and "electronic serials" "on-line journals".

The goal of E-journals subscribed by any library is to provide desktop access to electronic version of journals to its users and free e-journals of relevance to institute to this end. In addition to online journals, library Webpages can also contain several free, peer reviewed electronic journals/ database sites etc. Variety of information for each journal, including link to journal website can be stored at library web page. Using these links, users can visit the journal site and access the full text of articles. The users can be kept informed about the online status of e-journals regularly.

The growth of electronic journals parallels the growth of the web. E-journals can be an electronic version of an established journal, an "electronic only". Journal or a journal that issued in both electronic and print format. Some e-journals are digitally reformatted version of print format and may contain all or only portion of the print version.

In other words e-journals are those journals, which can be accessed electronically using different technologies such as World Wide Web, FTP, Telnet, e-mail, etc. There are two types of e-journals, those which are issued free of cost over the internet and those which are the digital equivalent of the printed journals and are published by the commercial publishers which require subscription. As publication of e-journals is quicker, they can convey up to date information. E-journals are also available on various storage media.

E-journals present new integration challenges for libraries and has certainly been a value added service. E-journals support paper-based and electronic methods of knowledge dissemination, provide remote access, permit simultaneous use by more than one user, provide instant access, offer search capabilities, and provide, and provide such feature as links. Frequently e-journals appear on the screen exactly as they do in print with similar page design and typeface. These are Portable Document Format (PDF).

Features of Earlier e-journals

Comparing earlier and latest e-journals we see great difference. E-journals have undergone a dramatic transformation in style and format since their initial appearance in the early 1990s. Most of now have full color web pages.

1. Simple files structures (one file equals are article or one file equals one issue).
2. Published by individual or groups of scholars
3. Disseminating by e-mail and the implied audience is

the individual subscriber.

4. Copyright restrictions are usually waived to the extend that proper attribution is made.

Features of Latest e-journals:

Now HTML based on use the web to disseminate specially formatted issues.

Issues or articles include graphics, multimedia or links to other Internet resources.

NEED FOR SUBSCRIPTION OF ELECTRONIC JOURNALS

Today, almost 90 percent of journals existing worldwide are available on Internet.

Online journals are the electronic versions of the existing printed version. Today, most of the journals and databases are available on online format, which may access through on-line subscription, i.e. electronic subscription. The On-line versions are similar to but not always identical to the printed versions. Among the publishers that offer subscriptions to parallel print and electronic versions are Academic Press, American Chemical Society, John Hopkins University Press, etc. These publishers have moved energetically into electronic publications. Now many publishers have provided electronic version of their printed journals over internet.

Online journals are the wave of the future. Clearly, online journals allow easy bridging of distances. Online journals are fast. There is no mail delivery lag, and the cycle of publication is therefore a lot shorter. Online journals are a much less expensive option from the point of view of printing and dissemination. They have no paper or ink costs, minimal connectivity cost, and mail delivery cost. World Wide Web in particular and the Internet in general, have opened new vistas and opportunities to extend the reach of messages via novel and exciting channels and modes of communication. Online journals are already becoming the mode of choice for academic publications.

Subscriptions that provide access to an online collection require an agreement between the publisher and the subscriber. If the subscriber is a library, the agreement is usually written as a contract. Although the detail of these agreement varies.

Articles can be put on the web as soon as they are ready, without having to wait for months for a space in a journal issue. It means that the information is much more up-to date than it can be achieved with print.

Many printed journals are available in electronic form over internet either free of cost or on subscription

We need e-journals because:

1. It allows remote access.
2. Can be used simultaneously by more than one user.
3. Provide timely access.
4. Support searching capabilities.
5. Accommodates unique features such as links to related items.
6. Saves physical storage space.
7. Contains multimedia information.
8. Does not require physical processing, receiving and binding.
9. Can be environmentally valuable.
10. Can be digitally saved.
11. Reduce certain work in the library such as circulation and filing.
12. No chances of multimedia /disfiguring of pages as in the case of print journals.
13. Solve the problem of missing issues.

14. In case of any eventuality/calamity such as fire, the resources could be still intact;

E-JOURNALS VS PRINTED JOURNALS

All publication aspects like manuscript processing, peer review, editing, layout and design are common for both print and electronic versions except printing and distribution. This process is different in electronic form. As printing, binding, transporting and mailing the printing copies to the subscriber is labour intensive, time consuming.

The most important advantage of electronic journals over the conventional journals is the saving in the turn-around time, i.e. the time lag in subscription, refereeing, revision, editing, composing, printing, binding and forwarding eliminated by using computer and telecommunication networks. This enhances timely publication and is suitable to the letter type journals where rapid communication is of utmost importance. The electronic version also offer Boolean search of the full text to browse and read only the selected items. Further when computer and communication facilities are available, the reader need not go to the library and need not have to sift to unwanted material as in conventional journals to search the relevant papers. Electronic publications may help in overcoming the restrictions on the length of the paper imposed by many scholarly journals.

Online journals are already becoming the mode of choice for academic publications. Last one decade has witnessed a great boon in scholarly electronic journals. Even though the electronic format can save at least 30 percent of the cost, saved on printing and mailing of paper versions, the saving may get offset with the extra recurring expenses which the publisher have to incur in maintaining the system used for storing the electronic journals and for providing uninterrupted service on the net. An electronic journal will have software and hardware costs of some kind in addition to the editorial cost.

Some of the drawbacks in printing journals are:

These include the delays experienced in communicating the research results:

1. The slowness in the flow of manuscripts; the peer evaluation process; the time required for editing, typesetting, page layout;
2. The ever increasing overhead cost such as printing, binding, packaging and mailing charges.

The major advantages of e-journals over printed journals are:

a. Multidimensional interaction.
b. Multimedia effects
c. Downloads
d. Cost effective option
e. Flexibility
f. Manipulation of text
j. Operating cost free.
g. Easy to have backup files.
h. Interactive

ADVANTAGES OF E-JOURNALS

Some of the advantages are:

Speed

E-journals allow for more speed in the scientific communication process. Electronic versions of current journals are published early on the net than their printed counterparts, many a time as much as 11 weeks ached.

Speedier delivery: e-journals allow far more speed than print version. Search is very fast, to the point and user friendly.

Easy Access

Search ability is one of the core advantage of an electronic format and it is also easier to find articles online. Online access allows users to search by subject, author, title, keyword etc. Use of Boolean operators facilitates formulation of more precise and complex queries to get maximum relevant hits.

Size

Electronic articles are not limited in size.

Monitoring: It is much easier to monitor the use of e-journals.

Multiple Accesses

It is possible to add experimental data, software, and even multimedia extension links simulations. It is possible to add experimental data, software, and even multimedia extension link simulations. Access is available to all users of the library at a time. For any researcher availability from a desktop computer means a significant increase in accessibility, especially for those who do not work within easy reach of the library are also keen on the fact that entire archives will be available, several peoples can read an issue at once, and they can not go missing.

Shelving Space

Electronic journals demands neither library space nor shelving costs nor can they be stolen from the library.

Availability

Electronic journals are available 24 hours and 7days a week.

Merging

Electronic journals can easily be merged with alerting service.

Maintenance

Economy in maintenance (replacement, wear and tear)

Delivery

E-Journals can be delivered directly from the publisher to the users desktop.

Distribution

The major advantage of e-journal is their global distribution, their hypertext links, the ability to access from different sites and the ability to search.

Retrieval

Most of the publishers of e-journals are provided key words, author search, thus reducing the role of additional indexing and abstracting.

Printing/Downloading

E-journals provide the facilities of downloading and printing the appropriate articles at the end user workstations.

Publishing

Cost involved in publishing and distribution of e-journals will be less than the print.

Archive

Some publishers' gives free access to back volumes with current subscription.

Remote Access

Remote access to electronic journals has removed the barrier of time and space. Users can search; download articles to their home computer in office, avoiding the need to visit the library personally.

Dynamic Hyperlink

Links are the mainstay hypertext format, and should be

exploited. Not only can paper link to those they have cited, but also with a bit of effort, they can be linked to those that cite them.

Interactive

The ease with which e-mail can be sent, or forms filled in means that there can be much greater feedback through the web.

E-journals have a facility for full text journal with images.

Search methods are available -subject guide, keyword search, and relevance search.

E-journals open up many existing opportunities and potentials for the libraries. They possess many advantages and also disadvantages.

DISADVANTAGES

Some of the disadvantages of e-journals are:

1. E-journals and articles are not physically present in the library.
2. Often not included in indexing and abstracting services.
3. Publishers change their day-to-day terms and conditions.
5. Lack of archiving and back files availability.
6. Require suitable training and technology.
7. Possibility of data manipulation by unauthorized persons.
8. Pricing and economic factors (initial cost of hardware and software is high)
9. E-journals are available in various forms and formats.
10. In the ever changing technical environment issues of credibility, accessibility and permanence need to be

addressed before electronic journals become wide spread.

11. **Difficulty in reading:** Reading of computer screens, archiving and disappearance of URLs, authenticity, search engines ignoring PDF files, etc. are some of the disadvantages. The main disadvantages of digital information are the limitations of the computer monitor. This leads to the problems with reading, particularly over four or five screens, annotation and portability.
12. **Data updating:** Who should archive the digital data/ whose responsibility would it be to upgrade old data to newer format? Etc.
13. **Publishers go out of business:** If publishers go out of business what will happen to the archives.
14. **Access after expiry or cancellation of subscription:** clear understanding is needed on this aspect before entering into an agreement with publisher.
15. **Perishable citation:** once printed, the details of a paper journal remain constants, thus finding them again is easy, and however websites change their URLs or frequently disappear altogether.
16. Can reach the users much before the print journals.

TECHNICAL REQUIREMENT OF E-JOURNALS

The basic requirements to access the e-journals on the Internet are as follows:

Internet Access: a minimum dial up access to an Internet node is needed to retrieve the files corresponding to the desired articles.

Hardware: A PC, a modem or network connection, a high-resolution monitor, a laser printer.

Software: Dial-up Internet users requires standard telecommunication software and applications for uncompressing and translating various storage formats. For journals used online Graphical Users Interface must be loaded on the user's computer.

TYPES OF E-JOURNALS

Electronic journals fall into several groups according to the method of payment/or licensing. Many publishers are allowing free access to the electronic version of titles one subscribes to in print, sometimes just for a trial period; some are making an additional charge for the electronic version from the start. Some academic journals are freely available online.

From access point of view some publishers are giving user ID and password authentication, but some are giving IP range authentication which can not be accessed through dial up connection.

Following kinds of e- journals can be identified:

1. Online journals
2. CD-ROM and
3. Networked journals

1. Classic electronic journals: some of the journals are available through internet application, which are also called as classic electronic journals. Originally they were distributed via-e-mail but now are available on the web.

Parallel electronic Journals

These types of journals are published simultaneously in the both form-print and electronic.

The online journal may be including the fultext of journals, only table of contents or selected articles and experts from print version.

Database model and software model

Another type of e-journal is called database model and software model. Under the database model articles reside in centralized database maintain by the publishers and subscribers are given permission to access the database and use search software on central computer to locate and download the articles. The software model provides a piece of software which runs on Internet connected computer to the database journal control computer.

When both printed and electronic (internet) versions are subscribed, the subscription charges for the internet version are nominal for example: Elsevier charges 10 percent over and above the subscription charges of printed journals.

While some e-journals are published in parallel with their printed versions 5-7 weeks early, the instantaneous internet journals are made available about 7-12 weeks in advance to their printed versions.

CD-ROM Journals

Commercial publishers have also made journal title available on CD-ROM. CD-ROM journals are usually fultext of individual or collected journals in various subjects and mostly electronic versions of existing print journals. The fultext journals and newspapers have been made available on CD-ROM.

Many electronic journals are available as offline products i.e. on CD/DVD. In this format journals are cheaper then printed. Therefore, in such case certain barriers such as Internet connectivity and bandwidth do not concern.

A large numbers of databases such as MEDLINE, BIOSIS, Compendex plus, Chemical Abstracts etc are available on CD-ROM as well as printed formats.

NETWORKED JOURNALS

The networked e-journals are based on mailing list software or client/server computing applications including WWW.

ONLINE JOURNALS

However, majority of the journals, both free and paid, are available online with download facility.

The online journals may be categorized as:

1. Journals, which are totally free online.
2. Journals with online access free along with print subscription.
3. Journals, which are online and priced (very few).
4. Journals with online access whose price marginally less than the print version.

The online journals are available through online host such as OCLC, Dialog and Bibliographic Retrieval Services (BRS).These are very costly journals.

The access could be through a password or could be through IP address. Sometime a small program, which locates on the workstation, may also be needed for the access.

Many publishers offer online journals along with the printed version, to the subscribing institutions on WWW at no extra cost. This has speed up the dissemination/delivery of the primary journals. For many publishers these attract new readers and additional revenue over and above the printed circulation, as well as facilitate content revision through feedback analysis.

E-JOURNALS VS ON-LINE JOURNALS

An e-journal is a fultext delivery system and differs from an online journal and conventional bibliographic databases available online. It is a fulltext e-publication, which may include graphics and images. The e-journals include a number of newspapers, magazines, BBSs, newsgroups, e-conferences etc.

SUBSCRIPTION OF ON-LINE JOURNALS:

Many publishers choose variants on the familiar

economic model of selling annual subscriptions to individual libraries or to consortia of libraries. Subscriptions that provide access to an online collection require an agreement between the publisher and the subscriber. If the subscriber is a library, the agreement is usually written as a contract. Although the details of these agreements very. A publisher like Blackwell offers a range of options through synergy of plus online and print journal system to ease transition from print to online. *http://www.blackwellscience.com/online/default.htm*

Material

When a library subscribes to a print journal for a year, it receives a copy of the journal's issues for that year, which it may then store forever. When a library subscribes to an electronic journal for a year, it typically receives a license for access to the publisher's online collection, which contains the current year's journal and those earlier issues that have been converted to digital form. The library is relieved of the burden of storing back issues, but it loses access to every thing if it does not renew the subscription the following year, or if the publisher goes out of business.

PROBLEMS FOR SUBSCRIBING ON-LINE JOURNALS

There are, of course, issue of copyright, ownership, privacy, the response of established publishers, the training of users, accessibility and universal access, and so on.

Some of the problems are listed below:

1. Due to regular increase of subscription cost of journals, problem is appearing to keep regular online access year wise.
2. Keep regular touch with publishers in case link automatically di-link.
3. Sometimes, local networking problems are appearing for online journals. In that case keep regular touch

system administrative.

4. Printed resources have certain benefits over the on-line subscription.

How to get online journals (full text-version) up to user's desktop (PC)

Procedure for having online access of any particular journal, the following steps should be followed:

1. Registration formalities/agreement between customer and publisher of journal for having online access of subscribed journals.
2. Download the registration form/ask them to send form by e-mail/mail or direct fills the online registration form.
3. Read carefully its instructions before filled it.
4. General conditions for full text access.

Filling of the form (on-line)

a. Internet Protocol addresses (IP) or IP address.
b. Institute domain name such as du.ac.in
c. Filling the customer number, this has received with print version, given by publisher.
d. Name of journals with their customer ID numbers that we are subscribing for publisher.
e. Institutes proper mailing address with phone numbers, e-mail, fax number, etc.
f. If extra information required for online access than attached payment detail.
g. Send the form to publisher by e-mail/fax/mail.
h. After receiving the filled form by the publisher, they will set up IP address ranges and other information in their server, and type of access such as multiple user access or single user access.

i. With authentication via user ID/Password

j. With authentication via IP address.

ON-LINE VS OFFLINE JOURNALS

Printed resources have certain benefits over the on-line subscription. With printed subscription, libraries owned might continue to access those issues they purchased during the lifetime of the subscription. With on-line subscription, library pay for access to the journals rather than ownership and at the end of a subscription, a library may no longer have the right a title. Where as users may access these resources without attending a library building within opening hours.

What is Online and offline access?

Online access today typically means that the users uses a web browser on a desktop computer and connects to the digital library website (or web page) over the internet and access the contents using the search and retrieval interface provided by the digital library. Online access requires that the server computer which hosts the digital library has dedicated connection to the internet. In offline access, the digital library is not accessible over a network. Offline access is possible in several ways-make available the digital library collection (complete or portion) on CD-ROM; handle user quaries over e-mail; provide limited online access locally where the digital library collection computer is located.

MANAGING E-JOURNALS

E-journals form an important part of library service. Due to the proliferation of e-journals it is very difficult for the librarians to manage them. If managed properly, electronic journals can be efficient source of saving money and space while improving access and fast information delivery.

These e-journals can effectively be utilized by taking the following steps:

- Identify scholarly journals available free of charge over the Internet.
- Develop criteria for selecting e-journals.
- Provide links from catalog entries to full text sites.
- Provide full text searching with most formats of articles such as PDF files, HTML articles and so on.
- Link brief cataloguing entries pertaining to electronic journals to the full text and related material.
- Determine cataloguing entry element to be included in the catalog record.
- Choose vendors who would provide usage statistics and archiving.
- Familiarized with licensing terminology, key issues and contracts.
- Create an e-journal home page.
- Includes e-journals in OPAC.

If the libraries want to play important role, they have to collect and disseminate information independent of the type of medium. Many of the e-journals have advantages of being free of subscription, but it should be remembered that they still cost money in terms of equipment and more important, of library personnel.

Most libraries are considering adding e-journals to their collection because they represent a less costly, faster means of collecting scholarly information. However it is a common feeling that electronic journals will not replace the traditional print format, but rather complement it as a new means of communication.

CONSORTIA

Consortia based Subscription:

What is?

Consortia based subscription or shared subscription

means a strategic planning through which numbers of institutions having more or less the same information needs and requirements for providing the library and information services to their readers agreeing to participate in collective and collaborative efforts to subscribe electronic information resources for their mutual benefits.

CONSORTIA SCENERIO FOR E-RESOURCES

Library consortium is a group of two or more libraries which have agreed to cooperate with another in order to fulfill certain similar needs, usually resource sharing. Cooperative purchase of e-resources is one of the key activities of a library consortium. It usually refers to cooperation, coordination and collaboration between, and amongst libraries for the purpose of sharing information. Consortia are basically, evolving a form of cooperation among the libraries, which come together to share resources electronically.

Some of the successful library consortia are:

1. CSIR (Council of Scientific and Industrial Research)

   CSIR e-journal consortium

   http://www.niscair.res.in

2. UGC-INFONET e-Journal consortium :

   http://www.ugc.ac.in/new_initiatives/infonet.html.

ACCESS TO E-JOURNALS

For accessing the e-journals there is a need of a specific application programme for reading, retrieving, and for downloading the contents of the journal. These are available in various formats such as HTML, PDF. Access to e-journals is provided either by publishers themselves or through e-journal portals. The libraries and information centers cater the information needs to a variety of users in different disciplines. To avoid the inconvenience to subscribing the e-journals through various publishers, e-journal portals, are the best option for subscribing the unlimited numbers of e-journals published through various publishers at a single gateway. There are various e-journal portals, providing access to various different e-journals ranging from bibliographic data to fultext retrieval.

The following are the some of the e-journals portals:

EMERALD

www.emeraldinsight.com

An acronym of the Electronic Management Research Library Database and launched in 1996 from UK.

Emerald publishes the world's widest range of about 100 world class e-journals on management, business strategies, accounting, economics, marketing, quality management, human resource management, material science and technology and 24 world class outstanding e-journals of Library and Information Science.

E-PORTALS AND E-JOURNALS

E-portals

E-portal is a mechanism that filters the overwhelming amount of information and provides a fast, easy and consistent way to get relevant information on a cost effective way to disseminate critical information to users in a right time. E-journal portals, integrates, captures and manages various e-journals published through various publishers at various places at a single web portal. In other words, e-journal portal is a single shop /gateway for subscribing all kinds of e-journals published worldwide. Thousands of e-journals are available through a single window of e-journal portal for serving to the libraries and information centers. Therefore, the importance of e-journals portal in providing information services is, very significant in today's context.

E-journals are called by various names such as e-journals, electronic journals, e-serials, and electronic serials. Jones W defines e-journals as "they are available electronically via a computer or a computer network, that they may or may not published in some other (physical) medium, but that they are not CD-ROMs or diskettes.

FEATURES OF E-JOURNALS AND E-PORTALS

The salient features of e-journals as described by Fecko (MB) in 1997 are as:

- They can be delivered to the desktop.
- More than one person can read them at a time.
- The entire text can be searched.
- They can include multimedia and graphics, in color, at marginal cost.
- They can publish more quickly than paper publications.
- They can be interactive; they can foster an on-line exchange of ideas by mail.
- They can make use of hyperlinks, both internally and to other publications.
- Articles can be retrieved directly though links from abstracting and indexing databases.
- The content can be reproduced, forwarded and modified.
- E-journal portals are the data warehouse of fultext and bibliographic records of e-journals.
- E-journal portals enhance the personalized selection of e-journals and their contents.
- They provide access to integrated set of users.
- They facilitate an intuitive access method for retrieving relevant information.
- They enable user to access any required information without having to know its location, format, or access method.

- They provide reliable, up-to-date, and relevant information at affordable cost.
- They provide Internet options for further extending access of e-journals within organization.
- They provide an opportunity to users to hyperlink other e-journals freely available on Internet.
- They provide quick and easy access to a myriad of data and systems.

Retrieve only the content needed for specific requirement.

E-BOOKS

Definitions

The collection in many libraries now includes e-books. The popularity of e-books has grown since their introduction in 1980s. The idea of e-book is not new; several factors have contributed to e-book emergence such as: technologies, internet, the web, print on demand etc.

The Association of American Publishers has provided the following definition of e-books:

"An e-book is literary work in the form of digital object consisting of one or more unique identifiers, Metadata, and a monographic body of content, indented to published and accessed electronically." E book is digital medium for communication of information. A book is in digital medium. It may be in CD-ROM form, may be available on-line with the help of Internet. It is easily accessible and is available 24x7.

The core of the definition is that an e-book is content, a digital object containing an electronic representation of a book, most commonly thought of as the electronic analog of a print book. This type of e-book has been delivered electronically on CD-ROMs, diskettes, and via network to terminals and workstations since the early 1980s.

According to **Lee (2002)**, an "e-Book is a term used to describe a text analogues to book that is in digital form to be displayed on a computer." He also included the definition of an e-book from the Hi-tec dictionary and The New Concise Oxford English Dictionary respectively as "a book that has been converted to digital form and could be read on a computer, usually through network services or CD-ROM. E books could expand over print media by adding specific features such as hypertext links, search and cross reference functions and multimedia" and "an electronic version of a printed book which can be read on a personal computer or hand held device designed specially for this purpose".

Thus, E-books are books that are available in digital format. E book can be defined as a text in digital form, digital reading material, a book in a computer file format, an electronic file of words and images to be deployed on computer screen, or read on a computer over a network, or viewed on a desktop/notebook/dedicated portable device, or read on all types of computers, or formatted for display on e-book readers. E-books are printed in light instead of ink.

E-books are books in file format in the computer, which can be read with specific software such as Acrobat e-book reader/glass book reader, net library e-book reader. It is interested to read with animation, sound, etc., they are faster, cheaper, and searchable and can print, make a copy, etc. E-books are ordered on-line and delivered electronically to your computer. E-books are quickly becoming an important alternative to paper books and thousands of e-books are downloaded every day.

The term e-book now most often is used to refer to digital objects specifically made to be read with reading applications operating on either a handled device or a parallel computer. An e-book is usually a collection of several digital objects or documents, consisting of content files, style sheets, metadata, digital rights, navigation, and other components. The contents consist of text documents and image documents. Metadata provides a summery about the book (e.g author, publisher, ISBN, and price), while dial rights management (DRM) files specify the rights of the owner of the book. All of these different documents are collected in one publication in a property format.

E-book is becoming a viable means of book publication. The rise in the popularity of personal digital assistants has allowed a stable technical platform to be used, which allows users to download books or chapters. They can be read away from the office or home. The major advantage of e-books is that it can be read on all types of computers including handheld devices. E-books contain audio, video and dynamic hyperlinks. It can be delivered instantly from anywhere in the world by downloads, e-mail file attachment, on diskette, or CD-ROM.

The contents of e-books are disseminated in digital form, which can be had with the help of personal computer or special purpose reader. E books are delivered to the users either through storage media like CD-ROMs or through the World Wide Web. E books are available on the web site are downloadable either free of cost or by paying fee. The availability of the usual types of reference books in electronic form makes the reference service easier. As information can be given within seconds, there is no scope for long-range reference service.

E-books can be considered as software objects as well as physical devices. Understood as a software object, an e-book is simply an electronic text.

Features of e-books

Some of the features of e-books are:

- E-books are accessed faster
- Cheaper
- Easily searchable

- Easy to print and copy
- Users can manipulate the text easily in desired manner
- Online purchasing is possible

ADVANTAGES OF E-BOOKS

E-book has many advantages such as hyper linkage, cutting, pasting, printing and multiple simultaneous user access.

Some of the advantages of e-books are given below:

- E-books provide multimedia information, full text searching, reference linking, and flexibility in searching and browsing, selection in different types of fonts, portability, and interoperability on a variety of devices.
- The instant delivery of material is a reality with e-books.
- Saving in shelves space and an end to lost or damaged titles for library and information centers.
- E-books are ordered on-line and delivered electronically to your computer.
- E-books are compact, convenient, and portable.
- Easy to download from booksellers to library's or user's laptop/computer.
- E-books empower you with control over the look and feel of your e-book with powerful features such as digital notes, dynamic display setting, search, and text-to-speech.
- The publishing process becomes quicker with electronic media. It is easier to make changes and distribute via Internet. The publishing cost of printing, binding, inventory etc. disappears. The electronic copies do not require physical storage space in warehouse of publishers.

- The availability and access to titles is quicker and more convenient to the readers.
- E-books provide a great hope for the environment by saving millions of trees that are destroyed every year for paper books.
- E-books are infinitely more portable than paper books when carried with you on a PDA.
- You save money with no shipping costs. Hence are cheaper.
- It is easier for authors to publish directly for niche market, without a publisher. Enhanced feedback can be achieved by direct contact with readers and integrated electronic feedback given by readers.
- For users who are frequent travelers, or who have to carry out research in remote places e-books offer a substitute for print books and provide easies portability.
- For teachers and students, e-books are very good classroom teaching tool and are a good device for those with low hand dexterity.
- Elimination of printing and distribution cost.
- Easy to replace when lost.
- Minimal processing for circulation.
- E-books are able accessed remotely. More than one person may be able to access the same e-book at a time.
- No loss of pages as case of traditional books.
- Scope for enlargement and reduction of pages.
- For publishers, e-books offer economies in publishing costs and involve no storage, shipping and handling charges.
- It facilitates access in digital form to previous and rare

documents that are currently under lock and key in collections around the world.

- For librarians, e-books do not go out of print, are easy to download, can be customized to suit individual needs (especially by those who may physically handicapped), allow many people to access the same book at the same time, are free from problems of being misplaced, and do not suffer from wear and tear or theft (Rao 2001, Teddd 2004)

DISADVANTAGES OF E-BOOKS

Inclusion of e-books in a library collection has presented some problems related to access, ownership, and protection of rights.

In spite of these advantages, e-books are still not very popular. Some of the possible reasons are:

- The technology for creating and accessing e-books (both hardware and software) is not yet mature.
- Not very convenient to use.
- Lack of awareness of software/hardware available for e-books.
- Incompatibility with hardware and software of e-books readers.
- Cost of hardware readers is high.
- Limited availability of titles.
- Problem in bibliographical control as vendor's listing does not provide sufficient bibliographical data.
- Problem regarding copyright, fair use, digital right etc.
- Difficulty in accessing computers or internet.
- User's basic reluctance or averseness to switchover the new media.
- There is high risk in buying a technologically obsolescence e-book reader.

- Some titles are available for downloading but are costly.
- There is no compatibility across different hardware/ software for using titles.
- Enough printed books in libraries already;
- The physical dimensions of an e-book are fixed and cannot be changed individually for each title .The hardware for e-book is fragile, non-flexible and the battery life determine access to material.
- Peoples are used to reading printed books and do not want to change the habit;
- A lack of awareness of e-books;
- Problems with printing and downloading.

FORMS OF E-BOOKS

E-book may be available in various forms:

- It may be available free on-line.
- It may be available under communication common license etc. E-books, which are available only on Internet in digital form or it, may be called online book.

TYPES OF E-BOOKS

E-Books are of following types:

1. **Multimedia Books**: these are a mixture of different works such as video, sound, animation text etc.

2. **Cyber Books**: these are fully electronic. These are not owned by one library. User can approach to these books from any corner of the world and at any time using their PC and Internet.

3. **Scroll-Media Books**: The text here is presented in a scroll form as in traditional book.

TECHNOLOGIES AVAILABLE FOR USING/ READING E-BOOKS

There are two types of technologies available for using e-books:

1. Online or Internet base.
2. Offline or specific e-book reader based.

In the online version the user can read the text through internet browser and this opens up possibilities of linking to other resources, cross text searching, utilization of dictionaries and so on.

For reading an e-book similar to paper book perhaps, a dedicated reading gadget is the best option. In these gadgets a touch sensitive LCD screen is fitted in e-book. Simple feather touch button monitors the book to move forward and backward. The gadget users have purchase specially formatted content either from online bookstores through their PCs or directly from the device maker via built in MODEM.

TECHNOLOGY REQUIRED FOR E-BOOKS

E-book hardware

Several portable e-book devices in a range of shapes, sizes are available. These may be -dedicated reading devices, desktop or laptop PCs. These use a monitor, LCD or touch screen device as screen.

E-book software

Functions such as search, user defined text size, color, network connection, read only contents, hyperlinks within the books, range of platforms and devices are supported and carried out by e-book reader software. A few of them are Acrobat e-book Reader, Franklin Reader, Microsoft Reader etc. Most of the reader software is free to download and support several operational systems.

There are several organizations, which offer access to

thousands of e-books. Some of them are:

Net library (*http://www.netlibrary.com*)

Questa (*http://www.questa.com*)

In the offline version users will read e-books through special e-book reader software, which can be downloaded, from the Internet. Much of this software is format specific, such as:

Abode reader in PDF format (*http://www.abode.com/product/ebookreader*)

Microsoft reader in LIT format Heibook reader in H1 format (*http://www.heibook.com*)

There are many e-book online 'stores' such as eBookmall (http://www.ebookmall.com), which offer downloadable e-books in a variety of formats.

Some of the important e-book sites are described below:

1. Gutenberg project on electronic books on-line.

http://www.promo.net/pg

Thousands of e-books are available in this site free of charge. The site is having browsing facility by author, and by title. It also provides advanced search facility by author or by title(words). Author wise list of e-books is available at *http://www.promo.net/pg/authors.zip* and title wise list of e-books is available at *http://www.promo.net/pg/titles.zip*

And current list of e-books is available at GUTINDEXALL at the FTTP site at university of North Carolina *http://ibiblio.org/pub/docs/books/guttenberg/GUTINDEXALL.*

2. University of Pennsylvania online book page

This site includes the different sections like, books online, news, features, archives. The online books listed on this page have been authored, placed online, and hosted by a wide variety of individuals and groups throughout the world. The local index of this page includes more than 15000 English works in various formats. All are free for personnel, non commercial use. Numbers of books on various subjects are available free of charge.

3. Electronic Text Center of Virginia University

Near about 141 numbers of books on various topics are available in the electronic text center of the Virginia University.

4. Coutts Library Services

www.couttsinfo.com

Coutts Library Service is a leading international supplier of books to academic, medical, professional and reference libraries.

5.Baker And Taylor

http://www.btol.com

Baker and Tayler is a leading full-time distributor of books, videos and music products to libraries and both traditional and internet retailers. Maintains one of the largest combined stock book, video and music inventories in United States .Access is convenient and easy through on-line or CD-ROM.

6.KHOJ

http://www.khoj.com/life_and_family/shopping/books

Khoj is the wonderful online book ordering sites listed at India's great search engine KHOJ.

7.English Book Depot

http://www.ebdbooks.com

India's premier landmark book store since 1923.This site has an ideal form for book ordering.

8.D.K. publisher and Distributor

http://www.dkpd.com

D.K.Publisher Distributor has database on the web from over 1100 publishers.

9. EBSCO Book Service

http://www.ebscobooks.com

EBSCO Book Service offers more than 2.5 million book titles from all disciplines and an extensive collection of audio and video products.

10. Bartleby Books Online

(*http://www.Bartleby.com*)

The Bartleby is one of the Internet publishers of literature and reference providing students, researchers and intellectually curious with unlimited access books and information on the web free of charge.

The following reference books are available free of charge from Bartleby Books Online:

1. Columbia Encyclopedia,6th ed.
   http://www.bartleby.com/65/
2. Anatomy of human body:
   http://www.bartleby.com/107/
2. world fact books 2001 *http://www.bartleby.com*
3. Roget's II: The new thesaurus, 3rd ed
   http://www.bartleby.com/62/
4. American Heritage Dictionary of English Language: *http://www.barleby.com/61/*

Encyclopedia of world history: ancient, medieval and modern: *http://www.bartleby.com/67/*

Free online books:

http://www.freeebooks.net

Free encyclopedia :

1. Encyclopedia Britannica:
   http://www.britannica.com

DICTIONARIES

1. Academic Press Dictionary of Science and Technology
   http://www.harcourt.com/dictionary
2. All words English dictionary with multilingual search
   http://www.allwords.com
3. Cambridge Dictionary
   http://www.dictionary.cambridge.org

GENERAL INFORMATION

Interactive unit converter

http://www.convert-me.com/em

Measurement converter

http://www.microimng.com/science

Calculator

http://www.calculator.com/index.html the processed information to the users.

Ordering from online booksellers like www.amazon.com, Bn.com, dkpd.com brings not only the 24 hours a day, 7 days a week benefits. It offers an Internet ordering system that is customized for the user's organization. The user enters his personnel information into an order form on secure web servers. Option can easily be added to choose quantities, enter purchase order numbers, choose billing and shipping information, and other data. The system shows the status of the data.

In addition to the electronic way, alternative options like a paper form for those customers who cannot use the Internet based system, are there to send orders-by fax or mail.

ACCESS OF E-RESOURCES

Access is provided after the registration, which is the part of the licenses by which the library provides information to the publishers to, enables them to be sure that the users from the organization have the rights to access. Libraries can provide link to e-resources through the proxy server after authentication by IP address. Users can also use e-resources by login through institutional networks by user name and password.

Many libraries provide access of e-resources on the website through A to Z list or subject wise list. The alphabetical lists of e-journals on web pages are maintained via text editor, HTML editor. Many libraries are providing online access directly from the publisher's website by the federated search system such as EBSCO host.

MANAGEMENT OF E-RESOURCES

Administration and maintenance of e-resources are important component of e-resources. Electronic resources comprise some of the library's most visible and expensive investments. Effective management of information about electronic resources can result in improved access, operations, with licensing agreement.

CHALLENGES ASSOCIATED WITH E-RESOURCES

The challenges that comes with e-resources includes technical issues, cost, copyright, equity of access , security, bibliographic control, licensing, user instruction, and issues of authority, quality, accuracy, instability, and mutability, and mobility of information.

Slow response time can be much more frustrating for users than waiting for another patron to return a print index to the shelf. Remote users trying to connect from outside the library may experience technical problems with no assistance available. Searching success depends on the quality of indexing, key words, and text markup and the effectiveness of the search engine.

Authorization and authentication issues may be complex. Libraries typically loose access to back files at the termination of a contract for an e-resources. E-resources can be extremely expensive .Librarians who seek to identify, monitor, and direct users to free web based resources face particular challenges tracking, organizing, and maintaining access to such online materials.

PROBLEMS POSED BY ELECTRONIC RESOURCES/ PUBLICATIONS

The electronic publications pose some problems related to their selection, organization and retrieval. The organizations of CDs on libraries are a big problem. Because some of the publishers are also providing CDs along with the books. The problem is whether we manage them separately or intact with the book. If we remove the CDs from the books and organized them separately on racks, the library staff may face some problems in charging and discharging of books and face problems in selecting the right CD of the book which is being charged. On the other hand if we keep the CD in the book itself, changes for its missing or damaged are very high. It is an issue the library staff has to have to tackle in the near future.

There are other problems also related to identification, selection, and acquisition stage regarding the electronic resources.

DIGITAL RESOURCES USED BY UNIVERSITY LIBRARY

In a university library digital information resources include:

Full text articles, databases, thesis and dissertations, e-journals, e-books, multimedia databases, etc. Other information resources such as university course calendar, university statutes, thesis and dissertation guidelines, etc are also needed by the users of an academic community. As these information resources are spread across different servers and in different home pages, academic users find it difficult to obtain the needed information for their work in a desired format at the right time. The university library have to provide links to various information resources according to user's need, by establishing digital information kiosks or centers.

At present with the supports of UGC most of the Indian University libraries are automated. At present more than 50 Indian universities libraries subscribing e-journals through UGC info net. Among the Indian university libraries, Indira Gandhi Memorial Library of Hyderabad and University of Delhi Library leading ahead in digital resources and digital library services. It has good collection of electronic resources on classic literature. It also provides finding aids and gateways, internet search tools, e-resources on public domain, World Bank documents and reports, etc. It also introduced electronic referencing whereby reference service is done through e-mail service. Indira Gandhi Memorial Library has digitized its books collection, which are not under copyright act. It also provides services such as full text, bibliographical search databases, and thesis databases. Majority of them providing OPAC service to its users. Some of the libraries are having electronic documents and e-journals. Most of the university libraries are having Internet connections and they are providing these facilities to their users in different nomenclature like cyber lab, cybernetic, internet browsing center, e-learning center, etc.

Recently University of Delhi has provided around 40 computers to its affiliated colleges along with the Internet connection. It has also subscribed to various databases such as j-gate, Science Direct, Nature, Scopus, etc.

7

Electronic Publishing (E-publishing)

INTRODUCTION

Due to exponential growth of publishing literature, scattering of literature, it is very difficult to control the ever-increasing volume of information published in journals. This is an era of information revolution. This is an emerging trend of shift from print-based media to electronic based communication media. Concept like e-books, e-journals are developing very fast. Most of the organizations such as companies, institutions, government institutions uses lesser and lesser paper documents in inter and intra-organizational communication. Due to the development of modern information technology, especially the personnel computers, the publishing industry has undergone many changes.

Until the mid-1990s, established publishers of scientific journals have stated about online publishing. While commercial publishing on CD-ROMs had developed into an important part of the industry, few journals were available online. Publishers could not make a business case for online publishing and feared that, if materials were available online, sales of the same material in print would suffer. By about 1955, it is become clear that broad reaching changes were occurring in how people were using information.

During the past few years, both digital libraries and electronic publishing have been consolidation in ever large organizational units. In libraries this is seen as the movement to consortia, in publishing it has been number of huge corporate mergers. Yet, even as these giants have been formed, the energy of the ants has continued .At present; it appears that giants and ants, such as Yahoo and Amazon.com are becoming the new giants. Two factors that will greatly influence the future of digital libraries are the rate at which well managed collections become available on the internet and the business models that emerge.

Libraries and individuals were expanding their use of online information services and other form of electronic information much more rapidly than their use of printed material. Print publications were competing for a declining portion of essentially static library budget.

That resulted in the shift of emphasis from conventional publishing to electronic publishing.

The electronic publishing products may include texts, graphics, audio, video, numeric and textual databases, and reference sources such as encyclopedias, dictionaries, directories, and computer programmes. The ultimate goal of electronic publishing is to provide fast and easy access to the information contained in the objective publications with simple, powerful search and retrieval capabilities. The ultimate aim is to save the time of the users.

WHAT IS ELECTRONIC PUBLISHING?

Electronic publishing means publishing in electronic form. It is basically a form of publishing in which books, journals and magazines are being produced and stored electronically rather than in print. These publications have all qualities of the normal like the use of colors, graphics and images and they are much convenient also. The activity of making works and other production available to the public by electronic means, e.g. through access to material stored in electronic databases. The term electronic publishing may refer to a range of activities that include composing manuscripts, formatting pages, typesetting books and produces databases.

DEFINITIONS

FW Lancaster has defined the Electronic publishing as follows:

"It is publication process where the manuscripts are submitted in e-format, edited, printed and even distributed to users in e-format by computer and communication technology. The published information distributed in the form of online, CD-ROM, Networks, and ISDN etc."

Therefore, the electronic publishing can be defined as the publication process where the manuscripts are submitted in electronic format, edited, printed and even distributed to users by employing computers and communication techniques. The process of creating and disseminating information via electronic means including e-mail and via the Internet is electronic publishing.

Electronically published materials may originate as traditional paper publishing or may be created specially for electronic publishing. Electronic publishing refers to publication of any documents in an electronic media. Electronic publishing include application of computer aided process by which informational contents are found, captures, shaped, stored and updated in order to judiciously disseminated to a chosen audience. The computer should contain multimedia and support some standard multimedia graphics output. Electronic publication comprises the publication of computer programmes, films, compact discs and other such media.

While the term "electronic publishing" is primarily used today to refer to the current offerings of online and web-based publishers, the term has a history of being used to describe the development of new forms of production, distribution, and user interaction in regard to computer based production of text and other interactive media.

According to other definition electronic publishing is a process for production of typeset, quality documents containing text, graphics pictures, tables, equations etc. with the assistance of data processing system. The synonyms for electronic publishing are computer aided/assisted publishing. The published information is distributed on state-of the art medium CD-ROM networks, online internet etc. (Perryman, WR. 1991)

Kist defined electronic publishing as "the application by publishers of a computer aided process, by which they find, capture, shape, store and update information contents in order to disseminate it to a chosen audience."

Grolier Encyclopedia defines electronic publishing as: the term e-publishing refers more precisely to the storage and retrieval of information through electronic communications media. It can employ a variety of formats and technologies, some already in widespread use by businesses and general consumers and others still being developed.

Electronic publishing is the dissemination of information in electronic form and its distribution to potential users either on electronic network such as Internet and local area networks or in standalone formats such as CD-ROMs and diskettes. The one of the objective is to make information more easily available. To make this information as widely accessible as possible, it is published "electronically' or in other words, via the Internet. In this way anyone in the world with a computer and Internet access can obtain the information, whenever they like, cost free. Although network distribution is now a days strongly associated with electronic publishing, there are many non-network electronic publications such as encyclopedias on CD-ROMs and DVD.

Electronic publishing or e-publishing is publishing information -books, reports, and information products, interactive media-in electronic format, available or accessible in several forms: on CDs as downloadable files or in 3.5 diskettes. Similar e-publishing matter can be transmitted through e-mail as attachments.

There are different types of electronic medium that could be used to publish any piece of information.

The electronic publishing products may include text, graphs, audio, video, numeric and textual databases, reference sources such as encyclopedias, directories, dictionaries, atlases and computer programmes. The products of electronic publishing are seen anywhere. These includes indexing, abstracting, full text databases, computerized library catalogs or OPACs, national and regional catalogues of library collections such as OCLC, digital libraries, reference sources, electronic journals, newsletters, and news sources which display graphic audio video and textual information. Most of such resources are readily available to users who have access to Internet.

The topic of electronic publishing covers a wide spectrum of activities in a variety of industries and professions. Most obviously related are the publishing, particularly newspapers and journals publishers, the telecommunication and broadcasting industries, libraries and other information providers, vendors and suppliers of computer hardware and software. Electronic publishing is the substitute of electronically generated material, which also includes the dissemination of text and graphics on electronic channels i.e. television and radio, cable TV and telephone.

In the most sophisticated interpretation the full capabilities of electronic media including motions, sound and other interactive features are exploited in the creation of completely new forms of publications. In general the fusion of computer and communication technologies with publishing means that any information publishing in electronic (machine readable) form, can be stored on magnetic tapes, floppies, CD-ROMs and other storage devices, making it readily accessible to any user.

E-publishing technology can be classified into two general categories:

1. One in which information is stored in a centralized computer source and delivered to the users by a telecommunication systems, including on-line database services and videotexts represents the most active area in e-publishing today and
2. Another in which the data is digitally stored on a disk or other physically delivered medium.

NEED OF ELECTRONIC PUBLISHING

Due to application of modern technology in the printing industry, a lot of development has been taken place in the field of electronic publishing. The electronic form of publishing has changed the traditional concept of publishing. The most important goal of the electronic publishing is to provide better accessibility, current information in a lesser cost. Other housekeeping jobs are taking little time to make ready bibliographic data and fultext data especially case of e-resources for the users thus following Ranganathan's fourth law of library science "save the time of the reader."

The conventional research journal and its current mode of publication will become obsolete in the next decade. Authors will input their articles on computer terminals where the material will be stored in machine-readable form. The articles could then be transmitted digitally to the editor. All reviewing, rewrite etc. will be done via the computer terminal, and the final product can be stored in a data bank for on demand access. Fee would be charged for each use of electronically stored information and, if desired, print copies could be taken for conventional distribution.

The ever-increasing amount of information, the difficulty in having informal, personal communication, the large geographical distances involved in certain routes of information acquisition necessities the advent of e-publishing. The increasing role of information in shaping of a society and the changing notion of information from something to know to something to have as any commodity has resulted in the need for improving the information services. Developments in recent time in information technology have made it possible to overcome many of the above problems. Application of information technology in libraries and information centers raised the efficiency of information acquisition, processing, storage and retrieval.

The electronic journals and document delivery system as answer to current copyright/photocopying problem. With an electronic journal it is possible to log every use made of the database, so publishers could be in the happy position of being able to collect a fee for every time an article is printed out. This is fairer system, but the charges will have to be higher than expected as there will be no longer be cash up front' subscriptions.

The video text promises the biggest opportunity for changes in the publishing industry and think it will have a major impact on newspaper and journal publishers. Economic and market forces have already changed the way the printed word is prepared, edited, and put together. Cost of traditional distribution systems will undergo big price increases forcing publishers to adopt electronic distribution systems to augment rather than totally replace present printed products. The author defines the need for a delivery or videotext system and the role videotext will play in the future of publishing.

The enormous growth of scientific information has caused serious problems of accessibility, storage, retrieval and dissemination to the libraries and research workers. Efforts have been made to provide access to information through indexing and abstracting services, etc. Alternative methods of information transmission have led to the development of electronic publishing. Electronic publishing does every thing, which has traditionally been done in the image assembly operation up to paste-up stage. It combines typesetting with the electronic creation and manipulation offline art and halftone in one system. In electronic publishing system the document is created using computer and disseminated electronically over networks in the final form. In a broad sense the term electronic publishing encompasses other communication techniques such as e-mail, videotext, electronic journals etc.

In the most sophisticated interpretation, the capabilities of electronic media including, text, graphics, motion pictures, sound and alternative features are exploited in the creation of a completely new form of publication, which is accessible electronically, transmitted and stored electronically. In electronic publishing system, the document is created using computer and disseminated electronically over networks in the final form. Electronic publishing products may include texts, graphics, audio, video, numeric and textual databases, and reference sources such as encyclopedias. The product of e-publishing can be read directly from a computer screen using a special reader or viewer or it can be read using browser such as Internet

Explorer, which gives the experience that the reader is surfing in internet, only difference is that it is offline.

E -publishing can also be read using special handheld readers called slates. Currently, Rocket book is the most widely known e-reader.

Electronic publishing is also known as e-publishing, on-line publishing, web publishing or Internet publishing. The term electronic publishing is primarily used today to refer to the current offerings of online and web based publishers, the term has history of being used to describe the development of new forms of production, distribution, and user interaction in regard to computer -based production of text and other interactive media.

E-PUBLISHING PROMOTING FACTORS

Some of the e-publishing factors are as follows:

1. Internet popularity
2. Digital library initiatives
3. E-resources convenience
4. E-publications availability
5. As an alternative publishing mechanism.

PROPERTIES OF ELCTRONIC PUBLISHING

Some of the important properties are as follows:

1. Lower per unit publishing cost
2. Longer medium life without data loss
3. Ability to utilized hypermedia links.

The publishing is done by different types of publishers such as:

1. Academic and Research Organizations
2. Scientific societies and associations
3. Government Departments etc.
4. Commercial publishing houses

The publishing may be for different types of peoples such as students, teachers, researchers etc. for variety of purposes educational, entertainment etc. The publishing may be specializing in various subjects such as science and technology, humanities, social sciences, arts and architecture etc.

USERS OF ELECTRONIC PUBLISHING

The main users of electronic publishing are:

1. Research scholars
2. Publishers and
3. Libraries

All the above-mentioned users are affected by the e-publishing.

USEFULNESS OF E-PUBLISHING

Usefulness to research scholars

The greatest benefit of electronic publishing is the richness of information that is available to the end-users. Users are now having access to information that print technology could not provide. Numbers of reference sources are now available in electronic format. For example various encyclopedias such as encyclopedia Britannica, dictionaries, etc. are available now available on electronic format. These dictionaries can provide audio information, which shows how certain words are pronounced which is much simpler to understand than the guides prided in the dictionaries in the printed form. Similarly illustrations, animation in digital encyclopedia can demonstrate the working of the computer. The advantages of electronic format are more as compared to print format. The electronic publishing allows faster dissemination of information than print technology because information may be made accessible on electronic networks weeks or months before it appears in print format. Electronic publishing gives greater freedom to researchers to disseminate their research results without having to go through the cumbersome route of finding a publisher who is willing to publish their results. Electronic publishing allows those scholars to bypass the publisher and disseminates their research results directly to other scholars and other interested persons.

Usefulness to the publishers

Publishers are using electronic publishing technology recent years because it speeds up the publishing process, make editorial changes easier to accomplish, and enables the relatively small publishers to effectively participate in publishing activities. Electronic publishing has opened up new markets such as publications of encyclopedias in CD-ROM format, creating and distribution of electronic databases of indexing and abstracting services, and electronic journals. In fact, since most of the publishers are now requiring their authors to send in their manuscripts in electronic format, it is relatively simple to load them on computers and make them available to readers and libraries.

Usefulness to Libraries and Information Centers

Libraries and information centers are the beneficiaries of the electronic publishing revolution. The emphasis is shifting to "access" from "ownership".

This trend is also known as "just in time" as opposed to "just in case" collection. Electronic publishing resources improved library services to their users and made their internal operations more efficient. For example users can now search vast databases, print results of their searches, download any information required and further incorporate this electronic information into their regular day to day work.

Electronic publishing is forcing libraries to shift more financial resources from print publications to the acquisition of electronic resources.

LIBRARY SERVICES AND ELECTRONIC PUBLISHING

The electronic information available in a library and information centers would directly based on the quality of information services. The downloaded information would be edited, revised or repackaged as per the requirements. Electronic publishing facilitates faster and better quality of services including value added products, enhancement in the number of clientele served with little or no extra inputs, marketability of information services, and networking and remote login for geographically, distributed users. These factors will certainly enhanced the reputation of the library and information center (Treese, Winn, 1994;Perryman, WN, 1991).

FORMS OF ELECTRONIC PUBLISHING

Computer aided Publishing

Computer aided publishing is getting the print of relevant or required matter/information that appear on a computer screen with the help of a printer.

THE PRODUCTS OF E-PUBLISHING

It may be in the form of:

1. E-journals
2. E-books etc.
3. Electronic databases
4. E-publishing on CD-ROM.
5. Print on demand.
6. E-mail publishing.
7. Web-publishing.

E-JOURNALS

The e-journal is a version of the traditional print or paper based journal, which is disseminated electronically. The full-fledged e-journal came into limelight only in the

1990s. E-journals are the useful source of information for researchers as they apply to scholarly research. These journals are now become an important part of Academic Library System. Electronic journals are those journals, which are available on electronic format. These journals are accessible to all users regardless of geographic location. Anyone in the world with services and the proper computer software and browser services can access on-line journals. This category includes newsletter, magazines, journals etc. Electronic journal may be defined as 'any journal existing in an electronic format that embraces all periodicals available electronically as well as in paper copy, including the text of periodicals accessible through on-line networks and those periodicals distributed in CD-ROM form'. E-journals are full text journals that are accessible via internet/intranet. Hypertext has made it much easier for libraries and other institutions to place their collection on the intranet for the users to access them.

E-journals are a fast developing feature of electronic publishing. Today there are thousands of electronic journals, scholarly publications that are available online via an electronic network along with print. The term "electronic journal" is almost as ambiguous as the term "electronic publishing".

BENEFITS OF E-JOURNALS OVER PRINT JOURNALS

Since access to e-journals is beyond any physical boundaries with the availability of excellent Internet security, libraries are forming consortia and subscribing to electronic journals at concesstional rates. Journals have always been one of the most important types of resources for research scholars. The libraries have traditionally focused on the purchase of journals; the electronic environment has opened up new possibilities. Electronic publishing offers authors the possibility of making their publications freely available on the internet. This also known as Open Access

(OA). If OA publishing continues to grow, the impact on publishers and libraries will be considerable.

E-Journals have several advantages over print journals:

Print journals have

1. Peer review process
2. Delay in publication.
3. Escalating cost.
4. Lack of selectivity.
5. Stoppage of subscriptions by libraries and
6. Copyright held by the commercial publishers.

ADVANTAGES OF E-JOURNALS

Electronic versions of journals are available in advance of printed version. Time lag in submission, referring, editing, composing, binding and forwarding which is eliminated by using computers and communication networks. This enhances timely publication and is suitable to the letter type journals where rapid communication is of utmost importance. This leads to further reducing the gap between the user and the end-user. Most of the publishers of e-journals are coming up with site license policy, providing multiple accesses.

Distribution

The major advantages of e-journals are their global distribution, their hyperlinks, and the ability to access from different sites and ability to search

E-Journals

1. Allow scholars to communicate effectively and efficiently.
2. Eliminate barriers and limitations.
4. Protect the copyright interests of both scholars and institutions.

5. Maintain quality by peer review and referee system.
6. Reduce costs.
7. Avoid delays in publishing and delivery.
8. Provides tools to help the communication process.

DARWBACKS OF E-JOURNALS

One of the major drawbacks of electronic journals at present is their delayed release. Though there are many publications, which are available only in electronic medium, in many instances, when the publication is issued in both print and electronic form, the electronic version is released after a gap of three to four weeks. Other problems include the necessity of training for the subscriber and readers and multiple copying licence/charges. Due to these factors, unlike their printed counterpart, e-journals are not open to all but somewhat restricted clientele.

E-BOOKS

The book is quite popular document to meet the information needs of the users. Books have traditionally supported the role of teaching and learning. Course textbooks, reading list materials and scholarly monographs and reference materials have all been important library acquisition for the students, research scholars etc. The e-book market has been much slower in maturing than the e-journal market. There are certain problems related to e-books such as the difficulty of reading e-books on screen, lack of interoperability between publishers etc.

A book may not have contemporary value that a journal has but it certainly has an archival and reference value. Publishing a book electronically is to achieve quick publishing and dissemination of information. A number of reference books such as encyclopedias to come out on CD-ROM. It is felt that the internet is not satisfactory platform for publishing full text of documents but CD-ROM is an appropriate medium for publishing books. A book length e-text is also available on floppy disc and CD-ROM. A book may not have contemporary value that a journal has but it certainly has an archival and reference value.

Electronic books or e-books are texts designed to be read solely on a computer screen using proprietary hardware devices, or multipurpose PC. E-books provides text that no space beyond that on the hard device. They have an amazing potential for enriching the books, both in the provision of accessory media and also in their capacity for providing cross reference, relevant information at the press of the button. Using the e-publishing language on internet like SGML presented and published attractively with multimedia effect especially for reference books such as yearbooks, encyclopedia etc.

Barnseley the CEO of Harper Collins pointed out that e-books offer publishers an end to unwanted inventory, no more returns, and no more out of print titles.

One of the new existing new developments, which may very well impact on the availability of books for library users, is the Espresso book machine. This is a print on demand machine that takes a PDF file and prints, collates, covers and binds a single paperback book in a few minutes. The machine is designed for the library and bookstore marketplace.

ELECTRONIC DATABASE

With the development of new information and communication technology, the development of databases has taken new shape. The database may consist of books, periodicals, reports and thesis can be converted into electronic form that allows access for public use through digital networks. The OPAC (On-line Public Access Catalog) shows how information could be published and that enables the users to search the document with various access point such as author, title etc.

Databases generally publishes information both bibliographic and fultext on CD-ROM as well as making them available for on-line retrieval. The prominent online publishers are DIALOG, EBSCO etc.

ON DEMAND PUBLISHING

On-demand publishing, or downloading, as it is describe in some literature, promises to affect library organization and functions dramatically. Anything that can be digitized can be transmitted electronically from central or regional storage over telephone lines, cable, fax, or satellite link to an appropriate receiver. We can digitize today virtually any sound or image. For the new electronic media, the barriers to on demand publishing or downloading are principally financial, legal, and organizational.

It is mix of digital and print publishing. The book is held by the publisher in electronic form and is printed out from the hard copy form only on order. This method helps to free publisher from the process of doing a traditional print run of several thousand books at a time. The technology involves complex laser printing systems and electronically formatted text that the printers can read. This technology is currently expensive. Because POD is still a method that uses paper and can not be delivered as cheaply and quickly as electronic books. In future consumers may decline towards print form and may create problems as electronic reading software and e-book reading devices.

ONLINE PUBLISHING

With online publishing, users are given access to more current material that can be economically distributed in packages.

ELECTRONIC PUBLISHING ON CD-ROM

Storage on CD-ROM has provided new dimensions for information storage and retrieval. Publishing of information sources such as abstracting, indexing, e-journals and reference sources are common.

The products of e-publishing can be read directly from a computer screen using special viewer or reader or it can be read using browser such as Internet Explorer, Netscape Navigator etc., which gives the experience that the reader is surfing in internet, only difference is that it is offline.

Some of these important electronic mediums for storage are:

a. Low capacity magnetic diskettes.
b. High capacity portable hard disk units.
c. Solid state disks of various kinds
d. Optical storage media
e. Computer network system local as well as worldwide

Each medium has its advantages and limitations.

Publications produced in electronic form are available in the following formats:

1. Standalone, discrete products like CD-ROMs.
2. Electronic Bulletin Boards.
3. Online interactive services
4. Information on networks.

CD-ROMS

CD-ROMs are now being accepted as standard storage medium. A CD-ROM can store about 650-700 MB of data. It enables about 2,50000 pages of A4 size to be stored in CD. The life of CD-ROM is about 100 years. It is one of the cheapest storage media. A good number of CD-ROMs are available on almost all the subjects. Multimedia databases, the most useful educational tools are now becoming popular. These are very helpful for the beginners in any subject. If the CD-ROM databases are subscribed and are available on CD-NET, many can access them on network from remote distances. Under this environment less space is required, as bulky volumes are not subscribed. CD-ROMs needs less space. Complex enquiries can be traced by Boolean expressions (and, or, not) and thus there is no need to subscribe secondary periodicals in printed media. Cost, which is considered as a major factor to decide whether or not one should subscribe to CD-ROM databases is no longer true. Now these are becoming cheaper and cheaper with the passage of time. The important factor relating to CD-ROM databases is the evaluation and that can be done on the following points:

1. Frequency of updating
2. Coverage by countrywide and language wise.
3. The quality of retrieval engine

Some of the advantages of CD-ROM are having good storage capacity (700MB) and fulltext searching is easy.

WEBPUBLISHING

With the development of various programming languages such as such as HTML, XML etc. HTML is widely used programming language .XML is valuable because it allows the publishers to create contents and data that is portable to other devices.

A web page is nothing more than a text file, a HTML file (Hyper Text Markup Language) - a simple computer language, a better description language. A set of codes determining what a page will look like in a web browser. Hypertext is to locate something in a book quickly from index or table of content. Markup comes from printing. It tells the typesetter how to put text and images on a page that will be printed.

ADVANTAGES OF ELECTRONIC PUBLISHING

Electronic publishing is increasingly popular in the fields like science. Electronic publishers are able to provide quick gratification for late-night readers, books that customers might not be able to find in standard book retailers and book by new author that would be unlikely to be profitable for traditional publishers.

The biggest advantage of e-publishing are the cost saving in printing and paper as well as better data storage and maintenance .It is most ideally suited for publications like journals, research reports and newsletters. It is also suited for all information that is dynamic or constantly changing. E-publishing finds great use and acceptance in academics, in the on-line publishing of educational books or tutorials. With increase in distance learning programmes , the need for quality educational material is on the rise. These types of reading material are more interactive.

The information in electronic format can potentially offers many advantages over one printed on paper to both users and publishers, which paper publication, cannot match.

Following are some of the advantages of electronic publishing:

1. Electronic publication can be more timely.
2. Binding/shelving is not required.
3. No chances of missing pages.
4. Eco friendly.
5. **Customization**: In electronic publishing only the information of interest are "delivered" and the user has some control over the appearance of the information both printed and on the screen.
6. The data in digital format can be quickly and perfectly duplicated into a new media.
7. Electronic archiving, copying at the other site, storage in hard disk, floppy, tapes offer very secure means of archiving.
8. Electronic documents can be accessed from anywhere

at any time and by any numbers of users at a time.

9. Electronic publication can be more timely. Library and information centers need not buy publications to access the information in it. They can have online access to the electronic journals and download or print the required material. Electronic publishing provides aids for connectivity, audio visualization, customizability, creation and revision of documents, interactivity, and rapid information retrieval.
10. Cost of publication is low.
11. Dissemination is faster in electronic publications
12. Provide greater interaction with users.
13. Electronic information can easily be managed by adding book marks and personnel notes to the sites or by downloading it to private files or databases for copying and editing.
14. **Reduce printing and distribution cost**: Only low costs are involved-as compared to paper form. No costs to authors, readers, or institutions; it is completely free for authors no much proof reading is required and therefore immediate publication of their work. The process of publishing is very easy and quick for authors. For the publishers production tasks can be automated. Readers can access full literature free of costs. Color pictures and diagrams are also completely fee.
15. Sound and video files are easily included in a publication;
16. The publication is searchable from anywhere in the world using search engines such as google. Speedy publication of documents, articles are possible.
17. Electronic publishing offers various attractive and interactive forms of presentations. Apart from texts, pictures, graphics it is possible include audio recordings, video, animation, computer programmes,

etc.

18. Electronic publishing is an effective way to spread research results. Electronic version of journals is available in advance of printed version.
19. Using the internet, one can effectively gets world wide distribution of a publication;
20. Any publication is guaranteed to be accessible on the Internet from the publishing date;
21. Since these documents are archived under a permanent Internet address, long-term research available on the Internet is ensured.
22. Immediate access to others electronic documents published online for verification of research and quotation is possible.
23. Speedy publication is possible. Your document is immediately accessible through the Internet. Time consuming interlibrary loan are no longer necessary. Publications of electronic journals save the turn around time. i.e. The time lag in submission, refereeing, vision, editing, composing, printing, binding and forwarding which is eliminated by using computer and communication networks. This enhances timely publication and is suitable to the letter type journals where rapid communication is of utmost importance. This leads to further reducing the gap between the author and the end users.
24. Research possibilities include direct search for author, title, year of publication, keywords, abstracts, full text search of the electronic document.
25. Immediate access to other electronic documents published on-line for verification of references and quotation is possible.
26. Puts no limit on number of users of the information and

publication will be accessible to both professionals and non-professionals.

27. Allows for instant correction and updating of information at any time.
28. Electronic documents are delivered with powerful mechanism to search easily.
29. Users can browse the content tables of forthcoming issues.
30. Offers all kinds of information that will not fit into the printed documents.
31. There is good number of search engines available to access and retrieve the appropriate article. Most of the publishers of e-journals are provided keywords, author search, term reducing the role of additional indexing and abstracting.
32. **On Demand Publishing:** The individual subscribers can be provided with only those documents, which match their profiles, and can be charged accordingly. On demand publishing also allows retrospective searching and SDI.

DISADVANTAGES OF E-PUBLISHING

The information in digital form is very helpful in many respects but there are lots of problems involved for accessioning this huge amount of information also.

1. In comparison to the printed form it is difficult to search the information in digital form.
2. Spot access to document is more comfortable then remote access
3. Non availability of latest information on the internet
4. Surfing on the net.
5. Lack of restriction on the information.
6. Limited band width takes longer time in downloading.

7. Require a power source to operate.
8. Discriminate between socio-economic groups.
9. Bad for browsing and nearly acceptable for reading online.
10. Readers can get lost and frustrated in current hypertext system.
11. **High Initial cost**: Publishers as well as library and information centers have to invest huge amount before benefits are expected.
12. **Incompatible Hardware and Software**: The non-compatibility of hardware due to the absence of common standards, and usage of different retrieval softwares by different publishers. The acceptance of electronic journals depends upon the user-friendly retrieval software, especially when the article is in acrobat format or Photoshop format.
13. Weak Infrastructure of computer and communication network: As prerequisite, EP necessitates the proper availability of a computer and communication network to the subscriber.
14. **Inconvenience to use**: ease of use i.e. reading at convenient time and place is not possible with EP. There are psychological feelings that researchers generally read more outside their workplace, thus requiring portable reading material.
15. **Delay in release**: In many instances, when the publication is issued in both printed and electronic forms, the electronic version is released after a gap of three to four weeks.
16. Less flexibility in use.
17. Non-availability of required information.
18. Less reviews.

CHANGING ROLE OF LIBRARIES AND INFORMATION CENTERS DUE TO E-PUBLISHING

The main aim of the library is to serve the users by providing high quality services and products to meet their information needs with the extensive use of the present information technologies. However, the emergence of new information technology such as Internet and electronic publishing continue to widen the role of library professionals. The computer makes possible a fundamental change in the way of information dissemination. Electronic publishing will remake technical services of the library and information centers.

In the changing scenario, libraries and librarians will continue to play an important role in handling conventional and electronic resources.

Libraries have already been influenced by the development of electronic publishing. The ultimate goal of electronic publishing is to provide fast and easy access to the information contained in the objective publications with simple, powerful search and retrieval capabilities.

8
Digital Library Services

INTRODUCTION

Digital libraries are meant to provide intellectual access to a wide range of users. Digital libraries are the organizations that employ and display a variety of resources, especially the intellectual resources embodied in specialized staff, but they need not be organized on the model of conventional library. Though the resources that digital libraries requires function similar to those within conventional libraries, they are in many ways different in kinds, e.g. for storage and retrieval. Digital libraries are dependent almost exclusively on computer and electronic network system and systems engineering skills rather than traditional skills of catalogers, indexers etc.

The concept of online services has changed dramatically over the past few years and similarly the way we search for and disseminate the information has also changed.

REFERENCE SERVICES

Traditional Reference Services

Traditional libraries provide a large number of services.

Many of these can and should be continued or extended in the digital library. All services are useful to the users.

First of all we should see what is reference service?

A full service digital library must accomplish all essential services of traditional libraries and also exploit digital storage, searching and communication (Gladney, Henery M et. al.1994).

Reference service in libraries is most often defined as direct personnel assistance to readers, seeking information. Three main functions of the library are acquisition, organization and dissemination. The dissemination function under which primarily directed service is reference service.

According to **Foskett**, "reference service is currently humanism in practice because the aim is to help people, in a way or other, to secure great happiness through the process of knowledge"

According to **Ranganathan** reference service is establishing the contact between the right user and the right document in a right possible way in a best possible time. We can say reference service is the process of establishing contact between a reader and his documents in a personnel way.

The main objectives of reference service in any library are:

- To satisfied the information needs of users.
- To assist the users to find their books/documents.
- To direct the users to find there required information.

Traditionally reference service can be categorized into:

1. Information services that involve either finding the required information on behalf of the user, or assisting users in finding information.

2. Instructions in the use of library resources and services and
3. User guidance, in which users are guided in selecting the most appropriate information sources and services. The main purpose of reference service is to keep the user well informed in their area of interest.

Now the question is whether these services are needed in the digital environment or not.

The traditional reference service is based on the following steps and it involves interaction between the librarian, the users, and the library resources in order to satisfy their information needs.

- Develop the essential elements of information.
- Collects the information.
- Record, sort, evaluate, and interpret the information.

Library reference service activities are the basic activity of the library. Reference service sometimes referred to as "reference and information services" refer to the personal assistance provided to the users in the pursuit of information. Provision of such personalized information services has remained the central theme of the library and information professionals. The importance of these services grew over time with the development of new information and communication technologies in libraries.

Great advances have been made in the automation of indexing and abstracting services, which are important tools for providing reference services. The applications of computer has made it possible to create large databases, leading to efficient and fast access to sources of information for current awareness service as well as retrospective search.

Some of the services, which are generally provided by the conventional libraries, are as follows:

1. Reference services.
2. Inter library-lending services.
3. Reservation services.
4. Referral services.

The reference service expended from directing users to print material to retrieving information from databases. By 1980, online searching became a standard part of reference service, requiring all librarians to have more technical skills than in the past.

Because of the development of new technology, communication and sharing of information changed.

DIGITAL REFERENCE SERVICES

The field of reference service is vast and dynamic and many new developments have taken place during the last ten years or so. The rapid developments have occurred in computer technology, telecommunication, printing reprography, etc. These developments have important implications for the provision of information and information services by libraries/information centers to their users.

Traditionally the role of librarians was to provide assistance and instruction. The concept of providing these services has changed. Today, librarians not only help the users in person but also virtually by using modern techniques such as Internet.

During the early period, libraries become interested in developing a system that would allow them to retrieve information faster and more accurately. To demonstrate the potential for the use of computer in libraries, various organizations developed a system that allowed users to search a bibliographic database through a computer using a standard telephone lines.

There are various terms used to the concept of digital services. Many dictionaries use same definition for "virtual" and "digital". Library professionals use both the terms, and everyone agrees that digital/virtual reference is a new type of service based on the same question and answer type of assistance provided in traditional in person reference. Digital or virtual reference provides the same type of service. The concept of library services has completely changed with the introduction of modern information technology. Some of the services in electronic environment are as follows:

It allows users to access information and assistance online, using e-mail, chat, video, voice software, or any other internet technology (Fig. 2).

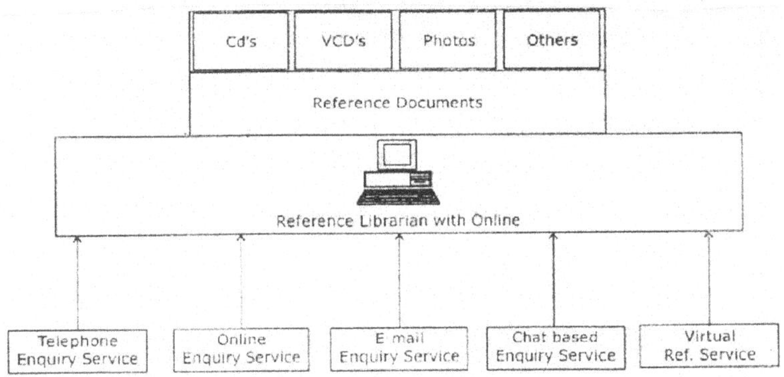

Fig. 2. Digital Reference Services

What are digital library services?

The term 'virtual reference", "digital reference", "e-reference", "internet information service" and " ask A service" are used interchangeable to describe digital reference services. Digital reference services generally based on e-mail or web based. Digital reference evolved from basic e-mail correspondence to more sophisticated systems that allowed librarians to show search results to the users. One of the first project was "See You See a Librarian" developed in 1996 by Eric Lease Morgan .The purpose was to investigate the possibility of providing chat communication between the librarian and the user.

Digital reference services use the Internet to connect people with people who can answer questions and support the development of skills. Digital reference requires not only reference service but also assistance in using hardware and software.

Why we need Digital Library Services?

Due to the changing scenario and advancement in science and technology, some factors have effected to convert the manual library database into digitized form.

We need digital library services to:

1. Increased volume of library activities/services.
2. Need for improved control over operation/collection.
3. Improved services to users in terms of -quality, user friendliness, regularity, efficiency, speed, etc.
4. Need to prevent duplication of efforts and work.
5. Need to operate with existing staffing patterns/ conditions.
6. Need for co-operation and shared utilization of information and resources.

ADVANTAGES OF USING DIGITAL LIBRARY SERVICES

The following are the advantages:

- Easy and effective retrieval search.
- Downloading the text, image, and audio with MM concept.
- Quick access through efficient search engines.
- Current information.
- Teaching and learning process in a live manner as in the classroom.
- Teleconferencing.
- Retrieval through web indexing/metadata.
- Meet the people of subject specialization.

- Vast statistical data.

SERVICES PROVIDED BY DIGITAL LIBRARY

Digital library provides numbers of services to their users (Fig. 2).

The following are the services, which are generally offered by the digital libraries :

1. Catalog database
2. Current Awareness Bulletin
3. Externally purchase Databases
4. CD-ROM databases
5. Remote Information Services
6. Internally published Newsletters, Reports and journals
7. Internet information Sources Mirroring and Cataloging
8. E-Mail
9. Bulletin Board Service
10. Netnews system
11. Audio and video communication
12. Electronic table of contents
13. Electronic Document Delivery Service
14. Electronic Thesis and dissertations
15. Reference Service
16. Electronic Publishing or E-publishing
17. Discussion Groups and Forums
18. Central Storage Facilities for hosting digital collections and indexes
19. Tools for loading, storing, searching, and displaying digital objects
20. Special collection Service, etc.

TYPES OF DIGITAL LIBRARY SERVICES

There are various types of digital library services. Some of these services are:

- Newspaper clipping service.
- Conventional library services.
- Web based Library services.
- OPAC to Web Pal.
- CD-ROM to web, databases.
- Manual to digital Reference Services.
- Document Delivery Services to Electronic Document Delivery Service.
- New Web based Library Services.
- Virtual Library Tour.
- Library Websites.
- Web based user education.
- Bulletin Board Discussion and list services.

I. Newspaper Clipping Service

This is an important service for research.

The research students are interested in newspaper information from these archives because of the librarian's efforts of selection, cutting, storing and indexing the newspaper articles.

1. Selection : The librarians can go through all the newspapers and mark relevant articles everyday of various subjects and topics.

2. Scanning and Saving : Selected articles are scanned and saved for developing database software in a required format indicating the name of newspaper and publication date after this process the newspaper goes to maintain a proper marked files.

3. Online searching and saving: The librarians can go through the online newspapers and select the relevant articles and saved for a relevant software development system. This is one way of newspaper collection.

4. Access and retrieval: The newspaper clipping service provides browsing and searching facility in various fields for the students like newspaper name wise, title, author, publication, date, etc.

SEARCH SERVICE

This is the most basic access service provided by the digital libraries to search the library collection. Online catalogs have been providing author, title and limited subject access to local holdings from a long time. The expectations for digital libraries is that the catalogs should seamlessly link to the digital collection of itself so those remotely located users can find and display not only the bibliographic information but also the primary information objects.

SEARCHING FACILITY THROUGH ONLINE PUBLIC ACCESS CATALOG (OPAC)

Catalogues and their access are the most visible aspect of libraries, particularly when they are on-line. The capabilities of the search system are generally going to be fixed by the software that you purchase. How you implement them and how the users use them is more under your control. Vocabulary control is an essential part of the cataloging process and is almost completely absent from full text searching. Searching using a controlled vocabulary is a service, which is particularly useful in the subject descriptions and makes for much better search precession than simple keyword searching. When controlled by a sensible thesaurus with descriptions and relationships it makes the user's job of finding the required meaning of a word much easier.

SEARCH PROCESS

During the search the librarian should provide a variety of accessible information to the user and then ask the user to if his/her question was answered. The follow up questions allow the librarian to verify that the user is satisfied with the material/information provided, and possible to refer the user to a library subject specialist answer the query the librarian may use either e-mail or chat. The reference interview will differ according to the method used.

E-mail reference

E-mail reference includes e-mail and web based forms. In E-mail service, the user sends the message and receives an answer at a later time. The user can usually finds a link for the e-mail service on the library's web page, with a form to fill out. When a query is sent, the system automatically matches the question with the information available in the archive where the most commonly asked questions are stored.

Chat Reference

The users generally prefer chat reference service to e-mail because it involves two-way conversation in real time, very much like talking to a reference librarian in person. Chat users can receive immediate feedback, thus they can use written language in the same manner used in person-to person conversation. Chat differs from e-mail because it provides real-time help. With chat, librarians can use a variety of tools to facilitate communication with the user.

Answering the question on-line

In answering the question on-line, librarians use the same criteria used at the reference desk. Librarian who work with digital reference tend to prefer web-based or electronic sources because they are easier to access and to share with user. One of the most important features in chat reference is the use of software with the ability to co-browse. This feature allows the librarian and the user to communicate while viewing the same web page.

II. Digitization of special collection

Special collection forms the core of the primary research collection of library. Whatever may the format, the common features of special collection are that they are unique, rare, require special handling and in limited availability just something that cannot be located in the open stacks. Equally important is that the material is valued as an artifact. Almost all the major libraries of the world are having digitized programme to provide greater access to its special collections through the digitization of material including photographs, maps, printed music, pictures, etc.

III. Service examination cell for the students

Librarians can arrange for the students motivation programme and they have to make separately arrangement for "service examination cell". In that cell having service examination documents for examples, UGC, GATE, GMAT, etc. and also make arrangements for "Group Studies Cell" for final years students. They have also conduct "how to prepare the service examinations and how to write the service examination"? It is more useful for the outgoing students.

FULTEXT SEARCH SERVICE

Search is not restricted to keywords. It covers the entire context available in the digital library system.

DOCUMENT DELIVERY SERVICE (DDS)

There has been a rapid increase in fee based document delivery services that use the network to order and /or transfer documents to libraries and often end users, bypassing the libraries.

Results of searches are available online. At time, there may be bulk transfer (such as e-mail attachment, FTP, etc.) if the access is restricted.

Digital libraries provide bibliographies on a subject or a combination of subjects can be created very easily.

CREATION OF BIBLIOGRAPHIES

Digital libraries can create bibliographies on a subject or a combination of subjects very easily which can be accessed online.

DISCUSSION GROUPS, FORUMS, NEWS

Since the library is on-line it is possible to run chat rooms or discussions on topics where the library is expert.

MARKETING SERVICE

It is possible to sell the contents on a "pay-per-view" basis or we can sell a subscription that gives unlimited access to all, or some section, of your library collection.

REGULAR E-MAIL UPDATES ON SPECIFIC SUBJECTS SERVICE

Users can subscribe to e-mail alert services on specific types of collections available in a library and remain updated on their subject area.

ONLINE TUTORIAL SERVICE

As an extension of their traditional role of providing library instruction sessions and developing instructional materials, librarians are designing online tutorials and courses that promote information literacy and encourage active learning particularly fine example are the University of Texas System Digital Library's TILT-Texas Information literacy Tutorials. The British Open University Library has developed SAFARI, a freely available interactive tutorial, as well as an information literacy course called MOSAIC (Marking Sense of Information in the Connected Age). Many libraries provide instruction to e-learners by making information available on their web pages, including frequently asked questions, library glossaries, research guides, and "how-to "pages.

Online tutorials usually operate on a model in which the learner interacts in isolation with a computer. Their effectiveness can be enhanced by the addition of more interactive forms of instruction. Librarians can also work with faculty to develop a library thread in a course discussion area, or to open a discussion forum on the library web pages.

FUTURE OF REFERENCE SERVICE

Reference services, sometimes referred to as "reference and information services", refer to the personnel assistance provided to the users in the pursuit of information. Provision of such personalized information service has remained the central theme of the library and information profession. The importance of these services grew over time with the introduction of new technologies and services into three broad groups:

1. Information services that involve either finding the required information on behalf of users, or assisting users in finding information.
2. Introduction in the use of library resources and services (broadly defined as information literacy skills) and
3. User guidance, in which users are guided in selecting the most appropriate information sources and services.

Reference question scan range from the simple fact finding type to complex questions requiring consultation, and often analysis, of one or more information sources. An important part of the reference service is the reference interview, which involve a personnel discussion between a user and the reference librarian. Based on the reference interview, the reference librarian is often able to filter the retrieved information in order to pick up the most appropriate source(s) for the given user at the given point of time. Librarian can also play an important role in providing the information services in anticipation of user needs. Such service includes various form of Current Awareness and Selective Dissemination of Information services.

These types of services that aim to keep the users abreast of the latest developments in their areas of interest, however, have not been provided only by libraries; online search service.

With the increasing availability of electronic information services and the emergence of the web and digital libraries an obvious question arises: is there a need for such personalized services?

It is obvious that the current digital libraries, and most of the digital library research projects, have focused on access to, and retrieval of, digital information rather than on the services that have been provided to the users by traditional libraries.

The web has alters the notion of traditional reference services, and a number of web based "expert service" are now offered by many library organizations. Now we can see some currently available web based reference services. Although these reference services are not necessarily offered by libraries, and they are termed differently, for example, as "expert service", they are used quite heavily, and they do not require a visit to the library to get answers to their questions. Now the question is what should be role of digital library?

The definition of digital library that came up in the March 1994 Digital Library Workshop emphasized that a full service digital library must accomplished all the essential services of the traditional libraries and also exploit the well known advantage of digital storage, searching and communication.

INFORMATION SERVICES AND DIGITAL LIBRARIES

The convergence of computer, telecommunication, information, and multimedia helped in the development of digital library services. The importance of personalized services grew with the introduction of new technologies and services in libraries.

A digital library must accomplish all the well-known advantages of digital storage, searching and communication. The richest online information is not beneficial to end-users unless they know what resources are available and how to extract the required information from the appropriate resources (Ming, Ding Choo, 2000).

Digital library should provide physical and intellectual access to a highly distributed, homogeneous collection of information resources.

Reference service is an important service provided by the modern library. Reference service helps the users to get right kind of information at right time in a right possible way. Many new developments have taken place during the last ten years in the field of information technology. These developments have important implications for the provision of information by the libraries/information centers to their users.

The field of reference service is vast and dynamic and many new developments have taken place during the last ten years or so. The rapid developments have occurred in computer technology, telecommunication, printing, reprography, etc. These developments have important implications for the provision of information services by the libraries/information centers/documentation centers to the users.

Great advances have been made in the automation of indexing and abstracting service. The application of computer has made it possible to create large databases, leading to fast and efficient access of sources of information for Current Awareness Services as well as retrospective search.

Automation in libraries has considerable impact on providing reference services such as indexing and abstracting services. The application of computer has made it possible to create large databases leading to efficient and fast access to sources of information for Current Awareness Service as well as retrospective literature search. With the help of keywords all the related terms and documents detail will come within a second with the help of computer. Even we can search interrelated books on a particular topic that was time consuming in a manual method.

REFERENCE SOURCES AND DIGITAL LIBRARY

A purely digital library should be in a position to lend reference books without restriction and may treat a reference book as an e-book like any other. Reference books are different from the other books they are even more different in an electronic context than in the physical library. When we think about e-books and reference books in the context of web systems and e-libraries it is very likely that we will need to answer some rather deep questions about what reference books are for; how they differ from other kinds of books; and how we can make reference books even more useful on the web than they are in physical form.

Reference books have appeared on the web in considerable number. Hundreds of dictionaries can now be consulted on the web, and most of them are there with no apparent commercial motivation, except in few cases the aim of developing 'brand awareness'. The Merriam Webster Collegiate dictionary is an excellent example of this. It is completely free and popular source. The website has garnered millions of pages of traffic in the five years. As web becomes a more commercial system traditional reference publishers have launched specialist subscription services built around major reference work, though which universities, public libraries and other institutions can obtain subscription access to major resources, such as the Oxford English Dictionary.

Reference sources on CD-ROM

Now a days numbers of reference sources like encyclopedias, dictionaries etc are available on digital media such as CD-ROMS etc.

Oxford Dictionary of 21 volumes available on CD-ROM. Cambridge Learner Dictionary has comes on CD-ROM. Where punctuation of British and English text is also there. National Geographic come on CD for 110 years.

In the eighties when reference works and abstracting journals began to appear on CD-ROM these were still used by the librarian on behalf of the users. The dictionaries, encyclopedias and abstracting journals were the most suited reference works for electronic delivery. Oxford University Press was one of the first publishers to make its dictionary available on CD-ROM.

Online Access

Access to online databases is provided through networks of computers and telecommunication systems. There may be Local Area Networks (LAN) provided access within a limited area or Wide Area Network (WAN) extended access to information at distant places. The Internet termed as World Wide Web (WWW) has several URLs representing sites on which data is stored under different broad heading used for classifying universe of knowledge. Emergence of subject gateways or portals that provide structured guide to internet based electronic information resources has been a much resent phenomenon. The subject gate ways restrict their operations providing linkages to third party sources.

The process of providing Reference Service online

The first step is the identification of the essential information in the request of user via e-mail or web interface, and then decide on an appropriate course of action. At this stage the librarian analyzes the query to determine the subject of the request and to identify the type of information needed. New questions may be checked against an archive of previously answered questions for appropriate answers.

REFERENCE QUESTION AND ANSWER SERVICES

The digital libraries provide communication channels like chat rooms, internet "news group" in which people interest to answer each other's questions, still many patrons come to librarians for answer to questions. Librarians can provide answers, references to literature or referral to other peoples or services. These form an essential part of the mission of most libraries. There are five ways by mens of which reference services can be provided in digital libraries.

FAQ Services: anticipate common questions and provides answer to those users can go to the FAQ service before requesting human assistance .Popular with the system related question.

Asynchronous exchange

Between patron and librarians -e-mail and online reference service.

Combined automated and human services: such as answer Garden services: which not only route questions through the FAQ list as they come in, but also capture new requests and human responses and automatically to the FAQ list.

Real time dialog with librarians: or content experts augmented by technology.

Created software Agents

Most advanced method is creating software agents that take into account the users context and act as human surrogate. Knowledge navigator video is the example of this type of agent.

Selective Dissemination of Information (SDI) Service

This service which is particularly important in special libraries sometimes also known as routing, alerting, or filtering. Filtering services are particularly appreciable to newswire, intranet " News" and broad cast media abstracting service, have been available since a long time, and will proliferate as more library contents becomes available digitally. Automated filtering service differs from retrieval services in that in filtering the corpus changes from period to period. And the query remains relatively stable. In some cases filtering services provide added value by abstracting primary information to users, where as search service typically bring documents which contain the primary information. In addition, digital libraries may also provide services that assist users in developing and maintaining profiles.

WEB SOURCES

Different types of information sources such as primary, secondary and tertiary sources can be searched through Internet. However, it must be noted that all the printed sources of the world are not available in Internet. Moreover, for consulting many Internet sources, password is required, and for obtaining the password, sufficient fund is required. Still, whatever is available free is also quite substantial, and usually very up-to-date. For example, in the case of many periodicals full text may not be available free, but the bibliographical details of the articles as well as their abstracts are available free in many cases. Hence, in any literature search it is always advisable to search Internet first. It should be supplemented with the search of the sources not available in Internet. If the library is allowed to obtain password for certain items, obviously, it will augment the literature search potential to a considerable extend.

While searching Internet is advisable to use an efficient

search engine like Google. For locating primary periodicals in Internet, searches can be conducted with the URL of the periodical if that is known. Otherwise the title or subject may be used. Various types of sources available on Internet are mentioned in a separate chapter on Internet.

SEARCHING INFORMATION ON INTERNET

Whenever a reader come with a query at the reference desk of a library, immediately the librarian starts thinking of the category of the reference book in which the information may be available. In the case of internet librarian looks for a good search engine like Google to place his query. On receiving the query, the search engine runs through millions of web sites in seconds to retrieve the information. The information thus retrieved may be relevant, or partly or totally irrelevant. For example, while searching information on Bhangra dance with the term 'Bhangra', one may get information on Bhangra dancer, costume, apart from information on Bhangra dance.

There are two different ways with which one may carry our search in the Internet, either he use the URL or the address of the web site or the subject heading. Just compare the situation with that of the library. In a library, if the reader knows the class number of the book, he straight away goes to the shelf and locates the book. Otherwise, he goes to the alphabetical part of the catalog, finds out the class number of the subject, and than goes to the shelf to locate the book. Here also if the searchers know the address of the web site, he straight away goes there. Otherwise, he use the subject heading to reach there. In many cases it becomes almost essential to know the URL.

SOME OTHER SERVICES

Some of the other services are:

Acquisition of Material

The traditional libraries store the books. However, the digital libraries acquire non-documentary material such as microfilms, optical disks etc. All these material are acquired by digital library as one of the functions, i.e. acquisition. The role of librarian in this function of acquisition is having great importance. The librarian selects the digitized material that would prove the library as a resourceful center, repository and transitory for passing the information in digital format.

Access and Discovery

Access and discovery function of digital library includes the environment of user's friendly access to information. This function promotes the index and digital or machine-readable catalog to access the required information through OPAC. In this discovery function viz searches, retrieval and delivery of information are being performed. In addition to this the location of documents is also searched by discovering the information to promote interlibrary loans and to cater the needs of users in regard to information.

Protection

The function of protection of materials to be stored or to preserve is performed by the digital library. The librarian or manager of digital library always thinks, either good or bad effects will be there in displaying the digitized information.

Facilities

The facilities of different services are necessary to access the electronic library from outside world, which include the work stations, network connections, downloading, printers and copiers. In the provision of facilities and services the different hardware and software are provided to mail the message and to display the information through bulletin boards. In this function of provision of facilities and services the entire information infrastructure is provided to access and to get displayed the digital information.

COLLABORATIVE NETWORK FOR REFERENCE

In this model, two or more libraries team up to offer reference service using any of the above online formats. The user would be forwarded to the library best able to answer the question.

TYPES AND FORMS OF DIGITAL/VIRTUAL REFERENCE SERVICES

Digital reference services can currently be broken down into two main types: e-mail and chat.

Libraries are using a couple of different means of running an e-mail reference service: using basic e-mail or web form. There are also a few different ways of operating a chat reference service: using simple chat software, web based chat rooms, and web contact center software.

E-MAIL REFERENCE SERVICE

The first type of digital reference was e-mail. E-mail was first used by librarians to communicate with one an other and, soon, with users as well.

The user sends the library e-mail with a reference query; supply whatever information he or she feels is necessary. The digital library may reply by e-mail, phone, fax, letter etc.

The around the clock and around the world accessibility of e-mail allows users to connect with librarians beyond the walls of library buildings and outside the usual hours of operation's-mail provides a written record of request and responses, permits the electronic transmission of search results, and allows librarians time to reflect on requests.

There are two basic varieties in e-mail reference service:

1. The service is assigned a simple e-mail address provided on the library web site. If user wants to submit a question, he/she can just click on the link, which is turn launches the user's e-mail software (such as Microsoft Outlook etc.). The user then fills out the e-mail and sends it to the library via the user's e-mail software.

Benefits of e-mail reference service:

The user sends the library e-mail with a reference query, supplying whatever information he or she feels is necessary. The library may reply by e-mail, phone, fax, letter, etc. E-mail is one of the most utilized services of the internet. We can send and receive information at very fast speed and at very low cost as compared to postal service. E-mail allow us to save paper and hence eco-friendly. We can attach graphics of video images with our reply.

1. It is possible by this method a user can talk directly.
2. One can conduct reference interview on the spot by exchanging a series of short messages.
3. It is useful for those with hearing or speaking impairments.

Drawbacks of e-mail reference service

E-mail reference services suffer from a numbers of drawbacks:

1. E-mail does not offer the instantaneous response and immediate gratification that patron have come to expect from the web.
2. It's difficult to conduct any kinds of an effective reference interview using e-mail, if a question needs a clarification, it may take three or four exchanges over several days just to figure out what the user really wants.
3. E-mail reference places most of the burden of

answering the question on the librarian at the reference desk the reference librarian works with the patron to help him find the answer instead of doing all the work for him.

Most reference librarians know how hard it can sometimes be to discover just what the users at the desk really want. Reference librarian can communicate with other collogues. They can participate in electronic discussion group, share information, experience, and ideas with other librarians.

One of the most serious concerns about e-mail reference services is their impact on the traditional face to face reference interview, particularly the absence of the verbal and non verbal clues that typically assist a librarian in effectively responding to a question.

E-mail reference service can be enhanced and supplemented with additional technologies that raise the level of interaction with real-time or live communication. Chat technology allows e-learners and librarians to send text messages back and forth instantly, using a form of communication that is familiars to most Internet users. There have been a number of library experiments with web contact center software, which is modeled on the private sector's online solution to providing customer support.

WEB FORMS

Users fill out an online form on the library's web site. The form asks the user to answer clarifying questions that will help the reference librarian responding to the query. The user sends the completed form to the library by clicking a button on the page labeled "send". The library may reply by e-mail, fax, letter, etc. While e-mail reference allows the users to write down the query in his own words, a web form structures the user's request somewhat, producing the user to supply additional information that will specify the request.

CHAT REFERENCE SERVICE

Chat Based Reference service

Chat, sometimes referred to as instant messaging, is real time communication between two or more computer users over the Internet. Every keystroke a chat user maker is instantly transmitted and appears on the monitors of all other users in the same chat session. Chat is very popular means of communication over the Internet.

Since the year 2000 there has been an explosion of interest in the library world of adopting chat technology, which allows the user and librarians to send short written massages back and forth instantly. The user and librarian may exchange a series of short messages to get to the heart of the user's request. Some chat programmes offer an open virtual reference room where one or more user can enters at a time and exchange messages with the librarian. There are three ways of running this kind of a service: with free, instant messaging software (such as CompuServe Instant Messenger), with a virtual reference room solution or with chat software purchased by the library.

Chat provides reference nearly in real time communication and interaction between users and information professional is also known as live reference or real time reference.

Virtual reference does not mean 24 hours a day, 7 days a week (24x7 services) availability. It means real time, synchronous service for users, available remotely and / or within the library. The library sets the hours and service levels it is willing and able to support.

CHAT REFERENCE USING SIMPLE TECHNOLOGIES

Users exchange short, text massages back and forth with the librarian. There are three ways of running this kind of a service: with free, instant messaging software, such as

AOL (instant manager) with a web-based chatroom, or with chat software purchased by the library. The users and librarian may exchange a service of short massages to get to the heart of the user's request. This exchange of messages is live and allows for negotiations of the user's enquiry. With most of these services, the user types in an opening query to get the attention of the librarian staffing the chat reference service.

CHAT REFERENACE USING WEB CONTACT CENTER SOFTWARE

Borrowing technology from online customer service, software for web contact centers not only allow for instant messaging, but they also offer give the power to librarian to control the user's browsers. A librarian can actually make the user's browser display a recommended web page, such as a search engine or the main page for the library's online catalog. As librarian pushes pages onto the user's browser, the chat window can also appear on both user's and librarian's screen, allowing them to have a typed conversation about the Webpages being sent to the user.

Web contact center software provides a higher level of interaction than does basic chat software, allowing for queuing and routing of messages, as well as enabling librarians to "push" web pages to users. Providing e-learners with a toll-free telephone number remains an effective and convenient reference services strategy, particularly for intricate inquiries .The telephone reference interview works best when both librarian and e-learner are working in front of computers connected to the internet.

ADVANTAGES

It feels somewhat like a live reference interaction; you can talk to the user directly.

1. You can conduct a reference interview on the spot by

exchanging a series of short messages to get the better idea of what's asked for.

2. It eliminates problem of mishearing what is said.
3. It is helpful for those with hearing or speaking impairment.
4. The user can save text of chat session to refer to later.

DISSADVANTAGES

1. It is only chat, you can "talk" back and forth with the patron and tell her to go to a specific address on the web to find information, but you can no actually take her through a database search.
2. Much more time consuming than regular voice communication because you have to type every thing out with spelling and typing error that can creep in.
3. Most of the chat software packages do not allow to queue and route questions easily, nor do they offer scripted message to handle routine functions and requests
4. The user may not have the same level of patience with the librarian's effort to help -users expect every thing to be instant, convenient and efficient.
5. If the user logs off permanently, it may not be immediately apparent to the librarian, especially if the librarian is busy looking something up in a book or on a computer for the user.

DIGITAL LIBRARY SERVICES PROVIDED BY A UNIVERSITY LIBRARY

University library generally provides the following types of digital services:

E-mail reference service

Many academic libraries and information centers are extensively using e-mail facility to provide online reference service to the students. E-mail reference has the advantage of providing more complete answers than what could possibly be given at a busily reference desk. When answering a question through e-mail, the reference librarian usually has more time to think about the question, the user's needs and if necessarily consults with other colleagues who have more related expertise or knowledge.

Email reference

E-mail reference includes e-mail and web based forms; e-mail service provides asynchronous service; that is, users sends the message and receives an answer at a later time. The user can usually find a link for the e-mail service on the library's web page, with a form to fill out. Some libraries and Ask a service provide archives where the most commonly asked questions can be found. When a query is sent, the system automatically matches the question with the information in the archives.

Ideally, the e-mail reference interview should consists of three e-mails, the first one sent by the user with the question, the second sent by the librarian with the information, and the last sent again by the user confirming that the information received satisfied his/her question. In order to conduct an effective e-mail interview, Abels suggests using one of two methods. With the first method, the patron is required to fill out a form specifying any limitations they have such a language, due date, or amount of information.

The second approach requires the librarian to respond to a question that is not clear with a list of questions that will help the librarian find the appropriate information. The second approach requires more time of librarian's time, and there is no guarantee that the user will want to answer the questions required to help them.

Telephone or online Enquiry Service

The users ask a question for reference librarian through telephone, at that time that information is readily available that is ready reference service. That is otherwise called as online enquiry services. The students directly came and get the relevant documents for the reference section that is called face-to-face method service.

Virtual Reference Service

Real time reference line on the web is the latest trend in virtual reference. Already some librarians are providing live web reference services to their users.

For examples:

http://www.cpi.org

The librarian and informational professionals are required to cope-up with the new technological changes, but at the same time one should not fear that the new emerging technology based services will replace the traditional services completely rather these are emerging as supplementary services to improve the information dissemination amongst the student community.

Enquiry Service Section

The librarian arranges for enquiry service section. They needed not separate place and also utilize for the circulation section, otherwise the librarian can arrange separate system for user terminal. The above said both the ways very useful for locate the documents to the user community.

Inter Library Loan Service

In this, facilities can arrangement for university librarians. The costly documents, rare collecting documents, government reports, abstracts, patents etc., these are all put in to one place, the universities undertaken colleges call get lonely in this documents. One college having a rare collection of documents, the same document wants to some other institution at the time the university can collect that document and give to the relevant institution.

The librarian can list out the free information sources and services in the internet service library:

Free online journals

1. *http://www.jodi.ecs.soton.ac.uk/*
2. *http://www.information.net*

Free encyclopedias

http://www.britannica.com

Free conference proceedings:

http://www.sla.org/content/events/conference/2002.annual/confpap2002/papers2003conf.cfm

(Special Library Association Conference, 2002)

Free newspapers

http://www.hinduonnet.com

Free dictionaries

http://www.pdictionary.com

Free abstract service

Some of the publishers or organizations provide abstracts of the articles of their journals.

For example: *http://www..wkap.nl/kaphtml.htm/to* CSEARCH

Free online catalog service

The students have opportunity to access free online catalogs of publishers, suppliers and other libraries, which greatly help in their learning process.

http://www.catalog.loc.gov/

(Library of Congress)

http://www.phiindia.com

(Prentice Hall of India)

http://www.schandgroup.com

(S.Chand and Co.)

Librarian should maintain an index of online E-journal, E-books and other information sources, which are freely available on Internet. This can form an important part of library collection.

Digital Library Service by co-operative Library System

In order to deal with the rising cost of reference sources and staff and also of the huge initial investment required for introducing new services in the libraries, many have gone co-operative model of digital reference service. Web based co-operative service initiated by many libraries. One of the advantages of web-based reference service is that users can ask for such services from a remote location at anytime of the day.

Electronic services allow the service to:

1. Enhance the service given to users;
2. Avoid the repetitive work;
3. Maximize the stock available by holding information and documents in electronic form. Library and Information Science have wide range of E-resources viz., standalone and network databases, CD-ROMs, e-journals, multimedia products, image collection, encyclopedias, reference material, daily news, information sources. Electronic information can be accessed via Internet from information providers, or from local network of libraries and information centers.

Publications produced in electronic forms are available in the following formats:

4. Standalone, discrete products (like magnetic disks, CD-ROMs)

5. Electronic Bulletin Board
6. Online interactive services

Information on networks

1. Collection in which complete contents of documents are created or converted into machine readable form for online access.
2. Scanned images, images of photographic or printed text, etc.
3. On line databases and CD-ROM information products particularly those with multimedia and interactive video components.
4. Computer storage devices such as optical disk, CD-ROM, DVD-ROM.
5. Database accessible through Internet and other networks.
6. Digital audio, video clips or full length movies.

COMPONENTS OF ONLINE SERVICES

An online service has usually the following components:

1. Database producer or information provider who collect, process and supply data in generally in the form of separate record of computer processing.
2. A host or search service that loads the records onto one or more databases on large computers and provides search software that enables many users to access simultaneously the database and records from remote location.
3. Telecommunication connections between information searcher's terminals or workstations and host using special networks and ordinary telephone line.
4. Computer terminals or workstation with appropriate communication facilities providing access to the

service.

FEATURES OF ONLINE DATABASE SERVICE

Some of the features are as follows:

1. Instant and personalized
2. Comprehensive
3. Short range
4. Long range

The database can be grouped on the bases of different attributes like subject scope, geographic and chronological coverage, periodicity of release of new information by database producers, frequency of updating, and type of information/records they contain. Hence, the databases can be classified as:

1. Reference database

Which refer and points the user to an other source, such as document, organization or individual, for additional information or the full text.

Bibliographic databases: which contain citations and often abstracts of the printed documents such as articles in periodicals, conference proceedings, reports, books, newspaper items for example, AGRIS, CASEARCH.

2. Referral Database

Which contain references to, or addresses and descriptions of, institutions, persons, audio visual material and non print media for further information?

3. Source Databases

Which contain original source data, or full text original information source or materials prepared specially for electronic distribution.

These include:

i. **Numeric databases**: containing numeric information

such as original survey data, scientific /technical data, etc.

ii. **Textual -numeric database**: it contain a number of data elements/fields some of which may contain numeric data, for example company reports, etc.

iii. **Full text databases**: containing records of complete text of an item, such as, full newspaper item, a technical specification, etc.

iv. **Software database**: containing computer programs that can be downloaded for use on a local computer.

In addition to above the bibliographical database can be divided in the following categories :

i. **Specific subject**: bios, Medline, etc.

ii. **mission oriented**: NASA, NITS, etc.

iii. **Problem oriented**: TOXILINE, etc.

iv. **Referral**: ULRICH Plus, etc.

v. **Factual**: PTI forecasts, etc.

vi. **Textual**: dictionaries, encyclopedias, etc.

FUNCTIONS OF AN ONLINE SERVICES

The functions of online services are:

1. Retrieval of records with some unique characteristics such as:
   - Bibliographical record by name of authors, a particular subject, etc.
   - Land record by name of owner, etc.
   - Hospital patient record -by name of patient.
2. Retrieval of a set of records likely to be relevant to a particular topic for example: all publications by S.R. Ranganathan.
   1. Retrieval of a group of records within a specific field. For example papers on evaluation of information system.

2. Selective retrieval of material to be provides a general or critical overview of some specific subject.
3. Verification of some facts. Retrieval of documents/information so as to gives an update on specific subject or entity.
4. Ascertaining an answer to a specific question.
5. Sequencing of a set of retrieved documents according to some estimate of probable relevance.
6. Arranging group of records in a helpful sequence either by sorting or partitioning.
7. Conversion of search terms from one system to an other.
8. Conversion of search terms from one language to an other.
9. Helping searcher to make all necessary decisions.

ROLE OF LIBRARIAN/INFORMATION PROFESSIONALS IN PROVIDING REFERNCE SERVICE IN DIGITAL ERA

The role of librarian had expanded to include reference service. It has now become the part of the profession. With the development of new technology the role of librarian has completely changed.

Today, librarians not only help the users at reference desk but also in cyberspace. They not only help users in person but also virtually. This new type of service, called digital or virtual reference, has emerged as the result of various factors, including the advent and wide use of the internet and the development of the software capable of providing synchronous and asynchronous service. Digital/ virtual service is quite new, but has quickly become popular because of demands by patrons to access information anytime anywhere.

Digital / virtual reference service allows librarians to help users to access information in virtual environment, using various methods such as e-mail or chat. Each type of service has positive and negative features. Although digital reference lacks the face to face communication that is an integral part of reference service , the reference techniques used and the scope of the librarians role have remained the same. With invent of the internet, libraries began to offer online services to their users. One of the simplest type is of digital/virtual reference service is online access to the library's catalog.

The contribution of library and information professionals to reference work has increased, rather than the reverse, as electronic information sources have proliferated. It was probably never true that users could use all of the resources of a library unaided, but many thought that they could. With the great variety of bibliographic databases, numerical databanks, electronic journals and general Internet resources that exists today, few users can make optimal use of them all. The software needed to search in these files, the command languages, and the facilities available for output or transfer of 'hits' to other files for further processing are so complex and varied that professional help is very often needed.

9

Internet and Digital Library Services

INTRODUCTION

In recent times, computer are being used for a number of applications, ranging from communicating to each other from remote corners of the world to gathering information, downloading software, playing games etc. The Internet is slowly emerging as a low-cost medium for information dissemination. The spread is enabling a shift from traditional communication pattern between organizations and individuals.

The methods of using computers have been taking new dimensions over the years. Initially computers were used as a single stand-alone machine, each kept in isolation from other computers. In course of time, computers were interconnected to form computer networks. Networking allowed sharing data as well as resources stored in one computer with another. More and more networks were formed in due course. As the number of the networks grew, computer networks located in different places were connected to each other to form larger networks. Computers spread their "Net" across the world, and thus emerged the area of Internet.

Internet can be called 'the information communication system established by the national and international linking of material stored on electronic database and made accessible throughout the world through telephone, cable and other telecommunication links'. Numbers of interlinked networks and thousands of computers are connected in the internet.

As the "inter networking" is getting stronger and stronger, different activities of people such as learning, teaching, communicating, banking and so on have been taking new shapes.

Internet is moving to be single most significant phenomena offering never-ending opportunities. The use of Internet in libraries is rapidly increasing and is changing the traditional functions and services of the libraries. Internet is being used as an efficient medium for access, storing and disseminating of information worldwide.

Today, library patterns are stationary in nature, gaining access to digital libraries by fixed workstations with low and high speed wired connections to the Internet. In the future, as society moves towards a ubiquitous computing environment to accommodate an increasingly nomadic lifestyle, access to digital libraries will be primarily by mobile workstations or wearable computers with low speed wireless connections to the Internet.

The Internet is a network of networks which links scientists, businessman, educators, students, research scholars and others. Internet based material includes e-books, e-journals, etc. The electronic materials available through Internet are either free of cost or subscription based. Many standard reference materials such as dictionaries, encyclopedias, directories and other reference sources are available through Internet. Many of these sources available on CD-ROMs are now available on Internet. The advantage of Internet material is that they can be updated periodically.

Internet is the gateway for libraries and information centers to electronic information era and different organizations; institutions, research centers and individual all over the world generate information in digital form on the Internet. Creation of digital resources with the establishment of digital library is the need of the day.

It is world's first digital information utility, and co-operative computer networks of networks that links libraries, schools, governments, corporations, individuals and others to each other and to vast information resources. It has revolutionaries the world of information access, storage and retrieval. New information distribution systems without boundaries. It is aimed at linking business to business, individual to individual, and organization to organization irrespective of time and space barriers.

Library and information managers are making advantageous use of many internet applications such as e-mail, FTP, Gophar, Telnet, Usenet, e-commerce, World Wide Web (WWW), Virtual/Digital libraries, On-line Journals, and Databases, web resources, etc. in performing almost all of their functions, in the area of information "acquisition", "organization", or "dissemination". Processing of document request gets expedited as incomplete or missing bibliographic parameters of documents (to be acquired), can easily be gathered from a host of sources, available on the net.

Digitization of academic and research papers, books, journals, newspaper clippings etc. are being taken up on a large scale to make then widely available. Digital contents repositories can also be shared within an organization to capture both explicit and implicit knowledge in a local network called an internet.

Meaning

The Internet is a massive network of networks, a networking infrastructure. It connects millions of computers together globally, forming a network in which any computer can communicate with any other computer as long as they are both connected to internet. Before we define the Internet, we must briefly explain concept of a computer network. A computer network consists of two or more linked computers, which can share data with each other. We can think of the Internet as a network of networks, that is the internet connects networks from all around the world, creating a giant network. Internet is the networking of computer networks around the world which facilitates transfer or sharing of information among all the computer users connected to these networks.

In short, internet is a worldwide communication system which links together thousands of computers In fact; it is a network of thousands of networks which communicate among themselves using a single set of software, which are generally known as protocols. These protocols are known as TCP/IP(Transmission Control Protocol/Internet Protocol). These protocols make sure of the connectivity to the right computer to interact. Internet provides interconnectivity among government agencies, educational institutions, libraries, companies, or anybody who has a personnel computer system.

With proper equipments like modem and with certain amount of fee paid to the access provides after an agreement with the provider one can connect oneself with the net. The resources can be accessed, viewed, downloaded, printed, retrieved from all over the world. Internet helps the users to use the ever-changing wealth of information stored on computer throughout the world. Copyright laws apply to this electronic information. Of course some may feel that posting information on internet means making it open for the public. It is true that much of the resources on the net can be obtained free but copyright still subsists on these materials. When a person access the electronically stored information and make a copy of it or part of it which is not covered by any license agreement, the facilitator may be held liable for infringement of copyright.

The Internet is a network of computers, offering information, communication and a wealth of online activities. The network of interconnected computers that communicate.

INTERNET VS DIGITAL LIBRARY

Libraries are significant for searching information. One might use the internet or a search engine to find these databases, deeper access to them require registration. You are still online, but you are no longer on the internet. You are in a library.

WORKING OF INTERNET

The working of the internet is associated with a new type of switching methodology known as 'packet switching'. In this technique the message or information is divided into separate packages, each of which is transmitted independently through the network. In other words, the internet works by breaking down all the information which needs to be transmitted into packets, which contain not only the data to be transmitted, but also information indicating where it has to reach, where it come from an to what other packets of data is it is related to. The advantage of this technique is that since the network has to deal with smaller standard size packets in a pre determine way; a faster transmission rate can be achieved. By breaking transmission into standard data packets, transmission across the Internet is made efficient and effective.

Internet is a worldwide communication system, which links together a variety of computers with distinctive software and hardware. These computers are interconnected to allow them to communicate by translating messages in to a mutually understanding language refer to as communication protocols. Protocol used by the Internet is called TCP/IP (Transmission Control Protocol/Internet Protocol). The protocol is a set of rules that two computers are required to follow when they communicate. These protocols enable data to be passed easily from one place to an other on the network. All the computer systems connected to the Internet must be in a position to communicate in TCP/IP language or have some arrangement to interpret and translate TCP/IP instructions. The end users need not know anything about how TCP/IP works. Users can communicate or talk through their local operating systems such as Windows, DOS, UNIX, etc. and programmes will take care of translating user's requirements into a form, which complies with the protocol. The computers which are part of the internet are called hosts.

Large volume of telephone lines and fiber optics cables provide the link for all these computers and the total capacity of a. line to transfer voice, data is called its bandwidth. The vast majority of traffic is carried on fiber optics cables that can rout billions of packets or bunch of information every day.

The secret to understanding the Internet is that it is populated by the two types of computers programs, namely server and clients. Servers are programs that provide resources and clients are the programs that we use to access these resources. E-mail, Usenet /news groups, FTP, TELNET, GOPHER, ARCHIE, WWW, etc, are among the prominent service of the Internet. Each type of service in the Internet has its own client, for example to access the www we need to use the browser such as Internet explorer or Netscape navigator.

As we know that Internet is collection of networks covering the world. These networks contain many different types of computers and there should be a tool to hold the whole thing together i.e. "TCP/IP" which stands for Transmission Control Protocol and Internet Protocol. A protocol is a set of rules describing in technical terms how something should be done. TCP/IP is the common name for a collection of more than of 100 protocols uses to connect computers and networks.

SOME IMPORTANT INTERNET TERMS

1. IP address

A unique number assigned to every computer, which is currently connected to the Internet. Every computer connected to Internet must have a unique identifier so that thing sent to it will not get mismatched. This unique identifier is called an IP address. An IP address consists of four numbers (ranging from 0 to 255) separated by periods (ex. 100.101.237. 211). There are two types of IP addresses; static IP address and dynamic IP address. Most computers use dynamic IP addresses, this means that every time you connect to the Internet you will receive new (most likely different) IP address. A static IP address never changes for a computer, so this is mainly used for servers.

If you want to connect to an other computer, transfer files to or from another computer, or send an E-mail message, you first need to know where the other computer is - you need the computer's "address"

An IP (Internet protocol) address is an identifier for a particular machine on a particular network; it is part of a scheme to identity computer on the Internet. IP addresses are also referred to as IP numbers and Internet addresses.

The IP address has the following characteristics in common:

- IP address are unique
- No two machines can have the same IP number
- IP address are also global and standardized
- All machines connected to the Internet agree to use the same scheme for establishing an address.

2. Domain Name

Since IP address are difficult to remember human use simpler names like www. sggscc. ac. in, this is called a domain name. Since computers use IP address and people use domain names, we need special computers called domain name servers to translate domain names into IP addresses. These computers have very long lists of domain names and their corresponding IP addresses. If a domain name server doesn't know the IP address it will contact other domain server to see if they know it.

No two organizations can have the same domain name. A domain names always contains two or more components separated by period, called "Dots". Some examples of domains names are: Microsoft.com, sggscc.com, IBM.com, etc. The last position of the domain name is the top-level domain name and described the type of organization holding the name.

The major categories of top-level domain names are:

Com—Commercial entities

Edu—Educational institutions

Net—Organizations directly involved in Internet operations

Org—Miscellaneous organizations that don't fit any other category, such as non-profit groups.

Gov—United States Federal Government entities

Country code: a two-letter abbreviation for a particular country. For example, " in" for India, "UK" for United Kingdom, etc.

Web addresses (Uniform Resources Locator URL): It refers to particular pages on a web server, which are hosted by company or organization. The format of URL is:

Protocol / Inter address / Web page address

http:// *www.sgggscc.com*

Protocol (Web) (host) (type pf sites)

1 2 (Domain Name)

3.ISP (Internet Service Provider)

An ISP is a company that acts as a middleman between your computer and the internet backbone. ISPs work on the same premises as any other telecommunications company (i.e. phone, cable, etc.).

4. Packet

The name of a chunk of data, which is being transmitted over the Internet.

5. Web site

A website is an electronic description of an individual, institution or organization that resides on the internet. It consists of several pages, although a user may or may not see the breakdown of each page. A collection of web pages that are linked together in a "web".

6. Web Server

It is used to store the web pages accessed by the web browser. They may not contain database of customers or product information, which can quires from the browser. A web server is a computer programme whose tasks are to store files and to respond to requests in HTTP and associated protocols. A web server runs on a computer connected to the internet. This computer can be dedicated one, a shared one that also runs other applications, or a personnel computer that provide a small web site. The actual processing that a web server carries out is tightly controlled by the HTTP protocol.

7. Protocol

A set of rules that two computers are required to follow when they communicate. It sends web pages from the web server to one's computer. In computing , protocol is a set of rules that are used to send massages between computer systems. A typical protocol includes description of the formats to be used, various messages, the sequences in which they should be sent, appropriate responses, error conditions, and so on.

8. Web

Stands for World Wide Web (WWW). Most web addresses have www after http://. It identifies the site as part of the World Wide Web.

Host: This name of web site. This name could be name of the company, business houses, etc. This name is a part of unique domain name that must be registered with a company called 'Network Solution' which has an exclusive authority to register domain name.

9. Types of Sites

This part of the web address tells us what type of site a web site have, for example .com stands for commercial site.

10. Website

A website is a collection of information that the user perceives to be a single unit. Often a website corresponds to a single web server; however, a large site may be physically held on several server may host many web sites.

11. Home page

A home page is the introductory page to a collection of web information. Almost every website has a homepage. If the address in a URL does not specify a file name, the server congenitally supplies a page called index.html. Thus, for example, the URL *http://www.loc.gov/is* interpreted as *http://www.loc.gov/index.html*

A homepage usually provides an overview of the website (typically in combination with an introduction to the site, a table of contents and some helps in finding information)

Small sets of information within a web site is also can be called home pages. It is common for information relevant to a specific department, project, or service to have its own home page within the website of a company or an institution. Every designer has slightly different ideas about how to arrange a home page. However, just as the title pages of books usually follow certain conventions, a home page usually provides an overview of the web site. Small sets of information within a web site also can be called home pages. It is common for information relevant to a specific department, project, or service to have its own home page within the web site of a company or an institution.

12. HTTP

In computing, a protocol is a set of rules that are used to send messages between computer systems. A typical protocol includes description of the formats to be used, the various messages, the sequences in which they should be sent, appropriate responses, error conditions, and so on. HTTP is the protocol that is used to send messages between web browser and web servers.

INTERNET ACCESS

You can connect to the Internet in one of two basic

ways, dialing into an Internet Service Provider (ISP) computer, or with a direct connection to Internet Service Provider (ISP). The difference is mainly in the speed and cost. In dial up connection, individual user connects to Internet by using a telephone line and a 56Kpbs modem. The ISP's server route traffic between customers.

Dial up connection: with a dial-up account, you use your modem to convert computer bit and bytes into modulated signals that the phone can transmit. These signals are received by a modem at your ISP and demodulated into bits and bytes for their computer. Modem is the short form of "modulation-demodulator". You usually connect to a local ISP and can surf and browse the internet. Dial up access is either by way of SLIP (Serial Line Internet Protocol) or PPP (Point to Point Protocol).

To establish a conventional dial up connection to the Internet, you will need the following:

1. An account with an InternetAccess Provider (In India, at present Videsh Sanchar Nigam Ltd (VSNL) is the Internet access provider. The account can be either TCP/IP or Shell.
2. A telephone connection.
3. A computer with serial port (or external modem) or an expansion slot (for internet modem).
4. A modem (external/internet)
5. A communication (or terminal emulation) software.

Configuring Dial-up Connection

1. Double click on **My computer** icon on your desktop
2. Double click on **Dial-up Networking** icon
3. Double click on Make a new connection icon
4. Specify a name for the connection in the text box
5. Click on next button

6. Type VSNL's internet telephone connection number
7. Type your city STD code
8. Close your counting from the drop down list
9. Click on NEXT button
10. Click on FINISH button.

Your dial-up connection called my connection is now ready.

Now let us make a shortcut icon for dial-up connection on your computer desktop.

- Select my connection and click on your mouse's right button to get yes or no menu.
- Click on yes button.

The shortcut icon for my connection has been created. With this, you complete configuring your setting for Internet.

Below is the list of software that your ISP will install.

The ISP (International Service Provider) is a company they provides access to the internet. In India the most common ISPs are VSNL, MTNL, Satyam online, etc. This can be via a dial-up connection using modem, or using a higher speed connection.

- Telecommunication software, including Weinstocks, or other Internet protocol transceiver software.
- A World Wide Web Browser like Internet Explorer or Netscape Navigator.
- An E-mail Program.
- Optionally your ISP may also install or give you an FTP program and a Newsgroup Reader. With all this software installed, you will be ready to access Internet.

Direct Connection

You can also get a direct connection to your ISP, where you have fixed cable or a dedicated phone line to the ISP. This option requires that dedicated phone lines to the ISP. This option requires that dedicated lines be leased through network provider and special hardware be installed on site, making these complicated operations. Dedicated lines can be normal telephone line, cable or radio frequency lines. Often the dedicated line is an ISDN (Integrated Services Digital Network) line, which is higher speed version of the standard phone line, but actually required two phone lines. ISDN can handle more than 64 kpbs to 128 kpbs. Most telephone companies offer ISDN at a slightly higher cost than the standard dial-up service that it replaces.

The benefits of ISDN include being able to connect a PC, telephone, and fax machine to a single ISDN line and use them simultaneously. However, ISDN is dropping out favour because of the increasing availability of higher performance broadband option.

High Speed Broad Band Connections

Various companies, cable TV services, and other suppliers such as networking companies and satellite service providers provide this service. These high-speed services are sometimes called broadband connections (e.g. SYFY Broadband Connection), because they use media that can handle multiple signals at once, such as fiber optics, microwave, and other technologies. Now the broadband technologies for the homes, educational institutes, business houses, etc are becoming available and are priced within the reach of many individuals, it is entirely practical to establish an internet connection at home that is at least 10 times as fast as a standard 56K modem link.

Features of SYFY broadband Connection:

- No telephone connection is needed, no modem required
- Wireless + ethrnet cable technology
- Upto 10 times faster and 50% cheaper than dial up

- 24 hour customer care
- Unlimited, hourly and data transfer plans available
- Free licensed antivirus package from McAfee

  E-mal of customer care is:

  customcare@sify.com

  Rates: 256 Kbps—1GB—— for 1 month=550Rs

  256 Kbps—400MB—1month =Rs400

  96 Kbps — unlimited use -for 1 month=Rs795

  64Kbps — 15 hours—1 mnth=Rs440

SERVICES AND TOOLS

The primary purpose of Internet is communication, whether it is scientific research, current news, data base searching, entertainment, conferences, electronic publishing or simple chat.

The following can be done on the Internet:

- Communication (e.g. e -mail)
- Document or file transfer (FTP)
- Interactive browsing
- Reading and posting to bulletin boards.

The basic tools and services that are commonly used for these activities are

1. FTP (File Transfer protocol)
2. Telnet (Protocol/service)
3. Gopher (Protocol/service)
4. Veronica
5. WAIS (Wide Area Information Servers)
6. WWW

FTP (File Transfer Protocol)

FTP is a mechanism that facilitates transfer of files from one computer to another computer. It is the movement of the whole electronic documents, images, sound. FTP refers to the Internet tool, which allows the movement of the file from one place to the other. Here 'file' means any digital entity such as document, image, graphics, sound, movies and software. It allows downloading of software, product up gradation and other things. It has become popular and most widely used tool because of a number of anonymous FTP servers available. An anonymous FTP server allows any user to download files or programs. Several public access files exist on computers on the Internet as anonymous FTP archives, which we can download on our computers. FTP servers also supply a small amount of text information. With the 'help' command one get online help to know more about any doubt.

FTP work on the client / server principle. A client program enables the user to interact with server in order to access information and services on the server computer. Files that can be transferred are stored on computers called FTP servers. To access these files, an FTP client program is used. This is an interface that allows the user to locate the files to be transferred and initiate the transfer process.

The basic steps to use FTP are:

1. Connect to FTP server.
2. Navigate the file structure to find the file you want.
3. Transfer the file.

There are two types of FTP connections, anonymous and non- anonymous. Anonymous FTP access means that you don't have to be registered user to connect to the remote host. No special account or password is needed. However, an anonymous FTP site will sometimes ask that user login with the name "anonymous" and use their e-mail address as the password. Non- anonymous, you will need private login name and password. There are two types of files transfers ASCII and binary. ASCII is for text transfer only. Binary transfers are for transferring anything else. If in doubt, use binary (bin).

Files on FTP servers are often compressed. Compression decreases file size. This enables more files to be stored on the server and makes file transfer time shorter. It is good idea to have current virus checking software on the computer before files are transfer to it.

Telnet

Telnet is a protocol or set of rules, that enables one computer to connect to an other computer. This process is also known as remote login. The user's computer, which initiates the connection, is referred to as the local computer, and the machine being connected to, which accepts the connection, is referred to as the remote, or host computer. The remote computer can be physically located in the next room, the next town or in another country. Once a connection to a remote computer is made, instructions or menus may appear. A variety of resources are available through telnet.

For example: library catalogues, databases, other Internet tools such as FTP, Gopher, and the World Wide Web, etc.

Telnet enables the Internet users to log into other remote Internet computers to access online database, electronic library catalogue and Internet information services. Accessing other libraries' catalogues can help you verify information for acquisition, inter library loan and copy cataloguing. The original idea behind telnet was to let researchers from different institutions share resources with one another. The www lets you access sites through telnet and use FTP to retrieve documents you find. Telnet, like most other services is based on the client/ server model. It is directly accessing another computer system's database or archives. Telnet basically means remote login. This is ability to access and control another computer on the Internet somewhere. Telnet can be used to search an archive such as library resources or even to access our own computer from another geographical location. Many computers on the Internet are set to allow telnet access. Some require login names and password, but many do not have restrictions.

Gopher

Gopher is a protocol designed to search, retrieve, and display document from remote sites on the Internet. The Gopher was created by the Microcomputer workstation center of University of Minnesota to find information on the Internet in a user friendly way. In addition to document display, document retrieval, it is possible to initiate on-line connections with other systems via gopher. Information accessible via gopher is stored on many computers all over the Internet. These computers are called gopher servers. Information stored on many kinds of non-gopher servers is also available via special gopher server that acts as gateways (protocol translator). It is a menu driven programme that allows you to click with information servers or 'Gopher holes' on the Internet to retrieve the information including text, sound, and images.

Users interact with gopher via a hierarchy of menus and can use full text searching capabilities of gopher to identity-desired documents. Gopher was created a piece of software to utilize some of the services that were becoming available on the Internet. User can read or access an item without having to worry about domain names, IP addresses, etc.

Over the years other tools or services have emerged which generally expands the scope of their activities. The most widely used is gopher, which displays organized resources. Gopher is an Internet search utility that offer easy access to online library guides FTP files and numerous internet information services. It presents information in a hierarchical system. The resources on a gopher system vary from site to site. Generally gopher includes full text documents (e.g. speeches, reference books, news items, etc.)

Veronica

It stands for "very easy rod in oriented net wide index to computerized archives" which permits the users to search gopher menus by keywords to find relevant menus more quickly.

Veronica usually is a menu item on a gopher or World Wide Web server. There might be several Veronica sites available on a given gopher or www server. These varieties enable a user to select a not - too busy veronica server. After the user selects a veronica, gopher asks the user for their search words. Successful search formed the Veronica returns a new menu of gopher item satisfying the condition of the search.

Veronica is one of the most useful Internet information hunting tools around. Unfortunately, because it is also the one that has the fewest servers, reaching a Veronica server can be very difficult.

WAIS (Wide Area Information Servers)

It allows the users to search text, sound or images from a single interface located anywhere on the network. It is suited for retrieving textual information. It provides a scored list of documents, which are relevant to the query. The tidal wave of interest in the internet came with the use of www or simply the web, the fastest growing internet function. It uses the concept of hypertext to link information

Hypertext refers to the system of direct connections among information sources displayed to the user by allowing jumping from one source to another, by pointing and clicking. The web operator using an Internet protocol called HTTP (Hypertext Transfer Protocol). The language used is called

HTML (Hypertext Markup Language), which is a subset of the powerful SGML (Standard Generalized Markup Language)

WAIS is an Internet search tools that is based on the Z39.50 standard. The Z39.50 standard describes a protocol or set of rules, for computer-to-computer information retrieval. WAIS also works on client / server principal. A WAIS client program enables the user's computer to contact a WAIS server, submit a search query, and receive a response to the query.

Client Server Concepts

It is constituted of two parts, two programmes, client and server, for each application. The client software runs on the local machine, the PC. The server software runs on an other machine, perhaps a main frame, the host or the server of the information we want to retrieve. The application works by the combination of both the pieces of software working co-operative together. A client without server, or server without clients, would be able to do nothing useful. The server programme is responsible for holding the data, which is to be made available, and for finding and returning data requested by the clients.

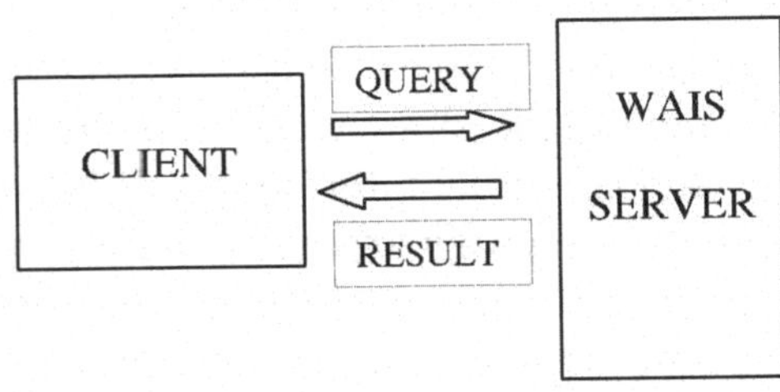

Fig. 3. Client Server Concepts (I)

When you request a search from a WAIS client, it contacts the server that handles the libraries / data bases you suggested. It asks each server in turn, to search its index for a set of works. The server WAIS has one really unique feature called "Relevance Feedback". It allows you to find articles that are similar to the articles you have already found.

Hypertext Transfer Protocol (HTTP)

It is a set of rules, or a protocol, that governs the transfer of hypertext between two or more computers. The WWW encompasses the universe of information that is available via HTTP. Hypertext is text that's specially coded using a standard system called Hypertext Markup Language (HTML). The HTML codes are used to create links. These links can be textual or graphic, and when clicked on, can "link" the user to another resource such as other HTML documents, text files, graphics, animations and sound.

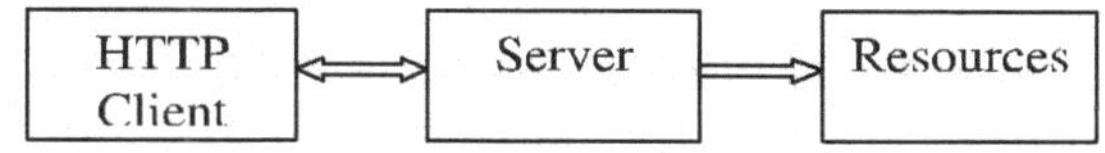

Fig. 4. Client Server Concept (II)

HTTP is based on the server / client principle. HTTP allows the client to establish a connection with the server and make a request. The server accepts the connection initiated by the client and sends back a response. An HTTP request identifies the resource that the client is interested in and tells the server what "action" to take on the resource.

Thus, when you select any of the hypertext links, you are identifying a particular resource and asking the server to send it back to your computer in a format that your computer can display or store

HTTP also provides access to other internet protocols like FTP, Simple Mail Transfer Protocol (SMTP), WAIS, Gopher, Telnet etc.

WWW (World Wide Web)

WWW is almost synonymous with Internet. Currently the most widely used facilities, the hypertext interface to the information on the internet. The www information is an advanced browsing service on the internet. WWW is a navigational tool that enables browsing of information linked to other related information. Website help in accessing universe of knowledge irrespective of their location. With help of www and related internet technology any organization and institution can make their presence on the internet. It is similar to gopher. However, instead of menu driven design it uses hypertext. This service is very useful. In a few minutes one can examine documents on a millions of topics located on a variety of computers at the internet sites around the world.

The www was originally developed at CERN, the European laboratory for particle physics and what started as means for scientists to exchange data (text, graphics, figures), came to be universally used with the introduction of the graphical browser. Mosaic was the earliest such browser developed at University of Illinois and distributed freely on the Internet. The last few years have seen several other web browsers, each having their own capabilities and features. The most widely used of these are Netscape Navigator and Microsoft Explorer.

The web is a subset of the Internet using a high level protocol (http) and supports text, graphics, audio-video and multimedia. On the Internet today, www is the largest information resource of easily accessible information.

WWW is fastest growing Internet tool for Internet tool for information retrieval. WWW is the set of servers on the Internet that are interconnected through hypertext. The hypertext is the method of presenting information where selected items that are highlighted in different color, can be expended at any time to provide other information about the item. These selected items are links, which allow to move from document to document and a server-to-server. The useful aspects of the web is the ability to browse through a list of subject headings to get an idea of just what kinds of materials exists on the internet in a given topic.

WWW is a method by which information can be published across the globe by just placing one soft copy of the document on the Internet web server. Millions of persons can search it, download it to their system and have it printed on their own printers. A few years ago e-mail, Gopher, WAISIS, FTP, Telnet, News services and mailing lists used to be distinctly different services on the net.

Over the past two decades World Wide Web has become an important source of information for scholarly literature. Web has become the major force in reshaping the way information is being distributed and used. The explosive growth on www has made it clear the impotence of Internet to libraries. Standard and sophisticated retrieval tools are required to search useful and quality information from the Internet.

Searching of World Wide Web

Millions of pages of information are available on the web; it is very hard to search the relevant information from the w-library. To retrieve relevant, consistent and useful information within a pleasant time, the uses should know about the tools and strategy for surfing e-resources or information through web.

WEB BROWSING

Web browsing is a facility, which can be utilized by users with the help of browsing softwares such as Internet Explorer, Netscape Navigator, etc. Surfing the net is an art to get any kind of information from all over the world. After entering in to these browsers we have to give URLs (Uniform Resource Locator) viz *http://www.du.ac.in* , which is an address of the website such as Alta vista, Info seek etc. One of the popular search engine is yahoo. To enter into this search engine, the URL is *http://www.yahoo.com* . After entering into any of the search engine, browsing is done either by giving desired keyword /title in search option or by selecting the appropriate titles from the front page.

There are some of the tips help us to browse net faster.

i. Using URL *http://www.internettrafficreport.com*, helps us to know the traffic for a particular country's network router. If we know in which timings the particular websites download fast, we can use those timings to visit the particular website. People from India can search Indian website at night.

ii. While browsing the net, the information displayed on the screen is stored in cache memory. So that, when the users goes back to the previous pages by clicking Back button those pages will be displayed from the cache memory. We can increase this cache memory size, if there is option.

COMMON FACILITIES PROVIDED BY INTERNET

Some of the facilities provided by the internet are:

1. Access to data stored on remote computers.
2. Access to wide selection of public domain and shareware software.
3. Exchange of electronic mail and other data files in a wide area environment.
4. Online real time interaction with other network users.
5. Receipt (and delivery) of electronic publications.
6. Participation in electronic media mailing lists and conferences, and
7. Access to remote sensing equipments, telescopes and graphic processors.

SERVICES PROVIDED BY INTERNET

A range of services is available on the net. These includes :

1. E-mail
2. Internet Relay Chat (IRC)
3. Internet Telephony
4. E- Commerce
5. Usenet/News groups
6. Information Search
7. Download and Uploads
8. Broadcasting

1. E-mail

The simple and the most widely used communication facility available on the Internet is the electronic mail service, which is commonly called, in short as e-mail service. It is used to send massages to other people or programs on other computer. Using e-mail facility people can send and receive massages over the Internet. The massages can be sent to a single person to a group of persons separately at the same time to this facility. Its speed is high and charges are low as compared to postal service.

The additional advantage is that massage need not always be text form. Graphic, sound or data, files can be attached with massages sent through the Internet. This communication method is so fast that massage reaches their destination within minutes. This saves time as well as ensures reliability. Copies of massage can also be sent simultaneously to different addresses at one go.

With an e-mail software program, you can write letters on your PC, address them to the destination e-mail address, and send them winging their way around the globe in a matter of moments. You can also enclose images and even video clips.

The elements that make up an e-mail address are:

drgurdevsingh @ hotmail.com

1 2 3 4

1 **User name** (identifies the address)

2 Separators

3 **Domain Name** (it is the computer address, with periods separating the parts

4 Suffixes

The suffix .com indicates a commercial organization based in the US. A company based in Indian would more commonly end with co. In, although .com and net are also frequently used. Other suffixes include gov for a government organization and edu. or ac. for an academic institution.

Running a mail program

We can start e-mail programme, usually by double clicking on icon or by choosing a program name from menu. To send mail massage, a user simply has to log on to his computer and use a 'mail program' to compose and send the massage.

Sending mail

All mail programs have a new massage or compose e-mail command, often located on a massage menu and they usually have keyboard shortcut for the command as well, such as Ctrl+N for new massage. When we start a new massage the programme will open a new window.

Type the address of the person to whom we wish to send the mail. The person's address must be of the form *username@address.domain*, where username is the person's identifier (the name they login with);address is identifier of the person's network and/ or machine on the network (the address might consist of several words - the host and the sub domain - separated by dots); and the domain is the three letter code including whether the address is a business (.com), a non profit organization (.org), a university (.edu), a branch of government (.gov), and so on .(some e- mail programme require special text before or after the internet, e - mail address).

There are two portions to every e-mail address, they are separated by '@' symbol which is pronounced as 'at'. The first portion identifies the name of the recipient and second is the electronic postal address e.g. gurdev@hotmail.com

Regardless of which mail programme you use, all electronic mail massages have two main components. The first is the header of the massage and second is the body of massage i.e. its contents.

Thus, the three most important fields are:

1. **To**: Where we must enter the username address of the recipient e-mail address usually have the form username @ address.

2. **Subject**: Is the area where we enter a title of our massage. Although this is optional, it is considered to give massage a title. People who receive lots of massages are more likely to, read if they can see at a glance that it is relevant to them.

3. **From**: This information is automatically entered into any mail massage that we send out. Its purpose is to inform the recipient of the senders e-mail address. The body of the massage is normally composed using an editor, which is built into the mail program. An editor is similar to a word processing program.

Microsoft Outlook Express which is included in the Internet explorer 4.0 package is very useful to compose and transmit e-mail massages

The new massage window is divided into two parts. The upper portion is header portion. The first box in the top window labeled to is for entering the e-mail address of the recipient. In the box labeled Cc enter the e-mail address of the recipients of copies of massage. BCC is the place for entering addresses of persons to whom blind copies of massage are to be forwarded.

To send massage to more peoples type e-mail addresses of recipients separating address with comma or semicolon. To import e- mail address from the address book, click the book icon in the new massage window next to CC and BCC and then select names from the next window. In the subject box type the massage title. After filling the details in the upper pane go to the lower pane, type the massage and then click the send button in the toolbox. If the massage is composed offline, the massage will be saved in the out box as qued and will send automatically when the system becomes online. The drafts of the massage can also be saved for later viewing. To get a print copy of the mail, click the print button. To delete mails select the mails and click delete. Deleted mails are sent to the trash folder from where they can permanently clear off on periodic basis. If required, format the massage by using larger fonts or making letters bold, italics and so on. Also a facility for checking spelling is available and this can be used by clicking the button on the toolbox.

Address Book

This is one of the features available in the mail client program. It enables e-mail users to store e-mail addresses and other details of their contacts. These can be imported to compose window while sending mails. To enter the address of person or to copy the address from the address book to the boxes in the compose window, click the icon appearing on the left of each box where the address is to be written. The address is displayed in the address book. From this window the selector can select e-mail address.

Sending Attachments

File can also be sent as attachment to massages. The attachment file can be a document, an image or a video file. For sending attachments, click on insert menu and select the sub option 'file attachments'. Names of the attached file appear in the attach box. Now click on the send button to send the massage with its attachments. When sending large files a compressed version of the massage can be sent. This helps the file to be transferred quickly.

Sending Replies

Massage can be replied easily by clicking on the reply button on the toolbar. On doing this the new massage window appears with the 'to address' automatically filled. The subject window is also automatically filled in.

Microsoft Exchange or Internet Mail or Outlook

E-Mail is an easy-to-follow guide to Microsoft's e-mail program, Outlook Express. It offers all the features you need to be able to send and receive e-mail over the internet. Outlook express provides a gateway to the world of e-mail. It provides a user-friendly interface that makes it easy to compose, send and receive e-mail messages directly from the main windows. E-mail messages can contain text, pictures, hypertext links to websites, and even self-contained file attachments. Outlook express has the additional benefit that if there are other people who wish to use your computer to receive their own e-mail, you can create multiple user identities so that their e-mail and contact details can be kept separately and privately from your own.

Outlook can handle internet mail, network mail from MSN. We can start it by double clicking outlook icon on your desktop.

To send a new massage with outlook select compose -> new mail massage (ctrl+ N). This will open a new massage window. Type on address and press tab to get down to the massage area. Type your massage and then click the send button.

To read a massage in your inbox, just double click its subject line. The massage will appear in its own window. To reply to the massage, select compose -> reply (ctrl+R). Outlook will supply the recipients address. Proceed as if you were sending a new massage.

To delete a massage, just highlight it and press delete. It will move to the deleted items folder until you specially open the folder and delete its contents (even then exchange will warn you that you are permanently deleting the massages). To exit outlook select file - exit.

To send mail select mail -> new massage (or press ctrl+N in windows, command +N on the Mac.). Type the address of the person to whom you wish to send the mail and press tab twice. Type the subject and press tab again then type your massage. When it is done, click the send button in the upper left corner of the massage window.

To check your mail with internet mail, select mail -> send and receive or press ctrl+M (or command +M). Unread mail will appear with a bold subject line. To view the contents of the mail massage in the lower pane, select its subject in the upper pane (or double click it to open it in a new window).

2. Internet Rely Chat (IRC)

IRC is the most popular tool on the internet, used by people to talk to each other using computer. It is used by people sitting at their homes anywhere in the world to talk to each other electronically using computer. It is generally called chatting. The chat takes place on channels.

Channels are the virtual locations on IRC networks where user meat to talk to one another. It is even possible to have conversation on several channels at the same time. Some channels will be topic specific, but others are less rigid and will be having a general chat. Channels have different modes. Most channels are public, but you can talk on private or secret channel, where it is possible to restrict access, for examples, to invite only. Channels are located on IRC servers, which often talk to each other and share channels, so that messages on one server are relayed to the same channels on the other IRC servers. To access IRC requires the use of an IRC client. One such client is available from *http://www.mir.co.uk*. Unlike any Internet service, IRC enable you to hold a spontaneous conversation, is real time, with a group of individual who may never physically meet. In most cases there is no constraint on the topic that may be discussed. Topic may be on spots, movie, books, gossips, etc.

Internet Relay Chat works as a client / server application, and the IRC servers are interconnected to form the user's perspective are large service.

To take part in IRC you need a client program. If your ISP has not provided you with an IRC client program, you can download any one of the client programs that are available on the web. Some of the IRC programs and the sites from where they could be downloaded are as follow:

1. mlrc (*http://papa.indstate.edu/winsoc-i/windows95/IRC/*
2. PIRCH (*http://www.bepl.lib.mid.us-frappa/*)

Once you join IRC, you can browse through the help manual to find the list of commands. Some of the most frequently used commands are:

/help - To get the list of all commands

/list - To view all available channels

/Join channel - To join channel

/quit - To quit from IRC server

/leave channel - To leave a channel

3. Internet Telephony

It is transport of telephone calls over the internet, no matter whether a traditional telephony device, multimedia PC's or dedicated terminals take part in the calls and no matter whether the calls are entirely or partially transmitted over the internet. The most significant benefit of IPT is money saving and easy implementation of innovative services. In the future Internet Telephony Service Providers (ITSP) may use a single infrastructure for providing both internet access and internet telephony.

4. E- Commerce

E- Commerce is a business methodology of conducting, managing and executing business transactions using computer and telecommunication network. Internet brought about a new concept called electronic commerce in the marketing and business. The internet probably continues to have an important role in electronic commerce including online ordering by the libraries. Books and journals can be ordered through web based ordering system. It is expected to improve the productivity and competitiveness of participating businesses by providing unprecedented access to online global market place with millions of customers and thousands of products and devices. Technical components of e-commerce are:

- Client or PC Workstation.
- Transaction Server.
- Database Server.
- Database Transactions
- Router (an internet working tool, which is used to interconnect these networks, which use the same high level protocols above the network layer. A router distinguishes data packets according to protocol types such as TCP/IP. Router forward traffic according to network level address.)
- Internet Communication Line

5. Usenet/News groups

Newsgroups as the Internet are rarely concerned with “news” in the sense of current affairs. They are essentially public e-mail discussion forums devoted to a wide range of topics and interests. Newsgroups provide a forum for people to discuss topics of mutual interest and share information- whether highly technical or just gossips. They can be excellent places to get advise if, for example, you have computer problem, participants (or subscribers to use the correct term) "post" messages to be seen and be responded to, either publicity or privately, by any reader of that newsgroup. The news group servers provide access to thousands of topic-based discussion group services that are open to every one. One can join the list by simply by sending e-mail request to the list.

News net is the name given to the large body of newsgroup distributed around the world by the computers known as news servers. These servers exchange information so that each one carries a copy of the most recent messages. Usenet is not strictly speaking, part of the internet, although Internet sites are used to carry its newsgroup. Most ISPs provide access to Usenet newsgroups, usually via their own news servers.

To view the newsgroup subscriptions window, choose Newsgroup form the tool menu. To locate a chosen newsgroup, type a keyword in the display newsgroups which contain box. To view the contents of a group, click the name in the list and click the subscribe button. To download a message, simply double-click on it.

It is global bulletin board messaging system consisting of various interest groups. Unlike list servers, which disseminate information on a specific topic from one person to many, news group's servers provide access to thousands of topic based discussion group services that are open to every one. A massage posted to news group may be read, forwarded, or followed-up a public response. Several news groups are well organized and science and technology professionals frequently use discussion format

6. Information Search

We can search any information from any part of the world within no time. A vast variety of sources are available on the internet free of cost. Various reference sources such as encyclopedias, dictionaries can be downloaded free of cost.

7. Download and Uploads

The terms upload and download often create confusion, as their definitions depend on the context. Download and upload refers to transfer of information between the computers. The person/computer sending the information refers to the transfer as an upload, while the person /computer receiving the information refer to it as a download. If the customer is sending information, it is an upload; if they are receiving information it is download. Most people use the term download when they are receiving a file and upload when they are sending a file over the internet. In either case, the information is transferred both ways to manage the download.

The act of transferring a file from one web server to an other, while technically a simultaneous download and upload is often called side loading. From the Internet user's point of view, downloading is receiving a file from an other computer. The File Transfer Protocol (FTP) is the Internet facility for downloading and uploading files. If you are uploading a file to another site, you must usually have permission in advance to access the site and the directory where the file is to be placed.

When you send or receive an attached file with an e-mail note, this is just an attachment not a download or an upload. However in practice, many people use "upload" to mean "send" and "download" to mean receive. In short, from the ordinary workstation or small computer user's point of view, to upload is to send a file and to download is to receive a file.

8. File Transfer Protocol (FTP)

This is mechanism that allows placing and retrieving of files over the Internet. It allows downloading of software, product up gradation and other things. FTP servers also supply a small amount of text information. With the help command one get online help to know more about any doubts.

Telnet : This is used to denote the networking over the telephone. Using telnet you can contact a host machine by typing host name of IP member and can transfer files, from the TCP/IP host to your own computer and can accessed databases.

Gopher: The Gopher was created by the microcomputer workstation center of University of Minnesota to find information on the Internet in a user friendly way. It is a menu driven programme that allows you to click with information servers or "gopher holes" on the Internet to retrieve the information including text, sound and images.

HOW TO GENERATE INFORMATION FROM THE WEB

The present trends in the field of information generation and transmission are due to the development in communication networks and accessibility of data stores extensively distributed on the electronic media. The www and electronic publishing on internet open up a major area which may be exploited, generating information which is continuously up to date and which is universally accessible.

In a very short period, web has matured into a globally distributed multimedia information retrieval system of impressive dimensions. Institutions and communities with shared interest are creating websites and scholars; learned societies and professional associations with home page continue to proliferate.

The information and library professionals are finding that their role is increasingly changing to that of inter mediator. While assisting and sometimes training users to access the vast store of information available on the Internet, they are also interacting to produce, organize and process information to make it available on the web.

The various kinds of information that they can generate on the web are:

1. Online Public Access Catalogue (OPAC), ranging from complete library collections to ones restricted to disciplines or subject fields for example OCLC and Library of Congress.
2. Databases, bibliographic or specialized may be prepared for general or free-based usage.
3. Notices, announcements of seminars or conferences or calls for paper etc.
4. Reports of summaries of research or academic activities, projects.
5. In-house publications, catalogues, browsers, schedule.
6. Electronic publishing of papers, reviews etc.
7. Home page which is a format most commonly used for a variety of information

The home page which is produced as a hypertext document can be designed using HTML tags, which allow the author to define standard features and to locate the hypertext buttons.

The followings are the objectives of website:

1. To improve the capacity of researchers, teachers and extension specialists to organize, to store, retrieve and exchange information.
2. To strengthen library's network through electronic access.
3. To provide current information to users.

4. To evolve mechanism of information sharing.

DESIGNING OF WEBSITE

Some of the points for creation website are as follows:

1. Purpose of website: first of all we should know the purpose of our website for which it is being created. It should be research oriented and educational. It should be attractive and informative.

2. Index page and site orientation: it is also called home page, which describe our organization, services provided, etc.

3. Site and domain name: determine a tentative name for the website. Name should be unique, short, descriptive and memorable.

4. Main graphics to highlights: "index" or "home page" should ensure simplicity, art, elegance and quick loading features.

5. Background color and texture: both color and texture will make website special. Make the text carefully so that it is easily readable.

6. Basic page elements: check page title, top of page, graphic, page background, text, last update, URL address, e-mail address including on every page.

7. Finishing touch: Horizontal rules, color lines, bullets, color balls, arrows and pointers, colorful "new" or "updated" markers. All these should be checked before final touch.

8. Photos and graphics: images could be black and white or color images .Types of images is like GIF, JPEG, etc. are to be decided. GIF files can be viewed by all web browsers and work best with images created in a graphics programme. JPEG images compressed better for photographic graphics, or those with color gradients and thus load faster.

9. Forms to user response: these are options, which return information from your user to you by e-mail.

10. Uploading and testing the page: there are three different practices followed each with their pros and cons,

i. Upload the page your self

ii. Send the pages to the Internet service provider on a diskette to upload for you.

iii. Have your web designer upload and test the pages for you. Any of these can be adopted depending on avail availability of facilities.

11. Registering and advertising website: The user should be able to find the website, and hence are needed to register it. There are several ways of registering a website.

12. Maintaining website: Once the website is up and running after testing all links and correcting the inevitable errors, we need to keep the website current. We need to handle the following:

a. Adding pages to describe new parts of organization i.e. new division created, new project started.

b. Updating links which have become obsolete. Also the website needs to be regularly updated with more emphasis on the information sought by most of the users.

c. Uploading images to match with the latest contents of the page.

d. Re-doing the "look" of the pages as and when required and necessary.

SOFTWARES FOR CREATING WEBSITES

There are various softwares available for creating websites.

Some of them are as follows:

MS Front Page, Netscape Computer, Hot Dog Express.

Among them Front Page is popular because toolbars and icon used are similar to those used in MS Word .It is a advanced software to create professionally looking websites. Lastly, it has been packed with MS Office 2000.

HARDWARE AND SOFTWARE REQUIREMENTS

To get the internet connection suitable hardware and software and an account with an access provider are essential.

1. Hardware Requirements

Any type of computer from mainframe to personal can be used for connecting to the Internet. The minimum hardware requirement for connection is a personal computer, modem and a telephone line. The computer used must be able to connect to the modem, and software is able to work on it. A high speed computer with a large capacity hard disk is an ideal choice. Present day computers are having 128 MB RAM or higher and fitted with VGA or SVGA monitors, can be used for this. To hear the audio, computer must be fitted with speakers.

The computer must have serial port for connecting external modem or a spare expansion slot for connecting an internal modem card.

A modem (internal or external), ideally a faster one (with a speed of 56 KBPS or more) is required.

What is Modem?

A modem is a device which converts electronic signals from the computer into analog signals (sound) which can then be sent over telephone lines. The process of converting digital data is called modulation. The reverse process is called demodulation. Thus, the device used for performing this process is called modulator/ demodulator or modem in short.

Modems are classified into two types, based on their

installation on computers - internal or external. External modems are placed outside the computers in separate casing and they are connected to computers using cables. Internal modems are fixed to expansion slots in the motherboard of the computer and they are not from seen outside the casing. External modems can be transferred from one computer to another easily, whereas internal modems can not be done so. External modems are costlier than internal modems.

How to select a modem

Speed of modem is an important factor to be considered in its selection. Speed is measured in units of bps or bits per second. Higher units such as kbps are used to indicate high speed and this is an acronym for kilobytes per second. It is always good to use modem with high speed, as file transfer rate of slow modem is less. With slow modems more time has to be spent for sending or receiving mails or visiting web sites. 56 kbps is current standard speed of a modem. Now a days computers are fitted with internal modem as a standard device.

The other things, which are required for Internet, are cables with sockets to connect to modem with computer and telephone (in case of external modem). A telephone connection is required. An Internet account is needed if we want to have internet access at our home and we need to sign on with an internet service provider (ISP). Some common ISP's are MTNL and VSNL.

2. Software Requirements

Every computer has a master control programme called operating system. Different application programs such as those for sending and receiving mails, transferring files between computers and so on are built with the operating system. The user has to select the application program for the particular operating system in which his computer is working. To run application program on character-based system, the user has to use appropriate command in the correct syntax. Program having Graphical User Interface (GUI) are common at present. Also available are internet ready computers fitted with internet ready keyboards and mouse.

A number of application and client programs for use in the internet have become a part of operating systems in recent days. Utilities for Internet working are also now available as freeware or shareware. Majority of these utilities is working on windows platform or Macintosh system. Therefore, for PC's the operating system must be at least windows 98 or higher version windows 7 is preferable because It has inbuilt components to support internet connectivity. For Mac systems the operating system must be at least Mac OS system 7.5.

Almost all the computers that provide Internet services work on UNIX system. UNIX is the family of operating system and this system can work in any type of computer. This is a multi user and multitasking system. Since it is widely used for the internet, many of the conversions felled in the internet world are based on this system.

A web browser such as Internet Explorer or Netscape Navigator. A browser is a client software program that allows the user to navigate the web.

FACTOR AFFECTING THE SPEED OF INTERNET CONNECTIVITY

1. Speed of Modem

A modem with minimum speed of 56 kbps or higher is recommended for good speed.

2. Quality of Telephone Line

Noise on the phone line running into your home can disrupt Internet connection with a modem.

3. Internet Traffic

Web traffic tends to expand throughout the day and peak around the early evening. If you plan to download software or wish to surf faster schedule such activities during off peak hours.

4. A faster processor (650 MHZ or higher) will allow you to surf web faster.

5. A computer with more memory (RAM) will help you to surf faster.

6. A highly fragmented herd disk can slow down web surfing considerably. It is a good practice to keep your hard drive defragmenter and optimized.

7. To further increase your surfing speed you can surf with two or more browser windows at a time. This will enable you to read the contents of one page while allowing another page to loading the second window. This may help to cut down the lag time and transportation. You may also consider turning off image loading and java in your browser. This may not affect the content of web page.

SEARCHING WITH INTERNET

To search for and retrieve the maximum information on the net following points needs to be kept in mind.

Retrieving information from net requires a lot of patience and devotion as the numbers of sites or web pages retrieved on any particular query are immense

While searching with Internet it so happens that within the stipulated time a proper solution to a given query may not be found, but experience shows that surfing the net leisurely retrieves an exact article/reference or what the user usually interested in. To remember these sites it is imperative that regular habit of noting down all these sites or adding them to the bookmarks be cultivated. This helps in assessing these sites at a later date, which is very convenient, and time saving task.

For doing the searches through Internet one can also go through web directory say yahoo.com. One can visit the site and decide the category to which it falls. Therefore, it generally takes longer time for a file to appear in a web directory through a search engine.

What is a search engines?

A Web search engine is an interactive tool that enable user to locate information available via the World Wide Web. Search engine provide fill-out forms and other interfaces so the user can type in a query, submit the request, and retrieve a list of resources that match the search criteria. The hypertext environment makes it possible to offer a link directly from the list of result to the resources themselves. Result may very from one search engine to the other. They tell the user what to look and they go out and get it. Unlike a librarian who has access to every item in the library, search engines have access to just a portion of internet. Search engines do however continuous search over the net on their own to find new information and new sources to add to their lists.

Search engines provide access to a major portion of the publicity available web pages.

Search engine are software which searches pages or web site on the internet. The response of the search engine comes in the form of "result", listing addresses of matching and relevant recourses. For giving the matching results, it runs the query terms (known as search string) against databases. The search engine indexes a portion of web documents as a full text database. The function of a search engine is a locator of information available on the Internet via the World Wide Web. It contains references to thousands of web documents. It provides an interface between a user and the related database. To provide information to users is composed of two parts, available information with data and methods of indexing of information. The interface presents the user with a place to type in a search string, which may be word, a phrase, a data, or some other criterion, and a way to submit the request.

Search engines are the most popular means of information on the www. There are several thousands of search engines. Some of them are very popular such as yahoo, Google, AltaVista, etc. Each uses different kinds of philosophy and programming design that is the reason why the user get different results in the same search strings on various search engines.

Realizing the role and value of search engines the following are some of the characteristics of the search engines :

i. Accessibility.
ii. Reliability.
iii. Search language capacity.
iv. Comprehensiveness.
v. Speed of access.
vi. User friendliness.
vii. Updating facility.
viii. Interfacing facility.
ix. Display of search result.

Though different search engines accomplish their task through different methods but some common ways of providing information to users can be explained as under:

1. Search information on the basis of information and defined keywords.
2. Indexing of keywords and related URLs (Uniform Resource Locators).
3. Making available the keywords or pages to users.

4. Earlier search engines used to index some thousands of web pages and documents and served 1-2000 queries but in today's scenario any popular search engines indexes billions of web pages and satisfies millions of queries. Some search engines use web spiders, which list out used terms used in web pages. This process is known as web crawling. These "spiders" read hundreds of pages in a second.

CATEGORIES OF SEARCH ENGINES

Search engines can be divided into four categories :

1. Robbot
2. Directories.
3. Met search engines, and
4. Software tools

General or Robot-driven Search engines

These search engines compile their own searchable databases on the web. Crawler or worm programme generate databases by means of web robots. These robots are programmes that reside on a host computer and retrieve information from sites on the web using standard protocols. Examples of such engines are:

AltaVista

Excite

Lycos

Hot boot

Info seek.

DIRECTORY BASED SEARCH ENGINES

These engines are also known as subject collection or as "subject gateways" and are created and maintained by human editors, subject experts, or by means of some automated indexing process. But they rely mainly only on people to identify and group resources .These directories offer access to the information that has been classified into certain categories. They group the Internet websites into categories such as Internet tutorials, universities, museums, etc.

Example: Yahoo, SOSIG, Look Smart, Magellan are some of the examples

These are best for browsing and for search of a more general nature.

META SEARCH ENGINES

Meta search engines do not crawl the web compiling their own searchable databases. These search engines utilizes databases maintained by other individual search engines. A meta search engine accept a single query from the user and sends it to multiple search engines in parallel. Meta search engines present the result of their searches in two ways:

1. **Single list**: most Meta search engines display multiple e-search results in a single merged list from which duplicate entire has been stored out.

2. **Multiple lists**: some meta search engines do not collate multiple engine search results but displays them instead, in separate list as they are retrieved from each engine.

3. The functionality of these engines depends largely upon performance of those engines.

They are attractive because users do not have to visit multiple search engines and re-enter their query. Mata search engines are useful in obtaining a quick overview on subject or a unique term.

Examples of Mata search engines are:

- Dog pile
- Interface Find

- Meta Crawler
- ProFusion
- Surfwax etc.

SUBJECT SPECIFIC SEARCH ENGINES

They concentrate only on a particular topic and often provide better access to information than powerful keyword indexes. Examples are Health A to Z (*http://www.Health* a to Z.com

These are alsi vailable Meth search, Agri Surf, Law Crawlers etc.

GEOGRAPHICAL AREA SPECIFIC SEARCH ENGINES

These search engines narrow down the search and the web is getting customized in different national and regional language giving space for the web pages in different languages. This too indicates the need of a geographical area specific search engine, since languages are geographic area specific search engine, since language are geographic area bound, generally. For example: as Chinese language contents becomes more redially available on the web, there are more than 10 Chinese search engines available on the net. Indian information on education, business, arts, sports, news, entertainments etc. can be retrieved though the search engine KHOJ (*http://www.khoj.com*)

USERS FRIENDLY SEARCH ENGINES

More than 2000 web search engines are available on internet. These are generally funded by advertising revenue. Some of the examples are; AltaVista, goggle, yahoo, Meta crawler etc.

Many popular search engines are Yahoo, AltaVista, AOL Search, Ask Jeeves, Google, Hoot boot, MSN etc. Google: *http://www.google.co./in* is most popular search engine on the net. It has access to Web pages in 12 languages. It can browse through about 10 million Web pages

Google:

Home page address : *http://www.google.com*

Search methods: keyword search

Database: very large

Operators: plus / minus, quote marks

Features

1. Return only pages that match all the terms in the query and also where the terms are in close proximity. It is very sophistical database and easy to use.
2. Minimalist, uncluttered search screen
3. Has the unique 'I am feeling lucky' button for fast results
4. Has its own software for rating pages.
5. Matches all terms used.

Yahoo:

Home page address: http:// *www.yahoo.com*

Search methods: Subject with coordinated keyword

Databases: I million subject sites

Operators: Boolean, plus / minus, quote marks, wild card and case sensitive

Features : In the case of keyword searches, it will return only sites that contains all search words. If there is no exact match then automatically referred to Google.

Alta vista

It is one of the best sites to search. It has also got the advanced search capabilities like combining the main keyword and its various aspects with Boolean operator i.e. AND, OR, NOT. Some of the special features include the provision of 'Refine' tool for acronyms. One can enter a keyword as usual in the search box and click on submit. The

'Refine your search link' option reveals a list of topics related to the term. Clicking on the topic will bring up a list of topics. For each topic, select require on exclude from drop-down menu in order to narrow down to the most specific term.

Home page address: http:// *www.altavista.digital.com*

Search Methods: Subject with keyword

Databases: full text

Operators: Boolean, plus / minus, quote marks, wild card and case sensitive

Features: Provides ways of specific search. One of the largest databases and most effective search systems.

1. Very large databases.
2. Online instructions available
3. Compact or detailed display of results

Infoseek

It only offers simple query options, but search words may be limited to particular fields such as with in document title, or eliminated precede the word with a sign "–" or required precede the word with a plus sign " + "

Home page address: http:// *www.infoseek.com*

Search Methods: Keyword with subject search

Databases: full text, 50 million web pages

Operators: Boolean, plus / minus, quote marks, wild stemming card and case sensitive.

Features: Provide an extensive list of popular sites accessible from the homepages. It is one of the fastest and most accurate tools on the w-library.

HotBot

It offers a simple search and an expert search .Simple search supports the booleon 'AND' and 'OR' operators.

Home page address: http:// *www.hotbot.com*

Search Methods: Keyword with subject, and provide an extensive list of popular sites under three categories.

Databases: full text Search

Operators: Boolean, plus / minus, quote marks, wild card and case sensitive.

Features: In case of keyword searches, it will return only files that contain all search words. If there is no exact match then automatically referred to google.

1. Many power searching options available via drop down menus from the main interface.
2. Indexes more than 110 million web documents
3. Offers natural language construction of searches.

PROS AND CONS OF SEARCH ENGINES

Although these search engines searches on enormous volume of information at impressive speed, there are some criticism too such as slow responses, the retrieval of duplicate records, the lack of precision etc. There is a risk of false ranking with the engines which follows 'meta tags'

USAGE OF INTERNET TO SOCIETY

Individual and professionals engaged in academics, research, business or similar activities more or less involved in using Internet. Because Internet appears to be the most powerful medium for exchange of information which works round the clock connecting people around the globe. The use of Internet is so widespread that it is not only confined to office and business workstations, rather it is being used at home for personal communication.

Some of the usage of Internet to the society are:

E-business: internet can be used to find business, product and services.

Education: the students can use Internet for educational purposes. Students can download topics of their interest. The concept of distance learning and virtual classrooms has emerged due to Internet only.

Travel: Internet can be used for getting tourist and event information. Tourists can find various relevant information such as weather conditions, maps, transportation facilities and schedule, etc.

Marketing and Sales: Internet can be used for selling products over the Internet. The emergence of e-commerce and virtual shops has been the outcome of the internet only.

Investing: Internet may be used to buy and sell shares on-line.

Patient doctor relationship: the doctors and patients to share their views about the treatment, progress, etc. may use Internet.

Finding People: directory services may be searched to find the phone numbers of the peoples and their addresses.

E-mail: electronically transfer of information including messages, text, graphics and pictures can be exchanged between two individuals. E-mail ensures delivery of messages most instantly.

Entertainment: The Internet may be used for the entertainment purposes also such as listening music, watching movies, playing games, etc.

Advertisement: Internet can be used for advertising a product or services.

Chatting : Internet can be used for conversation all over the world. Chatting enables to have on-line conversation with two or more peoples at the same time.

E-governance : The quality and efficiency of information and operations provided by the government can be improved with the use of internet. Citizens can receive information and can also file applications for renewal of licenses, file their income tax return, etc online.

Exchange and Auction: Internet can be used to exchange the goods and for auctioning of goods -directly to the consumers who needs them. Thereby, the need of the middleman is eliminated. Moreover, internet provides a perfect market place in with no single buyer or seller can affect the price of a product because all buyers and sellers have access to the same information and can have the information at the same time.

Conferencing: Computer conferencing can be established through internet. In this process, a person to person interaction can be held through the use of computers located in different places.

INTERNET AND INFORMATION SERVICES

A number of reference and information services are available on the web. Increasingly many of these services are provided by non library and commercial organizations. While some are free, others need payment. Most of these services are designed for registered users of the libraries concerned.

Although Ask Jeeves is basically a search engine, many researchers also see it as a web based information service because of two reasons:

1. Unlike in other search and Meta search engine, users can ask a question in Ask Jeeves , and in many cases can get an answer right away; and
2. Users can ask a question on a given topic, and Ask Jeeves comes up with a list of questions on the same or similar topics; the users can select any of these predefined questions, and then Ask Jeeves provides answer to that.
3. This is an interesting service and may be considered as a useful model for digital library reference and information services.

Internet service

Internet can be called 'the information communication system' established by the national and international linking of material stored on electronic database and made accessible throughout the world trough telephone, cable and other telecommunication links. 'Number of interlinked networks and thousands of computers are connected in the Internet.

As its name suggest, the Internet is an interconnected group of independently managed networks. Internet is the world's largest computer network, the network of networks scattered all over the world. The various sections of the Internet use almost every kinds of communication channel that can transmit data. The Internet is sometimes called an "information highway". Internet is one of the tools used for searching, retrieving information resources of various libraries and institutions all over the world. Hence, Internet is gateway to get the information in digital form. The internet can be put into many uses in the library, e.g., e-mail sending, etc. E-mail is the fastest, cheapest, and most efficient means for exchanging information and procurement of information products and interaction with other libraries. In short the e-mail combined with fast interactive protocol such as File Transfer Protocol (FTP) and World Wide Web (WWW) encourage collaborative work over the Internet. These tools allow the users to retrieve information from Internet site such as on-line library system.

The Internet is useful in the following ways for providing library services. Some of them are as follows:

1. To get information
2. To provide information on various subjects and topics
3. To compile information.

The various types of information are available on Internet:

1. Current events
2. Government information
3. E-journals, e-books, e-newspapers.
4. Directory type information such as name, address, telephone numbers, etc.
5. Downloading of various dictionaries, encyclopedias, etc.

The exponential growth of information in the World Wide Web and the numbers of users searching for information on the websites is increasing day by day. To cope with the situation digital libraries have emerged with tasks of massive digitization, storage, access, digital knowledge mining, digital reference services, electronic information services, search coordination, and manage the archive and its access. A digital library is a machine-readable representation of materials, which might be found in a library, together with conventional information sources, intended to help users find specific information. A digital library service is an assemblage of digital computing; storage, and communication machinery together with the software needed to reproduce, emulate, and extend the services.

Internet over the years has grown into an encyclopedia of gigantic dimensions covering every type of information for which we normally turn the pages of reference books and other information sources. There are different kinds of reference sources available to answer the queries of users. But in Internet one may find a conglomeration of all types of reference sources residing in the cyber space. Information contain in printed reference sources are in most cases found to be outdated by one year or more. But, in Internet information generally is quite up-to-date and often one gets the information in numbers of websites, which can be studded to choose the best one.

The development of information technology, especially

the Internet has made the reference service more meaningful. With the help of Internet this service can be provided more effectively and efficiently within a short period of time. It satisfied the information needs of users in a more efficient way. This form of reference service can be defined as digital reference service. Digital service is Internet based question and answer services that connect users with experts in various subject fields. In addition to answering the question, experts may also provide the users with referral to other online information sources. In case of traditional reference service it is provided by face-to-face interview in order to satisfy the information needs.

It is obvious that the current digital libraries, and most of the digital library research projects, have focused on access to, and retrieval of, digital information rather than on the services that have been provided to the users by traditional libraries. The web has changed notion of traditional reference services, and a number of web-based "expert services" are now offered by many non-library organizations. But the services provided by digital libraries are more authentic and preferable.

Digital reference services are Internet based question and answer services that connect users with individuals who possess specialized subject of skill experience. As opposed to static web pages, digital reference service use the internet to place people in contact with those individual who can answer specific questions and instruct users in developing certain skills. Digital reference services are also referred to as 'Ask a service, Ask a Librarian, etc. The digital reference service is an Internet based question and answer services that connects users with experts in a variety of subject field. In addition to answering the questions, experts may also provide users with referrals to other online and print sources of information. The question/ answer process in digital reference service is modeled after the methods practiced by reference librarians in traditional ways.

A library has now begun to offer web-based reference services.

Some of the currently available reference services are:

'Ask a librarian' is a web-based reference service, primarily designed for UK residents, provided by a network of public libraries in the UK. The site says "Mail us your factual questions and we'll send you an answer within two working days, if not before". A user has to put the query through an enquiry page, which is automatically routed to one of the participating libraries, which receives it as an e-mail massage. Within two days the library sends an e-mail message to the user with its response to the enquiry.

The British Library provides special reference services for business, patent, scientific, technical, medical and environmental information. These services ranges from answering simple question to finding answer to complex question involving online database searching, etc. while some of these services are free, for some others users need to pay. User can send e-mail with their queries.

USEFULNESS OF INTERNET TO LIBRARIES

The impact of Internet on the library operations including acquisition, cataloguing, reference and inter library loan has increased, electronic publishing has emerged, conventional libraries are transformed into electronic/digital library.

The internet resources are available in various forms of information such as e-books, e-journals, newsletters, archives, discussion list, reference tools such as indexes, bibliographies, abstracts, directories, encyclopedias, alerting services, on-line library catalogs, etc.

The www or worldwide web has made it enable the information just by clicking the highlighted terms and icons on the screen. Now it is very easy to access the information from the net. It can be used to access the information from the remote to read, download, and print the electronic books and journals besides some of the house keeping operations like acquisition and cataloguing etc. the internet services fall into two basic categories, Computer Mediated Communication (CMC) service and resource sharing services. The CMC allows users to exchange messages while resource sharing services allow users to access computing resources. There are vast resources of information available on the net (Fig. 5). The information available on internet are e-journals, preprints, electronic discussion forums, technical reports, contents pages of journals, standards, databases, library catalogs, reference sources such as dictionaries, encyclopedias, on-line educational materials and e-mail based reference services etc.

SOME OF THE INTERNET RESOURCES AND SERVICES USEFUL FOR THE LIBRARIES ARE:

1. Access to Various Internet Resources
2. Access to Online Catalogs of Libraries (Online Public Access Catalog)
3. Access to Various LIS Networks
4. Downloading of Bibliographical Records
5. Access to E-Books/Journals/Databases
6. Online Acquisition/Ordering of Library Material
7. Online Reservation of Library Material
8. Resource Sharing through Union Catalogs
9. Reference Sources
10. Discussion Groups
11. Newsgroups
12. Database
13. Distance Learning

14. Internet as an Information system.

Library Catalog

The internet gives access to the bibliographic records of millions of books and details of the holdings of the libraries around the world. One can check the new titles and even order them from a numbers of universities.

Electronic Journals

Hundreds of electronic journals are available in the different fields of study on the Internet for the benefit of the users.

Resources available on the Internet of librarian's interest

Following resources are available for library professionals for providing various types of information such as e-journals, magazines, databases various reference sources such as encyclopedias, dictionaries, and patents preprints, audio, visuals, etc.

Reference Sources

A numbers of reference sources are also available on Internet such as encyclopedias, dictionaries, directories, bibliographies, etc. Internet plays a vital role in library related activities in the following areas:

Cataloguing, classifications, reference services, serial control, OPAC, circulation, etc.

Internet as information system

The internet opened a totally new dimension. The convergence of media made it existing and created new challenges for libraries to grapple with. Libraries or information systems are defined by their function as systems that comprise of spectrum of activities from generation and location of information to dissemination and use of it. The nature of the activities in the internet information system also conforms to the components of an information system given below:

Generation→Storing → Organization → Retrieval → Dissemination → Control

These components are described briefly here:

From generation point of view, publishing information on the net, or e-publishing offered an alternative also to traditional publishing. Further, the information generated will not be restricted to any geographical boundaries and can be reached globally, thus widening its scope. The retrieval aspect depends to a large extend, on the description of the document with location of the document as the primary purpose. In the traditional library, the catalog performs this function. In the Internet parlance 'the book' or 'information item' is basically an Internet resource or most commonly a 'homepage' or 'web page'.

In addition to the familiar services other services could also be offered using the Internet as the base.

Some of these are as follows:

1. Reference service.
2. Referral service
3. Webb biographies.
4. BBS/Discussion forum.
5. Alert Services, announcement.
6. OPACs
7. Newspapers clippings service.

Discussion Groups

There are thousands of discussion groups available on the net for various subjects, which act as forum for discussion and even as a media for exchanging the information.

Discussion List

Hundreds of electronic discussion lists and conference

proceedings available over the Internet. They give direct access to scholars in their fields of interest with online help facility.

Online Public Access Catalog (OPAC)

Online Public Access Catalog also plays an important role information retrieval. They are broadly divided into :

1. OPACs, which are, used in a particular library using either multi-user system local area networks.
2. Those, which can be accessed by other libraries through emergence of Internet. These are very easily and quickly accessible on the Internet from any part of the world. The availability of these catalogs on web allows anyone to see the contents of various library collections at their home.

News Groups

There are many sites, which give news for various subjects and also bring out electronic newsletters. In addition to these there are thousands of Bulletin Board Services (BBSs) covering various subjects.

Databases

There are available different types of databases, which are over useful for example Carl Uncover is a database that contains over 17000 multidisciplinary journals published since 1988.

Distance Learning

1. Student of distance learning can have opportunity to get into the contact with faculty members to clear their doubts. Here, the use of computer and its services may be utilized. Computer Aided Instructions may be used for distance learners. These can be provided:
2. Providing reference materials to learners through e-mail.

3. Providing accessibility to the course material of one institution to the other institution.
4. Forming news groups /study groups to facilitates contact with other pear group for exchange of information.

Subject Directories

These are also known as subject guides, which allow peoples to browse information by subject. The search engines like yahoo.com and Altavista.com etc.

Besides, the above sources on internet, it provides access to software archives, directory of electronic serials, frequently asked questions (FAQ) documents, workshops etc.

Sharing Information through Internet

An Internet can foster the sharing the information in many ways. For example, an Internet can include public discussion groups set up to share ideas on particular projects, customers, or products. Publishers of information can be contacted easily via integrated e-mails.

Internet has become an effective tool for teaching and learning. It is significantly affected the efficiency and effectiveness of process of creation, accumulation and transfer of knowledge. Its role appears to be of paramount importance especially in the field of knowledge generation. Internet not only affairs interesting files to acquire information, but also provides with tools for actually doing research.

The vast interconnection of computer provides an ideal infrastructure for sharing resources. The Internet allows users to transfer files between incompatible computers and send message across the globe and login to databases. Thousands of kilometers away with the blink of an eye. It offers a variety of services to create, browse, access, search, views and communicates information on various topics.

The services of information available on Internet are electronic journal (e- journal), technical reports, library catalogue, e-mail based information services, reference services, contents page of journal etc. All these sources provide a great wealth of information, which can be utilized by the libraries in providing information to the user.

Library Without Walls

With the Internet connectivity the users of the library are expended worldwide. The valuable information present in the library can be uploaded to the library's website and be made available to user anywhere. The Library can be a depository of local information/resource to the worldwide community at the same time provides access to the information available all over the world to the local users depending on their needs and priority.

Assistance to Researchers

Internet can be a tool for accelerating the pace of research. A large numbers of technical reports which provide details of on-going or complete R & D projects and PhD thesis are available free of cost for example a welldeveloped systems called Networked Computer Science Technical Reports Library (NCSTRL) is providing web access to technical reports in computer science research. Besides technical reports campus Wide Information Services (CWIS) of many Universities providing Web access to a variety of information are also available. These provide access to research literature to faculty and students, directories, course details and research projects, library catalogues and other databases e.g.; CWIS of University of Michigan, CWIS of Punjab University (India) . The Libraries can assist patrons doing research by demonstrating various such databases and by obtaining information from these databases on a regular basis. Video conferencing makes it possible for researches to discuss latest development. The Special Library Associations such as American Library Association (ALA) and other associations support electronic conferences. These groups are helpful when one want to locate, say an important document, which is out of print. These facilities both for getting information and also supplying to others when needed.

Bibliographic Verification

Various types of libraries such as academic, public and corporate libraries all over the world have their catalogue available on line. The Internet offers a communication link to a multitude of library systems that have Online Public Access Catalogue (OPAC) generally available free of cost. These are useful for finding books not available locally, to identify and select books for local acquisition, bibliographic data verification and to search holdings of periodicals and monographs. These can be accessed through telnet, gopher and World Wide Web. Catalogues of very large libraries like Library of Congress (LOCIS) are example of Internet accessible library catalogues.

Library services

The reference librarians can extend the scope of their reference services with the information available in FTP archives, gopher servers and world web servers. This information is much more up-to-date then its printed counter parts. Various ready reference sources are available over the internet which help the librarian and library users and answers a relatively large percentage of factual questions e.g. at URL: http//www.refdesk.com/one can finds an excellent virtual library for reference source known as "My Virtual Reference Desk" encyclopedia' internet guide at URL: http.//www.BLAST.com/ is an other useful reference sources for the librarians. The American Society of Indexers provides an excellent site for reference work at URL: http // www.asindering.org/ref books .html. Other online reference works at URL: http//www.cs.cmn.edu/ reference .html provides access to various types of English dictionaries, language dictionaries, thesauri and quotations apart from the subject related reference sources.

Technical service

The Internet gives a tremendous boost to both circulation and inter library loan primarily through increased access to on-line catalogue such as Melvy and LOCIS. These allow a user greater convenience in compiling an on-line search. In addition to this, the user can check holding records at the office or at house to avoid coming to the library for a book that has already been checked out. Cataloguers can also benefit from using online catalogue in much the same way they use OCLC and RLIN.

Besides, well know books-stores around the world are offering their holdings over Internet.

It is possible to order a book from Blackwell publications:

http://www.blackwell.co.uk/bookshop.

Many sites of publishers tell the user about the books recently published, book reviews, electronic books, rare book dealers, mailing list, review of new books etc.

Current Awareness Services (CAS)

The tools available for current awareness on the Internet are table of contents of journals, discussion forums and Usenet news. Many publishers of science journals and documents delivery agencies today deliver content pages of their journals by e-mail, mostly free of cost. Content direct service Elsevier:http://www.elsevier.ni/ for example delivers content pages of about 900 journals by e-mail over the Internet much earlier to the full journals. Blackwell scientific: http:www.blacksci.co.uk/online) along with 8 other publisher have put content page of 250 journals on www, for which full text is also available since January 1977. IDEAL database of Academic Press (*http://www.*

Academic.press.com/) provide online journal library, containing more than 50,000 articles. Anyone with Internet access can freely browse and search journal table of contents and abstracts but authorized user can only access the complete articles. A very popular service is the "uncover" a general commercial contents database at URL *http://www.carl.org/carl* htm) run by CARL corporation. It provides web access to the content pages of 17,000journals.

All the above services mentioned above can be effectively used for CAS and SDI services by the libraries. They can deliver the information in a form compatible to their client's needs and requirement.

World Wide Web and Digital Libraries

The Internet, and World Wide Web in particular, is a crucial component of digital libraries because :

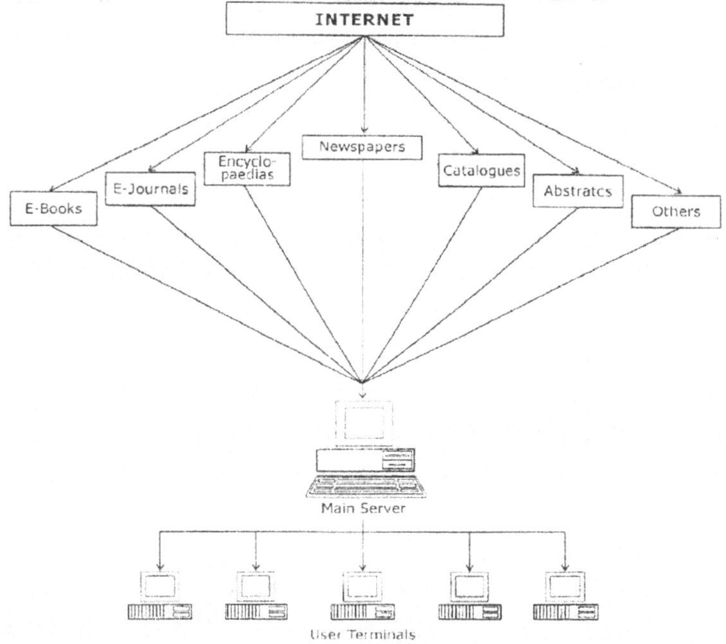

Fig. 5. Internet Services useful to the libraries

- As the internet expand, more people began to recognize the need to search indexed collections of information
- The Internet is like a library without a card catalog.
- Without the necessary mechanisms it is hard to find information on web effectively and efficiently.
- The desire to develop the necessary infrastructure to effectively mass manipulate information on the Internet is one of the primary driving forces behind the digital library initiatives in the United States and many other countries.
- The capabilities of the World Wide Web protocol make it an ideal tool to develop the interface of digital libraries
- The wealth of digital information on the World Wide Web makes it the most valuable source of information for digital libraries.
- The large numbers of people who now use the World Wide Web regularly makes it the most widely used mechanism to access digital information,
- On the other hand, trying to search for information in the web is a daunting experience for many users
- Despite the advances in search engine technology, current methods are not intuitive
- Many users are not used to elaborating an artificial text string to match their requirement
- Information returned by search engines is practically unorganized
- There is no mechanism to assist users in interpreting information retrieval from web
- There is no mechanism to assist users obtaining knowledge by filtering and cross-referencing information they obtain from the web.

- The objectives of digital libraries are to help users obtain knowledge by filtering and cross-referencing information they obtain from the web.

Internet, especially World Wide Web becomes so popular, which allows anyone connected to Internet to retrieve information on his/her desktop. The emergence of internet has changed the role of libraries radically. Now the library users have no barriers, as the entire information is available on web. Today, the libraries have important function of collecting; distributing and depositing of local information and resources available with them to users worldwide and also connect, retrieve and disseminates the information available across the globe to local users. All this could be possible only due to Internet.

Until, the emergence of world wide web, internet surfing was not an easy task for the common man not having some skills and knowledge of commands and the way of computers but world wide web or www has made it enable to reach this information just by clicking the highlighted terms and icons on the screen. Now, it is very easy to access the from the net. It can used to access the information from the remotes to read, download and print the electronic books and journals and in the reference service besides some of the house keeping operations such as acquisition, cataloging etc.

The web of today provides a basis for the building of digital libraries with better collection, better services, and better underplaying technology; much of the current research in the field of digital libraries can be seen as extending the basic building blocks of the web.

For the next few years, however we can expect to see the internet and web as the basis on which the libraries of the future are being built. Just as the crude software on early personnel computers has developed into modern operating system, the web can become the foundation for much generation of digital libraries.

WEB SOURCES

Information sources can be categorized as primary, secondary and tertiary sources. Primary sources are first hand sources contain original information it may be research work. Secondary sources are edited and modified version of secondary sources. It may be book, reference source etc. All these three types of sources are available in internet. However, it must be noted that all the printed sources of the world are not available in internet. Moreover, for consulting many information sources, a password is required, and for obtaining the password, some fee is required. Still, whatever, is available free is not always very up to date.

While searching internet it is advisable to use an efficient search engine like Google. For locating the primary periodicals in internet, searches can be conducted with the URL of the periodical is that is known. Otherwise the title or subject may be used. For example, a person can search for Journal of the American Society of Information Science and Technology by its title, abbreviation JASIST, sponsor, American Society of Information Science, its URL www.asis/ Publications/JASIS/jasis.html. And subject library science. It shows that information can be searched on internet by various approaches.

SOME IMPORTANT WEBSITES USEFUL FOR THE LIBRARY

Some important Websites on Internet which are very useful for library professionals are:

Books on Internet

It is new possible to surf the net and browse and purchase books from Indian or books written or purchase by Indians.

Some of the sites are:

1. www.Indianbookshop.com
2. www.bcindian.com

3. *www.Dkagencies.com*

Some other sites are :

1. **www.Indianbookshop.com**: It is one of the leading bookstores an internet which gives the widest coverage of books as all the major categories by renewed Indian authors. This site enable one to explore the information on various categories like culture, religion, science, history, sports, politics, etc.

2. **www.bcindia.com**: The site being one of Indians foremost and efficient online book source. The newly recorded books on any subject can be seen here. Order can be placed through Internet and books can delivered at the door step.

3. Information about Indian ministries, departments, states, union territories, organizations, Indian mission abroad, educational insititutions/universities, etc. can be obtained from *www.nic.in* is the URL for getting information on any of the above.

4. **http://www.ambook.org.so/bookweb/**: An American Bookseller Associations Websites devoted to information about books, authors and bookstores directory. Along with links to bookstores on the web.

5. **http://www.amazon.com**: these people claim to be largest bookstore. This site claim to have a catalogue of over one million books. With the help of this site libraries individual can do their books shopping.

6. **www.barnesandnoble.com**: The claim to have world's largest online book-seller.

7. **www.schoolgrou.com**: School's company limited. www, deals with text books in India.

8. **http://www.ambook.com.org.so/bookweb/**: An American Bookseller Assocations website devoted to information about books, authors and bookstore directory. Along with links to book stores on the web.

Free on-line E-Books:

1. *http://www.etext.libvirginia.edu/books*
   (The University of Virginia, USA)
2. *http://www.free* ebooks.net

INTERNET BOOKSHOPS

Internet Bookshops	URL
Amazon.com	*http://www.amazon.com*
Amazon.co.uk	*http://www.amazon.co.uk*
Blackwells.co.uk	*http://www.bookshop.blackwell.co.uk*
D.K. Agencies	*http://wwww.dkagencies.com*
Heritage Bookshop	*http://www.heritage.books/shoping.html*
Worldwide books	*http://www.woldwide.com*
Indian books	*http://www.indianbookshop.com*

Reference resources

Some of the **important magazines and newspapers** on net are:

General

1. *www.indiatoday.com*
2. *www.outlookindia.com*
3. *www.theweek.com*
4. *www.the-hindu.com/fline*
5. *www.mainstreamweekly.com*
6. *www.frontline.in*
7. *www.timesasia.com*

Business

1. *www.business-today.com*
2. *www.business-reader.com*
3. *www.businessworld.com*
4. *www.ijeb.com—Indian* journal of Economics and business

Entertainment

1. *www.filmfare.com*
2. *www.feminaindia.com*
3. ww.zeepemiere.com

Computer

1. *www.computersathome.com*
2. *www.pcquest.com*
3. *www.pcwindia.com*
4. *www.india-today.com/ctoday*

Economics

1. *www.capitalmarkst.com—capital* market
2. *www.indiainvester.net*
3. *www.epw.org.in*
4. *WWW.businessandeconomy.org*
5. *WWW.economist.com*

Newspapers

1. *www.timesofindia.com*
2. *www.expressionindia.com*
3. *www.decanherald.com*
4. *www.economictimes.com*
5. *www.tribuheindia.com*

Encyclopedias

1. **Wikipedia.org**: One of the more remarkable projects on the web. The online encyclopedia is work of 6000 volunteers covering huge range of subjects. It has a special focus on science and technology.

2. **Encyclopedia.com**: This websites, powered by a library, gives the internet browser the facility to look into any definition or topic on their dictionaries, thesaurus, almanacs and additional encyclopedias.

3. Howstultworks.com: An online encyclopedia an everything that makes the world around us ticks. It has a special emphasis on information technology related issues.

4. Eb.com: The biggest of then this entire Encyclopedia Britannica on web. Although, Encyclopedia Britannica in print form is still popular, the online edition provides greater convenience and is increasing gaining popularity.

5. Encyclopedia Britannica online: (htt:// www.Britannica.com)

6. McGraw-Hill Encyclopedia of Science and Technology: (http://www.mhreference.com/est.html)

7.Roget's Thesaurus: (http://www.thesaurus.com/)

Free on- line dictionaries

1. *http://www.pdictionary.com*
   (Internet Picture dictionaries)
2. *http://www.wesu.edu/library/odlis.htm*
   (Online dictionaries of Library and Information Science)

Others

1. Steel Authority of India—www.soil.co.in
2. Bharat Petroleum—www.bharatpetroleum
3. StateBank of India—www.statebankofindia
4. Reserve Bank of India—www.rbi.org.in
5. Videsh Sanchar Nigam Ltd.—www.vsnl.net.in
6. ICICI Bank—www.icici.com
7. *www.trade.india.com*: provides the trade information of India.
8. PKZid.delhi.nic.in: provides the patent information such as how to contact, mode of payment, how to apply, etc.

Documentation/Information Centers

WWW.insdoc.org: Information resources and services of INSDOC, a premier organization in the field of documentation and information science, science and technology services and systems is available from this site. Information regarding their services, products and publications, etc are available at this site.

WWW.nissat.org/centres.htm: NISSAT, the National Information System For Science and Technology plays a vital role in the field of information science and technology as it has the mandate to cover the entire spectrum of science and technology. The NISSAT web site provides information such as its objectives, activities, publications, etc.

Thus we can say that Internet over the years has grown into an encyclopedia covering every type of information and act as an important information source. Information contained in printed reference sources is in most cases found to be outdated by one year or so.

10

Digital Preservation / Archiving of Libray Reading Material

INTRODUCTION

Library is a central place where knowledge is preserved for future use. Libraries are established for the systematic collection, organization, preservation and dissemination of information. In the present era, the concept of library has changed and library is being transformed into digital library. Information and communication technology have transformed the way information is generated, persevered, archived and made accessible to the users. The modern library not only contains of books and periodicals but also possessed many other information materials that are called non-book material or digital material such as e-journals etc. The term digital preservation or digital archiving applies to the documents that are either "born digital" or stored online (or on CD-ROMs, diskette etc) to online databases.

Digital preservation refers to the various methods of keeping digital material alive into the future. It means taking steps to ensure the longevity of electronic documents or digital documents. That includes every thing from electronic publications on CD-ROM to online databases.

Due to wide spread transition of knowledge from print format to electronic format given rise to the problem of its preservation in digital form.

Today, information technology that is increasingly powerful and easy to use, especially like those that support the World Wide Web, have unlashed the production and distribution of digital information. Such information is penetrating and transforming nearly every aspect of our culture. If we are effectively to preserve for future generations the portion of this rapidly expending corpus of information in digital form that represents our cultural; record, we need to understand the cost of doing so and we need to commit ourselves technically, legally economically and organizationally to the full dimensions of the task.

Digital technologies increasingly serve to integrate information resources. Text, numeric data, images, voice, and video have heretofore resided in print or other analog media for storage and transmission. When they are encoded digitally, either by conversion or at the point of creation, these various kinds of resources shares layers of technology a common means of storage and transmission that allows them to be brought together and used in both old and new ways.

What is Digital Preservation?

Preservation encompasses activities intended to prevent, retard, or stop deterioration of materials or to retain the intellectual content of materials no longer physically intact.

Preservation includes selecting replacement copies, moving items to a protected area, and selected material for reformatting. Binding, rebinding, repairing, using protective enclosures, controlling use, monitoring environmental conditions, and conserving are preservation activities intended to prolonged the useful life of materials.

The term preservation here in our context includes:

1. Preservation of reading material on digital media such as CD-ROMs, microfilms, audio, video digital material etc.
2. Preservation of non-digital material such as written heritage, rare documents, fragile documents, etc. The preservation of these types of reading material would require the process of digitization. The digitization is referring to the electronic process of converting document (e.g. rare document) in a non-digital medium into digital form for the purpose of storage, retrieval and transmission. Digitization is the process of transferring print media into computer readable format.

We may classify material in two broad categories:

1. Born digital (Which has no analog of originals)
2. Digital reformatted.

Digital preservation is a process by which digital data is persevered in digital form in order to ensure usability, durability and intellectual integrity of information contained therein. Preservation is the activity of protecting something from loss or damage.

Preservation generally means keeping an object from harmful effect such as loss, damage destruction and the like on the other hand conservation focuses on three basic aspects, namely examination, preservation and restoration.

Digital preservation is preserving the digital medium that holds the digital information by storing it in the correct environment and following agreed storage and handling procedures; copying the digital information into newer, fresher media before the old media deteriorates.

Preservation concerns include deciding what to digitized, formats for texts and images, quality of images and costs. Digital preservation includes the preservation of print and non-print material in digitized form for effective, efficient and purposeful use.

Preservation is the activity of protecting something from loss or damage. Preservation can be done for betterment, improvement and advancement -a change for the better and for progress in development. Digital preservation includes the preservation of print and non-print material in digitized form for effective, efficient and purposeful use.

Digital preservation means taking steps to ensure the longevity of the electronic document in terms of the following (Mark et al 1999) :

- Data (this might be text, image, video or audio, stored in variety of formats and standards)
- Index to the data.
- Link to other data.
- Metadata.
- Software (relies upon hardware and operating system) and
- Storage medium, etc.

Hence, in preservation of digital objects the following measures taken into account are as follows:

1. integrity of digital material;
2. the physical presence
3. the preservation format
4. the digital material's functionality;
5. the location and reference of digital material
6. the authenticity of that materials
7. the context of preservation material and

8. the province.

There are three distinct but not mutually exclusive preservation applications of digital technologies, defined in parts by the possible purposes that the product may serve the end users.

1. Protect originals: The most common application of digital technologies in an archive or library is to create digital copies of sufficient quality that they can be used for ready reference in lieu of casual browsing through the original sources. Preservation goals are met because the original documents can be protected by limiting access to them. Example includes image reference files, which permit the identification of individual items requiring closer study.

2. Represents originals: A digital system could be built that represents the information content of the original source in such detail that the system can be used to fulfill most , if not all, of the research and learning potential of the original documents.

3. Transcend originals: in a very small number of applications, digital imaging promise to generate a product that can be used for proposes that are impossible to achieve with the original sources. This category includes imaging that uses special lighting to draw out details obscure by aging, use, and environmental damage, imaging that makes use of specialized photographic intermediates; or imaging of such high resolution that the study of art factual characteristics is possible.

Each of these applications places separate, but increasingly rigorous, demands on digital technologies .In such case, the use of an intermediate film or paper copy to felicitate the scanning process may or may not be necessary or advisable.

Thus, digital preservation refers to the taking steps to ensure the longevity of electronic documents. That includes:

1. The various methods of keeping digital materials alive into the future.
2. Typically centers on the choice of interim storage media, the life expectancy of a digital imaging system, and the expectation to migrate the digital files to future systems while maintaining both the full functionality and the integrity of the original digital system.
3. Include everything from electronic publications on CD-ROM to on-line databases and collections of experimental data in digital format.
4. To maintain the ability to display, retrieve and use digital collections in the face of rapidly changing technological and organizational infrastructures and elements.

WHY WE NEED DIGITAL ARCHIVING/PRESRVATION?

Digitization has changed the entire concept of use of information and its dissemination for the users. Preservation of reading material such as old and rare material related to cultural heritage of a country, decaying documents, etc. requires special attention.

Digital preservation refers to the various methods of keeping digital materials alive into the future. That includes every thing from electronic publication on CD-ROM to online databases and collection of experimental data in digital format maintains the ability to display, retrieve and use digital collection in the face rapidly changing technological and organizational infrastructure. It is very important for man to preserve and maintain the valuable knowledge and information contained in the books and other documents because it is important to preserve our knowledge and wisdom for the coming generations. Libraries place high value on preserving the irreplaceable contents of their collections, making the historical and cultural artifacts of our civilization available for future generation. Fire prevention systems, environmental controls, and microfilming initiatives guard against catastrophic loss of irreplaceable items. By preserving the documents in a library this knowledge can be made available to others who need it.

Digital preservation is a process by which digital data is preserved in digital form in order to ensure the usability, durability and intellectual integrity of the information contained therein. .

Preservation generally means keeping an object safe from harmful effects such as loss, damage, destruction and the like. The purpose of preservation is to ensure protection of information of enduring value for access by present and future generation.

It is difficult also because there is also changes in the technology say after 10-15 years. There is change in hardware, software, etc.

The holdings of the library are the priceless heritage of mankind as they preserve facts, ideas, thoughts, accomplishments and evidences of human development in multifarious areas, areas and directions. The past records constitute a natural resource and are indispensable to the present generation as well as to the generations to come. Any loss to such materials is simply irreplaceable. Therefore, preserving this intellectual, cultural heritage becomes not only the academic commitment but also the moral responsibility of the librarians/information scientists, who are in charge of these responsibilities. Besides, proper dissemination of library material is possible if the documents are in good and usable condition. This demand for the proper preservation of library materials.

Most of the libraries have paper based reading material such as books, periodicals, maps etc. These materials are susceptible to natural decay and deterioration.

There are other benefits of digitization besides preservation. Digital technology promises many easy to use features. Digital technology enhances access and functionality. Institutions typically select treasure for digitization not because they are in high demand, rather, by digitization; they seek to make their valuables better known and more widely accessible. The relevant considerations when selecting materials for digitization thus are not primarily about preserving the original, but about access. The new media and technology may be used to preserve documents for a long time. Digitizing as a means of preservation is quite beneficial. It helps to preserve rare and frail objects without denying access to those who wish to study them. Users can retrieve digitized books in seconds by searching for words, phrases or ideas. Several people can simultaneously read the same book or view the same picture. An other benefits is space. Electronic material occupies millimeters of space rather than meters on shelf. Digitization has become order of the day due to the significant advancement in computer and communication technology. Preservation includes, deciding what to digitized, formats for texts and images, quality of images and cost.

In 1991 the American Library Association published a preservation policy outlining the responsibilities of the library profession for preserving access to information of all forms. In 2001, that policy was updated to reflect changes brought about by the Internet. The policy states that:

"Librarians must be committed to preserving their collections through appropriate and non-damaging storage, remedial treatment of damaged and fragile items, and preservation of materials in their original format when possible, replacement or reforming of deteriorated materials, appropriate security measures, and life cycle management of digital publications to assure their usefulness for future generations."

Electronic publications may contain text, graphics, tables, sound, movies, or other type of material. As electronic media changed more easily than documents on paper, they are more vulnerable than print publications. Many institutions are trying to find appropriate answer to the question of how electronic documents can be prepared today for the technology of tomorrow. In this context, we need to address the uncertain durability and future availability of current storage media such as CD-ROM and magnetic tape and the respective reading devices. As evolving technologies do not necessarily replace previous ones, libraries theoretically have to provide all kinds of reading drives in panel.

The primary method of building digital resources is digitization. Digitization refers to the process of converting an item such as printed text, manuscript, image or sound recording, picture, picture or video into digital form. Digitization solves various traditional library problems such as conservation, preservation, storage, and space. The traditional concept of libraries which was completely based on print media is changing towards digital/electronic form with the help of information technology.

Digitization as a preservation treatment is becoming increasingly accepted in libraries. A digitized surrogate can add value through enhanced description and searching capability. Digitization has the advantage of reducing handling of the original artifacts and making it accessible to more people as a surrogate. The Digital Library Federation has developed a "benchmark" for digital reproduction of monographs and serials. It provides standards for optimally formatted digital contents that address quality, persistence, and interoperability. Digitization often is combined with conservation of the original or with microfilm reformatting. Libraries that undertake digitization as a preservation medium must have a robust hardware and software infrastructure and the resources to carry out the project and provide continuing access. Libraries should see that not to duplicate work done at other libraries.

Why Data Needs preservation?

The data may be text, image, video, audio, etc stored in variety of formats.

1. **The nature of the data** : Data is at risk because it is recorded on a transient medium, in a specified file format, and it needs a transient coding scheme (a programming language) to interpret it. The basic unit of data, the "bit" (binary digit), is represented by one of only two states :'1' or 'o' linked together in a 'bit stream' consisting of many millions of bits or electronic impulses. The kinds of digital data that concerns us here is complex and meaning derived from data can depend as much on how individual data objects are linked as on what those objects are.

2. **Data impermanence**: Digital data is in danger, not because it is inherently fragile or flawed, but because there is a continually accelerating rate of replication, adoption and redundancy of hardware, software and data formats and standards which may means that the bit stream may not be readable, interpretable or usable long into the future. All data is stored as a code and therefore require an element of decoding before it is recognizable and usable in a computing environment, even if open data standards are used.

Digital data does not have a long enough natural lifetime for us to wait for better media to come along. The life of data written even to optical media, such as CD-ROM or DVD, may be measured in years rather than decades. After 15 to 20 years require some very serious computer technology for storage. As yet, data storage has not found in stability equivalent of paper or microfilm, but the evolution of the technology may be around the next corner.

An other reason is that the rapid obsolescence of

computer hardware, software, and the accelerating rate of change in systems and software poses the greatest threat to the longevity of digital information. The lack of technologically feasible, viable and affordable method for preserving digital information is a major impediment to build digital libraries. Technology obsolescence is also a critical problem for libraries, archives, and other repositories that are attempting to acquire and preserve digital information.

DIGITAL VS NON-DIGITAL PRESERVATION

Digital preservation is different from the preservation of other media. Preservation of digital media require more attention than preservation of other media because we can read information written thousands of years back but digital preservation created a decades ago is in fear of loss due to improper preservation techniques. Digital preservation is for long-term storage of digital information. It is also error free storage of digital files. These files may be text files, images, audio, video, sound files. These files are decoded for access.

To keep the digital information for indefinite period, we need proper preservation tools, techniques and process.

In this chapter we are mainly concerned with first one that is preservation of digital material. While the chapter of preservation of non-digital material will be discuss in the chapter of digitization. Digitization is the process of converting non-digital material into digital format or computer readable format.

The topic of digitization is described in detail in separate chapter.

Digital preservation or digital archiving means taking steps to ensure the longevity of digital documents. It applies to documents that are either born digital or stored online or on storage media such as CD-ROMs.

CONSERVATION VS PRESERVATION

Very often the two terms 'preservation' and 'conservation' are used interchangeably but these two terms have different connotations. Preservation means preservation from deterioration or damage. It may be due to many factors such as biological hazards such as insects, lizards and fungi, climatic hazards such as light, heat, humidity etc., natural hazards such as floods, fire, earthquakes, environmental, etc. Oxford Dictionary (2nd ed) has stated that "the word 'conservation originated from a Latin word 'conserve' which means to keep to 'preserve'.

Conservation may be oriented towards specific objects while preservation is a broad based concept which includes protection, maintenance, restoration, and conservation. We can say that conservation a part of preservation. Conservation is not a single or one time activity, but it is a combination of numbers of processes which ultimately leads to achieve the goal of preserving a material. The total effect is that the deterioration of a material may be delayed to a considerable extent.

Many libraries of the world even the smallest, hold rare or unique resources that require preservation and conservation. Conservation is direct method of treatment in which an item is physically or chemically changed. This includes cleaning, deacidifying, repairing, rebinding, and reformatting. All conservation treatments entail the least instructive method possible, and use acid neutral or buffered materials, such as pastes, fungicides, and marbled papers, will be made in-house to ensure their quality. Conservation activities also include examination documents, treatment, and preservative care, supported by research and education.

In other words, conservation is a broader concept of an activity of which preservation includes one particular facet.

Many publishers, government agencies, professional

associations, trade publishers now use alkaline papers comply with national standards. Standards are concerned both with permanence (how long paper's shelf life is) and durability (how paper stands up to use).Several methods of deacidification have been developed.

While there is, naturally, no purpose in conserving documents without ensuring access these two aims are not always mutually achievable. Conservation means that access often has to be restricted in the case of rare or fragile object such as ancient manuscripts, fragile historic newspapers, brittle books. Access always result in a degradation of original objects. Digital archives necessarily embrace digital library functions to the extend that they must select, obtain, store, and provide access to the digital information. Many of the functional requirements for digital archives defined thus overlap those for digital libraries.

Many traditional libraries, archives and museums, as institutions, have taken and may well continue to assume digital library and archival functions.

DIGITAL ARCHIVES VS DIGITAL LIBRARIES

Digital archives are distinct from digital libraries in the sense that digital libraries are repositories that collect and provide access to digital information, but may or may not provide for the long term storage and access of that information.

Digital libraries thus may not be, in functional terms, digital archives and, in fact, much of the recent work on digital libraries is notable silent on the archival issues of ensuring

RELEVANCE OF DIGITAL PRESERVATION:

Today, information technologies that are increasingly powerful and easy to use, especially like those that support the World Wide Web, have unlashed the production and distribution of digital information .Such information is penetration and transforming nearly every aspect of our culture. If we are effectively to preserve for future generation the portion of this rapidly expending corpus of information in digital form that represents our cultural record, we need to understand the costs of doing so and we need to commit our selves technically, legally, economically and organizationally to the full dimensions of the task. Failure to look for trusted means and methods of digital preservation will certainly exact a stiff, long term cultural penalty.

Digital preservation means the planning, resource allocation, and application of preservation methods and technologies necessary to ensure that digital information of continuing value remains accessible and usable.

- The purpose of preservation is to ensure protection of information enduring value for access by present and future generations (Conway, 1990, 206)
- Through digitization there is unhindered access to contents over computer and communication network.
- Digitization may be considered as a means to enhance the life of material by preservation apart from the virtue of increased and easy access.
- As a number of users may make any number of copies, there are fair chances of at least one electronic copy to be available on the network for use in future.
- Digitized material can be easily searched and retrieved.
- Required less space for storage.
- Less likely to be damaged than print counterparts, as they have no physical form to yellow and decay with age, and loaning out a copy does not relinquish the original (Hodge, 2000).

The pursuit of knowledge is a process in which the emergence of new knowledge builds on and reconstruct the old. Knowledge cannot advance without consistence and reliable access to information sources, past and present. It is the archival function in the system of knowledge creation and use that serves to identify and retain important sources of information and to ensure continuing access to them.

FACTORS RESPONSIBLE FOR DETERIORATION

There are various factors, which are responsible for deterioration. These are:

1. Environmental factors such as light, heat, humidity, moisture, dust, etc.
2. Biological factors such as micro organisms, insects, etc.
3. **Chemical factors** : Acidic nature of the paper.
4. Human factors
5. Disasters such as floods etc.

Because of all these factors preservation is required. One method of preservation is digitization.

OBJECTIVES OF PRESERVATION

Heavy use of reading material result in wear and tear of the material, even for the newest materials. Libraries have been facing the problem of aging collection. The deterioration problem may be due to acidic nature of the paper, binding, glues, etc.

Deterioration is compounded by poor housing conditions, in which temperature, excess light, and humidity, extremes accelerate deterioration.

To reduce the effect of deteriorating factors such as temperature, light, moisture, flood, fire, fungus, bacteria, insects, pollution, dust and the impotent factors called "Human".

Some of the objectives can be summarized as follows:

1. To maintain the historical value of information.
2. To make it easy to use and handle
3. To make information survive longer
4. To provide worldwide accessibility.

CLASSIFICATION OF PRESERVATION

Digital Preservation can be classified into three types:

1. **Long term preservation**: continued access to digital materials or at least to the information contained in them, indefinitely.

2. **Medium term preservation**: continued access to digital materials beyond changes in technology for a defined period of time but not indefinitely.

3. **Short term preservation**: Access to digital materials either for a defined period of time while use is predicted but which does not extend beyond the foreseeable future and/ or until it becomes inaccessible because of changes in technology.

ADVANTAGES OF PRESERVATION

The preservation of documents in digital form has the following advantages:

1. Space saving.
2. Easy access.
3. Easy to handle.
4. Easy to transmit.
5. Time saving task.
6. Low cost.
7. Less manpower involved.

DISADVANTAGES OF PRESERVATION

1. Process of installation is complex and costly.

2. Lack of infrastructure: In developing countries like India, it is very tedious job to provide all infrastructure facilities at one platform as and when it is required.
3. Insufficient budget.
4. Shortage of expertise in India.

In country like India, libraries are facing many problems in digital preservation such as shortage of funds intellectual proprietary rights issues, less interest of staff, lack of trained staff etc. Now the government and many institutes are gradually realizing the need of digital preservation as UGC -infonet and other like programme is the innovative steps towards digitization and digital preservation.

CATEGORIES OF MATERIAL TO BE INCLUDED IN DIGITAL PRESERVATION

It applies to the documents that are either "born digital" and stored on-line or on CD-ROM, diskettes or other physical carrier or to the products of analog to digital conversion , if long term access is intended. The modern libraries not only contain books and periodicals but they also possess many other information materials that are called non-book or non-print material or digital material. The digital material can be classified as:

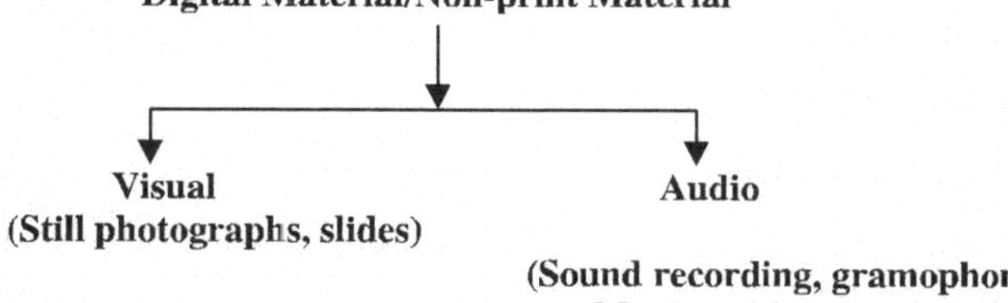

Types of Media for Preservation:

1. Microform Media:

  i. Microfilming
  ii. Microfiche
2. Magnetic Media
  i. Hard Disk (40 GB and above)
  ii. Floppy Disk (100 MB and more)
  iii. Cartridge Tape Disk (CTD, 40 GB and more)
3. Optical Media
  i. CD-ROM (600 MB) of textual information
4. Networking Media

Internet is a cheap and economical medium for preservation of information for longer and worldwide use. There are three important ways namely bulletin Board, Website and Portal being used for preservation and dissemination of information worldwide.

Aspects of Digital Preservation

Maintaining the accessibility of digital media is much more complex than with such non-digital media paper. For example, when a book is preserved in its original format, all aspects of the book are preserved-its physical presence, its format, its layout, and its contents. It is practically impossible to extract individual elements (e.g., content without layout) because they are inextricably linked. Digital objects in contrast, are easily decomposed into individual elements, and significantly more efforts must be made to preserve them as a "whole". In preserving a digital object, the following aspects should be taken into consideration:

a. The object as a discrete whole
b. Presentation
c. Functionality
d. Authenticity
e. Location information for reference
f. Provenance

g. Context

SELECTION OF MATERIAL TO BE DIGITIZED

The first step is to select the sources to be digitized. This is called target source.

The images /contents of physical media such as periodical articles, books, rare manuscripts, research papers, newspapers, newspaper cuttings, images, sound, film and audio video cassettes, photographs etc to be digitized is called target source. This is the material to be digitized.

Documents

They include text, bibliographic or full text, photographs, diagrams, maps, etc. They exist either in print or non-print form or also as single unit or collections.

CRITERIA FOR SELECTION OF MATERIAL TO BE PRESERVED

Digital preservation refers to the various methods of keeping digital materials alive into the future. Includes everything from electronic publications on CD-ROM to on-line database and collections of experimental data in digital format maintains the ability to display, retrieve and use digital collections in the face of rapidly changing technological and organizational infrastructure elements.

Librarians follow many of the criteria to select the print material for digitization. Such as its usage at present and in future, its contents, quality and the area matching the instructional objectives (Chapman and Kenny, 1996).

The libraries should select the material, which is in high demand but less number of copies are available. But before the libraries should see the copyright rules and restrictions.

The libraries find three types of materials as per copyright involved.

They are:

1. Copyright free.
2. Copyright owned and
3. Copyright bought.

Copyright free documents are usually government documents or old books whose copyright is either expired or not applied. The libraries can buy the copyright for certain documents highly demanded from the publishers. The library may digitized the copyright owned material of the institution like in-house reports, in-house publications, conference proceedings, thesis and dissertations and informal sources like lecture notes, manuals notebooks, etc.

Preserving digital information is difficult as the information itself in rapidly changes. Digital information is traditionally preserved by transferring the files at regular intervals to the latest new information carrier available. But the multimedia resource restore in digital format may not be possible without the original software and hardware.

BASIC DIGITAL PRESERVATION REQUIREMENTS

Long term preservation of digital information on a scale adequate for the demands of future research and scholarship will require a deep infrastructure capable of supporting a distributed system of digital archives.

A critical component of the digital archiving infrastructure is the existence of a sufficient number of trusted organizations capable of storing, migrating, and providing access to digital collections.

Preservation and digitization technologies

That includes:

1. **Hardware**: which includes scanners, computers, printers, data storage and data output peripherals.
2. **Software** (Image capturing, data comprehension)

3. **Network** (data transmission)
4. Display technologies.

Digitization and preservation requires certain technologies. These include storage technologies, variety of devices to store and retrieve information in digital form such as magnetic tapes/cassettes, floppy disks, hard disks, data tape, CD-ROM, smart card, processing technology creating the systems and applications software that is required for the performance of digital network; communication technologies primarily to communicate information in digital form; display technologies variety of output devices.

In order to preserve digital material, it is necessary to examine some basic requirements from the view of libraries, archives, and other custodians who creates and preserve digital material and from the perspective of users of digital materials.

The basic requirements for preserving digital information in different ways are contents, formats and style, and contexts; storage media; systems technology and metadata policies.

Digital imaging means taking steps to ensure the longevity of the electronic documents in terms of the following (Mark et al; 1999):

- Data (this might be for text, image, video or audio stored in variety of formats and standards)
- Index to data
- Link to the other data
- Metadata
- Software (relies upon hardware and operating system and
- Storage medium.

PRESERVATION TECHNIQUES

In the face of rapid technological obsolescence and to overcome the problem of media fragility, archivists have adopted the technique of "refreshing" digital information by copying it onto new media. Copying from medium to medium, however, also suffers limitations as a means of digital preservation. Refreshing digital information by copying will work as an effective preservation technique only as long as the information is encoded in a format that is independent the particular hardware and software needed to use it and as long there exists software to manipulate the format in current use.

There are two main approaches for preservation:

1. The first is the more conservative approach where the original technological environment is fully preserved for decoding the digital information in the future. This approach divided into two preservation techniques. The first is to preserve the working replicas of all computer hardware and software platform for future use.
2. The second is to program the newer computer system to emulate on demand the older obsolete platforms and operating system.

The Commission on Preservation and Access and The Research Group (RLG) formed a Task Force on Digital Archiving in 1996.The task force made some recommendations about the digital preservations.

There are various preservation techniques. Each preservation technique has its advantage and disadvantage.

The following strategies were purposed as components of a digital preservation.

Refreshing Data

Refreshing digital information by copying it from

medium to medium and the possibility of maintaining a complex set of emulators describe two distinct point on a continum of approaches to preserving digital information.

However, neither refreshing nor emulation sufficiently describes the full range of options needed and available for digital preservation. A better and more general concept to describe these options is migration. Migration is the periodic transfer of digital materials from one hardware/software configuration to an other or from one generation to computer technology to a subsequent generation.

The first and probably most common alternative for digital preservation is refreshing.

Refreshing relates to preserving media only. Refreshing is simply copying the digital files from one storage device to another of the same type. It involves transferring digital material to a new medium, for example changing from CD-ROM to DVD ROM. Changes to physical storage devices require this to be an ongoing process.

This method is viable only when the digital files are in non-proprietary format and independent of hardware and software. If the files are in a proprietary format, problems may arise when refreshing the media, as the format owner may have implemented changes to the specifications of file format. In such cases, difficulty may be experienced, when accessing the files. Hardware and software will still be required to read non proprietary formats.

The Task Force also proposed two solutions to deal with file format changes.

1. Emulation

Emulation refers to creating a new software that mimics the operation of the older hardware or software in order to reproduce its performance. Thus, not only the physical presence and contents are preserved but also digital objects could display original features, i.e. layout and functionality available with the older software. Emulation has recently attracted attention as a potential strategy to assists preservation, recognizing that digital material that is highly dependent on a particular hardware and software will not lend itself to migration. Emulation is used to provide backward compatibility for digital objects in subsequent technological environment .Ressel (1999) considers emulation is more like the 'just in time' option, where as technology preservation will have the necessary hardware and software 'just in case'.

This is strategy where the technology has grown from computer gaming arena. Rather than attempting to migrate files continually into new version of software. Which is compatible with new hardware that will run 'defunct' files on current or variant system' 'as if' they were running on the system they were originally designed for. Focus on the application rather the file product. Emulation tries to recreate application environments on which the original files can run .Ideally, a combination of refreshing with either Emulation or Migration should be adopted as a preservation strategy for digital information objects.

The advantage of this method is that it maintains the look and feel.

Disadvantage is that the complexity of creating emulator specifications. The large amount of information that must be preserved.

2. Migration

Migration is defined as the transfer of information intact to other medium. Migration involves moving files from one file-encoding format to another. Migration is the periodic transfer of digital materials from one hardware/software configuration to another or from one generation of computer technology to a subsequent generation. For example, upgrading a file type to the newest version of the software, which may have developed in house or procured from software development firm. Migration is the chosen method of copying information at the moment because its propose is to preserve the integrity of the document/file/program by making an exact copy of it the new generation of technology. This means that not only is the data copied to a new medium but the structure if the information and the way in which it is related, features such as retrieval abilities and report making, will also be transferred intact. But this can be a very difficult method of as there is limited experience in predicting when migration will be necessary and the search for the perfect new medium to transfer the format of the information can be difficult.

The purpose of migration is to preserve the integrity of digital objects and to retain the ability for clients to retrieve display, and otherwise use them inn face of constantly changing technology. Migration includes refreshing as a means of digital preservation but differs from it in the sense that it is not always possible to make an exact digital copy or replica of a database or other information object as hardware and software change and still maintain the compatibility of the object with the new generation of technology.

The advantage of this method is that there is no need to retain original applications.

The disadvantage is that

- Significant cost for long term preservation information degradation.
- Lack of preservation metadata.
- Need for continued diligence on the part of archivists.

1. **Harvesting**: The other way to copy digital information involves reformatting the information for use on a different medium. Reformatting the information to a simple standard format is done by harvesting.

2. Standardization: This is a strategy, which alleviates hardware/software differences, at their root: resource creation. The adoption of standard formats for digital contents and accompanying metadata ensures that resources will have greater interoperability and compatibility between variant systems and increased longevity.

3. Encapsulation: Involves wrapping the record to be preserved within human readable wrapper containing information that supports organizational preservation, and documents, the preserved information to allow it be decoded in the future.

The advantage of this method is that it maintains preservation information.

The disadvantage is that the knowledge about the format must be preserved. Systems required for capturing the digital information.

4. National and international initiatives in digital preservation: The cost of digital preservation is high. The cost is not preserving our digital heritage will be higher in terms of lost data and lost history, and there is no time to waste inputting strategies and practices in place to preserve key materials. Many individual projects and institutions are working hard on this problem, and there are also national and international initiatives collaborating to find long term solutions.

There are also a number of initiatives to establish national and international partnership to solve digital preservation coalition, together with international organizations such as RLG and OCLC. This has been set up to deal urgently with digital preservation issue in the UK within an international context.

5. Technology Preservation: Another method for ensuring ongoing access to digital objects would be to simply keep older technology available for use .The most obvious way to ensure that the object is preserved as it was created by preserving the environment used earlier to created and access the resources, i.e., to preserve the software and hardware environment that was used to access the resources when it was created. For some digital objects this may the best solution at least in the short run, because it ensures that the material is accessible by preserving the access tools as well as the object itself. However, in loner term, this is more problematic. For example, issues of space and maintenance for hardware and software as well as cost may make this an impractical solution for the long term. This method is used as an interim method when migration is not possible.

6. Digital technology Migration: Migration is the primary strategy articulated by most organizations that plan to preserve digital object. The task force on archiving of digital information defines digital information migration as "Migration is the periodic transfer of digital material from one hardware or software configuration or from one generation of computer technology to a subsequent generation" (Bullock, 1999).

It covers a range of activities to periodically copy, transfer digital information from one medium that is becoming obsolete or physically deteriorating to a newer one(e.g. floppy disk to CD-ROM) and converting from one format to another (e.g. Microsoft word to ASCII) and moving document from one platform to another (Eg. MS-DOS to Unix).The Experience of the National Library of Australia illustrate that even this simple form of migration, i.e., copying , may pose problem for some type of digital object, such as CD-ROM, floppy disk, etc. In copying these objects, it also needed to copy the executable programmes in languages that may become obsolete.

Migration certainly preserves the physical presence and the contents of a digital object. However, it may not preserve presentation, functionality and context. Successive migration may eventually result in unacceptable data loss. Migration is undeniable an important strategy for preserving digital object. However, it has yet to be tested and proven as a mechanism for managing complex multimedia objects over the long run.

PRESERVING ARCHIVAL IMMAGES

The main purpose of creating digital images, may be for the propose is to create images for the web, or, intranet use in each case the organization should create master images. These will be images captured at a high resolution, on which no manipulation or change is made. Copies of these archives files can be made and used for later projects, but the original capture files should always be maintained and preserved.

PRESERVING METADATA

Recording preservation metadata should be a key component of digital preservation strategy. This type of information will often be administrative or structural in manner, and will include information about the date of capture, the capture device, change history, and other information about the files, including relationship to other files. This metadata is different from descriptive information about the contents of the file, which may be used for resource discovery.

Some projects have developed extensive sets of preservation metadata.

CEDARS-Curl Examples in Digital Archives

United Kingdom project objectives include promoting awareness of digital preservation issues identification of strategic framework for developing digital collection management policies developing guide lines for long term preservation.

NEDLIB-Network European Deposit Library this

collaborative effort among European National Libraries aims to developing the infrastructure for a networked European Deposit Library, with a focus on preservation of electronic publications.

National Library of Australia Preservation Metadata for Digital Collections

The OCLC and RLG collaboration is also focusing on the OAIS (Open Archival Information System), which is an information model for handling archiving of physical and digital information.

DIGITIZATION AND PRESERVATION OF MANUSCRIPTS

The National Mission for Manuscripts (NMM) is the first consolidated national effort for reclaiming India's inheritance of knowledge contained in the vast treasure of manuscripts. The mission was established in 2003 by Ministry of Tourism and Culture with Indira Gandhi National Center for the Arts (IGNCA) as its nodal agency.

Digitization of manuscripts as means of protecting and documenting textual heritage has emerged as an important field in recent times.

With the advancement of information technology, digitization promises documentation and preservation of original text, facilitating at the same time, greater access for scholars and researchers.

What is manuscript?

The Antiquities and Art Tresures Act, 1972 lays down the legal framework for custody of manuscripts. Antiquities, defined under the Act includes "any manuscript, record or other document which is of scientific, historical, literary or aesthetic value and which has been in existence for not less than seventy five years".

Thus, the definition defines manuscript as:

1. A handwritten document.
2. which has scientific, historical, literary or aesthetic value and
3. Which is at least 75 years old.

In India the manuscripts are available at Khuda Baksh Oriental Library, Asiatic Society, Kolkata, and National Library Kolkata. Outside India, Sanskrit, Pali, and Prakrit manuscripts are available in almost all the famous libraries in Europe, Japan, Srilanka, Pakistan, Thailand etc.

PROCESS OF PRESERVATION

The preservation process can be divided into two processes :

1. Scanning documents and making image file: In this process the scanning of documents is an initial process. The documents should not be scanned below 300 dpi resolution. Basically, the resolution depends on the physical condition of the documents. The scanned images are typically stored in file formats like JPG, TIFF etc. The final output is converted to a light format like PDF. PDF format allow various security measures to be built into prevent a user from edition, downloading, or even printing.

2. Scanning and preparing fultext file: The scanned and processed images before being converted to PDF files, under the process to separate the text and media from the image files. The next process which is an important task is to rectify the errors and make text files error free with the help of Optical Character Recognition (OCR) process. This process also involves proof reading and checking quality of text files. After completion of all the above process, the text is converted into the mark up language like XML, HTML etc. along with complete tagging which enables the database to be integrated with any WEB applications.

The process of preserving digital information will vary

significantly with the different kinds of objects-textual, numeric, image, video, sound, multimedia, simulation and so on being preserved. Whatever preservation method is applied, however, the central goal must be to preserve information integrity; that is, to define and preserve those features of object that distinguish it as a whole and singular work.

In the digital environment, the features that determine information integrity and deserve special attention for archival purposes including the following:

Content, fixity, reference, province, and context. What digital archives are trying to preserve after all is the intellectual substance contained in information object.

The main function of any archive is to preserve the heritage and artifacts which make up the heritage.

Digital preservation involves copying the digital information into newer media before the old media become so obsolete that the data cannot be accessed. This is referred to copying or refreshing. In this process integrity of digital information is preserved. It is clear that the lifetime of a medium determine the period of time for which the information recorded on the medium is stored safely without loss.

There are three steps in preservation work:

1. Conservation.
2. Preservation and
3. Restoration

It involves mainly four phases in its processing:

1. Identification of documents
2. Collection/conservation
3. Storage
4. Discrimination.

STEPS FOR PRESERVATION

The preservation process involve the following steps:

Finding Information → Selecting Information → Organising-information → Digitizing Information → Preserving Information

Once an information object is identified for inclusion in digital archives, it needs to be accessioned, that is, prepared for the archives. The accession process involves both describing and cataloging selected objects, including their province and context, and securing them for storage and access. Standards for description are well developed for certain kinds of materials that are likely to be appearing in digital archives, such as monographs and serials. Because of the high degree of standardization, one might reasonably expect such descriptions eventually to accompany the digital object, thus, simplifying the accessioning process.

For other kinds of material, such as WWW pages, motion video and multimedia, relevant attributes are less well understood. Standards of description are less well practiced and one cannot reasonably expect satisfactory descriptive material to accompany the digital object. In all cases, special attention is needed in the accession process to creating, describing and talking the versions of the object in the digital archives to satisfy the various requirements for display and other forms of access and for long term storage.

In the accession process, selected digital objects also need to be made secure for indefinite future use. A digital archive may need to establish access control for its information objects and the means for authenticating them to future users.

Little used material may be stored most efficiently offline, usually in tape format. For objects in high demand, where retrieval time is at a premium, on-line storage in magnetic media may serve best.

In distributed network, they may need to be stored on-line in multiple locations. An intermediate solution is near line storage, where information objects may be stored on optical or tape media and loaded in a jukebox. Retrieval time in near line storage systems suffers by comparison to on-line storage, but is considerably more responsive to user demand than offline storage.

Depending upon the copyright status of the objects, digital archives may choose to make backup copies on their own or to make arrangement for other sites, which holds the same object, in the network of digital archives to serve as backup, or they may choose to do both.

Digital archives have an obligation to maintain the information in a form so that users over the network can find it with appropriate retrieval engines and view, print, listen to or otherwise use it with appropriate output devices.

Digital archives may use any or all these methods.

DIGITAL IMAGING TECHNOLOGY FOR PRESERVATION

Digital imaging technology is one of the reformatting options. Imaging involves transforming the very concept of format, rather than creating an accurate picture of a book, documents, photograph, or map on a different medium. The power of digital enhancement, the possibilities for structured indexes, and the mathematics of compression and communication together alter the concept of preservation.

The process basically involves taking a physical object and essentially making an electronic photograph of it. An image of the physical object is captured using a scanner or digital camera and converted to digital format that can be stored electronically and access via computer.

PROBLEMS/CHALLENGES/ISSUES OF DIGITAL PRESERVATION

Issues during the Process of Preservation are :

Issues such as media instability and technological obsolescence are threatening greatly to reduce the longevity of electronic publications unless they are carefully managed. Digital preservation is a very complicated process and many issues must be addressed before libraries can effectively preserve the digital material.

Some of the issues include:

1. **Technical obsolescence**: Technological obsolescence represents a far greater threat to information in digital form than the inherent physical fragile of many digital media. In the rapid race of information and communication technology era, the computer hardware, software, devices, process of recording, storing, and accessing information are being replaced with new products and methods at regular three to five years cycle.

It is costly and difficult for the vendors to assure that their products are either 'backwardly-compatible' with previous versions or those they can inter-operate with competing products.

2. **Migration of digital information** : It has always been a problem with the preservationists to make an exact copy or replica of a database or digital object as hardware and software chances makes the object incompatible with new generation of technology.

3. **Legal and organizational issues** : Current copyright law is unclear about the digitization of any information object; storing of the digitized image in archive; authorization of the digital objects ; changing file formats and also deletion of the digital object.

4. **Infrastructure** : Lack of organizational efforts for digital preservation i.e. building deep infrastructure which

involves multiple, inter-related factors, such a institutions, services, technologies, and qualified personals, capable of supporting a distributed system of digital archive.

5. Conceptual framework or standards

1. Absence of established standard, protocols, and proven methods for preserving digital information.
2. Lack of adequate research in the areas such as, framing key problems associated with digital information, defining critical issues, establishing standards for digital preservation, etc.

PROBLEMS AND CHALLANGES

1. Networked digital information technology is very good at transmitting data across space, but is not well suited for transmitting data across time. The evanescence of the medium creates many difficulties.
2. There is a problem of the lack of fixity in digital media. One of the greatest advent of typography was that readers of a document were well sure that they were all reading the same document (more or less). His advent of fixity facilitated a major advance in scholarly communication.

Digital preservation has raised many challenges of a fundamentally different nature. Some of them are in the area of planning, resource allocation and applications of preservation methods and technologies necessary to ensure that digital information of continuing value remains accessible and usable.

3. Durability problem: The durability of digital content has become problematic for a number of complexes and interrelated reasons as most of the documents exist only in encoded form, specific software is required for handling them. The digital component like hardware or software is also often changing their versions or processing capacity. Technology used is becoming obsolete and digital documents depend on them and digital documents become unreadable.

Maintaining the accessibility of digital media is much more complex than with such non-digital media as paper. For example, when a book is preserved in its original format, all aspects of the book are preserved -its physical presence, its format, its layout, and its contents. It is practically impossible to extract individual elements (e.g., contents without layout) because they are inextricably linked. Digital objects in contrast, are easily decomposed into individual elements, and significantly more efforts must be made to preserve them as a 'whole'.

In preserving a digital object, the following aspects should be taken into consideration;

- The object as a discrete whole.
- Content
- Preservation
- Functionality
- Authenticity
- Location information for reference
- Province
- Context.

Other aspects of this problem are non-technical issues such as management, funding, staffing, maintenance of digital documents and updated the development of policies for standard techniques and practices to prevent the loss of digital information should need to be well planned.

4. Form of Material: Digital materials are very short life as compared to traditional format. Recording media for digital materials are susceptible to worsening and catastrophic loss. Librarian and archivists are trying to preserve acid base papers, thermo fax, nitrate films and other fragile media for decades. In this situation magnetic and optical media are qualitatively different as these are the reusable media.

Digital materials are especially vulnerable to loss and deterioration due to being stored on impermanent media like magnetic and optical, which can fail suddenly from exposure to heat, humidity or faulty reading and writing devices. Hence, can not be relied upon for preservation of their contents for long. In comparison, information on paper or microfilm can survive for hundreds of years.

5. Media Problem: Advancement in the computer hardware, storage and software industries media obsolescence is a very common fact. When greater storage and processing capacities are available in market at lower cost, slowly old product's market will be surely down. So devices, processes and software for recording and storing information are being replaced with new products and methods on a regular three to five year cycles. Early attention to the difficulties in preserving digital information focused on the longevity of the physical media on which the information is stored. Even under the best storage conditions, however, digital media can be fragile and have limited shelf life. Moreover, new devices, processes and software are replacing the products and methods used to record, store, and retrieve digital information on breath taking cycles of 2 to 5 years. Given such rates of technological change, even the most fragile media.

The document created as digital form is equally vulnerable to technological obsolescence. For example, the short lifetime media are eight inch floppy disk, tape cartridges and reels. Hard sectored disks and seven track tapes those storage formats are inaccessible and more durable storage media are CD-ROM/DVD-ROM and optical WORM. There is lack of consideration of long term access requirements while creating digital information.

6. Software dependent Problem: The digital documents are in general dependent on application software to make them accessible and meaningful. But the problem is that software is also developing and changing versions. Coping media correctly at best ensure that the original stream of a digital document will be preserved. But a stream of bits can not make self-explanatory. Every software has different kind of encoding for which every computer needs some specific software to active the digital documents. A bit stream can be made intelligible only by running the software that created it or some closely related software that understand it. A particular digital document may require a particular word processing programme running on a machine with a special kind of computer processing chip and operating system. Other objects, such as an image file, may be readable using a variety of software programmes, but may be stored on disk in a format that is readable only with a special computer. For still other objects, like www document marked up in HTML, the hardware and software dependencies may be specified in a general terms because they are readable with a software browser that is available on almost any hardware platform.

7. Standards: The absence of established standards, protocols, and established methods for preserving digital information creates problems. Main objective of digital libraries are to organize the information, maintain the intellectual property rights and preservation, retrieval and visualization of digital materials. The main role of digital libraries and archives are the future accessibility of information and preservation of valuable materials. Digital preservation remains largely experimental and repeat with the risk associated with unproven methods. Moreover, digital preservation requirements have not been factored into the architecture, resources allocation or planning for digital libraries.

8. Intellectual Property Rights (IPR): An intellectual property rights is a big barrier for preserving the digital documents. Digitization of documents are involved with complex method for resolving the legal and practical question of migrating intellectual property that includes the creators and owners of intellectual property managers of digital archives and actual and potential users of intellectual property.

Conversion of paper in to digital or electronic form is expensive and time consuming. Some types of objects such as photographs, sound and video are readily digitiable but books, journals and maps are not. The fact that special hardware and software are essential to view digital objects compounds the problem. This is specially true in developing countries, where by the time the necessary hardware and software are acquired and installed a new version is released in the market. Also the problem of obsolescence is true even with such media for example DVD replacing CD.

9. Contents: The initial problem with digital preservation is the contents itself. When preserving objects in the analog world such as books and music we use all of their contents and store them in simple form. Dealing with the digital content requires us to the meaning of preserving the object. For instance, web sites have links that not only change but also point to dynamically changing sites. As the objects grows and changes over time, new question emerge about what it means to preserve a digital object.

10. Format and Style: Latest technological developments facilitate the digitization of recorded information in different forms such as books, maps, photographs, and sound recordings. New emerging formats such as hypertext, dynamic pages, geographic information systems, multimedia, and interactive video, etc. pose distinct challenges (for example, encoding and compression) for digital preservation. Libraries and archives are supposed to satisfy the requirements of their users by preserving material in format that enables the types of analyses that users wish to perform. But it is not possible primarily due to resource constraints. The potential users of digital material are varied, unpredictable, and almost endless (Gould).

CHALLANGES

Digital preservation has raised many challenges of a fundamentally different nature which are divergent compared to the problems of preserving traditional form.

There are numbers of issues that complicate the maintenance of digital objects over longer periods of time.

Deterioration of media: Stone tablets have a considerable advantage over today's digital media for long term storage. The problem of deterioration limits the useful life of today's digital media to between 5 to 50 years.

Evaluation in type of format of media: In addition to the concerns of physical deterioration of media, we must be aware of the challenge posed by the changes in the media type and format. In the relatively recent history of personnel computer use, we have seen an evolution from floppy disk to high-density zip disk. Optical storage technology is next, and there will be undoubtedly be continual change in storage technologies.

Change in applications and operating systems: New software constantly appears on the horizon, rendering older versions obsolete. The hardware required by applications and operating systems software also changes over time. Any information stored in a given software/hardware environment will eventually be rendered obsolete through technological obsolescence.

Preservation of processing results: Some digital resources exist only fleetingly as a program runs and cannot be preserved as static objects. Preservation of such resources requires maintenance of the program and the surrounding operating environment in operable form of course, not all digital resources have the same preservation requirements.

11
Digitization of Library Resources

INTRODUCTION

Library is a central place where knowledge is preserve for further use. At present libraries have become centers of information dissemination with the help of computer and communication technologies. In a digital world, libraries are emerging as a means of creation and dissemination of knowledge. Information today exists in many forms than just as printed material this lead to libraries into digital era.

Information and communication technologies have transformed the way information is generated, preserved, archived and made accessible. With the development of modern information technology, the concept of library has changed. Now more and more libraries are being transferred into digital libraries. A digital library is nothing but the extension of a traditional library. Digital libraries break the barriers of physical boundaries and allow the users to access the digital resources across the world.

A digital library is one which collect, stores and disseminates digital information. Digital libraries are libraries with the same purposes, functions, and goals as traditional libraries -collection, development and management, subject analysis, index creation, provision of access, reference work and preservation. Thus, library and information centers are moving from traditional to digital library era.

We use digital library to describe the situation where documents are stored in digital form. It means information is stored in binary strings of 0s and 1s. A digital library is a library that contains materials in digitized form or access to internal or external digital resources -that can be manipulated and delivered in many ways.

But what of the older documents on paper that occupy so many spaces of library shelves? The solution is digitization of reading material. It may be digitization of existing collection or selected collection such as rare books.

Digitization has bestowed upon librarians and archivists of the late 20th and early 21st centuries the opportunity to reexamine how they access their collection. In 21st century there has been a great emphasis as moving towards automation of information preferably into digital media. All the archival material has no other best option except digitization.

Voluminous information has accumulated over the years, in universities, and other organizations. There is an urgent need to have a sound storage system and effective retrieval mechanism to deal with vast bits of information available in different media.

The librarians and archivist.... Both collect, preserve, and make accessible materials for research; but significant differences exist in the way these material are arranged, described, and used.'

Among the items usually collected by the libraries are:

Published books, and serials, and in more recent times,

commercially available sound recording, films, videos, and electronic records of various types. Archives, on the other hand, tend to collect original records of an organization, unique personnel papers, as well as other effects of individuals and families. Each type of institution, given its particular emphasis, has its own tradition and its own methods of dealing with its collection.

The digital information resources include e-books, e-journals, and full text, CD-ROMs etc. Digital libraries can provide the users fast access to electronic information. They can provide remote access to the resources from many locations simultaneously.

For building digital collection, digital libraries have to convert the existing print resources into electronic form. They can also acquire resources in electronic form or provide access to external resources.

The creation of digital information from conventional is generally a two way format process.

The first stage is digitization. This is essentially the conversion of the physical medium into a digital representation of the physical medium. It takes no account of any information content of the original material.

With the increased availability of economical digital storage media, high speed scanners and high bandwidth networks, a digital library has received a boost in the last few years. The dream of digitizing the vast knowledge of mankind, and making it available online has now become a realizable goal.

WHAT IS DIGITAL INFORMATION?

Information can be divided into analog and digital. Traditional information is in the form of analog form. When this information in a binary code is fed into the computer, broken into 0s and 1s and put together in a binary code, its character is changed in quite precise way. Those bits of data can be recombined for easy manipulation and compressed for storage. Voluminous encyclopedias that take up yards of shelf space in analog form can fit onto a very small space on a computer device, and that same digital encyclopedia can be searched in many ways other than alphabetically, making possible information retrieval that would have been unmanageable if one had only the analog copy, on paper or microfilm. Digital information is not eye-legible: it is dependent on a machine to decode and represents the bit streams in images on a computer screen. Without that machine and without active human intervention, those data will not last.

FEATURES OF DIGITAL INFORMATION

One of the most important quality of information in digital form is that that by its nature it is not fixed in the way that texts printed on a paper are. Digital text are neither final nor finite, and are fixed neither in essence nor in form except when a hard copy is printed out, for they can be changed easily.

Some of the features of digital information are :

1. **Flexibility**: digital text is flexible. Flexibility is one of the chief assets of digital information and is precisely what we like about text poured into a word processing program.
2. It is easy to edit.
3. It is easy to reformat.
4. We can create endless number of identical copies from a digital file, because the file does not decay by virtue of copying.

What is Digitization?

Digitization is the process of converting any item; it being in printed format, manuscript, image, sound, film and video recording-from one format (print or analog) into digital. Basically it involves capturing an image of the physical object using various types of scanners and digital cameras and converting to digital format that can be stored electronically and accessed via computer.

Digitization is conversion of any fixed or analog media-such as books, journal articles, photos, paintings, and microfilms into electronic form either through scanning or networking. We can say digitization is the process of converting any item, it being in printed format, manuscript, image, sound, film and video recording -from one format (print or analogue) into digital

In simpler term digitization is the process of converting the information in the traditional library in to digital forms with the help of computer, network, software and other electronic components is known as digitization and the library which provide service digitally is identified as digital library. It can simply be defined as changing material in printed form into digital form by the process of scanning etc.

It can simply be defined as taking electronic snapshot or scanning of a document, such as photographs, manuscripts, etc. The digital image is sampled and mapped as a grid of dots or picture elements (pixels). Each pixel is assigned a total value (black, white, shades of gray or color), which is represented in binary code (bits, i.e. zeros or ones). The bits are then interpreted and read by the computer to produce an analog version of the original for display on computer screen or printing."

Digitization refers to the process of translating a piece of information such as a book, sound recording, picture or video into bits. Bits are the fundamental unit of information in computer systems. Turning information into these binary digits is called digitization. This digitization process can be carried through a variety of existing technologies.

Basically it involve the capturing an images of the

physical object using various types of scanners and digital cameras and converting to digital format that can be stored electronically and accessed via computer. "A strict definition might be the conversion of analog media to digital form (hence the fact that in many books "conversion" and "digitization" are synonyms). The original media or source material might be printed text or images. For most people digitization equates to digital imaging -that is to say, the creation of a still digital facsimile of a source item, such as a rare manuscript, photograph, slide, journal, painting, monographs etc.

Thus, digitization means acquiring, converting, storing and retrieving the information in standardized and organized manner, with the help of modern technical gadgets such as computers, scanners, etc.

Imaging of manuscripts, paintings and pictures is more than just an archival application of digitization.

Thus, we can conclude that digitization:

- Refers to various methods of keeping digital material alive into the future.
- Typically centers on the choice of interim storage media, the life expectancy of a digital image system, and the expectation to migrate the digital files to future system while maintaining both the full functionality and the integrity of the original digital system.
- Include everything from electronic publication on CD-ROM to online databases and collections of experimental data in the digital format.
- To maintain the ability to display, retrieve, and use digital collection in the face of rapidly changing technological and organizational infrastructures and elements.

DIGITIZATION AND DIGITAL LIBRARY

Library digitization is different from a digital library. Library digitization is the process of utilizing computers, databases, multimedia equipments, networks, video equipments and web technologies to electronically collect, classify, copy, compress, scan, store and transform conventional library information resources. Digital library focuses on the process of making diverse library information resources electronically available, while a digital library is a platform for accessing, collecting, managing, searching and storing distributed digital information resources over the internet and World Wide Web.

WHY WE NEED DIGITIZATION?

Library automation has helped libraries in improving library activities. It saves the efforts, time and manpower of libraries. In an automated system the information can be altered and updated without the respective work involved in the manual system. With the development of computer, any information can be turned into sequences. It saves the time for the users, staff and increases productivity, reliability and efficiency. With new advances in the technology, digitization has proven to be possible for nearly every title presently held by libraries.

Some of the reasons for digitization are:

1. Preservation of Documents : Most of the ancient manuscripts were written on bhurj patras. Ancient India was well developed in the subjects like, astronomy, mathematics, ayurveda, medicine, etc. Unfortunately many of these manuscripts were lost due to improper care. Some of them were destroyed due to water fungus, fire etc and other natural calamities. Book is one of the medium, which deals with comprehensive knowledge and information. Preserving the books and other rare material is a burning question, which the librarians of the past and present are facing. Therefore, it is urgently needed to find out some permanent solutions to preserve the library material in digital form. Pages of many old and rare documents are loosing out to the adversaries of time. These sources must be preserved in their original colors, texture, along with the text and graphics.

2. Easy Transmission of Documents : Digitization is an important precursor to a variety of applications and projects. Specifically, it increases the ease and efficiency of transmitting document. Images can be displayed on a computer screen; distributed to multiple destinations via e-mail; printed into any paper-based format; made available via a web portal or search database. Further, digitized files can be fully searched through character recognition.

3. Easy Handling of Rare Books : The handling and use of rare books, fragile books and non-book materials are not new problems to libraries. In recent years libraries are acquiring non-book materials and have been developing special collection at the accelerated rate. The rare and age-old collection of documents is deteriorating in many libraries because of excessive handling and exposure to non-archival conditions. Never the less, researchers and other users often seek access to the originals, or to reproduction of near original quality.

4. Easy Accessibility : Thus, in order to makes the library collection more accessible conversion of its rare collection into digital form is essential. It has become widely known, even to those outside the computer field, that digital imaging technology can provide worldwide access to documents by many users simultaneously, as well as completely faithful reproduction, regardless of the number of copies produced. If the library collection were digitized, it would be possible for both local and distant researchers to use digital image in lieu of the originals.

The collection covers rare books, maps, manuscripts, pamphlets, posters, newspapers, music, microfilms, archival material, slides and films, pictures, paintings, graphic materials, clipping files etc.

5. High Quality Reproduction : Digital technology has provided very high quality of reproduction of reality in terms of audio and video stimuli. It is also possible to have very compact storage capacity for a big volume of data and information. There is sudden change in the world of information because digital technology realizes quite high speed of communication and on-line access. The new technology is helping the library professionals to provide more accurate and better services to their users. Libraries are moving from experimental testing to planning large-scale preservation programmes using digital technology.

Before building of database, we have to see why digital database is required?

6. Growth of Literature : There is a tremendous growth of literature, which includes printed, text and media. The high growth of information demand for the new techniques in processing and distribution of information and to access and process this enormous sea of information and serve it to the seekers is the greatest challenge of the information managers. To store such sea of information physically is very time consuming, complicated and difficult task with the emergence of digital library, storage and retrieval has become easier, comprehensive and affordable.

SPECIAL FEATURES OF DIGITIZATION

1. Seamless access to voluminous information resources.
2. Support multimedia contents for accessibility of information.
3. Provide user-friendly interface to access the information.

4. Provide hypertext linkages to various databases.
5. Provide client server architecture.
6. Support advanced search and retrieval of information.
7. Linkages with other national and international digital library system through networks.

ADVANTAGES OF DIGITIZATION

A summary of advantages offered by digitization tends to come under the headings of increasing access, preservation and meeting strategic goals (i.e. raising the profile of the institution etc). The first, allowing increased access to the object is the most often cited benefit of digitization. An electronic facsimile of a page, for example, can be theoretically copied and distributed infinitely without any degradation in quality (if correct standards are maintained).Most importantly, a single copy can be mounted on a server) most commonly a web server), and this can be viewed and downloaded by a large numbers of users (possibly in the remote regions), simultaneously, and from any location in the world.

The clear advantage of such a system is that it liberates the document from the constrained of traditional access method. Take, for example, a digital image of a folio from a rare manuscript. Traditionally users may only be allowed access to the original item if they have an appropriate reader's card and a good and validated reason. Most importantly they would have to physically go to the manuscript itself, which may involve travel time, and/or money. However a digital facsimile of the folio was mounted on the web, for example, and made freely accessible, suddenly every one can look at the image from the comfort of his own home, office, or institution. This example also leads us to the second sited advantage of digitization, namely preservation.

Now let us look at what would happen if we did not digitize the item, and keep to the traditional ways of making this available to more than one person at a time. Here the only obvious alternative (outside of taking out secondary subscription, that is), would be to photocopy the article. The cost of the item is about 50 paisa per page. Now let us look at the two scenarios together. In, short it is clear that by the use of article on web we can save lot of money. By the use of article on web site, we can save money over traditional method of reproduction. By digitization method and delivery of it across network, it becomes cost effective.

The use of digitization can help in the preservation of original manuscripts and other such materials. It also has the potential to change the way scholars and activists utilize historical documents. Once document has been digitized, many benefits can be realized such as preservation of originals, through reduced handling; understanding; unlimited data life span; wide availability to the public; ease of access through digital libraries and on-line access; powerful searching and browsing possibilities; aid in research, education, and awareness programmes. The major boost to the development of the digital libraries comes from the web technologies that enable instantaneous online access to consortium. Digital libraries encompasses a whole range of information services related work such as organization of digital information, information retrieval, user interfaces, archiving and preservation, services and social issues and a set of standards for interoperability and value added services.

Today, access to most of such rare historical documents is quite difficult because of their wide spread distribution throughout the region. Many such collections are still not cataloged or replicated and simply remain unknown. This is primarily due to lack of interest, means, and knowledge. Often stored in poor conditions, these precious articles are prone to irreparable damage. Further, handling of original documents establishes risk of permanent loss, because no duplicates exist.

Digital technology has revolutionized the ability to create digital replicas of print materials, and institutions around the world and moving ahead with projects to digitize books, manuscripts, photographs, maps, architectural drawings, films, and sound recordings in their collections.

Though it is too early to comments on its advantages and disadvantages. However, one can visualize that by this conversion from paper to electronic document the old reports will be easily searchable and accessible by different persons at different places at the same time. It will enable resource sharing among different libraries and information centers all over the country. Databases can searched through LAN, WAN etc. It will save the intellectual resources of the institution, which have immense potential for further research and economic benefit for the country as a whole in addition to its archival value also. Finally there will be a better bibliographical control of each report. Documents stored electronically are very flexible. They are easy to revise, rearrange, format and combine with other documents. Throughout the process, data security has been ensured with utmost care for which some compromise had to be made with the speed of the work.

1. Preservation and conservation: Digitization is not a long-term preservation solution for physical collection, but does succeeded in providing access copies for materials that would otherwise fall to degradation from repeated use. Digitized collections and born digital objects pose many preservation and conservation concerns that analog materials do not. The use of digitization can help in the preservation of original manuscripts. It also has the potentials to change the way scholars and activists utilize historical documents.

2. Add value : Certain characteristics of objects, primarily the quality of images, may be improved.

Digitization can enhance legibility and remove visible flaws such as stains and discoloration.

Benefits of digitization are many. Some of them are summarized below:

1. The use of digitization can help in the preservation of original manuscripts. It also has the potential of change the way scholars and activists utilize historical and rare documents.
2. Once the document has been digitized, many benefits can be realized such as preservation of originals through reduced handling; unlimited data life span; wide availability of the public ease of access through digital libraries and online access; powerful search and browsing possibilities.
3. Today access to most of such rare documents is quite difficult because of their wide spread distribution through the region. Many such documents are still not cataloged or replicated and simply remain unknown. This is primarily due to lack of interest, means and knowledge. Often stored in poor conditions, these precious articles, documents are prone to irreparable damage. Further, handling of originals establishes risk of permanent loss, because of no duplicates exists.

Digitization is the only solution to this problem. Digital technology has revolutionized the ability to create electronic replicas of print materials such as maps, manuscripts, photographs, sound records films etc., and institutions around the world. Many libraries around the world have digitizing their collections.

DIGITIZATION VS ARCHIVING

The librarian and the archivist both collect, preserve, and made accessible materials for research; but significant differences exist in the way these materials are arranged , described, and used. Among the items usually collected by libraries are: published books and serials, and in more recent times commercially available sound recordings, films, videos, and electronic resources of various types.

Archives, on the other hand, tend to collect original records of an organization, unique personnel papers, as well as other effects of individuals and families. Each types of institution, given its, particular emphasis, has its own methods of dealing with its collection.

APPROCHES OF DIGITIZATION

There are several approaches available. These are as follows:

1. Retrospective conversion of collections: Essentially, starting at A and ending up a Z. However ideal such complete conversion would be, it is impractical or impossible technically, legally, and economically.

Retro conversion is the process of changing already existing catalog from traditional form to a machine readable form. Once the retro-conversion work is done, the database thus created becomes foundation for many innovative services and activities in information management and many other library house keeping activities.

1. Digitization of a particular special collection or a portion of one. A small collection of manageable size, and which is highly valued, is a prime candidate.
2. Highlight a diverse collection by digitizing particularly good example of some collection strength
3. High-use materials, making those materials that is in most demand more accessible.
4. Adhoc approach where one digitized and stores materials as they are requested. This is, however, a hazard method of digital collection building.

These approaches can be used alone or in combination depending upon a particular institution's goal for digitization.

12

Understanding Requirements for Digitization

INTRODUCTION

Building a digital library is expensive and resource intensive. Before embarking on such venture, it is important to consider some basic principles underlying the design, implementation, and maintenance of any digital library. When creating digital library systems containing valuable content, we are making important promises to both current and future use. Valuable contents should be handled with care and rendered in the highest quality possible and should not disappear. We need to understand how to preserve and safeguard digital material, so it doesn't become obsolete.

DEVELOPMENT OF DIGITAL LIBRARY

Some of the important points to be considered in developing digital library are:

1. Digital collection or material selection.
2. Conversion of existing print, audio and video into digital format.

3. Cataloging and Metadata creation.
4. Storing.
5. Creation portals or gateway to the electronic collection available on web.
6. Integrated access interface.

Digital collection

One of the important factors for the creation of digital library is the building up of digital collection. A digital library can have wide range of resources. It may be in conventional form or computer readable form. The digital resources are either deliberately created as digital or created in parallel to print. Numbers of publishers now a days providing CD-ROMs along with books. Future library resources are e-journals, e-books through databases and datasets in many formats. Now a days large numbers of information products are available on CD-ROMs. Libraries can subscribe to any of these database for providing bibliographic or fultext information forms an important input to the digital collection.

Access to external digital collection

Digital libraries can acquire permission to digital collections provided by external sources like other institutions, commercial publishers, recourses from other libraries and electronic journals through on-line access. Many of the commercial publishers like Academic Press, ACM etc are making their journals available on-line through websites. Many of the journals are available in print and as well as in electronic form.

REQUIREMENTS FOR DIGITIZATION

The following are the main technical requirement for digitization:

The technical requirements of the digital imaging

process (i.e. converting paper documents into digital image) to be made accessible over network includes:

The digitization process requires some of the basic components such as:

1. Basic requirements.
2. Hardware (Scanners, computers, Data storage and data output peripherals)
3. Software (image capturing, data compression).
4. Display Technologies
5. Network (Data Transmission)
6. Human ware

Information technology infrastructure and personnel comprise two critical resources required for digital library project. Actual requirements depend on nature of the digital library collection (one-off or live collection) and on factors such as volume of source material to be digitized, metadata requirements, document formats to be supported, search and retrieval expectations, and quality requirements.

Three important requirements are:

1. Hardware requirements : Hardware requirements include server computer for hosting the collection, desktop computers, digitization equipments, network connectivity, and other equipments such as scanners, digital cameras etc.

2. Software Requirements : Digital library software is another critical technology component. That includes: open source free digital library software, library automation software, commercial digital library software, and in-house software development. Each one has its advantage and disadvantages.

3. Manpower Requirements : An other component for digitization is personnel. Personnel comprise the most important resource for digital library apart from requirement of hardware and software components. Actual personnel required for a digital library project depends on the type and volume of the task carried out.

PLANNING STAGE OF DIGITIZATION

The digitization firstly requires the procurement of given number of reading material. The type of books varies in variety of ways such as, size of book, quality of paper, clarity of print, font face used, type of binding etc. Old and rare books which are very delicate and have deteriorated over time need extra care in handling apart from requiring special routine procedures to process them.

It is to be decided whether the project of digitization to be accomplished in-house or through vendors. There are arguments, both in favour and against either working in-house or outsourcing.

In-house digitization requires tremendous inputs in terms of infrastructure, expertise, funds etc. One will have to invest on organizational cost, equipments such as digital cameras, scanners, desktops, storage disks, staff training, softwares. All these will be obsolete by the time the project is over. Further, a digital converted version of a document must be fully functional. If what is digitized is unreadable or poorly indexed, then end users can not find what they need, or read it when they do find it. In such a case, there is a failure to provide both preservation and access, which otherwise requires a particular set of skill to accomplish.

In order to make digitization project a success, it is essential that the institution has a clear understanding of its goals. This will guide decision making about work standards and whether the work should be accomplished in-house or outsourced. The difference lies in the extent of immediate control needed over the work, range of activities that can be performed, efficiency, economics etc. Relatively few digitization vendors work with libraries and archives. Most work routinely for organization that want quick and cheap solutions, knowing little about quality control standards in preservation. Luckily, the situation is improving and enterprises with relevant experience are emerging on the scene. Even if an institution decides to do it alone, it is advisable to get some assistance from professional organization or vendor to do. The aim of the pilot programme is to assist the management in establishing requirements and ascertaining efforts involved in terms of time, human and financial resources. This would help establish feasibility of the programme and thus assist in deciding on the future course. The institution that holds the material to be digitized must own the responsibility for; selecting material to be converted; determine the purpose of digitization; verifying the quality of work.

To build useful collections of digital library resources, the objects must be cataloged so that they are easily accessible. Creation of these digital repositories demands the expertise and collaboration of computer and library professionals. Libraries, especially college and university libraries do not have digitization equipments and budget. There is no trained staff. In theory at least, vendors can be trusted to have at least equipments and fully trained staff. They also have a fair idea of what services can be offered and what it costs to provide them. But there is a problem in this system. If any vendor is willing to bring in equipments to carry out digitization on site, then that will offer some of the benefits of in-house work, e.g. original materials need not travel , closer oversight of the work.

A well-trained flexible staff, some sort of training manual and a clear workflow plan with timelines and built in goals are the best tools to help managers accomplish their tasks. These workflow plans may also demonstrate where it might be more economical to outsource portion of a project.

1. Various units related to the work of digitization should be closer to the library.

2. The storage and transfer of data frequently required. Since network transfer of such large quantity is neither feasible nor economical, it has to be physically moved in HDDs or DVDs.
3. Duplications must be checked before digitization. It may leads to wastage of time and resources.
4. Digital libraries are also meant of preservation of contents for the use of future generation. Hence maintenance of good quality in the digitization process is utmost important.
5. The objects must be catalogued so that they are easily accessible.
6. Creation of these digital resources requires expertise and trained library professionals.

The entire process of digitization consists of various stages such as procuring, scanning, image processing, quality checking and web hosting.

BASIC REQUIREMENTS FOR DIGITIZATION

The digital projects involve the following factors:

1. The intellectual and physical nature of the source material
2. The number and location of current and potential users.
3. The current and potential nature of use.
4. The format and nature of the proposed digital product and how it will be described, delivered, and archived.
5. How the proposed product relates to other digitization efforts.
6. Projection of costs in relation to benefits.

Technical architecture that required accommodating digital material that includes components such as:

- High-speed local networks and fast connection to the

Internet.

- Relational databases that supports a variety of digital formats
- Fultext search engines to index and provide access to resources.
- A variety of servers, such as Web servers and FTP servers.
- Electronic document management functions that will aid in the overall management of digital resources.

The resources supported by the architecture could include:

a. Bibliographical databases that point to both papers and digital materials
b. Indexes and finding tools
c. Collection of printers to internet resources
d. Directories
e. Photographs
f. Numerical data sets
g. Electronic journals

Within a co-ordinate digital library scheme, some common standard will be needed to allow digital libraries to interpret and share resources. The problem, however, is that across multiple digital libraries, there is a wide diversity of different data structure, search engines, interfaces, controlled vocabularies, document formats, and so on. Because of this diversity, federating all digital libraries nationally or internationally would an impossible effort.

1. Storage media: storage media is having diverse formats such as text, data, graphics, video and sound, different storage media like floppy disk, CD-ROM, DVD-ROM, etc. with different strength such as 2 years, 5 years, 10 years etc.

2. User's expectations: user's expectations is always changing, yet users, especially research scholars need both traditional documents and digital documents or old information and current information.

3. Institution's responsibility: Libraries, archives and other custodians have responsibility of conservation for their any properties. So institutes planned for digital materials including their maintenance, preservation and distribution.

4. Missions of parent Institution: First objective of libraries, archives and other custodians is to satisfy the user's expectation and user's requirements. They should preserve all materials in all formats.

It is to be noted that digital storage is not for only print documents, it is also a requirement for oral, cultural and those information are out of print.

But before going into the details of the above, we have to see the certain points in mind.

Digitization requires certain technologies. These include storage technologies variety of devices to store and retrieve information in digital form such as magnetic tape, floppies, hard disk, CD-ROM, processing technology creating the system and applications software that is required for the performance of digital network; communication technologies primarily to communicate information in digital form; display technologies; varieties of output devices.

Quality control procedures

The procedure involves taking pictures at highest resolution, keeping in view all the factors affecting the color, texture and other attributes of the source document to ensure the closest image representation of the original. Lighting conditions and equipments used are other important factors.

Quality and size of the original images can be varied, depending on the need and medium of reproduction. TIFF used for high quality to enable printability and IPEG format with varied degree of compression for on screen viewing, without loss of visible feature or texture of the original through human eyes. Even PDF format is beneficial and in some cases desirable.

Having good knowledge of originals

Having a good knowledge of contents of the collections that are intended to be digitized will make it much easier to decide on processes and techniques for converting the originals to digital form.

The conversion depends upon many factors.

Some of them are:

1. The format of the original: is it printed text, photographic material, video, audio etc.?
2. The condition of the original: will it stand up to automate procedures (if used), will conversion be required before scanning?
3. The size of the original.
4. The color contents of the original and whether that color is important.

The following issues to be considered for paper and photographic originals:

Photographic media such as transparencies print and negatives.

What size are the originals? Are they all the same size?

Groupings of the same items

It makes for a smoother workflow if items of a similar size are grouped together.

What proportion of the items has color contents? Is it important to capture the color?

Condition of the negative

What condition are they in, for example, are they dirty from heavy use?

1. If they are dirty a better scan will be achieved if the items can be cleaned first.
2. **Format:** What format are they in?
    1. Slides in sleeves or strips will take longer to prepare for scanning and may cost more if a bureau is scanning them.
    2. Glass negatives are prone to breakage and require careful handling.

Condition of the photograph

1. Are the photographs flat or have they bowed?
2. Bowed originals cause difficulties with focus and may need weighting down.
3. **Quality of original:** What is the quality of original?
4. A bad original (i.e. out of focus) will not be improved by scanning.

PAPER MEDIA

What size are the pages are all items the same size?

What general condition is the material in?

Pristine pages will produce a better result and the scanning process may be able to automate. Any damage in an original may be exacerbated by the scanning procedure.

1. Can books that are bound be stripped to loose pages for scanning?
2. Scanning from bound volumes is more complex and therefore expansive than from loose pages.
3. Is there any artwork? Is it black and white or color photographs or line art?
4. Color scanning is generally more complex and resource intensive.

5. Is it text size particularly small or large?
6. Very small text may need a higher resolution to extract the information.

Objects require a different approach. Artifacts, art works and sculptures cannot generally be successfully scanned using the techniques available for 'flat' media such as photographs. It will therefore be necessary to use photography, either traditional or digital, to get an image of the original.

CALCULATION OF SPACE REQUIRED FOR DIGITAL IMMAGE

Resolution is usually expressed in dots per inch (dpi) and relates to the density of information that is captured by the scanning equipment. Broadly speaking, the higher the dpi the more detail is being captured. The amount of resolution required to get a useful image of an item is determined by the size of the original, the amount of detail in the original and the eventual use for the data. For example, a 35 mm transparency will require a higher dpi than 5x4 prints because it is smaller and more detailed. An A4 sized modern printed document that is intended to be processed into a searchable text will need less resolution than a similar size photographic original.

Bit-depth relates to the level of color that will be captured. A 'bit' is the binary digital that represents the tonal value of the pixel. As an overview, a 1-bit image is black and white (the pixel has 1 bit and is therefore black or white with no shade in between), an 8-bit image has 256 shades of either gray or color (2 8 =256 shades), and a 24- bit image has millions of shades of color (2 24=16,777,216).

Digitization offers a compact alternative to paper media. It occupies a considerable amount of computer storage space. To store one page of information scanning requires more disk space as compared to character-coded text. The storage requirement in electronic document images depends on several factors such as:

- The linear dimensions of document
- The scanning resolution.
- Digitization mode employed
- Compression algorithm used to use the amount of information.

The following formula calculates the number of bytes required to store a single page of given size digitized at a specified scanning resolution:

$$S = \frac{(H \times R \times B) \times (W \times R \times B)}{8} \times \frac{1}{C}$$

S = the storage requirement per page in bytes

H = the height of a typical subject document in inches or millimeters.

W = the width of a typical subject document in inches or millimeters

R = the scanning resolution in pixels per inch or millimeter, along the documents horizontal and vertical dimensions.

B = the number of bits utilized to encode each pixel and

C = an image compression factor.

The calculation (H × R × B) × (W × R × B) yields the uncompressed page storage equipment in bits. The value of B is determined by the digitization of mode. With binary mode digitization of black and white documents, the most common scenario in electronic document imaging implementation, the value of B is one. Other possible values are eight for gray scale scanning of photographs, and 24 for color mode scanning. The most common resolutions are 200 and 300 pixel per inch, but lower or higher value are possible.

The higher resolution image requires 2.25 times more storage space.

Storage requirements are similarly affected by page size. Larger documents require additional pixels coding and occupy more storage space at all scanning resolutions.

Applying the above formula for a letter size page (11 × 8.5), we can calculate how much space will required scanning at 200 pixels per horizontal and vertical inch. In this example the value of;

$$H = 11$$

$$W = 8.5$$

$$R = 200$$

$$B = 1$$

$$S = (11 \times 200 \times 1) \times (8.5 \times 200 \times 1)$$

We get the value of S as 3.74 million bits per page in uncompressed mode. When it is divided by height we get 467,500 bytes. In this example, the uncompressed page storage requirement is 467,500 bytes. The amount is then multiplied by the reciprocal of the compression factor that is a fraction with the anticipated compression as the denominator and the value one as the numerator

$467{,}500 \times 1/10 = 46{,}750$ bytes.

The image compression methodology employed by electronic document imaging systems are based on standard algorithm. The two widely encountered examples are the CCITT Group 111 and CCITT Group IV algorithm developed for facsimile transmission by the consultative committee on International Telephony .It yields a typical compression of 10: 1 for the official documents and 15:1 for engineering drawings.

Librarian can play a very crucial role in giving priority for conversion into digitized form. They can help to form the strategies while selecting the material from the huge ocean of literature. When digitizing the material librarian should consider old and rare material, which needs more attention. They should also see whether the material is safe and successfully digitized and copyright permissions are obtained. The decisions to undertake the digital image capturing work in-house or by the vendor has to be made. The process of digitization also depends upon the value and condition of the source material as well as scanning equipments. Digitization work also requires IT specialists, specialist librarian having good knowledge of subjects, reprographic and scanning technicians.

13
Hardware Components Required for Digitization

Hardware components include the necessary equipments required for digitization such as computers, networking and other equipment requirements.

Tools (Hardware) needed for Digitization include:

1. COMPUTERS

1. Clients are the machines that reside on the user's desk.
2. The server for the digital library is piece of hardware where the library has control.

Server with high capacity hard disc and clients in the LAN, Web Servers and FTP server etc. Desktop computers are required for staff handling various tasks related to digitization project. Some of the tasks such as scanning, editing conversion, quality checking etc.

Desktop computers are also required for users for searching web. Staff also administer and maintain the digital library server and website.

A computer consists of two components:

1. Clients and

2. Server.

Server Computer

The server computer holds the digital library collection, run the digital library software which provides the searching and processing applications. The server also handles the communication with the user over the network. The server needs to be reasonably powerful (typically measured in terms of processor speed, for example mega or giga hertz), has adequate main memory (RAM), has large amount of hard disk storage and has good communication capability (network card and bandwidth).Option includes specialized servers or server class PCs .Ensure that the server is expandable (RAM, storage, CPU)particularly if your digital library collection size and its usage is expected to grow rapidly. Options for server Operating System include Windows 2000, UNIX and LINUX. This is mainly determined by the digital library software we plan to use. License cost may be involved if it is proprietary operating system. Plan for online and offline storage backup for the digital library collection and procedures for taking regular backups. You should also have a contingency plan if the server computer fails-for example by moving your collection to an other server. This requires that you have the required digital library application programmes supported on this server. An other option is to host the collection on one or more mirror servers located at different geographical locations.

Networking and location of the digital library server computer

Internet connectivity either through Dial-up connectivity, or V-SAT, or through lease line or through modem requires accessing the digital collection.

There are several options for providing online access to the digital library collection via the internet. If your organization already has the requisite network infrastructure (internet and internet connectivity) than you can take help from your network administrator to connect and configure your digital library collection server to be accessible over the internet. If the digital collection is small and does not require a dedicated server, than you host it on your library web server, if one exists, or on the institution web server, if this is permitted. If there is no network infrastructure in your organization and if you have the required resources, then you can obtain dedicated Internet connection to an ISP (Internet Service Provider)-but this could be expensive as this would require additional equipments like router, and DNS and Proxy servers. Maintaining this infrastructure will require more resources. An other option is to locate the digital library server computer in a data center or ISP, on payment of rental fee. You can also hire storage space on a server computer. Several issues however needed to be considered. Content updating may not be easy .Maintenance and trouble shooting the server or the collection may also be difficult. If you are hiring computer storage to host the collection, ISP may not provide the support for the digital library software you need.

2. CAPTURE DEVICES

Capture devices such as scanners, cameras, and flat-bed scanners.

These are digitization equipments needed for converting source material in physical/analog format to digital format .Digitization equipments includes scanners for scanning print publications, video and audio capture cards for capture/conversions of digital video and audio files, and digital cameras for capture/production of videos clips/still images. Requirement will be minimal if capture and conversion is largely outsourced.

3. SCANNING EQUIPMENTS

Digitization equipments can be separated “contact” and ‘non contact’s. Contact equipments, i.e. flatted scanner, require that the original be flat against the scan bed to get a scanned image. This approach will only work if your original is flat or can be pressed flat without damage to it.

Non contact equipment includes overhead scanner or book scanners and digital cameras that are able to obtain a digital image with the bare minimum of contact with the original.

Choosing the equipment for scanning your original will depends upon the characteristics of the collection : in general term, photographic materials are usually scanned on a flatted or a transparency scanner while bound volumes and oversized flat material such as maps and plans require a digital camera or an overhead scanner.

If you have a mixed media collection then it may not be possible to use one scanner for everything. A flatbed that is ideal for high speed, high volume paper scanning may not be capable of the resolution required for high quality scans of transparencies.

A digital camera studio set-up will be overkill for loose leaf paper scanning and for most general photographic materials.

Generally make sure that your requirement match the capability of the scanners that you buy. Look carefully the resolution that the scanner is capable of, the scanner will often be listed with a maximum optical resolution and an interpolated or software resolution. The optical resolution is the figure to look for -interpolated resolution uses software to 'guess' the values of pixels that are between those that the scanner can optically register. Interpolation should be avoided in an archive -quality-scanning exercise. Where resolution is listed as, for example, 600x1200 dpi the maximum optical resolution will be 600.

The dynamic range of the scanner is important. It describes the tonal density of the information that the scanner will be able to capture and generally speaking the higher this is the better , particularly for dense originals such as photographic prints and transparencies.

A good flatted scanner is often the keystone to a scanning unit. They range in price from few thousands to lacs. If this equipment is the key to the success of your project then investing in a good flatbed is essential.

Production level flatbed scanners usually have either an A4 or A3 sized scanning area. Larger one are available but are specialist equipment and therefore rather expensive. In order to choose a flatbed you need to know what size your originals are, whether they are reflective (i.e. light is bounced off them to capture the image , as in photographic print) or tran missive (light is passed through the original to capture the image , as in transparencies), the resolution and bit depth you will be capturing and the volume of the work.

Transparencies can be scanned on a flatbed if it is capable of sufficient resolution and has a transparency adaptor fitted that will shine light through the transparency into the scanning head. Scanning on mounted strips or single frame transparencies on a flatbed is difficult and time consuming because they have to be either placed in holders or taped to the scan bed to stop them moving in the heat of the light-using a transparency scanner can alleviate some of this effort and would be good investment if 35 mm is a considerable part of the collection.

SCANNERS

A good-flatted scanner is often the keystone to a scanning unit. Good scanners are required with at least 2400 dpi and high reliability and speed.

Some of the important scanners being used for capturing digital image are:

i. Minolta PS7000

ii. HP Scanjet 6300C
iii. Bell a Howell 1000 FB
iii. Kodak 500S
iv. Digital camara- Zentschel omini Scan 3000 Minolta PS 3000
v. Slide Scanner-Kodak PCD Scanner 4045
vi. Microfilm Scanner-Mekel M 500 XL sunrise SRI-150

Types of Scanners

Couples of years back, the scanners used to be expensive and the image quality was poor. Now the scanners today are based on high image quality and are less costly. There are now different types of scanners which vary according to the needs of its users.

Scanners are of various Types;

1. Flatbed Scanner
2. Slide scanner
3. Microfilm Scanner
4. Drum Scanner
5. Sheet fed Scanner
6. Digital Camera

1. Flatbed Scanner: It is the popular scanner used in libraries and archives. It is made up of a glass pane, which is illuminated with a bright light found underneath, and a moving optical CCD or CIS array. In the flatted scanner images to be scanned are placed faced down on the glass and the sensor and light source move across the glass pane reading the entire area. These are suitable for scanning papers, photographs and other printed material (Fig. 6).

Examples are: HP Scan jet 6300 C, Xerox Doc CS 620.

2. Slide Scanner: To scan transparent material that is smaller than 4x5, than slide scanner would be helpful. There are some slide scanners that can handle larger transparent format. Generally slide scanners can scan 35mm transparent source material.

Fig. 6. Flatbed Scanner

Examples are: Nikon LS 3510, Kodak PcD Scanner 4045.

Microfilm Scanner: These scanners are more useful in libraries and archives. These have adapters to convert roll film, fiche, and aperture card in small model.

Examples are: Makel M 500 XL

3. Drum Scanner: In a drum scanner, source material is wrapped on a drum, which is then rotated past a high-intensity light source to capture the image. Drum scanners are designed for the graphic arts community and, provide an extremely high level of resolution. They can scan transparent as well as reflective media, in gray scale or color. Since they cause great deal of stress to the document, they are not used for fragile and brittle formats.

Examples are: Juno CP -4000, Scan Graphics Scan Mate

5000.

4. Sheet Fed Scanners: In this type of scanner, as is indicated in the name, document is fed over a stationary CCD and light source via roller, belt, drum or vacuum transport.

Example: Kodak 500S.

5. Digital Cameras: Now a days number of digital cameras are pouring into the market. These are the most promising scanner development for libraries and archives. High-end digital cameras have no scanning limitations when it comes to size and shape, and can scan at a extremely high resolution. Overhead digital cameras provide great potential for scanning oversize materials, media in all formats, bound materials with the aid of a copy cradle and present lower risk to fragile materials by allowing face-up, contact free scanning (Fig. 7).

Fig. 7. Digital Camera as Scanner

Example: Zeutschel Ominiscan 3000, Minolta PS 3000

Digital cameras are developing for both the home and professional market and are priced from several thousands to lacs. Home use cameras are aimed at non-professional users for taking general casual photography.

There are two kinds of professional digital cameras. The first has developed from medical and industrial uses and is a complete unit. The second is where the film from traditional cameras is replaced with computer sensors which transmit the image to a computer rather than to film; this is known as digital scanning backs .The first type has been around for longer and has been used in imaging projects for several years. Digital scanning backs are developing for professional photographers as a replacement for traditional film cameras, although they are also being used in project work.

One of the advantages of the scanning back is that they used the lenses and camera body of a traditional professional camera.

Professional digital camera set ups will generally require the operator to understand the basics of photography and this is a cost that projects need to consider.

Printers

Halftonning/Non-halftonning: A subtracted mixture of inks or dyes produces printed color copy. In most cases, three colors , cyan, magenta, and yellow, are employed. However, all possible combinations of these three provide only a choice of eight colors. Printing devices able to render shades of color (or gray tones) may be categorized into those, which perform halftone, and those, which do not.

Non-halftone printers are able to control the density of ink through a modulation of the physical process of transfer of the ink to the paper, such as by controlling the temperature of a heating element applied to the due during a dye-substitution process.

Thus, for every printed pixel, non-halftone printers can renders a range of colors or gray tones.

Halftone a process of changing the density of ink placed upon a page based upon a very fine screen with variable hole size or density. In digital half toning, the intensity of ink placed on the page is determined by the density of (tiny) printed dots-each printable dot is either present or not; gradation of ton for a single dot can not be generated. Using the printing of magenta as an example, if the highest dot frequency for the digital halftone screen was 1,200 dots per inch, a fully saturated magenta would be created if every dot was filled; where as a lighter magenta would result from 50% of the dots being rendered.

Other Equipments Required

Some of the other equipments are also required such as CD-writer, label printing system, laser printers, CD-ROM backup system, UPS support, etc.

Other equipments needed are:

1. Scanning software like OCR, data compression devices. Storage devices for backup etc such as CD-ROM disk (R- and RW), DVD.
2. High speed LAN, WAN.
3. Storage system
4. Network
5. Display system
6. Printers: laser, ink jet, (latest models)
7. Uninterrupted power supply (UPS)(high power, 10-20 KV)
8. CD writer and other accessories.
9. LAN cards and other accessories.

Storage System

Survival of any record depended primarily on the physical longevity of its material. None of the today's digital media can be guaranteed to last long. Some, such as magnetic tape, have a frighteningly short life span. Others such as compact discs are more stable, but no one will predict their ultimate life. Unless someone pays attention, all digital information may be lost within a few decades.

Various kinds of technologies available for digitization

1. Digital imaging technology: Numerous and varied high resolution, fast full color scanners are becoming increasingly available at low cost, while high resolution computer monitors has become common place on desktops. The power of low end computer processors and the capacities of local magnetic storage now allow the manipulation of tens or hundred of megabytes of data in local storage. Compact Disk, Read Only Memories (CD-ROMs) and the never record able compact disk make the distribution and storage of hundreds of megabytes very convenient, while most "multimedia" computer systems are now sold with CD-ROM drives. For most organizations, the speed of access to Local Area Networks (LANs) and to the Internet have been increasing and the adoption of digital image compression standards by software manufacturers has eased the burden for the transmission of large images. Recently, the internet's World Wide Web, with its ease to use graphical interfaces displaying formatted hyper text and "click able" images and its simplified file transfer procedure, has become familiar territory to many less experienced computer users.

2. CCD Sensor Technology: Most scanners and digital cameras (except for some very high resolution devices) use charge coupled (CCD) image sensors. CCDs are solid state, silicon based devices and are available in either linier or area array configuration. Linear array CCDs sensors are able to sense a line of pixels during a single exposure and, therefore, can be used to capture a full two dimensional document image only through motion of either the document or the sensor along the direction perpendicular to the line of pixels.

Area arrays are able to capture a two dimensional image with a single exposure, but are much more expensive to manufacture, especially in the larger array sizes. CCDs are almost ideal image sensors. In their response to light intensity CCDs are inherently very linear over a large dynamic range and their solid state design makes them geometrically precise and dimensionally stable (Fig. 8).

Fig. 8. A specially developed CCD

3. The Tag Image File Format (TIFF): This format is probably the most widely supported image format. TIFF is now copyrighted by Adobe Systems Inc. of Mountain view, California and the current revised is 6.0. TIFF was developed to provide hardware and operating system independent means of exchanging raster image data between application programmes and scanning devices. TIFF is a very capable and expendable standard and can accommodate bitonal, gray scale, indexed (palette) -color, and full color images. It supports many color spaces, compression types, a wide range of image data storage format, including 1to 64 bit signed or unsigned integer and 32or 64 bit floating point. Because TIFF is a powerful and flexible standard, it's easy to develop software for writing TIFF files, but very hard to develop a universal TIFF reader.

4. Graphics Interchange Format (GIF) : The graphic Interchange Format is a de facto standard for 2D raster data, either monochrome or color table (indexed or palette color) of unto 256 entries. GIF is well suited for computer generated images, in which the pixel runs (sequential pixels of unchanging color) are long and, therefore, the compassion ratio is high. Because of its limited color range and run length based compression, it is much less suited color range and run length based compression, it is much less suited for the storage or transmission of natural scene or illustration images.

5. JPEG, JFIF, AND JTIFF: JPEG is actually a suit of (official) standards developed by the Joint Photographic Group hence its name for full color and continuous tone raster images. JPEG (ISO 109180 is not a file format, but rather an encoding format for compressed raster images.

14

Software Components Required for Digitization

INTRODUCTION

This is probably the most important and central aspect of the technology infrastructure for the digital library. Digital library software works with the web server (and the operation system) is providing various digital library functionality including creation, organization and maintenance, indexing, search and retrieval.

Several software options are available today for creation and provision of access to digital library collections. A clear understanding of the requirements and the features of the collection you plan to build are very important to access and select the option that best suits to our need. A good understanding of features expected of digital library software will also help you in making informed decision.

FEATURES OF DIGITAL LIBRARY SOFTWARE

A number of softwares are necessary at different steps in the process of digitization.

There are two types of softwares that would be needed for most digital imaging. Digital imaging is the process of converting paper documents including text, graphics or picture into digital image. Digital library software works with the web server (and operating system) in providing various digital library functions such as creation, organization and maintenance, indexing, search and retrieval.

Various types of softawares are available today for digitization of library collection. A good understanding of features expected of digital library software will also help you in making decision. Some of these are available free of cost. Some of them can be developed in house. Some of the softwares are also available commercially in the market.

The digital library software should have following features:

1. Support for different document types and formats.
2. Metadata support.
3. Online content updating.
4. Indexing and storage.
5. Search and retrieval (Metadata, full-text).
6. Multilingual support.
7. Access and usage management.
8. Interoperability support.
9. Collection administration.
10. Supports for standards compliance like Dublin Core.
11. Unicode and XML.

SOFTWARES

Numbers of softwares are needed for digitization.

Some of them are:

1. Server Class Operating System such as LINUX
2. RDMS
3. Web server
4. Desk Top Operating System.

5. Optical Character Recognition (OCR) software.
6. PDF converter.
7. Scanning Software.
8. Firewall and Protection Software
9. Library software for cataloging and searching digital resources.
10. Abode Acrobat Reader.
11. CD-Read /Write software.
12. Greenstone Digital Library Software for full text indexing and searching
13. Windows-NT Networking Software SQL Server Software, Data Base Management Software.
14. Web designing software like Java, Front page, XML etc.
15. RDMS (relational database) supporting the variety of Digital databases like ORACLE, My SQL etc.
16. E-print
17. CDS/ISIS for Windows
18. Fedora

Full text Search engines to index and provide access to digital resources.

Greenstone Digital Library Software for full text indexing and searching.

Some of the softwares are:

1. Scanner Software

Software that run the scanner is also very important. It should be straightforward to use and an ability to run batch scans will save time as the scan bed can be loaded with originals and more or less left to get on with it.

Scanning software that comes with the scanner. Color management software is essential to ensure that the digital representation is as accurate as possible. This can often be purchased with the scanner.

Using software called document-imaging system does the process of converting a document into computer-possible digital image. This software is usually limited in its functionality. Scanning software would be capable of saving file into standard formats such as TIFF, JPEG, etc.

IMMAGE SCANNING SOFTWARES

Some of the image scanning softwares are:

Normally applied to the image after it has been scanned.

To produce images of acceptable quality and to clean up and enhance the images, image-editing software is necessary. The choice of image editing software is based on the level of image manipulation. Some softwares are very basic and some are very advanced.

Example: Adobe Photoshop, Corel Photo-Paint.

Adobe PhotoShop: It runs on Macintosh, Windows, and UNIX. Very high functionality, suited to create and manipulate images. Typical image enhancement features available in this software are filters. Plug-inns, color management, crop, skew, other transformation image sharpening contrast, transparent background etc.

Corel Photo-Paint : Photo-editing applications like Corel Photo-Paintwork with bitmap images. It is possible to make drastic changes. Refine small details and intensify effects, when working with bitmaps. It is suitable to create and manipulate the images, easy to use interface, and usual high-end editing tools. It is possible to open vector based CorelDraw Files, which have been saved as CPT file formats, as it automatically creates bitmapped version of the original.

Some of the image scanning softwares are:

1. Optical Character Recognition (OCR) software.
2. Quick Scan

3. OPTIX
4. File Net
5. Fine Reader
6. Altris Software
7. Documentum
8. Jawa System
9. Power Office
10. ABBYY

Optical Character Recognition (OCR):

Once the text has been scanned it need to be run through the OCR program to convert it to machine readable encoded form. It allows to scan printed, typewritten or hand written text(numeral, letters or symbols) and/or convert scanned image to a computer readable format, either in the form of a plain text or a word document or an excel spread sheet, which can be used or reused in other documents.

FREE DIGITAL LIBRARY SOFTWARES OR OPEN SOURCE SOFTWARES (OSS)

What is Open Source Software?

OSS are computer programmes in which the source code is made available to the general public for use and/ or modification from its original design free of charge, open.

These softwares are available free of cost. Users can modify according to their needs. It also includes the right of distribution; therefore, there, they may be products that are based on other open source products. The software may be free, a developer or distributor may charge for services including special programming, installation, training and technical support etc. In general , the source code of OSS is widely accessible, freely available and reusable The most popular source license, the General Public Licenses (GPL), allow almost full use and reuse of source code.

There are numbers of Open Source Softwares (OSS) available such as Green Stone, Linux, XML etc. They are not only cost effective but also capable of handling DL challenges like content/metadata management; information dissemination etc .Extensibility is achieved from plug- Ins that are available under GNU public license. For instance, the excellent utilities and applications provided by the Linux such as Apache, Samba, MySQL, PHP, Open Office etc. greatly help in digitization, electronic resource management, web publishing and other activities of digital library with almost free of cost.

Several free digital library softwares packages are now available, enabling easy creation and sharing of information through digital library collections.

Some of the software packages are:

1. Greenstone Digital Library Software: From the New Zealand Digital Library. It is an Open Source Software, issued under the terms of the GNU General Public License.

It is software for creating, building, managing and distributing digital library collections. It provides a new way of organizing information and publishing it on the internet. Means to easily create searchable and browsable interfaces to digital library collections via the web etc. If the sets of files are well structured, then the software will create things like A-Z list of resources and field searchable interfaces. It builds collection with effective full text searching and metadata based browsing facilities that are attractive and easy to use.

Project provides a new way in organizing information and publishing it over the internet. It is available for both Windows and LINUX operating system. It requires PERL software to build collection. The aim of the software is to empower users, particularly in universities, libraries and other public service institutions to build their own digital libraries.

http://www.greenstone.org/

2. **ARNO** : Academic Research in the Netherlands Online, Tilburg University, The Netherlands *http://www.uba.uva.nl/arno*

3. **CDSWare** : CERN Document Server Software (CDSWare), CERN, Geneva, Switzerland *http://www.cdsware.cern.ch/*

4. **D Space**: MIT libraries, Cambridge, MA USA *http://www.dspace.org*

5. **Eprints**: is generic archive software by University of Southampton, U.K. The primary goal of this software is to set up an open archive for research papers, but it could be easily used for other applications such as images, research data, audio archives etc. It works on LINUX operating system and needs MySQL, Perl modules and Apache web server. *http://www.software.eprints.org*

6. Fedora Digital Object Repository Management System,University of Virginia, USA *http://www.fedora.info/*

7. **I-Tor** : Tools and Technologies for Open Repositories

8. Netherlands Institute for Scientific Information Services *http://www.i-tor.org/en/toon*

9. **MyCoRe** : Essen University Library, University of Duisburg-Essen, Germany *http://www.mycore.de/eng/index.html*

10. **ROADS** : This software is a programme intended to aid in the setting up and day to day running of WWW based catalogs of online resources. It works on UNIX operating system with HTTP Apache web server and Pearl language.

11. **SITESEARCH** : OCLC SITESEARCH software provides solution managing distributed library and information resources in a WWW environment. It works on both Widows NT and UNIX operating system.

All of these are available for Linux operating system

platform, a freely available popular operating system. Specific features offered by these packages vary, but since they were all developed to meet the specific requirement of establishing and provision of access to digital collection, you should considered them seriously for setting up your digital library collection.

IN-HOUSE SOFTWARE DEVELOPMENT

If you have in-house software development and maintenance support, another possibility is to develop the software in-house. Simple, database-driven web application can be developed to setup and provide access to your library collection. Open source database (e.g. MySQL and Post Gress) and programming tools (e.g. Perl, PHP, Python and Java) available for Linux operating system platform can be used for developing the digital library application. Advantage of the approach is customization of the application to suit your requirement. Disadvantage is the cost of development, as software projects are known to over run schedules. Maintenance may also be difficult if you do not have dedicated software team.

COMMERTIAL DIGITAL LIBRARY SOFTWARES

If you have sufficient funds, you have option of selecting several commercial digital library software that is available today. Some of them are;

1. ENCompass of Endeaver Information System.

   http://www.endinfosys.com/

2. DigiTool of ExLibris

   http://www.exlibris.co.il/, or *http://www.exlibris-usa.com/*

3. Visual MIS(Multimedia and Imaging Solutions) of VTLS

   HTTP://WWW.VTLS.COM/

4. TEMS of Artesia Technologies

http://www.artesia.com/

5. MuseSearch of Museglobal, Inc.

   http://www.museglobal.com/

1. DEVELOPING DIGITAL COLLECTION USING GREENSTONE DIGITAL LIBRARY SOFTWARE

Digital collection can be developed by using Open Source Software GSDL (Green Stone Digital Library). Digital collection page have the collection of audio, newsclippings, e-books, photo galleries, e-journals, question bank and video. Greenstone digital library software is a comprehensive open source system for constructing, presenting and maintaining information collection. It supports both Linux and Windows base operating systems. So the libraries can take the advantages of open source systems for their digital library activities.

The Greenstone digital library software is an open-source system for the construction and presentation of information collections. The aim of Greenstone software is to help the users, especially in universities and other public service institutions, to build their own digital libraries. It provides a new way of organizing information and publishing it on the internet or CD-ROM. It is very useful for the development of digital libraries and help to share the information and place it in the public domain. Greenstone also has interfaces in many other languages.

Making information available using this system is far more than "just putting it on the web". The collection becomes searchable, browsable, and maintainable. Each collection, prior to preservation, undergoes a "building" process that, once established, is completely automatic. This process creates all the structures that are used at run time for accessing the collection. Searching is based on various indexes, while browsing is based on various metadata such as author and title; support structure for both are created during the building operation. When new material appears it can be fully incorporated into the collection by rebuilding.

Greenstone includes a facility for "end user collection building". It can further be explained how end users find information in collections. Next, we examine the interactive interface for collection building, which extends Greenstone's domain of application by encouraging end user to build their own digital library collections. The structure of a collection is determined by its "configuration file", and we briefly show what this look like.

Greenstone collection range from newspaper articles to technical documents, from educational journals to oral history, from virtual art to folksongs.

Why Greenstone?

Greenstone was used in building the content repository after doing a comparative study of 3 open source digital library softwares namely-D-space, E-prints, and Greenstone.

Features	D-space	Greenstone	E-print
Open source	yes	yes	yes
Unicode Complaint	yes	yes	yes
Hindi Interface	no	yes	no

OVERVIEW OF GREENSTONE

Summary of facilities of Greenstone Software

Brief summary of Greenstone facilities are given below:

1. Accessible via web browser
2. Collections are accessed through a standard web browser.

The browser is used for both local and remote access-whether Green stone is running on your own personnel computer or on a remote central library server.

Features of Greenstone

Some of the features are:

1. Runs on Windows and UNIX: Collection can be served on either Windows or UNIX (Linux, OS/X) .Any of these systems a serve Greenstone collection over the internet using either an integrated built in web server or an external web server

2. Fulltext and fielded Search: Users can search the fultext of the documents, or choose between indexes built from different part of the documents. Queries can be ranked or Boolean; terms can be stemmed or unstamped, case folded or not.

Flexible Browsing Facilities: The user can browse list of authors, list of titles, list of dates, hierarchical classification structures, and so on. Different collection offer different browsing facilities.

3. Create Access structure automatically: Searching and browsing structures are built directly from the documents themselves; hands insert no links. New documents in the same format become available; they can be merged into the collection automatically. Existing Hypertext links in the original documents, leading both within and outside the collection are preserved.

Unicode is used throughout the software, allowing any language to be processed in a consistent manner, and searched properly. On-the fly conversion is used to convert from Unicode to an alphabet supported by the user's web browser. A "language identification" plugin allows automatic identification of languages in multilingual collections, so that separate indexes can be built.

4. Multi-language user interface: The interface can be presented in multiple languages.

5. Makes use of Available metadata: Metadata forms the raw material for browsing indexes; it may be associated with each document or with individual sections within documents. Metadata must be provided explicitly or derivable automatically from the source of documents. The Dublin Core scheme is used, with provision of extension.

6. Plugins and classifiers extend the system's capabilities: Plugins can be written to accommodate new documents type. Classifiers can be written create new kind of browsing indexes based on metadata.

7. Multiple langages documents: Unicode is used throughout the software, allowing any language to be processed in a consistent manner, and searched properly. On the fly conversion is used to convert from Unicode to an alphabet supported by the user's Web browser. A" language identification" plug-in allows automatic identification of languages in multilingual collections, so that separate indexes can be built.

8. Multiple-language user interface: The interface can be presented in multiple languages.

9. Multimedia collection: Green Stone collection can contain text, pictures, audio and video clips. Most non-textual material is either linked in to textual documents or accompanied by textual description (ranging from figure caption to descriptive paragraphs) to allow fultext searching and browsing. However, the architecture is general enough to permit implementation of plugins and classifiers for non-textual data.

10. Classifiers allow hierarchical browsing: Hierarchical phase and key phrase indexes of text, or indeed any metadata, can be created using standard classifiers. Such interfaces are described by Paynter et al.

11. Designed for multi gigabyte collection: Collection can contain millions of documents, making the Greenstone system suitable for collections up to several gigabytes. Compression is used to reduce the size of the indexes and text. Small indexes have the added bonus of faster retrieval.

12. New collection appears dynamically: Collections can be updated and new ones brought online at any time, without bringing the system down; the process responsible for the user interface will notice(through periodic polling) when new collections appear and add them to the list presented to the user.

13. Collection can be published on CD-ROM: Greenstone collections can be published, in precisely the same form, on a self installing CD-ROM. The interaction is identical to accessing the collection on web(Netscape is provided on each disk)- except the response time are faster and more predictable. For collection larger than one CD-ROM, a multi CD-ROM solution has been implemented.

14. Distributed collections are supported: A flexible process structure allow different collections to be served by different computers, yet be presented to the users in the same way, on the same web page, as part of the same digital library (Bainbridge et al, 2001) The Z 39.50 protocol is also supported, both for accessing external servers and (under development) for presenting Greenstone collections to external clients.

15. What you see-you can get! The Greenstone Digital library is open source software, available from New Zealand Digital Library (nzdl.org) under the terms of the GNU General Public License. The software includes everything described above: web serving, CD-ROM creation, collection building, and multilingual capability, plug in and classifiers for variety of different source documents types. It includes an auto install features to allow easy installation on both Windows and UNIX.

Greenstone is highly interoperable using contemporary standards. It incorporates a server that can serve any collection over the Open Archives Protocol for Metadata

Harvesting (OAI-PMH), and Greenstone can harvest documents over OAI-PMH and include them in collection. In India, a number of institutions viz., Indian Institute of Management-Kozhikode, National Center for Science Information, Bangalore and Association of Indian Labour Historians, Delhi are using. LIS professionals should come forward to make use of the opportunity and the University/ college administration should also come forward to depute the LIS professionals to undergo such training so that they can built their digital library. Any individual or institution can make use of the software to build digital collection.

This software can be downloaded from the website: **www.greenstone.org**

2. BUILDING DIGITAL COLLECTION USING D-SPACE SOFTWARE

What is D-space?

D-space is open source software for designing and developing digital consortium. It developed jointly by MIT Libraries and Hewlett-Packard (HP), is freely available to research institutions as an open source system that can be customized. The D-space system provides a way to manage research material and publications in a professionally maintained repository to give them greater visibility and accessibility over time.

D-space is one of the first OSS platform to store, manage and distribute the collections in digital format D-Space preferred software for academic non-profit and commercial organizations, building open digital repositories D-space preserves and enables easy and open access to all types of digital contents including text, images, moving images etc. It is groundbreaking digital repository system that captures, stores, indexes, preserves and distributes digital research material. As most of the world's contents are now being developed and disseminated in digital format, the software supports next generation digital archiving which is more permanent and sharable than current analog archive.

D-space capture the data in any format such as text, audio, video, and data. It redistributes the reading material over the web. It indexes the reading material and preserves digital work over the long term.

The D-space initiative is one of the largest digital asset management projects in the history. It enables academics to place their content in a free and trusted archive, get indexed, get it on the web, and make it easy to find associated metadata.

D-space is digital repository system captures, stores, indexes, preserves and distributes digital research material. Research institutions worldwide use this open source system in a variety of ways—as an institutional repository, a learning object repository, for record management and more. D-Space is freely available as open source software, you can customized and extend.

Features of D-space

- D-space is open source technology platform, which can be customized, and its capabilities can be extended.
- D-space is service model for open access and/ or digital archiving for perpetual access.
- D-space is a platform to build an institutional consortium and collections are searchable and retrievable by the WEB.
- To make available institution based scholarly material in digital formats. The collection will be open and interoperable.

What D-Space can do?

Jointly developed by MIT libraries and Hewlett-Packard

Labs, the D-Space software platform serves a variety of digital archiving needs. Research institutions worldwide use D-Space to meet a variety of digital archiving needs.

- Institutionnel Repositories (IRs)
- Learning Object Repositories(LORs)
- E-thesis
- Electronic Records Management(ERM)
- Digital Preservation.
- Publishing.

What kind of Content does D-Space Accept?

D-Space accepts all forms of digital materials including text, images, videos and audio files.

Possible content includes the following:

- Articles and preprints
- Technical Reports
- Working papers
- Conference papers
- E-thesis
- Data sets: statistical, matlab, etc.
- Images: visual, scientific, etc.
- Audio files
- Video files
- Learning objects
- Reformatted digital library collection.

Benefits of Using D-space

a. Getting our research results out quickly, to worldwide audience.

b. Reaching a worldwide audience through exposure to search engines such as Google.

c. Storing of reusable teaching material that we can use

with course management system.

d. Archiving and distributing material put on to our personnel websites.

e. Keeping track of our own publications/bibliography.

f. D-space is easy to use .We use web browser to submit contents and search or browse its collection.

g. To submit content, you upload the file(s) and add descriptive information including titles, author, publication information and keywords. This descriptive data is known as metadata.

D-Space enables easy remote access and the ability to read and search D-Space items from one location: the World Wide Web and offers the advantages of digital distribution and long term preservation for a variety of formats including text, audio, videos, images, and dataset sand more. Authors can store their digital works in collection that are maintained by MIT communities.

The choice of the software for digital database should be based upon the nature of collection, data formats, applications, user expectations and infrastructure. Any information resources mostly comprise of scientific articles published in various journals, research reports, and monographs. For such collection the system should have simple installation, configuration and management facilities D-space has the following features that have made it popular choice for designing digital databases.

D-Space offers the opportunity to provide access to all the research of the institution through one interface which can be made use by any institution. The repository is organized to accommodate the varying policy and workflow issues inherent in a multi-disciplinary environment. Submission workflow and access policies can be customized to adhere closely to each community's needs. In India, the Indian Institute of Science (IISc), Bangalore, Indian Statistical

Institute Library, Bangalore and INFLIBNET, Ahmedabad have established their digital collections using D-Space.

The software can be downloaded from:

http://www.sourceforge.net/projects/dspace/

E-PRINT ARCHIVE SOFTWARE

E-print is generic archive software developed by the University of Southampton. It is intended to create a highly configurable web-based archive. E-print primary goal is to be setup as an open archive for research papers, but it could be easily used for other things such as images, research data, audio archives- anything that can be stored digitally by making changes in configuration. It works on Linux operating system and it needs MySQL, Perl modules and Apache web server. It is intended to create a highly configurable web based archive and is a platform for building repositories of research literature, scientific data, student thesis, project reports, multimedia artifacts, teaching materials, scholarly collections, digitized records, images, audio, exhibitions and performances, anything that can be stored digitally, etc. and offers integrating advance search, extended metadata and other features such as Archive Documents, Multimedia and Data. All these are open source software and downloaded from the cyber space. E-prints Archive Software can be downloaded from:

http://software.eprints.org.

KOHA LIBRARY SOFTWARE

It is first open source Integrated Library Management System and in use worldwide to archive their library automation goals. Its important features meets the user needs including simple, clear interface for librarians and users, customizable search, circulation and borrower management, cataloguing module with integrated z39.50 client, web 2.0 , full acquisition system including budget and pricing information, ability to cope with any number of branches, patrons, patron categories, item categories, currencies and other data, serial system for magazines or newspapers, reading list for members, etc.

The CERN Document Server Software (CD Sware)

CD Sware: The integrated digital library system is a suit of applications which provides the framework and tools for building and managing an autonomous digital library server. The software is readily available to anyone, as it is free software, licensed under the GNU, General Public License (GPL). It covers all aspects of digital library management and compiles with the Open Initiative Metadata Harvesting Protocole(OAI-PMH) and uses MARC 21.Its flexibility and performance make it a comprehensive solution for the management of document repositories of moderate to large size libraries.

The technology offered by the software covers all aspects of digital library management. It complies with the Open Archives Initiative Metadata Harvesting Protocol (OAI-PMH)and uses MARC 21 as it is underlying bibliographic standard. Its flexibility and performance make it a comprehensive solution for the management of document repositories of moderate to large size. It can be downloaded from:

http://www.cdsware.cern.ch

Scout Portal Toolkit (SPT) Digital Library Software

Though the Scout Portal Toolkit is not digital library software. It allows groups or organizations that have a collection of knowledge or resources they want to share via the World Wide Web to put that collection online without making a big investment in technical resources or expertise. The SPT can be downloaded from the following:

http://www.scout.wisc.edu/Projects/SPT/

3. DEVELOPING DIGITAL COLLECTION WITH OCR SOFTWARE

The OCR can be defined as "high speed process of reorganization and translating machine printed or hand printed words, letters, symbols, and numbers into computer processed information. The data is directly machined readable while still being readable by people." The scanner and digital camera can be used for capturing of text and images. The scanned data can be stored in the form of CD, DVD, tape and Hard Disk. For text, this is scanned by using Optical Character Recognition(OCR) software, which recognizes the shapes of the letter of the alphabet and produces a file exactly the same as one produced by word processor used to type in the same text.

OCR software is the system developed to scan a document, read and recognize the scanned image of the printed document and save the output on text files, or any other digital format that can be saved, printed, edited and reused. It is generally designed for features like speed, word accuracy and for producing a document that leads as close to the original as possible.

OCR comprises of two steps in translating characters on a page into a digitized form:

1. Optical Scanning
2. Reorganization system

OCR software is used for building bibliographic databases and fultext retrieval system in the libraries and information centers. It is a method of direct entry of VCDs from hard copy. The software is consists of scanning the page into a bitmap image, recognizing the contents with it and translating it into a file that can be edited.

It is very much clear that no OCR software programme is hundred percent accurate. Accuracy, formatting, ability to handle columns and tables, image, quality, font and type size, preprocessing, templates, software compatibility are the main features of OCR software.

Criteria for selecting OCR software:

The following criteria for selection of OCR software can be used:

The OCR system requires installation into PC.

1. It should have ability to recognize a wide variety of typewritten and typed documents including books, magazines, reports newspapers etc.
2. It should able to maintain the layout of the original text.
3. It recognizes columns of text with a minimum of user intervention.
4. It provides on-line help while using the system.
5. It should come with engaging technical support from the manufacturer.
6. It should have ability to support different types of scanners like flat-bed, hand-held etc.
7. It should scan material at an efficient speed.

Others Software Requirements:

Other software you may need include: Digitization software like Acrobat, OCR software (e.g. Fine Reader), image editors, web server and browsers, word processing software including HTML/XML editors, and DBMS package. Many of these are available freely, both for windows and Linux operating system.

COST OF DIGITIZATION

It depends upon various factors such as type of material to be digitized, the number of documents to be digitized.

The Library of Congress Preservation Directorate

compared the costs of various preservation treatments for a single 300 pages book. The estimated cost are binding or boxing -$ 10, mass deacidification -$ 15, preservation photocopy - $ 65, microfilming- $ 185, conservation -$430, base level digitization - $ 1, 600, and enhanced digitization- $ 2, 500.The Library of Congress's base level digitization includes machine readable, minimally encoded text generated by fully automated process of Optical Character Recognition and text markup and basic bibliographic description. Enhanced digitization offers improved access through the addition of enhancements, such as essays and finding aids.

15

Human Resource Development Required for Digitization

INTRODUCTION

The success and failure of an organization depend mainly on its human resources. The human resource is the most important determinants of its success, efficiency and effectiveness. The same is true for the libraries also. One of the important and the key roles of human resource in the modern library is development of human resources.

Development of human resource means "employees of an organization are helped to acquire essential skills, knowledge and other capabilities required by the organization according to its standards in a planned process to meet the present and future expectations of the organization on human side in a conductive environment with result orientation." There is a strong need for training and developing the people of an organization in order to equiped them to accept challenges. If the human resources of a library are to be properly developed, they should be trained and educated. Human resource development is a continuous process. It enables the individual to gain their best human potential by attaining a total all round development. Human resource development promotes dignity of employment of every employee of an organization, and provides opportunities for teamwork, personnel development and carrier development. HRD must be able to develop overall capacity of individual employees of an organization, and discover and exploit their own potential for the common goals of the organization to which they belong, for the betterment of themselves and a country as a whole.

The library automation and network have totally transformed the nature and functions of library/information centers. Accordingly the library collection that is the media used for information has been changing from print to non-print media such as optical and magnetic media like CD-ROMs etc. Today digital storage and telecommunication media are playing an important role in the transmission and dissemination of information. The use of better and advanced technology in dissemination and retrieval of information is the need of the hour. The modern information society demands multimedia based information instead of traditional paper based information. As a result of increase in the production of electronic information, users are in a better position of having up to date information in the digital form. The informational processionals will have challenging and dynamic role to play in the digital information environment. The technology is progressively replacing the old methods of information storage, retrieval and dissemination. Now a days most of the reputed journals and books are available fultext form online.

The biggest challenge for library and information professionals now a days is to select, organize, consolidate, and disseminate information in order to satisfy the information needs of the users. Today's librarian is moving beyond the traditional roles of collection development and custodian duties to newer functions of translating, accessing, and marketing resources beyond the walls of the physical collection of library. The new technology has brought in a quantum change, wherein retrieval is done from online catalogs and text or through searching bibliographical databases. Hence the traditional role of librarian is being replaced by assisting users to perform online searching. This new role requires attitudinal change towards forms of materials available in various formats, location and selection of resources, integration and interpretation of the content in resources and demands. It requires special skills in dealing various information products, printed as well as digital format, and their use. In this changing scenario, informational professionals need to aware the collection of their libraries and attend meetings of special interest groups, conferences, seminars, etc. for updating their knowledge and skills to provide better services to the users.

NEED OF TRAINING

The explosion of digital information and the growth of online digital resources has led to a shortage of individuals with an understanding of the discipline of libraries, document management and archives who also have the technical knowledge and skills needed to create, manage and support digital information collection.

ROLE OF LIBRARIAN IN /MANAGEMENT OF DIGITAL COLLEXCTION/CHANGING DIGITAL ENVIRONMENT

In traditional libraries the role of librarian was knowledge manager, who acquire and collect, store, catalogued and retrieved the printed material as and when required by the users. Due to advent of the new information technology the role has seen sea changes. The librarians who were more of knowledge managers have moved from that role to become more of service providers. Most of the libraries have started using the information, communication and technology (ICT) to serve their communities in a more effective and efficient manner.

The role of librarians/reference librarians is changing with the changing environment. The reference librarians are able to serve their users better by accessing and showing their users how to access a wide diversity of electronic information sources. Although vast resources are available on Internet, even with the help of tools such as Netscape and web crawlers, is time consuming for the users. This will give an opportunity to reference librarians to redesign their responsibilities more and more towards instruction in the use of electronic resources.

Today most of the journals and databases are available on-line format, which may access through on-line subscription i.e. electronic subscription.

Today's librarian makes a significant contribution to achieve the user's goals with the help of new information technology. While in the past preservation of books was the main task of librarians. They were regarded as the custodian of books. With the advancement of knowledge, the role of librarian grew from a collector of books to a professional involved in very complex issues of organization, dissemination and access of information. The role of librarian in the electronic age has gained widespread acceptance all over the world. Now the information is available on various electronic media also. The handling and preservation of digital media is not an easy task.

The role of information professionals with respect to web is different from their role with respect to printed media.

The roles of librarian in the changing environment are:

1. To provide intellectual access to information in any format.

2. To evaluate available sources of information.
3. To organize and structure information.
4. To ensure the preservation of information.
5. To provide specialized staff to offer instruction and assistance in interpreting resources and accessing resources.

These services should take into account the information seeking behavior, information needs of the users. The library should help to identify and employ external databases, agencies, and to provide services in meeting information needs of users and to participate in consortia and networks to obtain access to information sources and services. In this changing scenario, a good reference service is bound to encourage the use of the library in the context of online services.

Therefore, in the changing scenario the librarian is supposed to perform the following services:

1. Determine the information needs of the users when interacting with them in person or through other communication channel.
2. Analyzes information sources and recommends to users in the context of the attractiveness, interests, and context level for each user.
3. Suggests specific works that releases to the user requirement.
4. Engages users in discussions about experiences related to their information needs and communicates interest in every user's experiences.

The reference staff encourages user awareness about information resources and fulfills information needs with complete, accurate answers to their queries. They provide instructions, guidance, and direction in using information resources effectively and finding material on Internet.

Librarians have organized information recourses through classification schemes and standardized methods of describing resources such as MARC. However, in the digital environment, there is a need to specify the format in order to access to web resources over the Internet. New organizational tools are being developed to accommodate these issues. One of the most significant is metadata. Metadata is defined as structured data about data and is format for describing an Internet or digital information resources.

The virtual library environment requires a new technical setup of competences for librarians, which are not previously required. Skills such as creating web pages, building and maintaining computer networks, etc. Keeping in view the above developments, the staff requires different skills. Librarians are needed a combinations of knowledge, skills, and professional qualities in order to full fill the multifaceted role. The information, communication and technology have necessitated the professionals to keep themselves abreast of the changing times. From acquisition of books to choosing their media for storage, the role has changed completely for library professionals.

NEED OF RE-ENGINEERING HUMAN RESOURCES IN DIGITAL INFORMATION ENVIRONMENT

In the information society of the future the ability to manage knowledge in different ways will be essential. The traditional skills of librarianship will either be transformed and/or supplemented employees will be involved in a lifelong learning process; be flexible to work in a variety of different projects and areas; be able to process and supply information to the satisfaction of their client communities, be able to market information and have a high level of expertise as appropriate in information technologies. A shift in paradigm of working styles, meshing traditional librarianship and IT approaches to information provision will occur.

In this context challenges for managers will be retain existing staff and to face the emotional and industrial issues of re-structuring and re-engineering of libraries.

The library and information professionals will have to play an important role in the digital environment. Librarian as an information manager is a crucial individual in management system of an organization who is responsible for his own library management. The emergence of electronic publishing, Internet, CD-ROMs, DVDs etc. has changed the role of librarians/information professionals from custodians of documents in printed form to information providers in digital form.

In the changed circumstances it is necessary to have efficient and highly skilled professionals who are proficient in handling electronic equipments for efficient and effective dissemination of information. The information professionals who are proficient in computers and keen enough to know the latest available electronic resources only can provide the right information to the users in digital era.

The development of technology is so dynamic that it is very difficult for the professionals to be up to date. The knowledge and skill acquired today will become obsolete tomorrow. The traditional lethargic library staff should be re-engineered in the effective manner by giving training and motivating them to acquire, process and disseminate digital information effectively and efficiently.

So, there is an imminent need of re-engineering the human resource development programmes for library professionals to handle the digital information effectively and efficiently.

1. The library staff should be aware of the process of digitization and modern equipments.

2. They should attend seminars, workshops and refresher courses on digitization and handling digital information.
3. They should be aware of the information needs of the users so that the problems can be solved effectively and efficiently.
4. To cop up with the current information technology environment, library professionals should have training for both in computers and human resource development area.
5. The training should be;
   i. Computer based and computer aided instruction based.
   ii. Web based.
   iii. On digital media storage and handling based.

What is re-engineering?

Michael Hammer and James Champy have defined the concept of re-engineering as:

"Re-engineering is the fundamental re thinking and radical redesign of business processes to achieve dramatic improvements in critical, contemporary measures of performance, such as cost, quality, service and speed"

Bob Smith has defined re-engineering as:

"The radical redesigning of the business policies and practices within the organization in order to streamline an operation and adept it to existing market realities."

Johnson A Edosomwan has defined the reengineering process as:

> "a coordinated, continuous improvement approach required to rethink, redesign, retool and reinvent new processes that will perform better than existing ones."

The training programmes should be chosen in accordance with the library requirements.

The library professional should be proficient in different network operating systems, database management software, application software, library management softwares and other automation softwares. SOULS, SANJAY, LIBSYS, OASIS, are some of the major library softwaes packages. By mastering these software packages enabling the library professionals to find more time for information provision.

The library professionals should have the following skills for developing digital libraries:

SKILLS REQUIRED FOR DIGITISATION

He should have knowledge about :

1. **Technical Skills** : Knowledge about microcomputer systems such as operating system, word processing, softwares, desktop publishing, computer networks, Internet services, hypertext and hypermedia, image processing, graphics file formats, photo/image editing, etc.
2. **Internet Knowledge** : Sufficient knowledge of Internet and its tools and utility. He should be well versed of the different search engines, websites and their URLs.
3. Formats for computer based cataloging such as MARC format
4. Online information retrieval and database searching, online access databases about journal articles, e-journals, etc.
5. Database development knowledge.
6. Library automation, OPACs, management of digital library services.
7. Archives and record management, interlibrary lending and cooperation, document delivery service,

copyright, information security, CD-ROM in a local area network, developing a website, methods for access to databases through internet, etc.

8. Conversion/preservation of printed documents, developing cooperative community WWW sites, evaluating websites.
9. Downloading of information and record format conversion, an advance application of MARC in ISIS. Preprogramming in ISIS, extension of classical WWW (client based and server based).
10. Identify user need.
11. Web designing subject specialization.
12. Know how to use ICT tools and match the query with the available resources on the net.
13. Communication skill for articulating his/her information needs.
14. E-collection of books and journals.

Besides all these technical qualities, they should response to the opportunities and challenges of the development in information technology with a high degree of enthusiasm and professionalism.

Computer based training technology is very well used as a media for lectures, tutorials etc. Web based training uses the Internet as its primary medium for instruction.

NEED OF TRAINNING

Training is an instrument of developing the employees or workforce by enhancing the skills and improving the human behavior, which result in organization development adequate enough for the accomplishment of objectives from time to time. It helps organization and individuals to develop themselves in consonance with the changing needs of the environment in which they survive, operate and progress.

The necessary alternative to recruitment is intensive internal staff training, which can be expensive. Some of the skills learning can be virtual, i.e. training course available on the net. It is important for existing staff to change their working habits and attitudes towards the functioning of library. There is already shortage supply of skilled personnel. In-depth knowledge of IT applications is required.

Introduction of new technology necessitates the library staff to learn new skills and undergo training to handle new information technology. The increasing need for well-trained peoples using sophisticated tools to perform more complex tasks has made well thought our skills training more necessary than ever before. Besides, over a period of time, such skills become out of date and need refreshing. For that purpose various universities and institutions has been conducting refresher cources. The library staff can become up-to-date on the developments in their field by undergoing such training programmes.

Trainings have to be imparted to staff in computer and communication systems, in user instruction and training and in current scholarly information. Many library users will have a need to learn the new ways of the digital order; the library will more than at present be a teaching organization.

Today, when libraries are making use of modern communication media such as e-mail, e-journals, satellite communication, online networks etc. the level of knowledge of library users is also on higher side. Knowledge of computer has become an important aspect as far as library professionals are concern. Once he has the operational knowledge in computers, he can develop his skills and realize the position of information provider.

FORMS OF TRAINNING

For the full-fledged digital library the existing staff members should have trained well to cop up with the emerging new information technological trends in the library with up-to-date knowledge.

Training could be given to the library professionals as a part of a continuing education programme, which could be in the form of workshop, short course, seminar, symposium, refresher courses organized by various universities. These professional courses/programmes will provide additional skills and knowledge to the library professionals to function more efficiently and effectively in their present positions and to prepare for additional responsibilities within the system. In other words training programmes add to the knowledge development of the professional who will be able to provide the right information at the right time which will result in the progress of the society. In order to impart latest developments faculty and library professionals must update their knowledge. Periodic national seminars and conferences organized by various professional bodies such as ILA, DLA, IFLA, IASLIC, etc. at international, national and state level provide opportunities for the professionals to update their knowledge. Various short term courses are also organized by various institutions provide new knowledge to working professionals.

TRANING PROGRAMME BY UGC AND INFLIBNET

They provide training on different aspects of librarianship from time to time. The contribution of INFLIBNET in this particular aspect is a unique effort as far as development of information professionals is concern. CDS/ISIS is a database management system, which will be very helpful for the library professionals.

UGC Refresher courses as carrier advancement scheme

UGC has made compulsory for teachers and librarians to attend refresher courses and orientation courses for promotion to next higher scale. The main purpose of this programmes are to refresh the subject knowledge of participants. The same is applicable for the librarians of colleges, etc.

Academic Staff Colleges

National Policy on Education 1986 with an aim at improving the status of teachers and librarians and proposed to provide opportunities for their professional and carrier development, orientation programmes have been formulated. They also organize refresher courses to librarians to refresh and add to their knowledge in their disciplines.

Lectures are organized in these programmes. Lecture on various current topics such as use of Internet, networks and networking, application of computers in libraries has been providing.

Library professionals want the library of the future to be a hybrid institution that contains both digital and book collections. Some library professionals envision a digital library "library without wall" in which users gain access to almost unlimited amount of information through home computers or at remote terminals located around the community. Traditionally, librarians have often organized and classified information in such a way that they can find the information on behalf of the user in other words the librarian as fulfilled physical role of advisor, interpreter and mediator for the user information needs. He should embrace the entire new information cycle from the creation, restructuring and representation of information to its dissemination and use.

SKILLS AND MANPOWER REQUIRED FOR DIGITISATION

Personnel comprise the most important resource for digital library not only during the initial creation and set up, but also for its operation, maintenance and provision of services. Personnel comprise the most important resource for the digital library apart from technology. Actual personnel required for a digital library project depend on the type and volume and task carried out.

The manpower, which are supposed to implement and manage the IT should be trained and retained in order to keep themselves abreast of the latest techniques and tools. Trained manpower is required not only in initial creation and set up but also for its operation, maintenance and provision of services. Since access to the digital library is easy compared to a physical library, more users are likely to access it. If the digital library does not meet the expectations of the users in terms of currency and quality of contents, they will lose confidence and are less likely to visit the digital library again. It is therefore important that personnel should have right skills and attitude to handle various tasks associated with digital library project. For running the digital library effectively the training to library employee is required. The training should be given to existing staff members to cop up with the emerging technological trends in the library.

Actual personnel required for a digital library project depends on the type and volume of the tasks carried out.

Broadly, personnel will be required for following tasks:

1. Project management
2. Selection and preparation of source material
3. Digitization and conversion
4. Cataloguing and metadata assignment
5. Quality assessment
6. System administration and maintenance of digital library server and website
7. System analyst/programmer for digital library application/interface development
8. Promotion and provision of services

A special skill is required for developing and managing

the digital library. Very few people will have skills required to construct the digital library. Developing a digital library is teamwork.

The following skills are required for developing a typical digital library:

- He should have technical skills such as knowledge of computer hardware and software.
- Database management.
- Cataloging (metadata).
- Computer programming.
- Web designing subject specialist.
- Preservation (document formats and long term storage media)
- Photography.
- Graphic design.
- Digitizing skills.

The staff should have knowledge about the:

- Information needs of the users
- Hardware and software dedicated to library functions
- Knowledge of internet and networking
- Can prepare website for the library
- E-journals and e-books and other e-resources

The strength of the staff required for the digitization projects depends upon the size and nature of the institution. In a smaller institution, a part time project manager (librarian) working with the two or three highly trained staff may be sufficient for completion of the small project. For part time temporary tasks, you may also consider seeking support from enthusiastic and hardworking staff from within the library or from other departments such as computer department. You can also take the advantage of student's assistance /intern programmes available in most educational institutions for employing students on hourly payment basis.

While hiring new personnel or re-deploying existing staff, it is important that their education and skills match the requirements of the job. Their responsibilities etc. should be clearly defined.

SKILLS REQUIRED

Skills include both hard (technical and IT skills) and soft (e.g. communication) skills. Apart from professional and technical skills, soft skills such as the following could be important:

- Communication skills;
- Ability to work in team;
- Flexibility;
- People skills;
- Capacity to learn constantly and quickly;
- Ability to work under pressure; goal oriented;
- Time consciousness; capacity to work independently;
- Presentation skills;
- Negotiation skills; and teaching/training skills.

Thus, apart from the professional and technical skills, soft skills such as communication skills, ability to work as a team, flexibility, people skills, capacity to learn constantly and quickly, time consciousness, capacity to work independently, presentation skills, negotiation skills and teaching /training skills.

Staff Training

Training is very important for the development of the skills required for the project. Training can be provided either in-house or by the outside institution. In-house training include special training programmes and on the job training. Staff may also be deputed to various relevant training programmes. It will be useful to prepare a training manual which will be very useful for the new staff.

Due to rapid change in the technology, requires constant re-training and re-positioning of staff. They must have up-to-date knowledge about the development in the field.

One of the main issues here is the degree to which libraries will digitize existing materials and acquire original digital work, as opposed to simply pointing to them externally

DIFFICULTIES IN DEVELOPING MANPOWER

1. Shortage of information professionals' skills in using information technology.
2. Lack of in-service training facilities.
3. Lack of enough trained personnel to maintain the database.
4. Lack of staff orientation towards computerization.
5. Lack of motivation.
6. Lack of awareness about the possible benefits of IT.

16

Process of Digitization

INTRODUCTION

Now a day, apart of conventional collection of a library is being converted into digital form. The process of conversion of paper documents into digital format is mainly with the help of scanners. Printed text, pictures and figures are transformed into computer accessible forms using a digital scanner or digital cameras. The important step involved in the process of digitization is scanning. Scanners are mostly using for converting print resources into digital format. Most scanning softwares generated by default TIFF (Tagged Image File Format). The scanned textual image (TIF) are not searchable nor can be manipulated like text files document (ASCII).The scanned TIF format are converted to text by the process of Optical Character Recognition (OCR).The OCR software allows the option of maintaining text and graphics in their original layout as well as plain ASCII and word processing formats. Though OCR software we can save the file into html, doc and other formats. The image can be browsed through a table of contents composed in HTML providing linked to scan images.

The purpose of digitization is to making the reading material available online in searchable and browsable form.

METHODS OF DIGITIZATION

Digital resources can be built by adopting the following methods:

1. **Digitization**: conversion of existing print and other media into digital format.
2. Acquisition of original digital work created by publishers, institutions and other scholars. Example: items would be electronic books, journals and databases.
3. Access to external materials not held in-house by providing pointers to web sites, other library collection, or publishers' servers.
4. Creation of the bibliographic database of print and non-print materials and such database to be made available via LAN and WAN.
5. Acquisition of need based digital resources in the form of CD-ROM, optical disk and multimedia version.
6. High bandwidth Internet connectivity.
7. Subscription of e-journals.
8. Facility to access commercial database via online in the related areas and
9. Creation of local digital contents available within the resource center.
10. Metadata creation.

ii. Conversion of existing print, audio, video into digital format:

Nowadays, a part of conventional collection of a library is being converted into digital form. The process of conversion of paper document into digital format is mainly with the help of scanners. Printed text pictures and figures are transformed into computer accessible forms using a digital scanner or digital camera (Fig. 9).

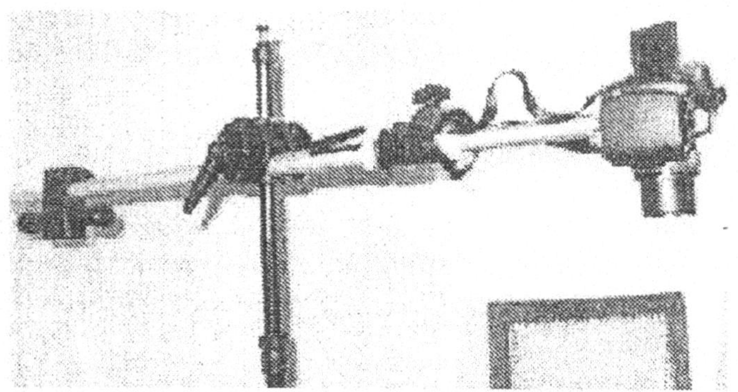

Fig. 9. Digitization with using Digital Camera

Scanners are mostly using for converting print resources into digital format. Most scanning software generate by default TIFF (Tagged Image File Format). The scanned textual image are not searchable nor can be manipulated like text file Document (ASC11). The scanned TIF formats are converted to text by the process of Optical Character Recognition (OCR). The OCR software allows the option of maintaining text and graphics in their original layout as well as plain ASCII and word processing formats. Through OCR software we can save the files into html, doc and other formats. The image can be browsed through a table of contents composed in HTML providing linked to scanned image.

SELECTION OF MATERIAL TO BE DIGITIZED /TARGET SOURCE TO BE DIGITIZED

The first step is to select the sources to be digitized.

The source may be images /contents of physical media such as periodical articles, books, rare manuscripts, research papers, newspapers, newspaper cuttings, images, sound, film and audio video cassettes, photographs etc to be digitized is called target source. This is the material to be digitized.

What material to be digitized?

Documents: They include text, bibliographic or full text, photographs, diagrams, maps, etc. They exist either in print or non-print form or also as single unit or collections.

The following in-house resources can be selected for the digital library :

1. **Digital resources**: Resources which are originally created in a digital format, such as electronic books or electronic journals and data sets and
2. **Non digital resources**: Those documents such as old manuscripts, drawings and other non print material.

In addition to that machine readable data files, various online databases and CD-ROM information products, computerized networked library systems, etc.

Digitizing resources produced /published internally

Many institutions bring out the following publications (in-house) on a regular basis in order to disseminate the work being undertaken. They are:

1. In-house journals.
2. Project reports/thesis submitted by the students, research scholars.
3. Articles published in other national /international journals.
4. News letters of the institution.
5. Annual reports.
6. Technical reports (consultancy/sponsored/R and D etc) generated in-house.
7. Technical brochures /pamphlets.
8. Regular course material.
9. Lectures.
10. Video/audio clippings, explaining working of some instruments, facilities, etc. available.

11. Publications/services from the library like CAS, SDI, select bibliographies on certain topics.
12. Newspaper clippings- recent and relevant information published in newspapers.
13. Internally created files (correspondence, communication, circular, office order, etc.) available in various file formats such as ASCII, PDF, XLS, etc.
14. Internally created records using databases such as dbase, access etc.
15. Internal reports and thesis, which require no copy right from the publishers /authors
16. Research papers published/presented by organizations at various forums.
17. Proceedings of the conferences /seminars/symposia/ workshops/tutorials conducted by the organization. Invited lectures delivered by eminent speakers.
18. Policies and plan documents.
19. Photographs and films produced by the organization.

Digital collection process may include digitization of entities such as books, manuscripts, palm leaves, periodicals, newspapers, paintings, movies, videos, databases, etc.

In digitizing libraries, there may be several rare documents and manuscripts of value, which may need careful handling while scanning. The document/manuscripts may be available as a single copy which means that if a part of paper is damaged it will cause severe loss of knowledge which is irrecoverable.

The conversion of textual, visual, and numeric information to electronic form encompasses a range of procedures and technologies with widely varying implications and costs.

The judgment we must make in defining digital

projects involves the following factors:

- The intellectual and physical nature of the source materials.
- The number and location of current and potential user
- The current and potential nature of use.
- The format and nature of the proposed digital product and how it will be described, delivered, and archived.
- How the proposed products relates to other digitization efforts.
- And projection of costs in relation to benefits.

There are so many steps involved in the process of digitization. The process basically involves taking a physical object and essentially making an electronic photograph of it.

STEPS INVOLVED IN DIGITIZATION

The following steps are involved in internal recourses:

1. Compiling a list of all the internal resources
2. Identifying suitable software for database creation.
3. Identifying suitable hardware and software(operating system and OCR)
4. Obtaining the all documents preferably in soft copy or hard copy(if soft copy is not available)
5. Input of the bibliographical data for each document submitted in a suitable software.
6. Editing the database: modification, addition and deletion.
7. Standardization of entry.
8. Digitization of document (if soft copy is not available) using a good scanner.
9. OCR (ing) the scanned document—to convert the image fie into editable text.
10. Convert the OCR(ed) documents into pdf files.

11. Providing links to the full text document (pdf files) in the data base.
12. Indexing the full text using digital library software such as GSDL.
13. Testing.
14. Making it available on the library web server and the campus Internet for search, retrieval and browsing.

THE PROCESS OF CONVERTING PRINT INTO DIGITAL FORM

It is to be decided whether it should be done:

1. In-house or
2. Through external agencies or commercial agencies.

The conversion of the materials can be done either in-house or through some external agencies or commercial agencies. Digitization unit can be set up in-house. Using an external supplier to do some job such as scanning means that the equipments and expertise of the third party can be exploited. Both approaches have their merits but there are certain situations where the choice is more clear-cut.

The reason for outsourcing may include where there is a large volume of work to be done in a short period of time or where the project has space, infrastructure or staffing constraints, which preclude the setting up of in-house facilities.

THROUGH IN-HOUSE SOURCES

The project can be done in-house for several reasons:

- The collection cannot be moved out of the institution.
- The collection is badly organized.
- The digitization needs to be phased in small amount over a long period.
- The digitization task is very simple.

But if we do in-house, some basic infrastructure is required.

There are some baseline infrastructure requirements for in-house:

- A production level scanner, which will be able to scan the originals to a suitable resolution.
- A powerful PC with lots of memory (at least 256 MB RAM)
- Plenty of system resources such as backup and write to media such as CD-ROM.
- Software to assists the digitization.
- Experienced/competent staff to run the equipment and to staff to oversee the process and quality assurance.

If we have the entire above infrastructure than it is possible to do digitization job in-house. A further reason why many projects are undertaken in-house is that the staff time, overheads and some consumable such as file storage can often be swallowed up by the institution and do not become apparent as a coasted factor of the project, thus making this appear to be cheaper option than out-sourcing.

THROUGH VENDOR OR OUTSIDE AGANCIES

Develop a tight specification of requirements and a contract that set out what you expect from the vendor, including technical procedures, output form as, handling requirements and time scales. It is important to see whether the vendor is a specialist in digitization of a certain type of material or all type of material. Some are specialists only in paper material some are specialist in color images. They may not be good at some media. The third party advice is important in this regard. Generally in the institutions tender/ quotation system is followed to select the vendor. Order is generally placed to the vendor who quoted lowest price. But one should bear in mind that the cheapest quote may not be form the best vendor or supplier for the job.

Before starting the process there are certain important issues, which are to be discussed first:

1. Copyrighted material are digitized and made available online, only with written permission from the author and the publisher.
2. The rare and old books and other related material such as palm leaf manuscripts, which are part of the Indian heritage, should be handling with care.

PROCESS OF DIGITIZATION

The process consists of following stages:

The creation of digital information from conventional is generally a two-stage process:

1. The first stage is to select the documents, which are to be digitized. Than these can be further categorized subject wise, and type of documents such as reports, maps, etc. Bibliographical detail is to be prepared for each of the document. For this purpose computerized database can be utilized.

   The first stage essentially the conversion of the physical medium into a digital representation of the physical medium (Digitization).
2. The second stage is the digitization process is to have the computer extract information from the digitized image. For text this is done by Optical Character Recognition (OCR) software that recognize the shapes of the letters of the alphabet and produces a file exactly the same as one produced by a word processor used to type in the same text. This stage allows some of the information from the original page to be made available to the computer. Thus, it is now able to index the text for retrieval and is also able to reformat the text for different forms of output.

Data capture

It includes manual data entry, Optical Character Recognition (OCR) or imaging using scanners (scanning process).

Document Numbering

Now the selected record are sent to section for numbering. Each report is to be given a unique number. It may be accession number of the book. Than the each page is to be numbered.

Manual Data entry

Manually entered digital text has the advantage of greater accuracy than some types of data (directories, numerical data base) not amiable to automated means of digitization. However, manual data entry consumes time, manpower money and other recourses. The re-keying or data entry or retyping is another mode of converting print text into digital form. This involves complete typing of the text. This process, although comparatively more accurate, is quite time consuming and costly. But corrections, modifications and changes in formats are easier to carry out.

The following are various methods in the process of digitization:

1. Scanning.
2. Image enhancement.
3. Corrections.
4. File format.
5. Compression.
6. QC.
7. Indexing.
8. Storage /retrieval.

Scanning process

In the second stage selected articles were went

through the process of scanning but one more step was included in scanning. Scanned articles (JPEG format) were linked to another field called image (scanned article).By clicking on the link the scanned page were displayed on the screen. The user could find both options of their choice of getting articles either in full text or in physical form. The user could also use 'expert search' in case of exhaustive search and 'guide search' in case of specific search (e.g. specific brand or product or company or agency or subject).

The process involves conversion of paper documents into an electronic image using image scanner, fax card, digital camera, and other image capturing devices and also played for acquisition of images (Fig. 10). The impotent step involved in the process of digitization is scanning, as explained above with the help of scanning. Scanning is the easiest option to obtain the replica of original source document.This is much less time consuming method than re-typing all of the text. However, system for transfer of paper document into image.

1.The scanning of the document is done with the help of an electronic image scanner. Scanning and capturing the essential components of the original material in digital form is the heart of the process of setting up a digital library. The creation of digital information from conventional is generally a two-stage process.

The basic conversion technique is scanning.

Scanning is a typical part of digitization that requires hardware that so called scanner that can be used to take digital pictures of objects. Scanners can be simple desktop machines or very large and complex systems that process thousands of documents. The fragility, odd sizes, and bound volumes of some library materials pose greater difficulties for scanning. Now the new scanning systems are emerged which uses pattern recognition technologies. They are high productive scanners that suit to library applications.The selected documents than to be scanned with the help of scanner. Flat-bedded scanner is generally used. Because if the document is old and there is a possibility of getting them damaged while passing through Automatic Document Feeder.

Fig. 10. Image Scanning using Digital Camera

An image of the physical object is captured using a scanner or digital camera and converted to digital format that can be stored electronically and accessed via computer.

Most scanning software generate default TIFF format which can be converted into PDF format using a number of softwares. The image can be browsed through a table of contents composed in HTML providing linked to scanned images.

A document is scanned by sampling its image on a grid of points. Each point is represented by a brightness code. In the simpler form only black and white are distinguished. With the resolution of 300 dots per inch (horizontal and vertically), good images can be made of most printed pages. If the resolution is increased to 600 dots per inch, or if eight levels of gray are coded, the clarity becomes excellent and halftone illustration can be represented. High quality artwork requires at least 24 bits per dot to represent color combinations. This creates very large files. The files are compressed for convenience in storage and processing, but even simple black-on-white text files need at least 50, 000 bytes to store a single page.

Scanning resolution

Resolution refers to the number of pixels that are used to describe a single image. Resolution affects the level of details that can depicted by the image file. The 3oo dpi (dot per inch) on an average is good.

The basic conversion technique is scanning. Scanning is a typical part of digitization that requires hardware that so called scanner that can be used to take digital pictures of objects. Scanners can be simple desktop machines or very large and complex systems that process thousands of documents. The fragility, odd sizes, and bound volumes of some library materials pose greater difficulties for scanning. Now the new scanning systems are emerged which uses pattern recognition technologies. They are high productive scanners that suit to library applications.

An image of the physical object is captured using a scanner or digital camera and converted to digital format that can be stored electronically and accessed via computer.

Most scanning software generate default TIFF format which can be converted into PDF format using a number of softwares. The image can be browsed through a table of contents composed in HTML providing linked to scanned images.

Once the document has been digitally scanned, the images are available for rapid distribution, reproduction, and on-screen reading. Such document images are commonly stored in Portable Document Format (PDF), or Tagged Image File Format (TIFF). One can have additional benefits by using Optical Character Recognition (OCR) to convert images of book pages into machine readable form -possible encoding of the document's text, dramatically reducing the storage needed for the book and allowing the text to be reformatted, searched, or used as input for text processing applications such as natural language processing.

The process of scanning can be in a small scale or it may in a large scale. It can be done in-house by the staff or it can be done by the professional vendors. If the scanning is required in a large scale than commercial scanners are required.

Scanning with the help of commercial scanners

The commercial scanners are different from the other scanners. Commercial document scanners are not like normal scanners. These scanners are usually high quality digital cameras with light sources on either sides of the cameras mounted on some sort of frame to provide easy access for a person or machine to flip the pages of the document. (Fig. 11).

Some models involve V shape book cradles, which provide support for book spines and also center book position automatically (Fig. 12 a & b).

The advantage of this type of scanner is that it is very fast, compared to the productivity of overhead scanners. This type of camera based book scanner is much more cost effective.

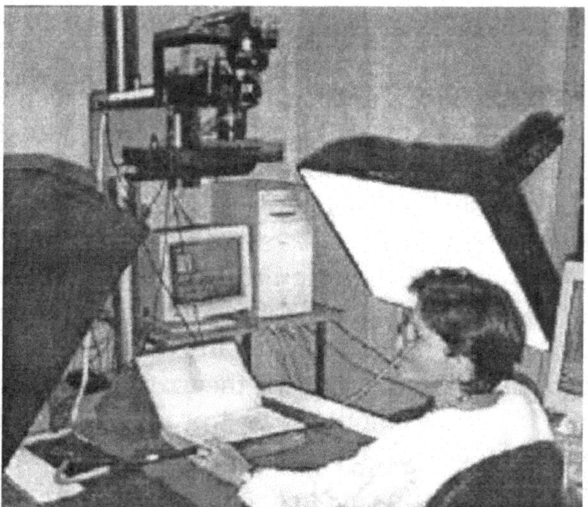

Fig. 11. Commercial Document Scanner

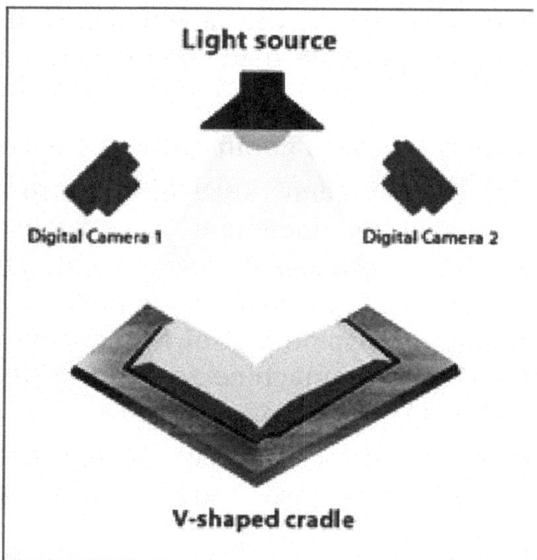

Fig. 12(a). Sketch of V-shaped book scanner

METHODS OF SCANNING

There are three main ways that a large organization is relying on:

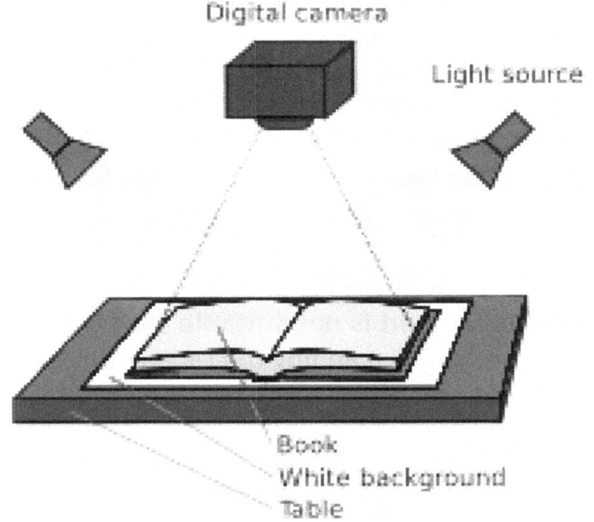

Fig. 12(b). Sketch of a typical manual book scanner.

1. Outsourcing
2. Scanning in-house using commercial book scanners and
3. Scanning in-house using robotic scanning solution.

1. Outsourcing

As for outsourcing, books are often shipped to be scanned by low cost sources such as India. Alternatively due to convenience , safety and technology improvement , many organization choose to scan in-house by using either overhead scanners which are time consuming , or digital cameras based scanning solutions which are substantially faster , and is a method employed by Internet Archives as well as well as Google.

2. Low Budget Scanning

The least expensive method to scan a book or magazine is to cut off the binding. This converts the book or magazine into a sheaf of loose-leaf papers, which can than be loaded into a standard automatic document feeder and scanned using inexpressive and common scanning technology. This is the traditional method, which includes cutting of the book's spine and scanning the pages in a scanner with automatic page feeder, with rebinding of the loose pages occurring afterwards. This is not a desirable solution for very old and rare books. It is a useful tool for books and magazines scanning where the book is not an expensive item and replacement of the scanned content is easy.

But this method is not suitable for rare and fragile books. The method of scanning the rare and fragile books is known as Robot scanning.

3. Robot Scanning

In recent years, software driven machines and robots have been developed to scan books without the need of disbinding them in order to preserve both the contents of the document and a digital photo archive of its current state. This recent trend has been due in part to ever improving imaging technologies that allow a high quality digital archive image to be capture with little or no damage to a rare or fragile document in a reasonable short period of time. Some high end scanning system employ vacuum and air and static charges to turn pages while imaging is performed automatically, usually from a high resolution camera located over an adjustable v-shape cradle (Fig. 12a). Images are then shuttled from the imaging device into various editing suites which can further process the images for either an archival quality file such as TIFF or JPEG 2000, or a web friendly output such as JPEG or PDF.

1. Optical Character Recognition (OCR)

The next step is OCR.OCR software is used for conversion of scanned text to machine-readable text that can be searched or indexed. A policy should be made not to make any correction for words not understood by the OCR software but retain the same in the image output because large numbers of documents may be produced by the conventional typing machine with a very small font.

Another simple digitization process is that of scanning printed pages to build a digital database of the text. This process uses OCR software that takes a picture of the page and then turns it into digital text, which can be edited or fully indexed. An other method is Optical Character Recognition is the technique of converting scanned images of characters to their equivalent characters. The basic technique is for a computer programme to separate out the individual characters and then to compare each character to mathematical templates. Despite decades of research, Optical Character Recognition remains an inexact process. The error rate varies with the legibility of the original. If the original document is clear and legible, the error rate is less than one percent. With the low quality materials, the error rate can be much higher. For many purposes, an error rate of even a fraction of a percent is too high; it corresponds to too many incorrect characters on every page. Various processes have been devised to get around these errors. One technique is to use several different character recognition programmes on the same materials in the hope that characters that others may resolve cause difficulty for one programme. However, all high quality conversion requires human proofreading.

When the individual words have been recognized, the next stage of conversion is to identify the structure of a document and to tag headings and other structural elements.

An alternate method of conversion, widely used in practice, is to retype the document from scratch and add markup tags manually. This approach is often cheaper than a combination of automatic and human processing. It is usually carried out in the countries where labor cost is low.

The basic technique is for a computer programme to

separate out the individual characters and then to compare each character to mathematical templates. The two well known available OCR techniques are Xerox Text Bridge and Caere's Omni page Incorporation technology. Retaining the page layout is the major problem in OCR. Now number of softwares are available for retaining the layout. The process of retaining the page layout is software dependent. The process of OCR results in computer possible file that is less accurate than re-keying of the data. The Acrobat 2.0 provides several options for retaining not only the page layout, but also the fonts, and to fit text into the exact space occupied in the original. In image + text solution or OCRed text is generated for each image where each page is an exact replica of the original and left untouched. The OCRed text is generally not corrected for errors since it is used only for scanning. The PDF normal gives the clearest image on screen display.

2. Compression

Scanned image required good amount of memory storage. In order to have economies on storage space, images are to be to be stored in a compressed form.

Cleaning job is required at this stage. Now the scanning of the documents to be done. A4 to A0 size maps are stored in hard disk.

3. PDF (Portable Data Format) conversion

The OCRed output is than converted to PDF file, sometimes through in-built technology of the OCR software or sometimes by separate software for PDF conversion. Interlinking of text pages, maps/ plates are done with the PDF file by book marking.

4. Checking

Before storing in the CD, checking of every stage is required by professional staff. Checking is required at the following stages:

1. Document identification stage
2. Post scanning stage
3. OCR checking and PDF conversion stage
4. Metadata creation and indexing stage.

The OCRed output is than converted to PDF file, sometimes through in-built technology of the OCR software or sometimes by separate software for PDF conversion. Interlinking of text pages, maps/ plates are done with the PDF file by book marking.

5. CD cutting

Scanned and checked records are than transferred to CDs with backup in duplicate.

Standardizing the soft copy format (data from text, audio, video, etc.)

1. Editing, final formatting
2. Inputting documents into a document management system

   (Using/w like Data scan. Omni Docs)
3. Open database connectivity

   (Networks, Web)

6. Indexing and Processing:

Indexing: Indexing of documents converted into an image or text file is the second step in the process of document imaging. It is the second step after scanning is over. The processor indexing a text database. Scanned images are just like pictures describing. An image system typically stored large amount of unstructured data in two files is traditional file that has a text description of the image along with key to second file. The second file contains document location. The user select a record from first file using a search algorithm. Once a user selects a record, the application key into the location index, find the document and display it.

Digitized documents need to be processed using standards, protocols and indexing systems. Classification using library systems also hold much promise. Metadata application should be a major component of the digital information processing.

7. Data Processing

Text in the convertible document may require conversion of special characters; images may need enhancement, implications or compression. In many cases a simple conversion from print to digital is not enough.

8. Storage of Digital Resources

Digital resources can be stored in CD, DVD, tape and hard disk. Usually the things to be digitized will be image, text, audio and video. The text, image and photographs after scanning is stored in the JPEG (Join Photographic Expert Groups) and GIF (Graphics Interchange Format). These two formats are widely used for storage images because they are small, fast and capable of displaying any type of picture. Audio files can be saved in way, mp3, midi, etc. format. Recently developed MP3 format is very compact and takes less space while quality of audio is also better compared to other formats. The digitized video files are saved in .mov or .avi, divx, mpeg file formats.

9. Access to Digital Information Available on Web

The web provides the hypermedia based systems that allow rapid access to a wide variety of networked information resources. One can browse the different web sites, which are scattered geographically and have access to the major resources from which one can download the information. Some of the major portals sites or gateways that provide access to electronic resources are:

http://mel.library.mi.us/

http://bubl.ac.uk/

http://edoc.com

So digital libraries can develop their collection through the integration of a number of resources and media types. Digital libraries can also provide access to electronic resources through library home pages.

Third step is to transfer scanned image from hard disk of scanning workstations to external storage devices like CDs DVDs etc. The image storage device may be either remote or local to the retrieval workstations, depending upon the imaging system and document management system. The most difficult problem is that of storage. The page image has to be stored on a storage media. A large capacity storage device has to be used, like optical disks-CD-ROMs, magnetic tapes, etc.

The digitized information needs to be recorded in proper digital medium, which may be a hard disk, magnetic tape, optical devices such as CD-ROM, or networks with workstation to access.

10. Retrieval

After the storage of scanned image is the retrieval of the needed data from the digital collection files. The digital image is also called "bit mapped page image". In this process scanned images are retrieved through two files are for text description and second for location of text/document. The text description file or the traditional file links to second file i.e., document is identified then it can be viewed on monitor taken as print out.

In this process scanned images are retrieved through two files one for text description and second for location of text/document. The text description file or the traditional file links to the second file i.e. document is identified than it can be viewed on monitor taken as printer out.

PROBLEMS IN DIGITIZATION

There are many advantages of Digitization however, it also poses some problems:

1. Cost

The first problem to digitization is the cost involved. It is very expensive, especially to undertake it alone and in house. The cost of digitization is about $ 2 to $ 6 per page.

It shows heavy expenditure for the process of digitization. It means stealing of acquisition budget.

An other problem in the development of a digital library is copyright and IPR.

Copyright has been called the "single most vexing barrier to digital library development". Copyright and IPR issues are governed by the constitution of various countries and through international treaties like the Berne Convention.

DIGITIZATION OF SPECIAL COLLECTION

Digitization of reports, rare books and such material

A library consists of not only books and journals but also some special collection such as maps, reports, photographs, thesis, press clippings etc. These types of material required special attention. Digitization is the best solution for keeping/preserving these materials for the longer period of time. This type of material forms the primary research collection of the library. Whatever may be the format, the common features of the special collections are that they are unique, rare, require special handling and in limited availability or just some thing that cannot be locate in the open stacks. Equally important is that the material is valued at an artifact. Special collection may use digitization as a preservation techniques but its real value is related to the increased access to special collections. Almost all the major libraries of the world are having digitization programme to provide greater access to its special collections through the digitization of material including maps, reports, rare books, thesis, dissertations etc.

The rare and old collection of documents is deteriorating in many libraries because of excessive handling and exposure to environmental condition. The digital imaging technology can provide worldwide access to documents by many users simultaneously as well as completely faithful reproduction, regardless of the numbers of copies produced (Fig. 13).

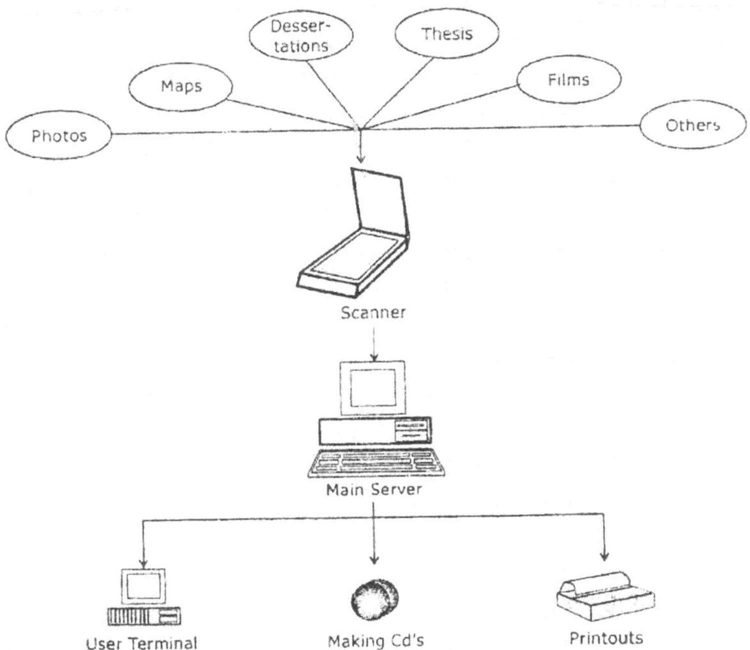

Fig. 13. Digitization of special collection

It is the process through which an array of technologies for browsing, displaying and applying packages that ultimately helps in access.

PROCESS

Identification of documents: First step is to identify

the documents, which are to be digitized. Documents may be photographs, drawings, maps, etc. prepared a list-contained author, title, accession number etc. scanning of documents on flat bed machine because old documents may damaged while passing through the ADF (Automatic Document Feeder). Before scanning a unique number is required for identification. This number may be accession number. Each document should be numbered sequentially. The quality of scanned document depends on the scanning resolutions. Resolution refers to the numbers of pixels that are used to describe the single image. The scanning resolutions are measured in terms of dot per inch or dpi then the scanned image required compression. The scanned image required good amount of memory storage. In order to save storage space images are stored in compressed form. Some of the images like maps can be stored in hard disk. Now the scanned images are to be converted into machine-readable form by OCR (Optical Character Recognition) the OCRed output is than converted into PDF Files. It can be done through inbuilt technology of the OCR software or sometimes by separate software for PDF conversion. Interlinking of text pages, maps, diagrams are done within the PDF file by book marking. Before storing on storage devices such as on CDs checking of the text is required in all the stages such as documentation stage, post scanning stage, OCR and PDF conversion stage, metadata creation and indexing stage. Scanned and checked items are than transferred to CDs with backup in duplicate. Next step is metadata creation for indexing. For easy searching and retrieval of reports different parameters viz, author's titles, keywords are used (Fig. 14).

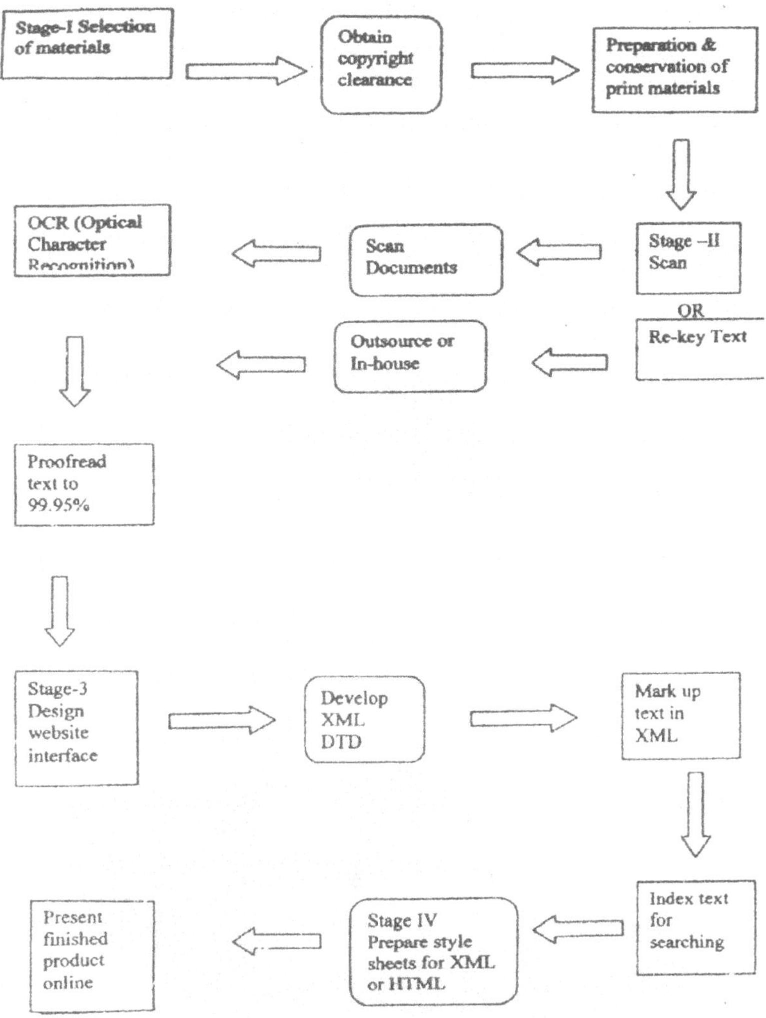

Fig. 14. Process of Scanning

Digitization can be done by the process of creating digital files by scanning or converting analog materials. The technology used for digitization of analog object is called scanning and the equipment is called scanner. Scanners are imaging technology or OCR technology for digitization. Imaging process create photo images of the papers document and later on may be converted to PDF format or can be saved as Jpeg or bit map image as per policy of standard adopted for digitization. The image can be read only and cannot be edited.

The OCR technology allows converting the scanned image to the electronic format able to format either in the form of a plain text or word processor document format, ready for editing.

Fig. 15. Modern Book Scanner

Rusbridge has divided resources for a digital library into four categories i.e. legacy, transition new and future. Legacy resources are largely non-digital resources including manuscripts, print, slides, and maps, audio and video recordings.

Transition resources, are primarily designed for another medium (mostly print) are those which are being or have been digitized, making the transition into the digital world. The conversion into digital form is just to ensure better access and to reduce dependence on physical libraries. These are either digitized images or ways that are converted to list by the process of OCR.

A digitization project can cover a wide range of complex activities and it is often easy to lose track of the underlying project aims and objectives.

17

Information Access/ Retrieval in Digital Libraries

INTRODUCTION

A digital library enables users to interact effectively with information distributed across a network. Digital libraries are a metaphor for access to collections of electronic documents through a network. The classic research area dealing with the electronic search for documents is information retrieval. During the last 30 years the topic of this discipline evolved from electronic catalogs to the management of fultext and multimedia documents. So, from the first viewpoint digital libraries and information retrieval are not that different. Information retrieval has to leave the controlled and uniform conditions of professional information providers. It is confronted with a vast variety of servers, formats, indexing, strategies, and query mechanisms.

Digital medium is fast replacing the paper medium. Similarly traditional libraries being replaced by digital libraries. Information in digital libraries is digitally stored and accessed. The recent development in communication technology, networking, use of the Internet and electronic resources has brought revolutionary changes in the dissemination of information process. The new technology is mainly being used for communication, database searching. It has also changed the concept of archiving. The organization, storage, access, preservation and retrieval of information have become easier now. The quality of information one receives through digital system i.e. in the forms of hyper books, CD-ROM and digital retrieval systems.

INFORMATION RETRIEVAL SYSTEMS

Information retrieval deals with representation, storage and access to documents or information surrogates. Usually, an information retrieval system is considered to have the function of "leading the user to those documents that will best enable him/her to satisfy his/her need for information. According to Bulkin the goal of information retrieval is system is for the user to obtain information from the knowledge resource which helps him /her in problem management.

All types of information retrieval systems whether it is manual or computerized comprising three stages:

1. Indexing
2. Storage and
3. Retrieval.

1. Indexing

Indexing is the process of allocating index terms or key to record or document represented in an information retrieval system. The term was used to locate an item(record or document).With the invent of computers and the availability of text in digital form, alternatives to manual indexing are available and are essential to cope with the proliferation of information in the documentary form. Thus, automated techniques are absolutely necessary. It is important to develop algorithms for automatic indexing. In other words, a computer can select index terms in accordance with a set of instruction. Selection will depend upon word occurrence. The index terms that may be assigned are drawn from a standard list or computerized thesaurus, on the basis of word occurrence in a record or document. Such terms will be selected and assigned by the indexers on the basis of indexer's subjective assignment of the contents of the document. In either case, computer acts as a reliable tool for arranging as well as displaying of the index terms.

2. Storage

The second aspect of information retrieval is storage. Information retrieval systems may use the computer itself to storage both the document files as well as index files, and also to maintain databases. In that case, the information must be stored in specially designed data structures to support the processes above.

3. Retrieval Capabilities

The third aspect is retrieval capabilities. The retrieval process is the most important issue and basically depends on how the information contained in the system has been indexed and how it is stored in the system. In other words, the indexing and storage aspects determine, to a large extent, the search strategy to be adopted for retrieval of information. An other factor which influences the retrieval process is the system user and the queries that are submitted to the system which do not, in general, change the system. The user's needs may not change with the availability of a particular system, although they may become more sophisticated as the user's experience with the system increases.

DIGITAL RETRIEVAL SYSTEM

The organized collection traditionally called "libraries" and the searchable on-line versions of these are called "digital libraries". The basic purpose of digital libraries is to enable searching of electronic collections distributed across networks, rather than merely creating electronic repositories from digitized physical materials. Traditionally, information retrieval has been a task for professional librarians. The trained reference librarians interact with on-line services of specialized materials and report results to querying user. Although public computer networks have long been used to access specialized information services, it has taken the recent rise of the internet to make literature searching directly available to widespread users.

The internet is the world's first digital information utility, an all purpose network that lets anybody send anything digital to anywhere, without argument. An Internet is a popular and widely used network. In traditional setup, physical/geographical distance is one major constrain for access which does not exists in the Internet environment or digital environment. The ways of accessing information and library operations have undergone metamorphic changes.

These network information system support search and display of items from organized collection. In the historical evolution of digital libraries, the mechanism for retrieval of literature have been particularly important. There is rise in the document search, from multimedia browsing across local area networks to distributed search on the internet. By 2010, the visions will be realized, with concept search enabling semantic retrieval across large collection.

The networked information systems needed to support such access have steadily improved as the underlying computing and communications infrastructure has improved. The recent advent of WWW searchers and digital libraries has developed popular interest in these issues.

INFORMATION RETIEVAL TECHNIQUES

The development of communication technology and computer technology has developed a number of advanced models of information retrieval techniques that has been employed in various fields of research and development.

The retrieval techniques may broadly be divided into two headings:

1. Exact Matching Techniques.
2. Partial Matching Techniques.

1. Exact matching technique

This technique is a widely accepted phenomenon that is implemented through Boolean, fultext string searching methods. The primary advantage of this technique is that, it is easy to understand and use, as it is available on most systems. The disadvantages with this that are, it looses the opportunity of getting many relevant texts which match the query. It further neither ranks the documents nor takes care of the relative concepts either within the query or within the text

2. Partial matching Technique

Here, the information can be retrieved employing various sub techniques such as, individual, network, clustered, probabilistic etc. According to the requirement the relevant techniques are to be adopted for retrieval of information.

Since the beginning of on-line information retrieval more than 30 years ago, the base functionality has remained the same. A collection of literature is maintained and indexed, which the user access by means of a terminal connected to a server across a network. The user specifies a query by a set of words, and all documents in the collection that contains those words are returned. The fundamental technology for searching large collections is finally changing, so that information retrieval in the next century will be far more semantic than syntactic, concept rather than word.

Although the software has remained largely unchanged, the hardware has improved dramatically as computer and networks have become faster and cheaper. As a result, the "document" has changed from a citation with descriptive header to the abstract to the complete multimedia contents, including text, figures, tables, equations, and data. Similarly the size of the organization able to serve a collection to the users has decreased, so that there are now hundreds of thousands of servers distributed around the world, instead of a few hundred at central site.

Today, the online information retrieval available with internet web searches enables interaction with information sources distributed across the international network. The functionality has changed dramatically from the previous generation of multimedia text abstracts retrieved using special purpose public terminals from a single large central computer center to the present generation of multimedia documents retrieved using general purpose personnel computers from multiple small distributed file servers.

INDEXING AND ACCESS/RETRIEVAL

Once the content is selected and acquired it should be added to the collection in such a way that users will be able to retrieve it effectively.

Several WWW based services use a hybrid approach by manually crating a classification system and than using automatic techniques to assign objects. The most ambitious effort to automatically indexing large volumes of documents till date is the work of Schatz and others. Currently researchers are actively applying existing text retrieval techniques to the cross language retrieval systems as digital libraries because more global consisting of multiple language documents.

BIBLIOGRAPHIC DATABASE SEARCH

The first attempt was centered on text search of technical citations. The contents were the text of a bibliographic citation of journal article, which include the title, author, journal, and keywords of the reference article. A search query was matching specified words to words in the field of citation.

The hardware capability of the central mains frames of this period largely determined the functionality of the information retrieval. Disk space mandated the collection of citations rather than the complete text of articles. The output devise was a paper typewriter, mandating a short display, such as a title or citation. The network was a telephone line, used as one of the first packed switched networks. The items were not yet actual documents but pointers to physical documents.

These systems were well suited to generating a bibliography -for example, exhaustively printing all articles that contained the keywords "information retrieval" and "computer networks" for the references of a paper. Although the systems were intended for searching and location desired items, their slow speed and precise queries limited their effectiveness in browsing, and their primary users were professional librarians generating bibliographies for scientists.

The collections of citations that the online systems handled became known as "bibliographic databases". Generated by the abstracting and indexing industry, bibliographic databases were extended over time to include searchable abstracts of the articles.

RETRIEVAL

Most retrieval systems for images, video and audio recording and other non textual objects have depended on text items such as title, creator name, or manually assign subject heading for retrieval.

Most present day document retrieval system employs specialized personnel to index documents. However, many providers of repositories for electronic documents are not able to use this successful but extensive method. An alternative is the use of automated indexing tools for full text documents. They are faster and less expensive and they can be taken advantage of structural information like HTML or SGML tags) included in electronic documents. In addition they can incorporate specific views of specific users.

TEXT SEARCH; RETRIEVAL TECHNOLOGY

The basic technology for searching bibliographic databases is still the primary method for large scale information retrieval; when there is a large collection to be searched, the retrieval method used today are those developed for bibliographic databases 30 years ago. These text retrieval methods rely on indexing the documents so that selected items can be quickly retrieved. A user sends a query from his terminal across the network to a server. Software at the server searches the index, locates the document matching the query, and returns these documents matching the query, and returns these documents to the user terminal.

To support retrieval by word matching (find all the documents containing the particular word), an inverted list index is built. The documents are scanned for words, omitting a few noise words such as 'the' and "of" and a list is built for every word. These lists are called "inverted" because for each word they contain pointer to the documents that contains the words. The index consists of the inverted list in alphabetical order by word. It can be used for fast search of a specified word by scanning the index for that word and then using the attached pointers to retrieve the matching documents.

As computer became more powerful, the scale of documents for information retrieval becomes greater. That is, as it became technologically and economically feasible to provide faster networks and larger disks, it became possible to store and retrieve more than just a citation. First, the abstract was added, and this is the economic level that today remains the standard for the literature. Then, video terminals became the mode of display, so that text could be viewed more rapidly that with teletypewriters. This led to the extension for abstracts to so-called" full text". An online fultext article contains all words within an article but exclude non-textual materials such as figures, tables etc.

RETRIEVAL ISSUES

The success of the digital library depends upon the efficient retrieval .The system should have a flexible search language with on-line help at every stage. Further the system can be enhanced with the search options such as Boolean query or providing a drop down menu of the subject strings from which the user may be able to choose from pre-coordinated strings.

A set of search queries and syntax may be provided to direct the users to formulate the search queries. The retrieval set should be available with abstract so that they reflect the contents. Further links can be provided to full text documents to the extend possible.

The case of retrieval of information using the Internet as a source poses an entirely different challenge. From the user point of view, Internet has a solution for every information need. But how can the web documents are traced at the time of the need? The various search engines available on the net are hardly adequate tools to give impressive information services to the users. Most of the search engines searches the terms in the title or the first few lines of the documents. There are also efforts at document description such as the Dublin Core set of elements. In any case the indicators are in the direction of continuous search for improving search on the net.

DOCUMENT SEARCH: MULTIMEDIA BROWSING

By the 1980s, fultext search had become established commercially in online retrieval systems. This same era saw the initial development of bitmapped personnel workstations and local area networks in research laboratories. This technology made it possible to provide new functionality to the established ideas of text search, most notably in the areas of multimedia documents and distributed browsing.

As the computer model changed from central shared mainframes to distributed personnel workstations, it profoundly changed information retrieval from text search to document search. The increased speed of both the workstations and networks brought an expansion in both the basic document and the basic retrieval. Multimedia slowly became possible, so that pictorial materials, such as graphics, images, and videos, could be included in the documents and accessed from collections across the network. It means interactive display of color pictures from remote sources become technologically feasible.

The increased speed across the network meant that multiple sources could be searched within a single query while still maintaining effective user interaction for the return of results. Multiple collections could be stored in physically distributed locations, yet searched as single, logically coherent collection. This was an interactive realization of the transparent information gateway technology pioneered in 1970s and commercialized in the

1980s.In the new computer environment; the network speeds enabled federation across sources to be done dynamically.

QUERY INTERPRETATION

A good query has to be general enough to cover all relevant documents and specific enough to select only relevant ones. To achieve a high specificity we use the rules defined for the indexing tool and, in addition, a set of domain specific rule. These rules are managed by an abducted system, i.e. a system for hypothetical reasoning. It constructs the possible interpretation of query terms corresponding to alternative paths in the inference network and negotiates them with the user. In this way user is able to select his/her intended interpretation of an unstructured query. An other way to enhance a query is to add related terms either as a substitute for or as an addition to existing query terms. Such related terms can be synonyms, associatively related terms, more general or more specific terms. To find such related terms we use co-occurrence analysis based on large corpora of documents of the respective domain. This corpus-based method allows the fast creation of such associative thesauri, which are specific to given domain and time.

DIALOG MANAGEMENT

Most retrieval sessions consists of a series of searches each based on the results of previous attempts. During this interaction the user elaborates his/her query. For many inexperienced users the cognitive load of managing the search and scanning the documents found is very high. In a digital library environment the situation will be worse due to the heterogeneity of the various systems and servers.

To help users in this situation we develop a Dialog Management System that keeps track of the interaction; it is able to offer context specific interactions of user actions and propose further steps in a context sensitive way.

SERVER SELECTION

The special problem of digital libraries is the selection of appropriate servers for a given query. This is a kind of 'meta search'. This includes the static descriptions like retrieval engines available, formats of queries, domain of server, average load, prices, network bandwidths, etc. In addition we plan to use knowledge discovery method to get information about a server.

18

Major Problems, Issues and Challanges in Building Digital Library Resources

INTRODUCTION

The impact of information and Communication Technology services has influenced every facet of library and information services in libraries and providing new opportunities and challenges to library professionals. The information revolution and knowledge that is available on the web have created new challenges to the library professionals.

PROBLEMS, ISSUES AND CHALLANGES

The major issues and challenges that the library and information professionals face in the present digital era for providing digital information services to the knowledge society are:

1. New generation of learners.

2. Copyright.
3. Privacy/confidentially.
4. Online/virtual crimes and security.
5. Technology challenges.
6. Manpower.
7. Collection of digital e-resources.
8. Organizational structure.
9. Preservation/archiving of digital resources.
10. Lack of clarity in vision.

Privacy/confidentially

Maintaining privacy/confidentiality in an other problem in accessing online information. To control pirating of software, copying or downloading all the contents of any e-resource at a time, right to obtain information and right to withhold or ban the access is essential and so there is a delicate challenge between piracy and right to information. Now almost all the users are having their own e-mail account and they are often sending and receiving important information and even secret programmes and databases through e-mail itself and storing them for future usage. So marinating piracy from e-mail is a big issue. Protecting one network from another to maintain confidentiality of information is an other problem in securing databases on Internet and intranet.

Technology Challenges

The explosion of information available on Internet poses problems to the access of information.

Manpower Issues

Lack of skilled manpower to maintain the e-resources and to provide proper e-information service to the user is an other problem. Core competencies of library staff are expending to include technology skills, personnel skills, learning teaching capacity, team skills, leadership skills etc. Hence library education must be redesigned to meet the new challenges and issues evolving in the knowledge society. Adequately skilled staff should be recruited to meet the increasing demand of trained staff.

Collection of e-resources

Collecting the material and making them available to the current and future users is another core problem. That challenge is for the librarian to contribute to establish realistic collection -development policies covering acquisition of and provision of access to electronic resources for users now and in the future. With the increase in the electronic resources, librarians and libraries are no longer just collecting and caring the print material. Unlike a print material, electronic resources cannot be considered a permanent addition to a collection. Payment for product covered by a license is a payment to use the information product for a period of time that is usually specified in a contract. This payment is not for the outright purchase of the product or for ownership of all the rights to that product. A digitized collection means that libraries share the use of the collection with other institutions, not only locally, but also globally. It is the publisher who dictates how much access will be provided, which issues will be available, and how much that access will cost.

Procurement of books

Considerable attention needs to be paid towards identifying and procuring books that are useful to broader communities of users. With the help of user study it can be found out the most accessible books. All the books may not be accessed most of the time. Yet an other problem is that many people do not agree to the fact that digitization is the only way of preserving the books. Some are apprehensive about the possible rough use and the resultant damage to the books by the scanning center staff especially for the old and rare books

Before discussing major issues and challenges, it is important to know that:

What does it take to establish a fully functional digital library?

One of the greatest challenges in the establishment of a digital library network in the country like India is Internet connectivity. The lack of networked infrastructure and inappropriate pricing patterns can also prove significant hurdle for fledging. Dial up access, using telephone lines emerge as an immediate connectivity solution as existing network infrastructure can be tapped. Due to limited bandwidth and slower speeds, dial up is suitable only for basic e-mailing and browsing.

1. **Knowledgeable staff/Lack of Experience**: Any organization that intends to establish a digital library must have a knowledgeable and skilled staff. They must be hardworking, committed, and loyal to their parent organization. They must be extremely sensitive to the information needs of the clients they serve. Digital libraries are considered but many to be a challenging area. The development of an infrastructure for the networked resource discovery and retrieval of highly distributed, autonomously created, and diverse electronic information is required. Above all, this infrastructure will need to be managed by professionals who understand information needs and uses.

2. **Provision of digital content**: The digital library must contain information resources. It may either be new material prepared digitally from scratch (I.e. born digital), or it may be old material, converted into digital form (i.e. digitized). It may be bought, donated or converted locally from previously purchased library stock. Digital contents then need to be stored and retrieved. Information is widely

found as text stored as characters and images acquired using optical scanners. More recently, audio and video, plus interactive material is accumulating rapidly in the digital form both newly generated and converted from older material.

3. Searching of digital information resources: After storing information in a digital library, mechanisms ought to be in a place for one to accurately identify and locate the piece of information sought.

According to Wikipedia, most of the digital libraries provide search interface, which allow in formation resources to be found. These resources are typically deep web (or invisible web) resources, since search engine crawlers cannot locate them. Some digital libraries create special pages or sitemaps to allow search engine to find all their resources.

4. Retrieval of digital information resources: Retrieval systems are necessary for users to obtain the information they require from the digital libraries. Whatever the case, retrieved information must be delivered to the user. A digital library must also have some form of preservation mechanism. In that way, there has to be a means of ensuring that what may be available today is still available tomorrow.

5. Interoperability: Digital libraries are at the heart of interrelationships between several information service-related disciplines like library management, archives management, document management, knowledge management and e-commerce systems. This brings about the need for the different kinds of systems to talk to each other.

Miller defined the term interoperability as:

"....the ongoing process of ensuring that the system, procedures and culture of an organization are managed in such a way as to maximize opportunities for exchange and reuse of information, whether internally or externally."

Interoperability, in digital libraries, allow organization and communities to retain their specialist practices, while putting high level standards and protocols in place for sharing information.

6. Sustainable Funding: Digital librarians need to establish the financial resources to pay for and sustain digital libraries. Funding digital libraries is the single most frustratating obstacle facing librarians in the present day. Digital libraries are bound to change the social system by which information is collected, transformed, managed, disseminated and preserved, both in the present day as well as in the future. So the sufficient backing of funding is essential.

So there is a need of fund raising and fund management, if at all their libraries are to strive in the medium and long term.

The following are some of the encouraging factors that have nudged the information society towards developing digital libraries, as mentioned by Hariharan et al (2002) and Deegan and Tanner (2002):

- Information can be saved digitally and therefore genres immediate access to high demand and frequently used items;
- There enhanced intellectual control along with new finding tools and support searching capabilities;
- Links are provided to access bibliographical tools;
- Manipulation of texts and images is improved by enabling the enhancement of digital images in terms of size, sharpness color, contrast, noise reduction and so on;
- Duplication of digital resources is easy;
- The potential for integration into teaching materials by presenting the critical mass of reading materials is provided;

- The burden of cost of delivery is reduced;
- There is encouragement of use by providing enhanced resources in the form of wide spread dissemination of unique collection;
- More than one user can make use of single information resource, simultaneously;
- Provides timely access;
- Saves physical storage space;
- Capable of supporting and creating multimedia information resources thus allowing the simultaneous integration of different media (images, graphics, sounds, videos and so on);
- No mutilation of pages due to high use or otherwise can occur;
- There is an increase use of library resources and web-base resources through internet or intranet, making it easy to receive or transfer information both from as well as to any part of the internet, instantly;
- Support resource sharing among libraries by providing efficient and seamless access to materials held remotely;
- There is the capability of keeping an electronic archive/history of resources previously accessed.
- There is possibility of several libraries forming a consortium or consortia of access to bibliographic database, abstracts, fultext journals and even e-books online, by spending only a nominal amount.

7. Creating effective digital library poses serious challenges : The integration of digital media into traditional collections will not be straight forward, like previous new media (e.g. video and audio tapes), because of the unique nature of digital information—it is less fixed, easily copied, and remotely accessible by multiple users simultaneously.

Some of the serious issues facing the development of digital libraries are:

The first issue is that of the technical architecture that underlies any digital library system. Libraries will need to enhance and upgrade current technical architecture to accommodate digital materials. The architecture will include components such as:

i. High speed local networks and fast connection to the internet

ii. Relational databases that support a variety of digital formats

iii. Fultext search engines to index and provide access to resources

iv. A variety of servers, such as web servers and FTP servers

v. Electronic document management functions that will aid in the overall management of digital resources.

The resources supported by the architecture could include:

1. Bibliographical databases that point to both paper and digital materials
2. Indexes and finding tools
3. Collections of pointers to internet resources
4. Directories
5. Primary materials in various digital formats
6. Photographs
7. Numerical data sets and
8. Electronic journal (E-journals)

Though these resources may reside on different systems and in different databases, they would appear as though there were one single system to the users of a particular community. The problem, however is that across multiple digital libraries, there is a vide variety of different data structures, search engines, interfaces, controlled vocabularies, document formats, and so on. Because of this diversity, federating all digital libraries nationally or internationally would an impossible effort.

8. Building Digital collection: One of the largest issues in creating digital libraries will be the building of digital collection:

1. **Digitization**: converting papers and other media in existing collection to digital form.
2. **Acquisition**: access of original digital works created by publishers and scholars.
3. **Access**: access to external material not held in house by providing pointers to website, other library collection, or publishers' servers.

One of the main issues here is the degree to which libraries will digitize existing materials and acquire original digital work, as opposed to simply pointing to them externally. This is the old access versus ownership issue.

How can specific materials to be processed by a given institution be identified? Who collects and/or digitizes what materials could be based on factors such as:

Collection strength, unique collection (if the library has the only copies of something); the priorities of user communities (such priorities will justify holding the materials locally); manageable portions of collections (what is reasonable for any one institution to collect or digitized?);

Technical architecture (the state of librarie's technical architecture will also be factoring selecting who digitizes what); skills of staff (institutions whose staff does not have the necessary skills cannot become a major node in a national scheme)

1. Digitization: One of the primary methods of digital collection building is digitization. Digitization is conversion of any fixed or analog media such as books, journal articles, photos, and paintings -into electronic form through scanning, sampling, or in fact even reeking. An obvious obstacle to digitization is that it is very expensive.

There are several approaches available to decide what part of collection to digitize?

- Retrospective conversion of collections—essentially, starting at A and ending up a Z.
- Digitization of a particular special collection or a portion one. A small collection of manageable size, and which is highly valuable, is a prime candidate.
- Highlight a diverse collection
- High-used materials, making those materials that are in most demand more accessible.
- An adhoc approach where one digitizes and stores materials as they are requested.

9. Metadata: Metadata is another issue central to the development of digital libraries. Metadata is the data that describes the contents and attributes of any particular item in a digital library. Metadata is a critical element for searching information through a database especially, when the information available in an invisible space like the internet, unlike a conventional library. Metadata is important in digital libraries because it is the key to resource discovery and use of any document. Incomplete and incorrect Metadata is an other problem. In order to do fruitful search, correct metadata is required. Due to varied sources of reading material, collected for digitization in multiple languages and due to lack of standard formats, metadata is missing, incorrect or incomplete or sometimes difficult to interpret. Inaccurate metadata hinders fruitful search and retrieval of resources, which brings in scope for duplicate entries of the same book.

A major challenge exists to develop methods of

consistently and uniquely identifying and retrieving networked information, no matter what format they are or where they reside. Metadata standards are still in their infancy. It has been found that given the complexity of metadata issues, a solution to the global resource discovery problem remains distant.

The function of metadata is to standardize the structure and contents of indexing or cataloging information. There are few universally recognized standards of classifications that are being used around the world for digital resource management purposes.

While there are formal library standards for metadata, namely AACR, such records are very time consuming. To create and require specially trained personals. Human cataloging, though superior, is just too labor extensive for the already large and rapidly expending information environment. Thus, simpler schemes for metadata are being proposed as solutions.

Every book that is scanned and stored is associated with metadata for identification and search and retrieval. Identifying the metadata that should be preserved along with the digital objects is debatable topic.

Each digital book object contains three forms of metadata:

1. Regular metadata: Regular metadata contains information about the book like title, author, date of publication, publisher, ISBN, keywords, subject, language etc. We follow the widely understood and accepted Dublin Core format and extended with a few extra fields like edition information of the book etc. This metadata primarily helps us to identify, categorize and retrieve the book.

2. Administrative metadata: This metadata consists of administrative details of the book, like the location of scanning of a book, the source of the book; details of scanning of book etc. may not be of interest to the book readers but are useful to the operational organization. It can be used to trace the progress of the project, generate report and identify bottlenecks, in scanning process etc. For example, we could trace the scanner producing low quality scans etc.

3. Structural Metadata: This metadata contains information pertaining to each page like the size of each page, whether the page is blank, or has an important context attached to it like the beginning of chapter, end of chapter, index, preface, table of contents etc. Such information enables us to improve the navigation of the end user through the book and also improve search and retrieval system.

Each digital book object contains all the three forms of metadata. Regular metadata is entered by source librarians or the contractor hired librarians before digitization begins. Administrative metadata is gathered at the contractors end and also automatically detected by learning techniques.

While they are still in their infancy, a number of schemes are have emerged, the most prominent of which is the Dublin Core, an effort to try and determine the "core" elements needed to describe materials.

Lack of common metadata standards-ideally, defined for use in some specified contexts-is yet another barrier to information access and use in a digital library, or in a coordinated digital library scheme.

While metadata standards are protocols per se, metadata systems are those that describe a set of metadata elements such as title, author, rights, date and so forth for a given disguisable material such as Dublin Core, MARC, SHOE, are metadata systems, of which Dublin core is more widely adopted around the world.

At present digital library initiatives in India make use

of Dublin Core for web based publications, encoded Archival Description (EAD) for archiving and Visual resource Association (VRA) for visual data. Consortia such the INFLIBNET and INDEST are involved in developing Indian metadata standards and software applications as part of the Open Archives Initiative Protocol for Metadata Harvesting (OAI-PMH). This would be used to automatically extract metadata information from digital libraries and enhance interoperability. This would also enable users to access all information repositories of participating institutions of the OIA.

10. Duplication : The duplication of a book can be identifying only using metadata of a book like the title, author, publishing year, edition etc. However if metadata is incorrect, missing or incomplete, it makes the duplicate detection more difficult.

11. Data Management : Assembling the data and making it available for easy access is one of the most important phase of any digitization project. Each mega scanning center is responsible for gathering the metadata and the scanned contents from the contractors operating as its scanning locations. The data is to be enabled on the web and also preserved for future use. Enabling many tera bytes of data for access to everyone in a highly reliable manner is needed for the success of the effort put into digitization process. Finally, digital preservation of the collections for a long future still remains a very significant problem faced by any digital library.

12. Software Issues : Greenstone is digital library software used for building and distributing digital library collections, organizing information and publishing it on the internet or on CD-ROM. Produced by the New Zealand Digital Library Project, it integrates functions such as metadata, full text search and retrieval, multilingual support, support for multiple document formats and administration. Greenstone is open source software, issued under the term of the General Public License.

The aim of the software is to empower users, particularly in universities, libraries, and other public service institutions, to build their own digital libraries. The Indian Labour Archives were one of the first Indian digital library initiatives to use Greenstone.

In India, at present, Information Library Network (INFLIBNET), a consortium incubated under UGC, is actively involved library automation, database creation, software development, Human Resource Development, Information services and networking. They have also developed a software SOUL, based on relational database management, which is used for cataloguing, archiving as well as enabling online public access of resources. The National Informatics Center (NIC) of India has also developed digital library software-DelSis, that is used by the Developing Library Network (DelNet), which is also an effort to network libraries and for resource sharing.

13. Digital Rights Management: Digital right management involves way in which the digital library operator manage issues of IPR those of ownership of material made available on the digital library, how one controls access to as well as dissemination of copyrighted material. Several methods of managing digital rights do exist now a day from which one could choose to adopt the more convenient one for their purpose.

Examples include: Naming, Identifiers and persistence

The fifth issue is related to metadata. It is the problem of naming in a digital library. Names are strings that uniquely identify digital objects and are part of any document's metadata. Names are as important in a digital library as an ISBN number in a traditional library.

They are needed to uniquely identify digital objects for

purposes such as:

- Citation
- Information retrieval
- To make links among objects
- And for the purpose of managing copyright.

Any system of naming that is developed must be permanent, lasting indefinitely.

The unique name and its location must be separate. This is very much unlike URLs, the current method for identifying objects on the Internet.

A global scheme of unique identifier is requited, one that has persistence beyond the life of the originating organization.

Three examples of schemes proposed to get around the problem of persistent naming are PURLs, URNs, and Digital Object Identifiers.

PURLS: these are persistent URLs. They are a scheme developed by OCLC in an attempt to separate a document name from its location and there fore increase the probability that it will always be found.

Uniform Resource Name (URN) : URNs are a development of the Internet Engineering Task Force (IETF). A URN is not a naming scheme in itself, but a framework for defining identifiers. They contain a naming authority identifier (a central authority given the task of assigning identifiers) and an object identifier(assigning by the central authority). Like PURLs, URNs must be resolved, through a database or other such systems, into actual URLs.

14. Digital Object Identifier (DOI): DOI is an initiative by the Association of American Publishers and the (American) Corporation for National Research Initiatives designed to provide a method by which digital objects can be reliably identified and accessed.

Administrative: For building and working with digital library the long -term organizational, fiscal, and institutional commitments will be necessary. Management of the technical infrastructure for "digital library" services will be a significant obstacle for most libraries, especially as budgets continue to shrink and the costs of developing and maintaining collections increases. Administration of the digital collection locally, is harder and more expensive than managing a comparable print collection.

Some rights management functions could include:

- Using tracking
- Identifying and authenticating users
- Providing the copyright status of each digital object, and restriction on its use or the fees associated with it.
- Handling transaction with users by allowing only so many copies to be accessed, or by charging them for a copy, or by passing the request on to the publishers.

BARRIERS THAT HAMPER PROGRESS IN DEVELOPMENT OF DIGITAL LIBRARIES RESOURCES

Digital libraries offer many advantages but also poses some challenges and problems such as:

a. Interoperability among different media input and formats
b. Rapid changing digital world
c. Copyright/licensing problem
d. Motivation and training
e. Heavy dependence of information sources/products
f. Customization and maintenance.

1. Lack of infrastructure: Lack of organizational effort for digital preservation i.e. building deep infrastructure which involves multiple, interrelated factors, such as institutions, services, technologies, and qualified personnel, capable of supporting a distributed system of digital archive.

2. Conceptual framework of standards: Absence of established standards, protocols, and proven methods for preserving digital information.

Lack of adequate research in the areas such as, framing key problems associated with digital information, defining critical issues, establishing standards for digital preservation, etc.

3. Migration of digital issues: It has always been a problem with the preservationists to make an exact copy or replica of a database or digital object as hardware and software changes makes object incompatible with a new generation of technology.

The following can be listed as the setbacks that are likely arise when creating digital libraries:

- The initial cost of digitization and preservation files is prohibitive. This comes about due to the relatively high cost of purchasing the required hardware and software for setting up the library.
- Special training is required and thus special skills to set up and maintain the digital library.
- The user has to accept the media, thereby making user sensitization a crucial factor to be considered. This is because the authenticity and credibility, hence acceptance of the digitized information resources may have a lot to be desired.
- Bandwidth problem in accessing multimedia resources and full text journals is a major communication barrier (particularly in a large majority of the third world countries).
- Scanning and electronically storing the original documents of the entire paper based collection is time consuming and labor intensive.

- Intellectual Property Rights (IPR) issues may not be clearly interpreted or correctly applied and enforced in different parts of the world.
- Some librarians are worry of the new technology and hence may be reluctant to adopt changes.

To manage the Digital libraries there is a need of specialized and trained staff:

Library staff is most crucial component of any digital library. We live in the age whereby information users not only have the knowledge but the capacity of generating information on their own, as well. Therefore, there has to be a unique set of professionals who are specially trained to distinguish between information that is palatable to any given set of users, from that which is not. Librarians fit this role perfectly and being information gatekeeper and gateways, they already have the know-how of matching user needs with information resources, predominately in traditional libraries.

Digital librarians are required for the following purposes:

- To manage digital libraries;
- To organize the digital knowledge and information resources;
- To disseminate digital information from computer held digital information;
- Provide digital reference services and other electronic services;
- To provide knowledge mining from the emerging knowledge warehouses;
- To handle the task of mass digitization, digital storage process and digital preservation;
- To provide universal access and retrieval of digital knowledge, ultimately access to all knowledge

resources available in digital form;

- To catalog and classify digital object and digital knowledge.

In an other school of thought, there is a belief that the information professional who manage a digital library is, in fact a knowledge manager. In that regard, Devenport, Delong and Beers (1998) highlighted that knowledge management is carried out with a view to:

- Creating knowledge repositories;
- Improving access to knowledge;
- Creating a knowledge environment;
- Managing knowledge as an asset.

2. Lack of trained manpower: Core competencies expected of digital librarian:

Sreenivasulu (2000) proposed the following skills and competencies that a properly qualified digital librarian ought to demonstrate:

- A good command of various internet skills beyond the level of an ordinary users, including on-line searching and web publishing.
- Knowledge and command of multimedia, digital technology and digital media processing techniques
- Knowledge and skills of handling digital information systems, online and optical information involving the management of a CD-ROM/DVD-ROM network station and the conversion of print media into digital media.
- Networking knowledge of using both internal and external networks, including the establishment of personnel networks, intranets, external knowledge resources and extranets.

Tennant (1999) also identified several skills that are supposed to personify the digital librarian's knowledge reservoir. Some of them are similar as sited above.

Optical Character Recognition (OCR): Scanning a printed will capture an image but in order to make it searchable, a good knowledge of OCR technology is required.

Imaging technologies: Digital librarian must be aware of the various ways in which surrogate of physical items (for example, journal articles) can be captures. They must be familiar with the typical manipulation required to edit and save it different formats.

Markup language: Digital librarians should have knowledge of Hypertext Markup Language (HTML) and also a suitable combination of other web authoring tools (such as SGML, XML, scripting language e.g. Jawa Scriptor Vbscript and so on).

Cataloging and metadata: digital objects require organization and description. Digital librarians must understands the way in which metadata can be captured. They should be familiar with standards such as Machine Readable Catalog (MARC), Anglo American Catalog Code(AACRII), Z39.50 protocol, Dublin Core and so on;

Indexing and database technology: Digital librarians must be familiar with a variety of tools from simple and easy indexing and searching tools to complex relational or object oriented database systems.

User Interface design: The digital librarian should be able to write the functional specifications and work with other knowledgeable professionals to achieve the desired goal of developing a user friendly computer interface with library automation system, in case the library has one.

Programming: Digital librarians need not to be full-time programmers, but it would be an added advantage if they were familiar with programming languages such as C, C++ or Java. Knowledge of handling open source software such as D-space or Greenstone would definitely come in handy.

Web technology: Digital librarians must know their way around the Internet and be well versed with web technology.

Project Management: Digital library projects need skilled management. Digital librarians should be good communicators and relates well with people both inside as well as outside the organization. Projects initiated need to be complete on time and within the stipulated budget.

The management of digital libraries demands the invoking of revolutionary skills and techniques, previously not commonly applied in traditional libraries. According to Hasting and Tennent (1996) :

"Digital librarians must thrive on change. They should read constantly (but selectively) and experiment endlessly. They need to love learning, be able to self-teach and be inclined to take risks. And they must have a keen sense of both the potentials and pitfalls of technology."

There are some barriers such as copyright issues, economic issues, rapid change in technology, bandwidth limitations, lack of trained manpower, and multilingual contents are some of the factors hamper global access of information in digital form.

ISSUES

Some of these issues are :

1. Economic, Social and Legal Issues: There is always a cost in its creation, its production, and its dissemination. Digital libraries introduce new and uncertain economic realities and relationship into libraries. Where the costs of accessing information were once hidden to patrons, the digital era is likely to require customers who will be required pay fees for access to digital services and collections. The major obstacle is digitization. Digitization is very cost intensive. Especially when one goes single-handed towards digitization. For digitization to succeed in the developing countries, the socio-economic conditions have to strong to a digital library.

The legal issues are both national and international. They range across several branches of law, including copyright, communications, privacy, obscenity, national security, and even taxation.

The social context includes authorship, ownership, and the act of publication, authenticity and integrity.

Social and technical issues often relate. For example, the cultural and social atmosphere determines how electronic thesis and dissertation will be managed on a particular campus, or across broader boundaries involving states or nations.

Legal issues also become more visible with digital libraries.

There often was little concern over copyright issues when preparing a dissertation that would largely go unread, sitting on a shelf in a local library. However, with the potential of thousands of downloads from around the world; authors must be very careful not to include a copyrighted image or other contents without permission.

PRESERVATION ISSUES

Preservation of the storage medium such as tapes, hard disk, floppies, has a short life span when considered in terms of obsolescence. In the rapid race of information and communication technology era, the computer hardware, software, devices, process for recording, storing, and accessing information are being replaced with new products and methods at regular three to five year cycle.

There are three issues of preservation:

1. It is costly and difficult for vendors to assure that their products are either backwardly-compatible' with previous versions or that they can inter-operate with

competing products.

2. Preservation of access to contents—this form of preservation involves preserving access to the contents of the documents regardless of the format. While files can be moved from one storage medium to an other, what happens when the formats (e.g. Acrobat, PDF) containing the information becomes obsolete. There is the problem of the lack of fixity in digital media. In a digital medium the fixity is lost. One can have no assurance that a digital text conveys the original expression of an author. It may have been altered internationally or unintentionally. As now there are many document presentation schemes, we have even lost the reliability of citation formulas.
3. **Fragility of material**: Apart from fixity, there is problem of fragility of the media. Random Access Memory (RAM) is completely evanescent and transitory. Digital files are mostly stored on magnetic media. The media become unstable and if no refreshed on a regular basis. The longevity of other media for digital storage (CDs) remains uncertain, as they can be less stable than paper codices stored in an appropriate environment. So there is a durability problem.

Thus, the increasing complexity of digital objects (incorporating text, images, audio, video in various formats) and their increasing software dependence (e.g. storage in database)

The rapidly increasing number of digital objects and proliferation of documents standards and formats

a. The lack of planning to incorporate preservation needs in systems and lack of availability of off the shelf products supporting preservation needs;
b. The lack of consideration of long-term access requirements when creating digital products.

c. The absence of widely accepted standards, which will assure over time.

d. Copyright/Intellectual Property Rights that may interfere with the ability to preserve digital objects through systematic copying; Current copyright law is unclear regarding digitization of any digitization object; storing of the digitized image in archive; authorization of digital object; changing file formats and also deletion of the digital object.

e. Unstable storage media (diskettes) whose lifespan is limited;

f. Lack of technical expertise in collection managers and preservation experts.

These solutions are based on the recommendation of International Conference on Digital Libraries organized by TERI in December 2006.

1. Enact Digital Library Act

Since digital library is a new concept for the country like India. There is a need to enacting first Digital Library Act which provides for:

1. Differential reduction in copyright period for all kinds of publications.
2. Vesting copyright to the authors.
3. Publicity funded materials should be freely accessible.
4. Build in clear and extensive provision for fair use of copyrighted material.
5. Develop new models of stated funded compensation to the authors.
6. Compulsory deposit of digital copy of new publications in addition to printed copy.

2. Establish consortia for content creation:

1. Countries should strengthen content creation activity

by establishing consortia for content creation aimed at:

2. Capturing traditional knowledge that still has been recorded but resides within the communities.
3. Archiving cultural assets of the country like songs, music, folklore, speeches, etc.
4. Archiving scholarly publications.
5. Building repositories of scholarly publications, government publications and reports, institutional reports, etc.

Certain percentage of budget meant for education sector must be earmarked exclusively for content creation.

Democratization of information: Countries should aim at democratization of information so that the information at the point of use is available for free.

In this regard following measures are important:

1. Place all contents on the internet.
2. Make provision for internet access through public library system.
3. Establish network of community knowledge centers.
4. Make access user friendly, tailoring it to the needs of individuals.
5. Use open access and open source technologies for information dissemination.

Capacity and capability building in digital library: To meet the manpower demand for establishing, developing, and expanding digital library activities, there is an urgent need to build new capacities and capabilities. In this, regard, the countries need to set up institutions of excellence. Such institutions can take up following different approaches to curriculum development, education, research, and training in digital library field. Creating a new discipline labeled "digital library studies" which would be a symbiosis of knowledge components from the fields such as library science, knowledge management, scintometrics, management, and computer science.

Usability of the digital library

Being digital is not necessarily commensurate with being useable. Considerable study of what users need, how they use information, and whether digital formats serve their needs effectively is still required. Undertaking large digitization initiatives without a fundamental understanding of user need might result in complete failure of the exercise and lack of support from users and the management.

The reasons this substitution will not easily occur are many: user resistance, limitations on use, poor digital products design, or the medium may not be effective to satisfy the user requirements. The challenge here will be “span both print and digital materials ...(and to) ... provide a coherent view of a very large collection of information”.

19
Copyright and Digital Library

INTRODUCTION

Copyright protects the creator. It is the right to reproduce, to publish, and to sell the matter and the particulars form of creativity related to literary, musical artistic or dramatic work. It deals with all forms and methods of publish communication-printed publications, sound and television broadcasting, films for public exhibition in cinemas, etc. The copyright allows the original creator to enjoy a kind of monopoly over his creative work in a tangible form of expression.

Copyright had come into existence after the printing process become mechanized which enabled reproduction of books and monographs, in large quantities. With further advancement in the technology such as photo duplication, need for protection became all the more a necessity. For instance, with the emergence of computer technology, the copyright has assumed an other dimension as it is now quite possible to duplicate, print, transmit, and share electronic documents with a mere click of the mouse, at almost, no additional cost.

The protection of copyright subsists without formalities. Registration is not necessary. Copyright law protects the form of expression, not the ideas. Once an idea is expressed in tangible form the protection of copyright exists. Any work, good or bad, even if it fails to serve the purpose for which it was intended, is protected by copyright act. The practical value of copyright law depends on the extent to which it is effectively implemented. It serves as an incentive to authors and their assignees to create and disseminate knowledge.

DEFFINITON

It refers to the right given to the author to reproduce work, distribute copies and publicly perform and display his /her works. Copyright is a legal protection for a limited period, against unauthorized reproduction of any published and unpublished literary, scientific and artistic work, in whatever form of its expression, provided such work is made available in tangible form. In other words, if a work is available either in printed form, , in micrographic, or electronic format including HTML , or a computer program/ graphics which can set on papers, magnetic media, sound records, video disc or saved in a computer floppy or even on hard disk, , it comes under the preview of the copyright. The copyright Act grants exclusive rights to the creator of the work to adopt, change, publish, distribute, perform, and display the work publicly. Thus, the creator alone possesses such a control over the work and not the person having access or possession over the same. The creator, however, is free to transfer his rights to anybody for an economic consideration or otherwise. In this context, it is hereby clarified that copyright protection does not extend too many categories including ideas, facts, concepts, guidelines, slogans, procedures, academic course contents, methods, and systems. However, the manner in which an author expresses his/her ideas or method is legally protected under the copyright.

THE COPYRIGHTED MATERIAL

The copyrighted material can be a book, a picture, a sculpture, music, or anything that is the result of a person's creative mind that take a physical shape and has no function other than the beauty and creative of the thing itself. Copyright only protects the expressive elements of a broad range of works-including books, graphical works, dramatic works, choreography, musical compositions, sound recordings, films, sculpture, architectural works in the forms of an article, paper or book, not the idea as such.

OBJECTIVES OF COPYRIGHT

The objective of copyright is to encourage creative activities. This act is also helping to make the creative work available to all. A copyright owner sells the right to companies /individuals to market the works for royalties. Copyright enables the author to obtain economic returns from his intellectual creation, and also encourages the dissemination of the knowledge to the mankind. Thus, it provides incentives to authors and subsequent motivate them to take up more creative works and the society at large is benefited due to the dissemination of knowledge. Hence, the copyright provides a proper balance between the authors (copyright owners) in getting the remuneration of their intellectual labor, and on the other hand, the users at large are rewarded in obtaining the fruits arising out of the reasonable access to the work. The Copyright Act attempted to balance the rights of authors to benefit from their writing and stimulate creativity and the need of the readers to have ready access to information.

Copyright law gives author several broad rights and also subjects these rights to exceptions , such as "first sale doctrine" (the copyright owner has no right to control the distribution of a copy of a work after he or she sold the copy) and "fair use" (the legal privilege to make unauthorized use of a copyrighted work for good reason) . For example US Code, grants libraries and archives the right to create reproductions of their own holdings during the last 20 years for any terms of copyright for purpose of preservation and replacing deteriorated materials if the item cannot be obtained at a reasonable price. An important restriction applies to digital copies, which must be used within the library.

The purpose of copyright law is to balance the rights of creators to earn a living from their works against the need for public access to their work. This is done by providing copyright exceptions that allow "fair dealing" with copyright work It is through such exceptions that prescribed libraries have the right to copy extracts of copyright works for individual users in the digital world. There are number of limiting principles and exceptions to the rights.

The intended purpose of copyright is to balance the rights of the public for access to information and creative expression with the rights of its creator and to provide incentives for the advancement of knowledge and creativity.

Libraries and archives are permitted to make up to three copies of unpublished copyrighted works for the purpose of preservation, security or for deposit for research use in another library or archive. This is also applicable if the work is damaged, deteriorated or lost, or the format of which has become obsolete.

1. Fair use is an other criterion.
2. First sale doctrine- according to which the owner of that particular copy of the work may sell or transfer that copy. Libraries lending and marketing of used books are governed by the first sale doctrine.

It allows people and organization to reproduce copyrighted materials under certain circumstances without receiving permission from the author or owner of copyright.

A fundamental principle of copyright is that its protection runs not to the ideas manifested in a work of authorship, but only to their expression. Not only the traditional works such as books, periodical article, photographs, motion pictures, paintings, sculpture, etc. eligible for copyright protection, but also are sound recordings, computer programmes, computerized databases and other high works.

Copyright in different counties have different approaches.

In the United States, copyright applies to almost all literary works, including textual materials, photographs, computer programmes, musical scores, and audio and video tapes. A major exception is material created by government employees.

COPYRIGHT ISSUES

An important issue that the present day library professionals are facing in providing digital information service in the large scale of piracy of software and plagiarism. The cost and timeliness in retrieving the information are also considered .When negotiating access with publisher, the librarian must agree to certain restriction on photocopying or distribution of digital material. Despite copyright notices and efforts to educate employees and users about Intellectual Property Rights, electronic publications can be easily forwarded to people outside the licensed user group. The library is responsible for maintaining the awareness of all users about copyright issues.

The contents are protected by copyright law regardless of whether they are published on paper or on the internet. Contents may be born digital, turned digital, and gained digital. Contents cannot be used without the authorization of right owner. It is therefore necessary for the persons involved in writing and distribution of books, articles, etc. to be well conversant with the copyright issues. Each and every country has their own copyright law. Copyright laws of all the countries have certain things in common.

In the present era of open access where content is being made available for free use, the creators of the contents are concerned about the violation of the copyright.

PROBLEMS WITH TURNED DIGITAL CONTENTS

With regard to the turned digital content, digitization of out of copyright material has not been a problem. Other than uploading digitized content on website, digitization is being undertaken by to preserve old, brittle, and crumbling documents for posterity.

Under the Article9(2) of the Berne Convention for Protection of Literary and Artistic Works(1886) the libraries can digitized the contents but uploading the same for public access requires permission of copyright owner. While libraries can be more liberal in digitizing contents such as thesis and other in-house generated contents. The disadvantages of turned digital content includes large size of the resultant scanned file which can become time consuming to download for voluminous publications. With regard to copyright issues, digitizing "out of copyright" material and institution owned copyrighted material such as dissertations and thesis is easier but obtaining permissions from copyright owners of other desired materials is a daunting task.

PROBLEM WITH GAINED DIGITAL MATERIAL

So far the gained digital content is concerned, the digital library is under contract or has obtained licenses for using such content. Depending on the license terms and conditions, the digital library has to sensitize the users and make them literate and aware so that there is no violation of copyright in general and also specifically about the agreement that the terms and conditions in the agreement are honored.

Born digital content can be categorized into exclusive digital wherein the analog version is not developed at all. This could include creating curriculum focused content, e-books, learning objects or other multimedia content where analog counterparts are not meat to be created or are not required. The other type of born digital content type is digital for print. In this type, the content is created in digital form for dual purposes which include hoisting the content in digital libraries and also having a print counterpart of the content developed. Many books and journals publishers follow this model of content creation.

PROBLEM WITH BORN DIGITAL MATERIAL

The problem with born digital content is that content creation can be a time consuming task taking a long time to populate a digital library. Further, resource requirement in terms of manpower and financial resources would be high for the content creation process. Recently, with institutional repositories and archives gaining popularity and in some instance being mandatory, the content creation keeps the digital requirement in perspective although a print counterpart such as a journal or a thesis is also produced.

INDIAN COPYRIGHT ACT AND AMENDMENTS

The Laws of copyright were framed in order to protect an author against piracy of his /her work. This right is not a right, which arises under common law, but is a right which has arisen by statutory protection.

In the early days of printing there was no copyright. In the ninetieth century, the United States had copyright protection for American authors but none of foreigners; the books of European authors were nor protected and shamelessly copied despite the plea of various authors.

The government of India has passed the International Copyright Order 1958, according to which any work first published in any country which a member of Brene or Universal Copyright Convention will be accorded the same treatment as if it was published in India.

In India the Copyright Act, 1957 covers literary work, dramatic, musical and artistic work. It also subsisted in cinematograph, films and sound recordings. This reflects that the protection that is sought to be given by the Act is wide and includes all kinds of work. Originally the copyright term was fixed at 50 years. With an amendment to the Act the period was increased to 60 years with effect from December 1991. The Act was amended in 1984 to check widespread piracy within the country. It prescribed increased punishment for the infringement of copyright and to make the provision of the act applicable to video-films and computer programmes. The Act was again amended in 1992 to extend the term of copyright Rabindranath Tagore's works, which are of national importance by period of ten years.

The Copyright Act was again amended in 1994 to extend the protection to composers of Indian music. Performer's rights were recognized particularly with respect to live performances. It also protects computer programmes and computer generated works. The copyright owners enjoy the right does not allow others to make copies of the work. The owners of the right also enjoy the right to prepare derivative works and to distribute copies, the right to perform work publicity.

Interestingly, prior to the amendment Act of 1994, the definition of literary work had a very wide definition, including "tables, compilations and computer programmes, that is to say, programmes recorded on any disc, tape, perforated media or other information storage device, which, if fed into or located in a computer or computer based equipment, is capable of reproducing any information. Unfortunately this clarity has disappeared with the 1994 amendment Act where the definition of literary work has been constructed by including computer programmes tables and compilations including computer databases".

New knowledge cannot be created without reference to already existing literature and knowledge. Libraries, museums and archives play crucial role as custodians and disseminators of knowledge and must continue to do so in order to carry out the educational mission. They must maintain a balance between the interest of the creators and copyright owners and the public. Copyright is important to ensure the continuity of writing, performing and creating information. Intellectual Property Right covers every thing created by using human intellect.

In United States, copyright applies to almost all literary works, including textual materials, photographs, computer programmes, musical scorers, and video and audiotapes. A major exception is materials created by government employees.

It is observed that Indian Copyright Act does not address the issues related with digital environment .If the existing provisions, which are meant basically for the exclusive applications to the printed work, are extended to the electronic publications, the vast majority of the digital work would remain unexploited. Since the published work constitutes an important ingredient as basic input to the educational, and research programmes, the revision of the Act must ensure that all the digital products and services be made available to the mankind. Therefore, the forthcoming amendments in the Copyright Act should be such as to promote use and also to protect the economic interest of the copyright owners. Then only can we say that the balance in the copyright has been achieved which was having distortions in favours of the copyright owners, earlier.

COPYRIGHT ACT AMENDED IN 1994

That includes:

1. In case of a literary, dramatic or musical work, not being a computer programme-
    1. to reproduce the work in any material form including the storing of it in any medium by electronic means;
    2. to issue copies of the work to the public and not being copies already in circulation;
    3. to perform the work in public , or communicate it to the public;
    4. to make any cinematograph film or sound recording in respect of the work;
    5. to make any translation of the work; and
    6. to make any adaptation of the work.

In case of computer programme:

1. To do any of the act specified in clause (a)
2. To sell or give on hire, or offer for sale or hire, any copy of the computer programme, regardless of whether such copy has been sold or given on hire on earlier occasions;

INTERNATIONAL COPYRIGHT LAW

The International Copyright Law provides protection to all creative works or productions of the human mind in the field of literature, art, and science regardless of their manner or forum of expression. There is no copyright of ideas. It subsists only in the material form in which the ideas are translated.

RIGHTS COVERED UNDER COPYRIGHT / RIGHTS TO AUTHOR/PUBLISHER

Copyright provides the following mandatory rights:

1. to copy the work or any substantial part of it;
2. to issue copies of the work to the public;
3. to perform, show or play the work in the public;
4. To broadcast the work or to include it in a cable programme service; and
5. To make an adaptation of the work or to do any of the above in relation to an adoption.

Rights covered under the copyright (in general) are as follows:

1. Right for reproduction

1. Rights for modification/adoption or creation of derivative works.
2. Rights for distribution of work to the public.
3. Right to recite, play, dance, or act with or without the aid of a machine i.e. rights to public performance.
4. Rights for display in public.
5. Exclusive right to make copies.
6. Exclusive right to sell copies.
7. Exclusive right to protect his/her works from copying by means of copyright Act.

In relation to computer programme, adoption means "an arrangement or altered version of the programme or a translation of it" copyright never stops anyone working on the same lines, upon the same sort of basic idea, and copyright cannot be effective against anyone who produces something independently. Ideas are not protected by copyright.

COPYRIGHT AND LIBRARY SERVICES

Photocopying service is an important part of library services. The most common kind of infringement that arises is in the form of direct copying and photocopying. Contrary to popular belief, photocopying work may be totally illegal, as it may be violative of some person's copyright in the work, which includes the exclusive right to produce further copies. Other form of infringement is arises when it requires additional copies of a particular work in the library.

ACTS NOT CONSIDERED TO BE INFRINGEMENT OF COPYRIGHT

The following acts shall not be constitute an infringement of copyright, namely the making of copies or adoption of a computer programme by the lawful possessor of a copy of such computer programme, from such copy-

1. In order to utilize the computer programme for the purpose for which it was supplied; or
2. To make backup copies purely as a temporary protection against loss, deterioration or damage in order to utilize the computer programme for the purpose of which it was supplied.

COPYRIGHT IN ELCTRONIC ENVIRONMENT

Copyright law is the one of the main issue faced in the electronic environment. In the electronic environment it is easy to create or duplicate electronic copies of the texts etc., but the illegal copying and copyright violations may result in losses to electronic information publishers.

Copyright is applicable in electronic environment such as for copyright in electronic works like computer programmes, databases, satellite broadcasting, electronic publishing multimedia and resources on the internet.

RIGHT OF ELECTRONIC ACCESS

Copyright law grants exclusive rights to authors for copying for educational purposes and also copying privileges to librarians and archivist but these rights are applicable within the preview of the work in digital form. Displaying, downloading, copying, transmitting or printing of copyright works in electronic form has to be performed under contract license. Thus, a crucial role has to be played by information professionals for both controlling and facilitating access to the growing number of local and remote electronic information resources. Therefore, a need is felt for statutory rights to use copyright protected material in all formats.

COPYRIGHT AS A BARRIER TO DIGITAL LIBRARY DEVELOPMENT COPYRIGHT MANAGEMENT:

Copyright is one of the most serious barriers to digital library development. Digital objects are less fixed, easily copied and remotely accessible by multiple users simultaneously. It is important to develop mechanism for managing copyright.

The library though has already paid the cost of the product, is debarred inn lending the product even on inter library loan. If the library provides services at several different locations, providing services of such leased digital products, say through local intranet network is prohibited. Even downloading the information for forwarding through e-mail is not permissible .The revision of the Copyright Act should ensure that such artificial barriers in the digital products are removed so that the information flow takes place smoothly. If these barrier are not weakened, small information centers would be deprived of sharing the fruits of accessing the digital information, due to budgetary constraints, though its impact would be felt in all the libraries.

It is unlikely that libraries will ever be able to freely

digitize and provide access to copyrighted materials in their collections. Instead, they will have to develop mechanisms for managing copyright, mechanism that allow them to provide information without violating copyright, called rights management.

Some rights management functions could include, for examples:

1. Usage tracking.
2. Providing the copyright status of each digital object, and the restriction on its use or the fees associated with it.
3. Identifying and authenticating users.
4. Handling transactions with users by allowing only so many copies to be accessed, or by charging them for a copy, or by passing the request on to a publisher.

2. Copyright/rights management

Copyright has been called the single most vexing barrier to digital library development. Copyright protects the owner's creative or intellectual work. Digital collections and services will be strongly effected by future copyright and licensing regimes, as well as prohibitive costs for digitization and support of technical infrastructure. Copyright could become an insurmountable barrier to the development of digital collection. In fact, copyright could end up preventing libraries from providing open access to the digital information they collect.

It unlikely that libraries will ever be able to freely digitized and provide access to the copyright materials in their collection. Instead, they will have to develop mechanisms for managing copyright, mechanisms that allow them to provide information without violating copyright, called rights management.

Copyright is one of the most important barriers to

digital library development. The problem of the libraries are that they are for the most part simply caretakers of information, they do not own the copyright of the material they hold. So libraries will never be able to freely digitized and provide access to the copyrighted material in their collection. They have to develop a mechanism for managing copyright.

3. Preservation

An other important issue is preservation. In the preservation of digital material, the real issue is technical obsolescence.

The digital storage media such as hard disk, tapes and floppy disk have a very short life span due to rapid technology obsolescence. The computer hardware and software, which used for storage and retrieval, become obsolete and they are replaced by better technologies.

DIGITAL LIBRARY AND COPYRIGHT

The basic purpose of digital library is to convert printed book into digital form provided copyright of the work owned by library is expired or the book is public domain. If this is not the case then one needs to know the necessary formalities like getting permission from the copyright owner or author etc. Seeking the permission from the copyright holder is complex process because it requires finding the details of the individuals who holds the copyright of a book, containing them and tries to negotiate for compensation for digitizing the book for preservation. For example Digital Library of India, which is under the Universal Digital Library (UDL), has books that are both in and out of copyright. It is explicit policy of the Universal Digital Library to adhere to the copyright policies of all countries.

ULD is using the following conservative guiding principles for displaying contents:

1. For those books that are either out of copyright or permission to scan has been granted, with the display of entire contents of the books free to read. Any book published before 1923 is deemed as being out of copyright.
2. For books under copyright , they displays only the title page and other selected pages not exceeding 10 % of the pages, under the fair use policy .Any book published after 1923 is deemed under copyright unless:
   a. The book is in public domain(e.g. government publications and other approved not for profit societies)
   b. Explicit permission has been received from the author or publisher or
   c. There is authenticated information to indicate that this book should not be in copyright.
3. An author or owner of a book published after 1923 is free to request that the entire contents be displayed on the UDL website.

Downloading and redistribution of electronic information is very easy. Anybody can cut, copy, paste the complete document and can distribute to any numbers of persons across the network, but it is very difficult to track down such an unlawful action. On June 9, 2000 the president of India gave his approval for Information Technology Act which legalizes the affixing of signature on electronic records by the subscribers to authenticate the records and verify it for the use of "public key" of the subscriber.

The Information Act is available on Internet (URL *http://www.navvi.co/cyberlaw/iibill2000*)

Copyright issues are the most important concerns in the digital environment. The ease with which the digital work can be duplicated, copied, re-distributed and used by multiple users coupled with heir compactness and relative invisibility have made the producers of the digital media, products to focus their attention on controlling the use of digital works.

A major unsettled issue in the emerging networked digital library environment is that of copyright. The emergence of digital library environment has left many questions unanswered. Prominent amongst these are:

To what extend the present copyright laws, made largely for the print media, are appropriate in the new environment :

If they are not suitable, what re-adjustment and re-definitions have to be made and

What new laws have to be framed?

How are agents like libraries going to be affected?

How will the publishers responded to new environment?

Now all forms of works can be stored, transmitted and disseminated electronically. With the development of technology and electronic communication the copyright and related rights are expanding very fast. WIPO (World Intellectual Proprietary Organization) is trying to develop new standards for copyright protection in cyberspace. WIPO Copyright Treaty, 1996, WIPO Performance and Phonogram Treaty, 1996 aim to prevent unauthorized access to resources on Net.

Electronic copyright is to be treated in the same way as copyright. Now all forms of works can be stored, transmitted and disseminated electronically. The term electronic work covers on-line databases, CD-ROMs, computer programmes, related documentation (both in print and electronic forms) used as manuals by programme users, computer networks including the internet and the resources available on the net, multimedia, electronic publishing and satellite broadcasting.

Computer works are also protected by copyright just as literary works are protected. Copying of computer programmes can be literal and non literal. In literal copying the programme code it is copied and in case of non-literal copying the programme code is not copied. Only the structure of, interfaces, methodologies etc. of the programme are copied. In case of computer works both the actual programme code and the structure of the programme can be protected under the copyright law.

The problem that is worrying scholars, researchers, educators and consumers of modern information is the possible impact of those new technologies may have in the copyright law and consequent burden on information users specially in developing counties.

The demarcation line between "copyright" and "no copyright" material is based on individual cases. For example one may be permitted to make a copy of a computer programme for the purpose of backup but one may not be permitted to copy an image from an electronic document to use in one's own document.

Digital publications can broadly be classified as:

1. Offline, such a computer floppies, CD-ROM products, or
2. On-line products, such as the Internet sites.

Again, both the products can either be allowed to be accessed free of cost or at a specified price. If these are distributed free of cost, the same if desired, can be downloaded without payment. Yet, the basic implication of copyright Act is, whatever may be the situation, deriving profit out of the accessibility of the publications, without authorization, is prohibited. Similarly, sharing the same with someone else, on a regular basis is not permissible. In other words, making such publications available at a price or otherwise without specific permission attract the penalties, prescribed in the Act. On the same logic, generating multiple copies of documents violating the spirit and the provision of the Act. Of course, one can consume the contents of the publications for his own study. Acknowledging the source, to generate upper strata of the knowledge, can freely use ideas, embodied in the documents.

Copyright is a serious problem for developing digital libraries. Indian copyright Act is salient about the copyright applications in digital environment. For designing and developing digital library one need to take permission from copyright holder with some conditions, which are beneficial to the copyright holder.

COPYRIGHT OF OUT OF PRINT WORK

Licensing is required in case of digitization of out of print work. Out of print work is defined as a work that is not commercially available, as declared by the appropriate right holders, regardless of the existence of tangible copies of the work as normally understood. Generally, it is allowed for a digital library to digitize and provide access to out of print works to users through closed network. It is not limited in respect of territory, but the library may not provide access through open network. A license can be prepared which grants the library a non-exclusive and non transferable right to digitize and make the licensed work available to the users in closed networks. The right holder is entitled to payment and retains copyright in the work.

DIGITAL PRESERVATION AND COPYRIGHT

Indian digital libraries are in view that digitization may be the only means of ensuring that cultural material is available for future generations and may therefore essential to enable continue access it. Similarly preservation should be justified

Preservation involves in the reproduction of work in

any form and preserves it for future use. Many countries have laws, which permit libraries to make copies either for preservation or meet their activities. In some legislations publications specifically excludes making a work available to the public by the means of an electronic retrieval system. Therefore, to digitize a work and then make it available over a LAN or WAN, could lead to claims for damages by the copyright owner.

PRINT BASE LIBRARY COPYRIGHT AND DIGITAL BASE LIBRARY COPYRIGHT

In traditional print based library copyright was violated by photocopying or by photocopier. In this era, the risk of violation was less as library photocopiers were best placed in highly public areas were library users are clearly visible to each other, and above all, in areas where library staff can supervise activity at the photocopier. The cost of photocopying is also high, so users are generally taking their relevant part of information from the document. But the digital library services are different from print photocopying services. As library move from the physical medium to the digital, library staff is increasingly confronted with the challenges of addressing copyright and other Intellectual Propriety Rights (IPR) issues related to digital information.

Advances in technology through introduction of cable television, computers and the Internet have demanded a review and reviewing of copyright laws.

Multiple digital copies of right protected material can easily be made than in the print world at a click of a mouse button or e-mail can send a file to the whole world in few seconds. The digitally networked interface has ability to download materials, to make any number of perfect copies and distribute these with virtually no extra cost. It allows copyright works to be copied, manipulated and disseminated with minimal effort and cost that cannot be matched using analog technologies. Users have access to online copyright material on their PC at remote location such as their home or office where library has no control of copyright violation.

ELECTROCOPYING AND COPYRIGHT

Electro copying is a term for the conservation of the printed material into machine-readable form using document image processing and OCR technology. It is quite clear infringement of copyright to convert, without prior permission, items into machine-readable form and to store them on a database. Scanning of the material in preparation for sending down a network without permission is "adaptation" of the work, and therefore, is the infringement. Sending the material down a telecom network is infringement. Similarly printing out copies at a remote terminal without the permission is infringement.

FAIR USE DEALING AND COPYRIGHT

The Indian Copyright Act provides the leverage to the public to copy a part of the publication for self-study. This is called "fair use". However, this statement is quite ambiguous, as it does not set parameters of defining and determine, as unto what extent copying is permissible. It might base on the special circumstances. In case of computer programmes nothing can be inferred as to what is constituted as "fair use", as either a programme can be used in full measures or not at all.

Libraries and information centers the world over, have been the major organized buyers of the copyrighted material in printed form such as books, journals, addresses, reports, and so on); analogue form such as maps, graphic, publications, drawings etc). In respect of printed publications, for example, after a book or monograph is added in a library collection, the copyright owner does not have control on the copy as it can be used multiple times, by several persons, to browse, read, or photocopies etc.

Similarly it can also be shared with other libraries by lending it to them on inter-library loan. On the same analogy, after a book is sold, it can be read multiple times by the purchaser, lent, resold and even destroyed. The copyright owner does not have any rights over the sold copy. Of course, rights of reproduction are granted only as an extension under the "fair use". If the same logic is applied to digital product, without having the reproduction rights, the work would not be exploited at all. Similarly if such rights are granted, without any limitations, the author would get no return for their creations. On the other hand, if libraries were asked to pay for each and every usage of electronic products, particularly in an online environment, the cost would not be able to afford the same.

An other aspect of the Indian Copyright Act is concerning the registration with the Copyright Board. In the case of printed publications, this can be easily compiled with as the further edition of a book might appear only after several years. On the other hand, in digital environment, updating the documents takes place very frequently, sometime daily. It is very difficult to have the registration updated every time. The United States has allowed dispensing with this requirement. Of course, the date appearing in the computer is a proof of the updating which can be used to establish the ownership. The same can be incorporated in the Indian Copyright Act.

Fair use is legal right that allows certain uses of copyright information without permission of the copyright owner. Under fair use, a reviewer or a scholar has the right to quote short passages, and an article or a portion of a book may be photocopied for private study. The boundaries of the fair use are deliberately vague, but there are four basic factors:

1. The purpose and character of the use (including whether such use is of commercial nature or is for

none-profit educational purpose),

2. The nature of the copyrighted work, the amount and a substantially of the portion used related to the work as whole, and
3. The effect of the use on the work's potential market or value.

In general fair use allows reproduction of parts of a work but not the whole, single copies rather than many, and private rather than commercial use. Only legal precedents can clarify the exact distinction. Court case are so expensive that many important copyright issues (even with regard to traditional print materials) have never been tested in court or have addressed only in the lower court. How much of the reproduction may be considered, as a fair will depend upon the circumstances of the case. In case of artistic work fair dealing will involve two-dimensional reproduction of the work or miniature models of the work. To take long extracts and attach short comments may be fair. The publication of the whole of the work cannot simply be justified on the ground that it was required for research or private study.

FAIR USE AND INDIAN COPYRIGHT ACT

Section 52 (a) of the Act provides that 'fair dealing' with a literary, dramatic, musical or artistic work not being a computer programme for the purpose of:

1. Private use, including research;
2. Criticism of review,

Whether of that work or of any other work, shall not constitute an infringement. The Act does not define it but it is clear that it does not connote reproduction but only a partial use for a bonafied purpose. While the Act supplies this bonafied purpose, viz., private use, including research and for criticism or revision etc. It depends upon the following:

- The quantum and value of the matter taken in relation

to the comments or criticism.

- The purpose for which it was taken.
- Whether the work is published or unpublished, or circulated (if unpublished)
- The likelihood of competition between the two works.

FAIR USE AND US COPYRIGHT ACT

Para 107 of the US Copyright Act 1976 lists out the following factors to the considered in deciding whether use is fair:

1. The purpose and character of use.
2. The nature of the copyright work.
3. The amount and substantiality of the portion used in relation to the copyrighted work as whole.
4. The effect of the use upon the potential market for, or value of the copyright work.

THE TIME PERIOD OF COPYRIGHT

Time period is varies from country to country. Historically, a copyright has had a finite life, expiring a certain numbers of years after the creator's death.

The Indian Copyright Act protects the interests of the owners for printed books and monographs, for a fairly long period extending up to 60 years after the death of the author. This long duration of the protection was perhaps fixed at a time when information explosion was taking place at a very slow pace as compared to the same in the present context of the digital products. The long time span as kept to eliminate any fair chances of getting the work exploited commercially, without the proper authority. In the digital environment, this time span needs to be drastically reduced to a few years as by then the new information sources, which might emerge, would make the older information obsolete, reducing the economic value of the earlier information to a negligible level. In this respect, it is observed that by reducing the time period of the copyright protection, dissemination of the digital information would take place several folds, without jeopardizing the economic stakes of the author.

Copyright protects the copyrighted material for certain period but after that period the public may enjoy freely those intellectual materials. A clear time frame should be established after which intellectual material can be made available free to everybody. This period is varying from country to country. Duration of copyright period is also different from country to country with regard to signed copyright conversions. For example, USA it is 70 years, in India it is life plus 60 years.

INFRINGEMENT OF COPYRIGHT

The most significant infringing act is that of 'copying 'the work. It also includes the production for commercial purpose. The most significant infringement act is that of "copying" the work. The act of copying is defined, as involving the reproduction of the work, or of a substantial part of the work, in any material form. This also includes "storing the work in any medium by electronic means". Thus, for example, the use of some form of scanning device to transform text into electronic format will constitute an infringement of copyright.

Indian Copyright Act

Section 14 of the Indian Copyright Act, 1957 (amended) described certain activities which are 'exclusive' rights for authors. These activities when done by unauthorized persons or without the explicit permission of the copyright holders, amount to be breach or infringement of copyright. Or which leads to copyright infringement. That includes the following:

1. Reproducing the work in any material from including the storing of it in any medium by electronic means.

2. To perform the work in or communicate to public.
3. To issue the copies of (publish) the work to public not being in circulation.
4. To produce and publish any translation of the work.
5. To make any cinematography film, or a sound recording.
6. To do in relation to a translation or adoption of the work any of the above specified act.
7. To sell or give on hire, or offer for sale or hire any copy of the computer programme, regardless of whether such copy has been sold or given on hire on earlier occasions (Govt. of India 1996).

As per the Indian Copyright Act 'the making of not more than three copies of a book (including a pamphlet, sheet of music, map, chart, or plan) by or under the direction of the person in charge of a public library for the use of the library if such book is not available for sale in India'

Therefore, three copies of such a book can be made and kept by a public library for the use of the library. It is therefore clear that libraries themselves can make and keep copies of such work.

INFRINGEMENT OF COPYRIGHT IN DIGITAL ENVIRONMENT

Digital libraries are digitizing, compressing, uploading, downloading, copying and distributing protected works to any place in the world. The expending power of this network allows mass storage and online delivery of protected material. The users are downloading the contents of a book, or listen to record music from cyberspace.

While this presents immeasurable opportunities, there are also many challenges for owners, users and collective management organizations. (WIPO, 2008).Some of the features which can control infringement in digital libraries are:

1. Reproduction and Redistribution : A security system that can be implemented through which file can be locked to the computer on which it was first opened only from that computer only.

2. Networking : these files cannot be used in multi-user, network environment.

3. Printing : the plug in limit the number of times the document can be printed. Printing a part of the document will be interpreted as the one allowable print attempt; it is recommended you to print the entire document instead.

4. Copy and Paste : you cannot copy and paste from document.

5. Viewing : dedicated software to view the document. There is no limit to the numbers of times a document will be viewed on the single computer it is locked to.

Acquisition agreement of non book materials such as CD-ROM databases have put burden on the librarian to educate copyright restriction to the users and enforce quantity of copying and also the method of copies to be made, which is a difficult task for any librarian to monitor each operation of the search (particularly in the networking environment such as LAN, WAN etc.).The new generation authors today 'keyin' their complete work on computers and more often than not store the data on CD-ROMs itself, thereby wishing the traditional hard copies (paper copies) goodbye. How would the same be protected? As the material is stored on compact discs, would the same be treated as 'literary work'?

Now the question is whether lending a CD-ROM to someone to use amount to infringement of copyright?

Would copyright data from a CD-ROM to floppy disc amount to infringement?

COPYRIGHTABLE ITEMS

Fletcher in 1990 provided a general summery of items of copyright.

1. **Text:** exclusive rights

2. **Graphics:** copyright when fixed in a medium.

3. **Software:** source and object wide usually covered by programs copyright.

4. **Music:** composer, publisher, recording company and musician have rights over a recorded programme.

5. **Film:** every frame copyright.

a) COPYRIGHT IN CASE OF LITERARY, DRAMATIC OR MUSICAL WORK, NOT BEING A COMPUTER PROGRAMME

1. to reproduce the work in any material form including the storing of it in any medium by electronic means;
2. to issue copies of the work to the public and not being copies already in circulation;
3. to perform the work in public, or communicate it to the public;
4. to make any cinematographs film or sound recording in respect of the work; and
5. to make any adaptation of the work.

COPYRIGHT IN CASE OF COMPUTER PROGRAMME

Software programes are recorded on magnetic media. Software programmes are essentially intangible items and it is required that they shall be treated as intellectual property. This is the reason why copyright is usually made applicable to them.

1. To do any of the acts specified in clause (a)
2. To sell or give on hire, or offer for sale or hire, any copy of the computer programme , regardless of whether such copy has been sold or given on hire on earlier occasions (Govt. of India 1996).

INTERNET AND COPYRIGHT

Copyright Act is also applicable to information put up on the Internet. It may be e-mail message, material loaded on FTP sites etc .Copying of ones homepage is copyright infringement. Copying ones logo or trade mark is also infringement. By clicking on the hypertext link the text sought is transmitted to the user. Therefore, the user is not simply viewing something which exists but having it transmitted to his own PC. This constitutes the copying of the work. The work was not only copied by the person doing the search but also the work is passing off to the other.

REASONS FOR INFRINGEMENT OF COPYRIHT

Some of the important reasons for violation of Copyright -particularly in library and information centers are:

1. Shrinking budgets.
2. Non availability of books (out of print, ban on books etc.)
3. Delay in supply/procurement of books/journals.
4. Higher cost of books/journals (specially foreign publications)
5. Urgent need.
6. Ignorance of Intellectual Property Rights.
7. Language need for translation.

Abuse of copyright

Pagell in 1990 provided a list of what he considered to be the area of abuse for numbers of products:

Books: photocopying, translating, and reporting.

Journals: photocopying.

Machine readable data: copying of citation records, abstracts, fultext articles, CD-ROMs and software copying.

Computer programmes: copying, translating, and cloning of computer programmes.

LAWS OF LIBRARY SCIENCE AND COPYRIGHT LAW

The main objective of Copyright Law is 'protection' of work/resources from duplication whereas the objective of library is to 'use' the resources effectively. Here the term 'use' not only includes reading but also photocopying, downloading, etc. The laws of library science have developed over a period of time. These laws are generally identified as the philosophical principals around whom any library development would be oriented. Modern day information accessing through internet, CD-ROMs, are nothing but implementation of the laws of library science. On the one side law says that 'books are for use' but on the other hand law of copyright restrict the use of books/ information. The laws of copyright were framed in order to protect an author against piracy of his work. This right is not a right which arises under common law, but is right which has arisen by statutory protection.

20

Storage Media For Digitization and Preservation

INTRODUCTION

In ancient libraries, documents were presented in different types such as clay tablets, silk, metal and palm leaves. With the rapid development in both papers and printing technology, there is tremendous growth in publications. It is estimated that millions of pages are being printed every minute at global level.

Digital library seems to be computerization of traditional library. It is heterogeneous library, which contains both hard copy and soft copy. It has the paper documents as well as electronic documents. With the emergence of computer technology, paper documents are changed drastically

Publications produced in digital forms are available in various formats such as CD-ROMs, DVD-ROMs. There are different types of digital medium that could be used to publish any given piece of work. The common storage media in digital libraries that are being used today are: microfilms, floppy disks, CD-ROM etc are minimized and submitted for large volume of conventional documents.

Electronic publishing products may include texts, graphics, audio, video, numeric and textual databases, and reference sources such as dictionaries, encyclopedias, directories, and computer programme. The CD-ROM has provided to be a suitable medium for publishing full-text databases.

STORAGE MEDIA FOR DIGITAL LIBRARIES

The ideal storage medium for digital libraries would allow vast amount of data to be stored at low cost, would be fast to store and read information, and would be exceptionally reliable and long lasting. Rotating magnetic disc is the standard storage medium in modern computer systems. Sizes range from a fraction of gigabyte to arrays of thousands of gigabytes. Disks are fast enough for most digital library applications, since data can be read from disks faster than it can be transmitted over networks. When data is read from a disk, there is a slightly delay while the disk heads are aligned to begin reading; than data is read in large blocks. These performance chrematistics suits digital library applications, which typically read large blocks of data at a time.

What are optical Storage Devices?

Optical storage devices are a storage medium from which data is read and to which it is written by laser. Optical disk storage is relatively new alternative to magnetic storage. Optical disk can store much more data as compared to magnetic storage media, such as floppy disk. Today, the most popular alternative to magnetic storage media storage system is optical systems. Optical disks differ from magnetic disk storage by the way data is stored and read from the storage media. Optical storage is relatively new secondary storage media. It is also a random access storage media. It can store enormous amount of data on a small size single circular disk.

A laser beam is used to read and write data on these reflective disks, so they are also known as laser disks. In this technology a laser is hit a layer of magnetic media spared over the surface of the disk. When data is being entered, heat from the laser produces tiny spots on the disk surface. Digital data is burnt into the surface of a plastic disk coated with a low melting point metal by a laser beam. To read the data, the laser scans the disk, and a lence picks up different light reflections from the various spots. The presence or absence of a hole correspond to one bit and can be read by an other layer. This technology offers high capacity storage at a low cost, and in a form allowing rapid access (analogous to magnetic disks).

Optical disks are becoming a very inviting option for users. They are less sustainable to environmental fluctuations, and they provide more direct access storage at a cost that is much less per megabyte to storage than the magnetic disk alternative.

The most widely used type of optical storage media is the Compact Disk (CD), which is used in -CD-ROM, CD-Record able, CD-Re-writ able, DVD, DVD-ROM, DVD-R, DVD-RAM, DVD-ROM.

Features of Optical Storage Media

1. In it information is permanently stored.
2. The information from the memory can only be read and it is not only possible to write fresh information onto it.
3. Since it can store large amount of structure data—bibliographic, full text, multimedia and image type, the CD-ROM has brought about a revolution in the information world.

Storage Capacity: The storage capacity can be calculated as: numbers of sectors X number of bites per sector. Typically, the optical disk contains 3,30,000 sectors, each sector contains 2352 bytes of data.

Background and History: Historically, two industries have been the main driving forces behind the huge advancement in optical storage technology. These are IT (Information Technology) industry and the entertainment industry. In the IT camp one can find high-tech giants such as Dell, Apple, Phillips, Toshiba, and NEC; on the other hand big movie players such as 20th century Fox, MGM, and Universal Studios are world leaders and music players such as T-Series, HMV, in India are the forces in the entertainment industry.

According to Wikipedia, a fellow by the name of David Paul Gregg developed an analog optical disk for recording video and had it patented in 1961 and 1969. The Music Corporation America (MCA) acquired the patent.

On the other side the physists of the Netherlands based Phillips Corporation begun their first optical disk experiment in 1969. Six years later, Phillips and MCA joined forces in creating the laser disks, which was first introduced in the United States in 1978.

Traditionally, Personnel Computers have used the physics of magnetism as the primary means of storing data for later use. Floppy disks, hard disks, zip disks, and back-up tapes all work by magnetizing small areas on the surface of the disk.

In the resent years magnetism has been complemented by optics as a storage mechanism

CDs

The Compact Disk is the result of collaboration between IT industry giants Phillips and Sony in the 1980s. The CD, as the medium become popularly known, offered an excellent replacement for the large music vinyl records of the time, and as such these disks were in fact audio CDs. These are two companies developed the Compact Disk (CD) in 1980s. A digital audio medium meant to supplement standard for CD's evolution into CD-ROM (CD-Read Only Memory) went beyond audio, adding software, computer games, movies, encyclopedias, and more. These CD-ROMs were not limited to audio data, as they can also hold software, text and video.

CD-ROMs mainly differ from audio CDs in terms of error correcting code. While it might be tolerable for any audio CD to have errors (e.g. from time to time the music skips while playing), it is definitely not tolerable for computer programs, as even the smallest software defect can render the whole program unusable. This means that CD-ROMs have to contain a large amount of error correcting code needed to safely store data.

The yellow book data formatting system for CD-ROMs follows this hierarchy; every byte is encoded in a 14 bit symbol, 42 consecutive symbols then form a frame, and 98 frames then form a CD-ROM sector.

After the yellow book came the Green Book, which added graphics to the CD-ROM, as well as the all-important ability to interleaved audio, video, data (in essence, multimedia). In short, the Green Book spaces made the CD into a true multimedia medium.

After the trio books, the standardized CD-ROM file system called High Sierra came, which allowed the optical disks to be read by computers running under Windows/MS-DOS, Apple, UNIX, and virtually, any computer.

As if the yellow and Green Books were not enough, the Orange Book came trudging along, bringing with it the technical details for the CD-R (CD-Recordable). This technical advancement gave people a less expensive means of storing data in CDs, as well as unfortunately giving software, music, and movie pirates the power to make illegal copies to CDs.

First generation optical disks were initially used to store music and software. For example CDs and magneto-optical disks. Second generation optical disks came into use in 1990s and are able to store large amount of data (which is needed in good quality digital video). Examples of these are: DVDs, Minidisks, etc. Lastly, most third generation optical disks are not yet in the market, but are looking to be the prime players in the near future. Vastly superior in data capacity, these disks will be able to store High-Density (HD) video and massive video games. Examples of these are HD-DVD, Blue Ray Disks, Versatile Multiplier Disks, and Holographic Versatile Disks.

Working of Optical Disk

Optical storage devices make use of the pinpointed precision possible laser beams. Laser beam is coherent in nature i.e. light energy is perfectly aligned in the same direction, which helps in focusing laser on an extremely area. Optical storage devices focus a laser beams on the recording medium, which is a spinning disk, same as phonograph record. Some areas of the disk reflect the laser light into a sensor called a lands, where as others scattered the light called as pits. As the disk rotates past the laser and sensor, a spot that reflects the laser beam into the sensor is interpreted as a 1s and the absence of a reflection as 0s. A laser can read an optical disks surface, where pitted areas represent binary 0's and landed areas represent binary 1s.

Advantages and Limitations of Optical Disks

Advantages:

1. **Low cost**: cost per bit of storage is low and it can store enormous data.

2. Reliable Storage medium: The optical disks are more reliable than magnetic storage; because optical storage disk derives do not have read/write heads. Thus, no chance of crash into the disk surface.

3. Read Large Blocks of Data: The data is organized in a single spiral track. This makes optical storage ideal for storing music and videos as it can read large blocks of sequential data.

4. Easy to Handle: Optical disk are compact, lightweight easy-to store and easily portable.

5. More Data Storage Life: Optical disk have data storage life more than magnetic tape or disk (more than 30 years app). Thus used for archival purposes.

6. Permanent Storage: Data stored on optical disk is permanent as it cannot be erased or overwritten.

Limitations

1. It is not reusable medium.
2. It is read-only medium.
3. Data recording and reading require a complicated mechanism than magnetic disk.
4. Data access speed is slower than magnetic disk.

Uses of Optical Disks

1. For distribution of software, electronic version of journals, magazines, books, conference proceedings, etc.
2. For storing multimedia applications, such as video games, movies, music, etc.
3. For archival data, this is not frequently required.

Life of Optical Disks

The life span of these disks is difficult to predict. It depends on two factors: 1.external factors, such as accidents, heat, humidity, direct sunlight, sub-standard manufacturing process, old/damaged burning hardware (lasers, lances, etc.), and other situations can effects the physical condition of these disks, and consequently the data contained in it.

Not all disks were created in the same way. Material used varies from one manufacturer to other.

In general, manufactured or pressed disks are more tolerant of damaging condition than home-burned CDs and the like simply because the differ in the way the data is stored: pressed disks have their data literally pressed onto them, while recordable types use dyes that change color or reflectivity under the heat of a laser.

The re-writable media are considered much less reliable than plain CD-R/DVD-R disks. It is advised that you stay away from storing permanent and rare data in RWs, unless perhaps you have backups elsewhere.

Types of Optical Disks

Optical Disks technologies still emerging and have yet to stabilize, however, at present there are three different types of optical disks in common use are:

1. Read only
2. Record able and
3. Erasable

Optical Storage Types

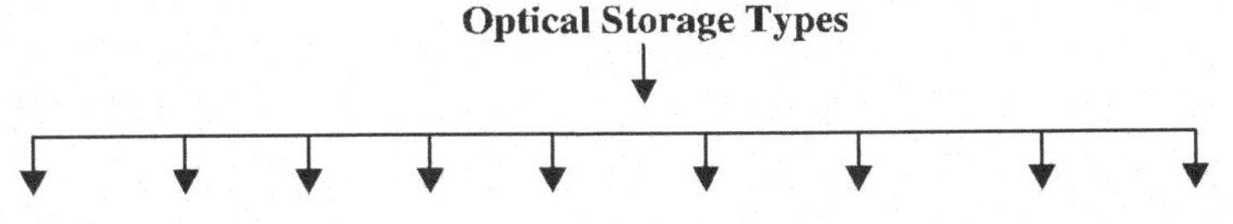

Fig. 16. Optical Storage Type

The most widely used type of optical storage medium is the Compact Disk (CD), which is used in CD-ROM, DVD-ROM, CD-Recordable, CD-Rewritable and Photo CD system

1. Read Only Disks

The compact Disk Read Only Memory (CD-ROM) introduced in 1985, the audio CD in 1982, is basically an optical disc. It is in the form of CD-ROM had become increasingly important as a medium of storage and dissemination of information during 1990s. The CD-ROM technology is being used in libraries in the area of bibliographic databases. But some applications are also there.

CD-ROMs

Stands for Compact Disk Read Only Memory, which simply means your computer can read data from these disks but cannot write data back. CD-ROM uses the same technology that is used in music CDs. A standard CD-ROM is 12cm (5.25 inches) in diameter and it can store about 650-660 Megabytes of data. It means that it can store 250,000 A4 pages of text. A megabyte being approximately a million bytes, a byte being the equivalent of an alphabetical letter or a numeral. Most of the computers today still come with CD-ROM drives—drives are the mechanisms that spin the disks—but this technology is being superseded.

CD-ROM is a medium for storage and distribution of large volumes of computerized information. It is known as "Read Only Memory." Because information stored on CD-ROM disc by the publisher can not be erased or rewrite. There are large numbers of reference books published by the publishers on CD-ROMs. CD-ROMs are now being replaced by DVDs (Digital Video Disks or Digital Versatile Discs) which is having more storage capacity, several times higher than CD-ROMs. DVDs are very useful especially for the storage of multimedia information. It has 4.7 GB memory which can store feature length movies. The double layered discs approximately 8.5 GB and double sided and double layered disc is 17 GB. CD-ROM drives will not play DVD but DVD drives will be backward compatible with CD-ROM and CD-R.

CD-ROMs has begun to be accepted as the media of publishing, which is particularly suitable for large volumes of information. CD-ROMs are now increasingly being used as a standard storage medium based on ISO standards.

It is an optical storage media and information is stored in them in digitized form unlike magnetic media. CD-ROM is pre-recorded disc allowing the user for reading only.

In the electronic information era, CD-ROM plays an important role as an efficient and compatible storage medium. CD-ROM is used to store and deliver large amount of information in the form of data, text, graphics etc. Apart from electronic books and journals, various other information such as software, games, music databases, abstracts, pictures etc are available on CD-ROMs. To read information contained in CD-ROMs, a CD-ROM player/drive and a microcomputer are necessary. CD-ROM products are just decades old, but they have already made an impression on the library profession.

CD-ROM has begun to be accepted as the media of publishing, which is suitable for large volume of information. It is very inexpensive storage media. It is very useful for libraries. The major applications of CD-ROM includes bibliographic database, reference books such as encyclopedias. A large number of data bases are available on CD-ROMs on almost all the subjects.

A CD is a thin layer of aluminum sandwiched between two layers of plastic. This Aluminum has a spiral track that contains millions of tiny pits (1s). As the CD spins a laser beam shines on the track. The "holes" on the CD are called pits, while the unburned areas around these holes are called "lands". These pits and lands are written in a single continuous spiral near the CD hole; if unwound, the spiral would extend to more or less 5.6 kilometers long.

Grolier's Academic American Encyclopedia was first published in CD-ROM in 1985. 20 volumes consisting of 9,000,000 words or 10,000 pages, consumes a mere one fifth of data capacity of one 12 cm diameter disk. The 1990 edition of Grolier's Encyclopedia included full color photographs for the first time. The encyclopedias on CD-ROMs are much cheaper than their paper equivalent.

Some of the significant CD-ROM developments during the past few years include:

- Development in the multimedia CD-ROMs
- Growth in the full text CD-ROMs
- Declining hardware and software prices
- Increased number of users
- General acceptance of CD-ROM in libraries
- Increased number of CD-ROM publishers.

Benefits of CD-ROM

1. Very low information distribution cost.
2. Considerable saving of time in information retrieval.
3. Extensive sorting, searching and retrieval.
4. Vast storage capacity (650 MB of data). Among the various storage devices, the CD-ROM is one of the best storage media because of its excellent features such as huge storage capacity (can store more than 1,30,0000 pages)
5. More information on less space for less money with more permanency and ease of access of data.
6. Light weight and portable.
7. CD-ROMs are not vulnerable to magnetic fields, which can destroy the data on a disk.
8. Reliable and durable. Optical media are extremely durable and reliable under normal use. Because the surface of the disk is never touched by anything but

light beam. One reason optical technology is so reliable is that the read head is several millimeters away from the disk surface.

9. Cheaper in comparison with other high capacity storage medium. It is providing to be a low cost publishing medium for high volume reference publications such as encyclopedias, abstracting and bibliographic databases.
10. Easily available.
11. Permanent store: the data cannot be erased nor anything can be written on it again. It is Read Only Memory Only.
12. Low error rate.
13. Long life.
14. Random access.
15. Easily transportable.

Applications of CD-ROM

CD-ROM applications include reference material, games, and software distribution. Thousands of pages of book or document can be recorded on it and which can be read through a computer and a print out can be taken instantly of the text at a very nominal cost. CD-ROM has revolutionaries the encyclopedia industry. Now most of the popular encyclopedias such as Britannica, dictionaries and indexing journals and their back-volumes are coming in the handy CD-ROM formats. Today, a large number of organizations around the world are publishing scientific data, bibliographies and full text information on CD-ROMs. Database which do not need to be up-dated quite frequently, and retrospective databases are most suitable for CD-ROMs. On CD-ROMs we can keep not only copies of rare and valuable literary works, scholarly studies, technical research but also out of print books. CD-ROMs has revolutionaries the encyclopedia industry, totally replacing some print encyclopedias. These are available one fourth the price of hard copy.

CD-ROM has evolved as an effective information storage and dissemination media in libraries and information centers. The major application of CD-ROM include bibliographic database, encyclopedias, dictionaries, etc. A large number of CD-ROM databases are available on almost all subjects. With audio, video and graphic facilities, the CD-ROMs could become multimedia resources for libraries. CD-ROM plays a vital role in transfer of information including its storage of data in libraries and information centers. Hence many libraries particularly university and special libraries have adopted CD-ROM technology and has become a common service in their libraries to provide effective and efficient service in an electronic information environment.

Disadvantages

One of the disadvantages is that CD drive is still slow, while on the other hand a good hard drive, by comparison faster and can transfer 10 MB of data per second as compared to 900 KB of data per second by CD drive.

The other reason is that you cannot write to portions of a writable CD-ROM that already have data written on them. You can add to data that was written to the disk in on earlier session but you cannot delete or change what is already there.

Data Storage on CD-ROM

Data is laid out on a CD-ROM disk in a long, continuous spiral that starts at outer edge and winds inwards to the center. The data is stored in the form of lands, which are flat areas on the metal surface, and pits, which are depression or holes. The depth of all pits is uniform, but their length varies.

Information is recorded on a 12 cm disk-using laser to each billions of tiny pits into a thin metal lair that is very much closer to the top surface of the disk than the bottom. Thus, the user should be more careful of scratching the top. Printed side of the disk is generally, the bottom of the disk. It beautifully reflects a rainbow of colors due to diffraction. To read the data, a low power laser light scans the disk surface. The pitted area does not reflect and thus interpreted as 0(Zero) as bit where as smooth areas are reflected and are interpreted as 1 (one) bit. On a full CD-ROM, the spiral of data stanched almost three miles long. As disk rotate past the laser and sensor, a spot that reflect the laser beam into the sensor is interpreted as a 1 and the absence of reflection as a 0. A laser can read an optical disk surface, where pitted areas represents binary 0s and landed areas represent binary 1s.

CD-ROM speed

Compared to hard disk drive, the CD-ROM drives are quite slow, in part because the laser reads pits and lands one bit at time. An other reason has to do with the changing rotational speed of the disk. Like a track on a magnetic disk, the track of an optical disk is split into sectors. However, the sectors are laid out quite differently than they are on magnetic disk.

Sectors near the middle of the CD wrap farther around the disk than those near the edge. For the drive to read each sector in the same amount of time, it must spin the disk faster when reading sectors near the middle and slower when reading sectors near the edge. Changing the speed of rotation takes time -enough to seriously impair the overall performance of the CD drive.

As we know that CD is a thin lair of aluminum sandwiched between two lairs of plastic. The aluminum has a spiral track that contains millions of tiny pits (1s). As the

CD spins a laser beam shines on the track.

To manage the enormous data files on CD-ROMs we use special indexing methods. The indexes on CD-ROMs contain information on how to find virtually every single word on the CD-ROM.

CD—R (CD-Recordable)

CD-Rs are WORM (Write Ones, Read Many) disks that gives people a cheaper means of storing data in compact disks. Unfortunately, the arrival of these low-cost, easy to use CD-Rs also helped to spread software, music, and movie piracy.

CD-Rs are look like regular CD-ROMs except that they are gold colored instead of silver. This is due to the use of gold instead of aluminum, which is used in regular CDs. This disk contains 0.6 mm wide grooves that guide the laser for writing data.

WORM is an ideal medium for making a permanent record of data i.e. it can be a feasible alternative to magnetic tapes for archival storage. These disks are ideal for archival purpose allowing organization to store large volumes of documentation on one disk. For instance 12 inches disk can hold about 2.5 GB of data at a cost of few hundred rupees. Storage capacity 5.0 GB is now available. But, the major problem with WORM technology is the absence of any industry standards.

Advantages

This is the newer technology that overcomes CD-ROM's read-only limitation-CD-R stands for Compact Disk Recordable. Popularly uses are copying music and archiving data. The best feature of these disks is their low cost. The cost is Rs 20 per disk if purchase in bulk. These are ideal storage media for archival proposes, allowing storing large volumes of documentation on a one disk.

Limitations

The biggest limitation is that you can record data onto them only once. CD-R drive can be attached to a computer a regular peripheral device. CD-R drives allow you to create your own CD-ROM disks that can be read by any CD-ROM drive. After information has been written to part of the CD, that information cannot be changed. With most CD-R drives, however, you can continue to record information to the other part of the disk until it is full.

Applications

1. Many financial institutions such as banks use WORM disks to store a record of each day's transactions. The transactions are written to an optical disk and become a permanent record that can be read but never altered.
2. Another popular application of WORM is in information systems, that require the merging of text and images that do not change for a period of time. A good example is 'electronic catalog'.

CD-RW (Compact Disk Rewritable)

CD-RW overcome the write once limitation of CD-R. You can rewrite and erase data multiple times. It's a technology that's becoming increasingly popular in PCs, in many cases replacing the Zip and tape backup drives. CD-RWs represent the next step in CD technology after CD-R. These disks use the same standard size of CD-Rs but are more expensive than CD-R.

Advantages

Now CD-RW drives available at somewhat higher cost that provides true auxiliary memory that can be coded (unto about a million times) and read back and are thus a type of WMRAM (Write Many, Read Many) disks.

It allows users to record and erase data so that disk can

be reused again. CD-RW with such a drive, re-recording of data can be done by first erasing the old information through intense laser action that heats each amorphous stripes to the temperature just below its melting point where it recristallizes, than after a few millisecond of cooling to complete the process, a less intense laser action is used to record new information on it.

Keep in mind that CD-Rs are not rendered obsolete with the availability of CD-RWs. CD-Rs can still be used as cheaper back-up media, as well as more secure storage unlike CD-RWs.

CD-Rs can only be written once, which means you cannot accidentally erase the stored data with another written process.

Recording and Writing Process:

Recording and writing process for CD-RWs use different magnitudes for laser:

- High power to convert alloy from crystalline to amorphous state
- Medium power to melts alloy in order to bring it back to its crystalline state.
- Low power to use in reading the CD-RW (that is, to sense the alloy to its state)

Use of CD-RW drive

Using newer generation CD-RW drives, however, user can write and overwrite data onto compact disk with a CD-RW drive in the same manner as in the floppy disk. A new type of CD-RW does not need to be attached to PC, but can be, if needed. These drives features a large built-in hard disk, which can record data or music from the user' PC or from an audio or data CD. The device stores the data on its disk and then can copy the data onto a fresh CD-R or CD-RW disk. This type of drive is handy because it can create CDs without typing up resources on the user's PC.

Erasable Disks: Magneto-Optical Disks

A hybrid disk called magneto-optical (MO) combines the best features of magnetic and optical disk technologies. A magneto-optical disk has the high volume capacity of an optical disk but can be written over as a magnetic disk. It is 5-1/4 inch disks and can store 1000 MB. The disk surface is coated with plastic and embedded with magnetically sensitive metallic crystals. To write data, a laser beam melts a tiny spot on the plastic surface and a magnetic aligns the crystal before the plastic cools. The crystals are placed in such a way that that some reflects lights and other do not. Later on, when a laser beam reads the data, only the crystals reflect light are picked up.

Some of the Disadvantages are:

- Magneto-optical disks are too expensive and do not offer anywhere near the kind of reliability that users have come to expect of magnetic media.
- The access time in magneto-optical disks is relatively slow, about the same as a low-end, Winchester disk.

As optical disk technology matures to offer reliable, cost-effective, read/write operation, it eventually may dominate secondary storage in the future magnetic disks and tape to today. The technology need to improve further in order to be widely accepted. As magnetic disks dominate over magnetic tapes similarly, these days optical disk technology is advanced to offer reliability, cost-effectiveness, read as well as write operations. I may eventually dominate secondary storage.

DVD (Digital Versatile Disk)

Formally known as Digital Video Disk has the same 12 cm size as a CD but it is called "Versatile" because it appears destined to replace not only the laser disk and audio CD for entertainment but also the CD-ROM for use as an auxiliary computer memory. DVDs are produced using the same concept of pits and lands applied to CDs.

DVD technology uses a higher frequency and shorter wavelength laser to etch pits, to make a CD. So, the surface of DVD contains microscopic pits, which represents 0s and 1s of digital code, which can be read by laser. When reading the disk, the laser starts at the bottom layer then goes to the top layer.

Furthermore, the DVD spiral tracks are denser than these of a CD. Although the diameter and metal thickness of CD and DVD are same, yet capacity of DVD is 4.7 GB each side. Dual-layer DVD disks can hold 17 GB of data. Dual-layer disks have silver colored surface where as single layer disks have gold surfaces.

DVD can hold around two hours of high-quality digital video (using MPEG-2 Compression), plus digital audio, usually using Dolby Digital or Digital Theater System (DTS). Like CD-ROM and LD-ROM, an ordinary DVD is DVD-ROM, that is, its pre-recorded pits-encoded information can be read but not re-written. It is used for mass distribution of pre-recorded software programs and multimedia.

DVD-ROM drives can be useful for watching DVD movies on your PC or playing computer games. Despite their capacity of DVD-ROMs, software makers have continued to distribute their programs primarily on CD-ROMs because of the urbanity of CD-ROM drives.

The difference between the CD and DVD is shown in the table below:

Types of DVDs

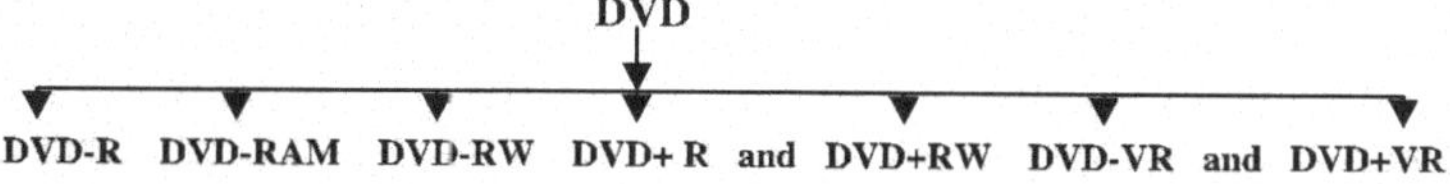

Fig. 17. Types of DVDs

1. **DVD-R**: DVD-Recordable, are the first and most popular format of recordable DVDs. Similar to CD-R, this technology lets you record data onto disks, but only once. DVD-R disks currently have seven to eight times the capacity of CD-R disks, though both the drives and disks are more expensive.

DVD-R drives can create CD-R disks and crate or re-write CD-W disk.

These are two types:

1. **DVD-R** : Authoring or DVD-RCA are highly expensive and uncommon disks used for professional needs, as they allow recording of any data; 2. DVD-R General or DVD- (G) is more available to consumers, but do not allow copying of protected DVDs.

2. **DVD-RAM**: The DVD-RAM format was developed by Panasonic according to the specifications of the DVD, but logically works like a hard disk.

This is a competing, and incompatible, technology. You can not read DVD-RAM disks with most other DVD drives, and DVD-RAM cannot create disks that can be read by CD-ROM drives or CD players, a big limitation compared with DVR.

3. **DVD-ROM**: DVD-ROM uses disks that are similar to CD-ROM disks but typically hold seven to eight times more data. Despite the greater capacity of DVD-ROMs, software makers have continued to distribute their programs primarily on CD-ROMs because of ubiquity of CD-ROM drives. DVD-ROM drives can be useful for watching DVD movies on your PC or playing computer games.

DVD-ROM drives, like CD-ROM drives, cannot record data, though they can read most types of CD and DVD disks. The speed ratings of DVD-ROM drives are not comparable with those of CD-ROM drives—a 12x DVD-ROM drive is faster than a 48x CD-ROM drive

4. DVD-RW: This technology lets you record, erase and record data. Because it is a new technology, it is expensive. Some DVD-RROM drives can not read DVD-RE disks that have been written to multiple times.

Just like the dual-state CD-RWs, DVD-Rewritable disks change state under a laser for it to be re-written on. Specification requires that DVD-RWs should reach up to 1000 instances of these re-writings. One drawback of this disk is that because they have relatively lower reflectivity and are consequently mistaken as dual-layer DVDs, re-writable DVDs are compatible with only around 70% of the players out there.

5. DVD+R and DVD+RW: The DVD-RW and DVD+RW formats are basically competing formats to their "dash-R" or "minus-R" counterparts, but with some noteworthy differences. DVD=RWs provides for: loss less linking (no need to re-record a whole disk if only part of its needs updating, better error handling, easy write or Mt.Rainer technology (transforming the disk into an ordinary floppy or hard drive), twice the maximum writing speed of DVD-RWs. DVD-R and DVD-RW copy protection is called VCPs, or Video Contact Protection System for DVD+R/+RW.

6. DVD-VR and DVD+VR: Like most DVD disks, DVD-VRs and DVD+VRs(DVD Video Recording Disk) were made for videos. This is taken as step further, though, as these video recording formats allow you to crate videos on these disks so that they can be edited fully. Features such as additing new video content, changing menu backgrounds, inserting chapters, splitting clips, or removing unwanted scenes are now possible with the DVD VRs. But this also added compatibility issues: support for VR editing may only be found in specialized or high-end hardware and software as of now. As for the "minus" versus "plus" formats, the same rule of thumb regarding incompatibility applies: DVD-VRs are not usually payable in ordinary DVD player and must be in

DVD-VR compatible devices. The same goes for DVD+VRs.

7. **HD-DVD**: Toshiba released the first HD-DVD player in Japan on March 31, 2006. The US release followed shortly on mid-April. On May 2006, the company released the first PC-equipped with on HD-DVD drive.

A single sided HD-DVD can hold 15 GB of storage, while a dual sided one can store 30 GB. The medium's main proponent, Toshiba, has announced a triple sided disk that can hold 45 GB. The HD-DVD's size is similar to that of CD and the DVD is 120 mm in diameter.

HD-DVDs are meant to use the IHD interactive format, which will allow interactive content to be written for these disks.

A lot of major players in the movie industry support the HD-DVD format, which only bodes well for its cause.

Comparison of Characteristics of CD and DVD

Characteristics	DVD	CD
Size	12 cm	12 cm
Versatility	Very versatile because destined to replace laser disk, audio CD for entertainment CD-ROM	Not very versatile as DVD
Technology used to each Pits	DVD technology uses a higher frequency (shorter wavelength) laser to each Pit. The packing of the Pits/holes is 0.74 microns for DVDs	CD uses lower frequency laser than DVD to each Pits. The packing of the Pits/holes is 1.6 microns in between for CDs
Spiral Tracks	DVD's spiral tracks are more dense than CD circumferentially	Spiral tracks are less dense circumferentially
Capacity	8.5 GB (single side) 17 GB (when recorded on both sides) It is 13 times more than CD	660 MB
Error correcting	Read-Solomon Product	CD uses Cross Interleaved

code	Code (RS-PC). It is ten times robust than the code used on CD	Read- Solomon Code
Eight to Fourteen modulation for recording	EFM Plus 8 bit to 16 bit modulation	EFM 8 bit to 14 bit modulation used

APPLICATIONS OF DVD IN LIBRARIES

The important applications of this technology in libraries are as follows:

1. Large and fultext databases.
2. Mixed databases.
3. Quick reference databases.
4. Archival purposes.
5. Cost effective mass storage for networking purposes.
6. Preservation media for multimedia libraries.

MULTIMEDIA

Multimedia technology integrates the following medium:

1. text
2. images
3. graphics video
4. Animation
5. Sound or
6. music

It is interactive on the lines of hypertext and hypermedia. Multimedia databases are now becoming very popular

ADVANTAGES AND DISADVANTAGES OF DIGITAL MEDIA

The decline in the cost of disks is one of the marvels of technology. Magnetic disks are coming down in price even faster than semi conductors. In 1998, the price of disks was a few hundred dollars per gigabyte. The technology is advancing so fast that digital libraries can confidently plan that in ten years time the cost will be no more than five percent and very likely will be less than one percent of todays. Digital libraries use huge amount of storage. A page of ASCII text may be only a few thousand characters, but a scanned color image, only one inch square, requires more than a megabyte (one million bytes).An hour of digitized sound, as stored on a compact disk is over 600 megabytes and a minutes of video can have more than gigabytes of data before compression. To reduce these storage requirements, large items are compressed, including almost all images, sound and video. The basic idea of compression simple, though the mathematics is complex. Compression method can be divided into two main categories. Lossless compression removes redundant information in a manner that is completely researchable; the original data can be reconstructed exactly as it was. Lossy compression can not be reversed; approximations are made during the compression that lose some of the information.

In some applications, compression must be lossless. In most applications, however, some losses are acceptable. The JPEG compression used for images and MPEG used for video are loosely methods that are calibrated to provide images that are very satisfactory to a human eye. Compression methods reduce the size of data considerably, but the files are still large. After compression, a monochrome page of scanned text is more than 50,000 bytes. MPEG compression reduces digitized video from 20 or 30 megabytes per second to 10 megabytes per minutes.

Since digital libraries store millions of these items, storage capacity is an important factor.

Replica is a basic technique of data processing. Important data that exist only as a single copy on one computer is highly vulnerable. The hardware can fail; the data can be obliterated by faulty software; an incompetent or dishonest employee can remove the data; the computer building may be destroyed by fire, flooding, or other disaster. For these reasons, computer center make routine copies of all data for backup and store this data in safe locations.

DISADVANTAGES

Disks have weakness of reliability. The data on them is easily lost, either because of a hardware failure or because a programme over writes. To guard against such failure, standards practice is for the data to be regularly copied onto other media, usually magnetic tape. It is also common to have some redundancy in the disk stores so that simple errors can be corrected automatically. Neither disks nor magnetic tape can be relied on for long term storage. The data is encoded on a thin magnetic film deposited on some surface. Sooner or later this film decays.

Digital storage media are "fragile" with a limited shelf life. The digital information on those media, even if they do survive will be rendered unreliable by obsolescence of technology. To preserve digital information, digital libraries will continually have to "migrate" information from one digital hardware and software configuration to another.

- Preservation of storage medium- tapes, hard drives, floppy disks, has a short life span when considered in terms of obsolescence.
- Preservation of access to content- this form of preservation involves preserving access to the contents of the document regardless of their format.
- While files can be moved from one storage medium to another, what happens when the formats containing the information become obsolete?

21

Development and Management of Digital Library Collection

INTRODUCTION

The three important functions of a library are collection, storage and dissemination of information. The effectiveness of two functions depends upon the collection.

Collection development is a vital process in building up a library collection.

Library collection is an important component of a library. It is a group of continuous activities, which serve as the backbone for all library services. Collection development implies selection, acquisition and evaluation of the library collection. Collection includes both print and digital collection. With the development of Internet and information communication technology the collection development policy has been changed to include the digital content in a collection. Technology has changed the mode of publishing and information market has been flooded with various e-resources. Collection comprises of monographs, textbooks, reference sources, journals, standards etc. Collection development is also related to budget and help in proper utilization of library budget. One of the problems that libraries are facing is how to manage funds for resources. Budget is a very difficult process for the librarians. Librarians do face the problem of how to manage the funds for the resources?

Collection development is a continuous activity. One of the elements of a developed digital library is its digital collection/documents.

Libraries maintain the various kinds of collection such as print and digital. The digital collection includes audio-visual material, CD-ROM, images text, etc.

Digital resources are very different from traditional resources. For their management collection evaluation is needed.

What is collection Development?

Collection development is a wider term, which involves formulation of a systematic general plan for the creation of a library collection, which will meet the information needs of the users. The word 'development' implies necessarily qualitative improvement of the collection. It also includes the systematic development of an already existing collection. The collection includes print and non print material. It includes text books, reference books etc.

Library collection have always been at the heart of the libraries, be they digital, traditional brick and mortar, or hybrid between the two.

Collection development according to G Edward Evans is "the process of making certain the information needs of the people using the collection are met in a timely and economical manner, using information sources produced both inside and outside the organization."

According to Hendrick Edelman "collection development, selection and acquisition are terms, which represent a hierarchy. The highest level is collection development, which is the planning function." According to Magill and Hickey "collection development includes assessing user needs, evaluating the present collection, determining selection policy, coordinating of selection of items, weeding and storing parts of the collection and planning for the resource sharing."

Collection development as a planned, systematic development of a collection, based on the objectives of the library. It is totality of activities, which leads to building up a library collection. It may also be defined as a planned, continuous cost effective and preferential acquisition of qualitative, relevant materials to meet the need of users and the objectives of the library. Collection development therefore is not only to be viewed from the growth in volumes and titles but in the quality of acquired materials in enhancing effective information, delivery and the usage of such to lessen users disadvantages and frustrations. It is only in this perspective that the word 'development' could be meaningful in relation to collection.

Although there is a wide spread availability of electronic resources, particularly that on internet, still this will not diminish or eliminates the need for collection development in libraries in developed or developing countries. But instead, collection development is to incorporate the new challenges in the acquisition process, such as site licensing, copyright issues, and how access will be provided to various electronic resources. About half a decade ago, recommendations on basic criteria for selection and purchase of the electronic era had been outlines as; content, relevance, usefulness, cost and accessibility.

Unlike print resources, decision regarding acquisition of electronic resources is directly tied to the availability of, or willingness to purchase suitability technology to use the resources. The selection process of electronic resources may also take into consideration the amount of user instruction required and potential demands made upon the library's other resources and services. The ongoing cost likely to be incurred such as of subscriptions and maintenance must be examined.

The interested aspect of collection development presently is that the cost of technology is going down but unfortunately the cost of information continues to ascend. This implies that libraries can only become more involved in any communication including scholarly, through the support of governments, parent organizations/institutions/societies/ communities and co-operative efforts (networking)

WHY WE NEED COLLECTION DEVELOPMENT?

The ever increasing needs and requirements of the users cause the growing demand of documents and information. The exponential growth of literature has its impact on library holdings. As we know library is a growing organism. Library is growing in terms of its collection. No library, whether it is large or small can store all the material. Individually no library, however resourceful it might be, could afford to build comprehensive, live collection to satisfy the actual as well as potential information needs of the users.

The physical limitations of storage naturally impose the necessary for selection and weeding out materials for proper collection and development. The financial constraint is also an important factor for such control. On the other hand cost of the reading material has been increasing at a very fast rate and the library budget have not expended at the same rate as the cost of reading material. Making decision about the purchase of individual items for library collection requires a clear understanding of the various needs of the users and the determination of overall priorities.

A comprehensive, balanced and updated collection of documents is an essential activity for providing effective library services. Libraries therefore need to identify, select, procure and organize documents for use.

Traditionally the process of collection development consists of identification, selection, acquisition and evaluation of a collection of library resources based on their information needs of the users. Library has to collect a wide variety of documents to satisfy the information needs of the users. A cooperative collection development programmes , on the other hand , will allow the users to have access to a wide variety and amount of information sources. Thus, a cooperative collection development programme will be in the interest of both the patrons as well as the librarians.

The application of information and communication technology in the libraries has made a significant impact on organization of collection and services of the libraries. Role of libraries and information centers has changed due to applications of information technology. The quality of services has improved. There is shift of print collection to digital collection. Electronic resources comprise some of the library's most visible and expensive investments. Effective management of information about electronic resources can result in improved access, operations, etc. Users now can access information from remote areas at any time 24 hours and seven days a week. Due to the shift of formats have force the libraries to change their functioning. All these changes require libraries to have well prepared collection development policy keeping in view the information needs of the users. A balance and need based collection adequate to meet the present and the future information needs of the users.

PURPOSE OF COLLECTION DEVELOPMENT

Collection development implies selection, acquisition and evaluation of the library collection. Collection in order to see that both print and non print material in the library are really useful to the users. Therefore, collection development dispenses away with arbitrary selection and acquisition of documents. It require periodic evaluation of the library stock both to improve its collection as also to weed out the irrelevant, outdated and unnecessary documents from the library. It also means user's needs should be kept in mind while building up collection. The quality of library services depends upon the quality of its collection.

The purpose of the library collection development is to find out the user's information needs to:

- Fulfills the library's obligations to the user community to provide relevant nascent information.
- Find out the users information needs
- Select and acquire documents that are really useful to the users.
- Adopt systematic and judicious spending on document collection keeping the objectives of the services in mind.
- Periodically review the collection for weeding out unwanted and outdated documents from it.

COLLECTION DEVELOPMENT POLICY

The collection development policy is a written statement that is both a planning tool and a communication device. It is meant to clarify objectives and to facilitate coordination and cooperation, both within the library or library system and among cooperative libraries within a region. It is used to introduce present and future board members, staff, community group and others to your library's policy and procedure. It provides for the basis for the systematic development of library's collection. It will provide a community a better understanding of the library and library staff with more interaction with its community. Collection development policy is a tool on the basis of which the library bases its collection. It is the course of action adopted for the developing the collection or stock in a library.

The document selection is important in collection building. It varies from library to library. In academic libraries teachers, library committee, librarian, etc generally do it. The book selection tools include publisher's catalogues, book reviews, bibliographical tools etc.

COLLECTION DEVELOPMENT PRINCIPLES

- Collection should be described so that a user can is cover characteristics of the collection, including scope, format, and restrictions on access ownership, and any information significant for determining the collection's authenticity, integrity and interpretation.
- A collection should be sustainable over time. In particular, digital collection built with special internal or external funding should have a plan for their continued usability beyond the funded period.
- A good collection is broadly available and avoids unnecessary impediments to use. Collection should be accessible to persons with disabilities, and usable effectively in conjunction with adaptive technologies.
- A good collection respects intellectual property rights. Collection managers should maintain a consistent record of right shoulders and permission granted for all applicable materials.
- A good collection mechanism is to supply usage data that allows standardized measures of usefulness to be recorded.

- A good collection fits into the larger contexts of significant related national and international digital library initiatives.
- A well-defined policy based on explicit selection criteria is to be in place before efforts to build a digital collection among the other resource centers.
- Collection description is important from the point of view of resource discovery and understanding the characteristics of information such as scope, format, and restriction on access etc.

Some of the important points to be considered in developing digital collections are:

- Acquisition of digital collections (of various forms and types)
- Conversion of existing print material into digital format.
- Archival of digital collections and storage media.
- Integrated access interface (integration with existing databases)

PRE-REQUISITION OF COLLECTION DEVELOPMENT

The library has to formulate a clear policy of acquisition, periodic evaluation of the collection and the systematic weeding out of document in order to have better collection.

- Identification of the purpose and mission of the library/parent organization.
- Formulation of library's collection development policy by library committees or library staff.
- Matching between user's requirement and institutions aims and objectives.
- Budgetary provisions and the contingent problem.
- Working out the strategies for implementing the

policies and programmes.

- Maintaining, revising and updating policy statement.

Collection development is a continuous process, which involve the users, the library staff and the subject experts on selection team. It is not an end in itself, but a means to develop a need based up-to date and balance collection fit to meet the information /documents needs of the users.

Evaluation of collection

Collection development is a dynamic process which involves both teaching and non teaching staff. Various factors such as information needs of the users, availability of resources, usefulness of resources etc. are to be periodically and earlier collection policy statement should be suitably revised.

Weeding out policy

Weeding out of unwanted material is very important. Each and every year numbers of books and other reading material to be added in the library. Removing of the unwanted or outdated material should be weeded out. Each library should conduct evaluated study of its collection from time to time. Weeding out may be due to some factors such as contents of the documents have become outdated, a particular item has not been used since long, the documents have become mutilated or damaged. For this purpose, a policy statement and action plan need to be made.

METHODS OF BUILDING DIGITAL COLLECTION

The digital collection may be built through either or both the process:

The creation of digital information from conventional is generally a two way format process. The first stage is digitization. This is essentially the conversion of the physical medium into a digital representation of that physical medium. The conversion of textual, visual, and numeric information to electronic form encompasses a range of procedures and technologies with widely varying implications and costs.

1. Digital documents may be created by digital conversion of existing printed or other analog materials.
2. Existing digital documents may be gathered from the web or from digital sources such as CD-ROMs.

The digital conversion process is costly because of labor involved both in processing time and in project management. It is the process, which requires careful planning to ensure that the full information value of the original material preserved.

The new digital resources are either deliberately created as digital or are created in parallel to print. Publishers are increasingly moving to XML or SGML format. Further digital resources are - electronic journals, electronic books through database.

Some of the important points to be considered in developing digital library are:

1. Digital collection.
2. Conversion of existing print into digital format: options for conversion.
3. Creating portals or gateway to the electronic collection available on the web.
4. Integrated access interface.

There are various methods of building digital collection.

Digital resources can be built by adopting the following methods:

1. Acquisition

Acquisition of original digital works created by publishers, institutions and other scholars like electronic books, electronic journals and data set. CD-ROM networking technology is now available for providing web based simultaneous access to CD-ROM databases on the LAN as well as WAN. The libraries have option to subscribe to these full text databases as a part of their digital library. Thousands of CD-ROM databases are currently available from multitude of CD-ROM producers including silver platter, which alone produces more than 250 information products on CD-ROMs.

2. Buying Access

Access to external materials not held in house by providing pointers to web sites, other collections or publisher's service.

Majority of digital collection would be provided by external sources like commercial publishers, collection mounted by scholarly societies, resources at other libraries, electronic journals sites etc. Internet has long been a favorite media for experimenting with electronic publishing and delivery.

3. Content Creation

Institution may have dissertations, in-house journals, annual reports, technical reports etc. that may be included in digital collection. The documents composed on world processing packages or desk top publishing packages can be converted into HTML, as a defecto language of the web and PDF using tools like Acrobat or Acrobat exchange. HTML, as a de fecto language of the web and PDF as a defecto standard for online distribution of electronic information can be employed to facilitate transition from computer possible files to a format accessible on the web.

CONVERTING OF EXISTING PRINT MEDIA INTO DIGITAL FORM (DIGITIZATION)

The existing sources of information may be in print media. These sources can be converted into digital media by scanning the materials. This is most popular method of converting the existing sources of information. The scanned image is stored, as a bit mapped image file cannot be edited. Hence OCR software is to be used to convert these scanned images into editable text formats.

OCR (Optical Character Recognition)

Optical Character Recognition means converting an electronic picture of text(such as letter) into a form of text- such as word processors, DTP, spread sheets and data bases. OCR products look at a picture of a character and convert it into an ASCII or ANSI character that applications programmes can utilized. This conversion process is called "recognition". There are several OCR softwares. OCR also allows converting files into a variety of formats such as PDF, DOC, HTML, RTF, ASCII etc.

CONVERSION OF HARD COPY OF THE DOCUMENT INTO DIGITAL FORMAT

Now days, the existing selected conventional collection of a library is being converted into digital form. This process of conversion of paper documents into digital format is mainly with the help of scanners. Printed texts, pictures and figures are transformed into computer accessible forms using a digital scanner or a digital camera.

4. Access to External Digital Collection

Access to external materials not held in house by providing pointers to web sites, other collections or publishers' services. Digital library can obtain/acquire access permission to digital collections provided by external sources like other institution, commercial publishers, resources of other libraries, and electronic journals through on-line access. Many of the commercial publishers like Elsevier, Academic Press, and ACM are making their journal available on line through websites. Many other commercial publishers are making available print and electronic versions of their journals. Some of the materials are available only in electronic form. In the present time, the web provides the hyper media based systems that allow rapid access to a wide variety of networked information resources. One can browse the different web sites which are scattered geographically and have access to the resources. One can download the information.

Some of he major portal sites or gateways that provide access to electronic resources are:

http://bubl.ac.uk/

http://mel.lirary.mi.us/

It can be concluded that digital libraries can developed their collection through the integration of a number of resources and media types.

So a digital library may have:

1. A collection acquired in a digital form.
2. A collection digitized in house.
3. It can access to gateways to electronic collection available on the web.

Portal site: The portal sites or gateways redirect a user to the holders of the original digital material. It may provide its own indexing and search services or may combine original resources from a number of different providers.

Digital resources for a digital library can be categorized under following categories:

Legacy, transition, born digital, legacy resources are largely non-digital resources including manuscripts, prints, slides, and maps, audio and video recordings. Transition resources are primarily designed for another medium (mostly printed).

Born digital/new digital resources are either deliberately created as digital or are created in parallel to print. Publishers are increasingly moving to XLM or SGML format. This includes electronic journals, electronic books, etc.

INTEGRATED ACCESS INTERFACE

We can also develop digital collection by combining one or more methods discussed above.

Some of the important points to be considered in developing digital library are:

1. Digital collection or material selection
2. Conversion of existing print into digital format
3. Cataloguing or metadata creation
4. Storing
5. Creating portals or gateway to the electronic collection available on the web
6. Integrated access interface

1. DIGITAL COLLECTION

One of the largest issues in creating digital libraries will be the building of digital collection.

Creation of Digital Collection : The creator may be human author or originator, or a piece of equipment such as a sensing device, satellite or laboratory instrument.

Several key practices are being involved in the archiving projects. First, the creator may be involved in assessing the long-term value of the information. Secondly, the preservation and archiving process is made more efficient when attention is paid to issues of consistency, format standardization and metadata description in the very beginning of the information life cycle.

The digital contents may be:

1. **Born digital**: These materials are from the beginning in electronic format as an originating source.
2. **Digitized**: It means materials are converted to a digital

format from an initial analog form.

A digital library can have a wide range of resources. Building digital libraries begins with creating digital content and collections. Creation is the act of producing the information product. It can obtain both conventional documents and/or digital or computer possible form. The conversion of digital form is just to ensure better access and to reduce dependence on physical libraries.

The new digital resources are either deliberately created as digital or created in parallel to print. Publishers are increasingly moving to XML or SGML format. Future digital library resources are electronic journals, electronic books, through databases and data sets in many formats.

The acquisition of documents, which are already available in digital format, like CD-ROM database is a part of transition. Now a days a large number of information products such as databases are available on CD-ROM, like MEDLINE, LISA, etc. Libraries can subscribe to any of this database for providing bibliographic or fultext information forms an important input to the digital collection.

Acquisition of digital collection

CD-ROM networking technology is now available for providing web based simultaneous access to CD-ROM databases on the LAN as well as on WAN. The libraries have option to subscribe to these full text databases as a part of their digital library. Thousands of CD-ROM data bases are currently available from multitude of CD-ROM producers including Silver patters which alone produces more than 250 information products on CD-ROMs.

Quality Control Procedures

The procedure involves taking pictures at high resolution, keeping in view all the factors affecting the colors, texture and attributes of the source document to ensure the closeted image representation of the original. Lighting conditions and equipment used are other important factors.

Quality and size of the digital images can be varied, depending on the need and medium of reproduction. TIFF format is used for high quality to enable printability and IPEG format with varied degree of compression for on screen viewing, with out loss of visible features or texture of the original through human eyes. Even PDF format is beneficial and in some cases desirable.

The second stage is to have the computer extract information from the digitized image. The scanner and digital camera can be used for capturing of text and images. The scanned data can be stored in the form of CD, DVD, tape, hard disc and other such medias. For text, this is scanned by using of Optical Character Recognition (OCR) software, which recognizes the shapes of the letter of the alphabet and produces a file exactly the same as one produced by a word processor used to type in the same text.

Information handling activities goes on changing with the changing technologies. Information management is not only about managing the process of selection, collection, processing, controlling and dissemination of information but also effective use of information and knowledge stored in primary, secondary and tertiary resources both in print as well as in electronic format. Positive and consistent collection development policy is a necessity for any meaning full library development. It may be traditional library or digital library.

By its nature, digital collection development requires extensive use of technological resources. In the early days of digital library development, when collections were typically small and experimental, a wide variety of hardware and software was utilized. Today, the leading digital library developers are putting substantial collections on-line. Some of the collections include millions of digital objects.

The process of collection development and management are undergoing a transformation as well. This is due to the effect of great many and diverse digital resources and tools that can be used in collection development and that are generally and easily available through the Internet.

The following technical points to be taken into consideration in the development and use of digital collection:

1. High bandwidth computer linkage supporting multimedia documents transfer among the resource center.
2. Open communication protocols (client-server) for information retrieval.
3. Information access tools like browser, display and search engine.
4. Metadata describing the data.
5. Electronic publishing tools.
6. Data compression.
7. Digital storage devices.
8. Scanning and conversion technology.
9. Multimedia for integration technology.
10. Advanced information retrieval tools such as indexing.
11. Security.
12. Intellectual Property Rights (IPR).

STORAGE CAPACITY

Storage capacity is required for mix media types that may store in a digital library, such as:

- Text, which is relatively compact.

- Graphics, which can be data intensive.
- Audio, which is highly dynamic.
- Video, which is highly dynamic and data intensive.

Storage capacity should be expandable in economical increments and should not require redesign or re-engineering of the system design as requirements grow.

The main purpose of maintaining digital collection is to preserve the rare material, improving access by making the information available on the web, or both.

Like print collection, the management of digital collection is also essential.

The digital collection management is a new concept. It was started by the libraries like Library of Congress and other academic and research libraries in the late 1980's.Libraries have already been influenced by the developments in electronic publishing. At the lowest level of effect, it is now common place to them to make electronic publications available.

Among the unique needs of libraries is the incorporation of the Dublin Core plus metadata scheme and support for Z39.50.

There were a few open-source alternatives to the expensive commercial products available as early as 2002, among them D-space *www.dspace.org*, a software package developed by MIT and Hewlett-Packard; Greenstone (*www.greenstone.org*).

VENDORS

There are several digital collection management systems designed for the libraries by various vendors such as:

1. Endeavor's ENCompass for digital collections (*www.endinfosys.com*)
2. ExLibris' ContentDM (*www.exlibris-usa.com*)

3. Innovative Metasource (*www.iii.com*)
4. Sirsi Dynix's Hypeion Digital Media Archive and Horizon Digital Library (*www.sirsidynix.com*).

Libraries that launched digital collections on PCs, Web servers, and as special on integrated library systems before purchasing a digital collections management systems, have sometimes moved them to the new system, but just as often have created links from the digital collections management system to wherever the older digital collections were mounted.

All the products developed for the library marked have the ability to import, catalog, edit, store, search, retrieve contents and metadata(bibliographical information about digital documents), and generate statistics. They generally do not include hardware and software for the digitization of source documents. It is assumed that libraries will do that in-house on their own equipment or will contract it out to a firm that specializes in digitization.

IMPORTING DOCUMENTS AND METADATA

The ability to import digital documents is a standard component of all of the products. The documents can be downloaded from a digital storage media, by FTP, or directly from any TWAIN scanning device. The documents can be images (GIF, JPEG, PDF or TIFF), plain-text, HTML, audio, or video. Generally, only a few parameters are required to load documents. It is also possible to load metadata that already exists for the documents being imported.

CATALOGING

The bibliographic information for a document in digital form is generally referred to as metadata. There are several options, including MARC21, for EAD, TEI, and Dublin Core, but the most widely used for text is MARC 21, for archival materials it is EAD, and for images it is Dublin Core. TEI (Text Encoding Initiative) was developed so that scholars could encode their own text, but it has had only limited use.

Several products offer an option of cutting and pasting information from the actual document to facilitate cataloging. Most of the systems do not limit the number of fields of metadata that can be crated. At a minimum, the metadata will include the name of he author, title, and language, the source, date, condition, access restriction, access restrictions, and content description. The metadata can be linked to a single document, also known as an object, or too many.

After the documents have been cataloged, virtual collections can be created. A single document can appear in several virtual collections.

EDITING

Digital contents can be edited, including reducing high resolution JPEG or TIFF documents to lower resolutions or creating thumbnails. Metadata cannot be created, but edited on a digital collections management system.

STORAGE

Storing digital files demand substantial disk storage capacity because digital files other than text files can be extremely large, especially color images and videos. Multiple disk drives are recommended in order to limit I/O (input-output) connection, thus improving response time.

SEARCHING

Searching can be done directly against the digital collection management system or through an interface from library's patron access catalog, portal, or web server. When a portal is used, simultaneous searching can be undertaken not only against the document on the digital collection management system, but also against other electronic sources within the library or on the web.

Because they have been developed for libraries, the system supports Z39.50 in addition to XML and HTTP gateways.

Searching may be limited to specific documents, individual collections, multiple collections, or may encompass all collections.

Searching can be done either against both the full-text of the documents and the associated metadata, or against just the metadata. Non-text a document searching is, of course, limited to searching the metadata. In most cases, searching can be natural language, Boolean, proximity, wildcard, truncation, date and date range, and pattern. Pattern searching makes it possible to find words with incorrect or missing characters either in the search term or the body of the text.

Most of the system return merged result sets. Some also return relevancy-ranked results.

All the systems include an image viewer for JPEG and TIFF files, enabling image manipulation and printing. There is also the option of including thumbnails for faster retrieval and display, with the option of clicking to the higher resolution image. A user may be limited to viewing only the thumbnail when there are restrictions on access is subject to the payment of a fee.

Security generally includes patron authentication to control access to the documents based on the profiles of the document and the users. For example, some documents may be subject to copyright, access restrictions required by donors or the desire of a library to charge for printing or downloading. Some categories of users may not qualify for access because they are not registered borrowers, are not adults, or are delinquent borrowers.

STATISTICS

All of the systems include a number of reports that summarize loading, cataloguing, editing, and searching activity.

COSTS

The cost of digital content management system is related both to the number of documents and number of concurrent users supported. An entry level systems supporting fever than 10,000 documents and ten concern users will cost minimum of $ 25,000, including $ 7, 000 or so for software licenses, $ 14000 for hardware, and $ 4,000 for training and other services. Annual hardware/software maintenance cost are a minimum of $ 3, 000 per year after the final year.

Libraries that require a small system may wish to consider a hosted service. Most of the mentioned in the list will mount the documents on a hosted server at the vendor's site for an annual subscription fee.

As the size of the system increases, it becomes more cost effective to purchase the system.

SOURCES OF INFORMATION

Currency is extremely important when seeking information about digital collection management. The web sites of the vendors cited in this TechNote are highly current sources of information. Also highly current is D-Lib Magazine (*www.dlib.org).It* characterized itself as the "magazine of Digital Library Research". The Digital Library Federation (*www.diglib.org*), a consortium of "libraries and related agencies that are pioneering in the use of electronic information technologies to extend collection and services" also has highly current information on its Web site.

Three good examples of digital collection maintained by public libraries are those of the Chicago Public Library (*www.chipublic.org/digital/digital.html*), the New York Public Library (*http://www.nypl.org/digital*).

Other useful sources of information are *http://www.ifla.org/II/metadata.htm.* for metadata, *http://www.libraries.mit.edu/guides/subjects/metadata/standards/tei.html* for TEI, *http://www..loc.gov/ead/ag/agappc.html* for EAD, and *http://www.dublincore.org* for Dublin Core.

COLLECTION DEVELOPMENT AND RESOURCE SHARING

Because of the changing information needs of the users, interdisciplinary nature of research, increasing prices of the reading material, limited budget, documents available in various languages and formats force the libraries to adopt certain measures. It also made the collection development a difficult task. Resource sharing is the best method for optimum utilization of resources and also to solve the problem of scarcity of budget.

Resource sharing includes:

- To develop the relationship with other libraries of the region to share the resources.
- By becoming the member of national and regional networks to share spare resources
- Contribute information to share with professionals and
- To retrieve and disseminate information from internet/ World Wide Web for members but the authenticity of the information should be checked. There is need to retrieve information from reliable sources.

CHALLENGES AT COLLECTION AND DEVELOPMENT PROCESS

Digital library face some challenges at collection and development process which are as follows:

1. Technical architecture.

2. Copyright management.
3. Preservation.

1. Technical architecture: Libraries will need to enhance and upgrade current technical architecture to accommodate digital materials. The architecture will include components such as:

1. High speed local networks and fast connection to internet.
2. Relational databases that support a variety of digital formats.
3. Full text search engines to index and provide access to resources.
4. A variety of services, such as web servers and FTP servers.
5. Electronic document management functions that will aid in the overall management of digital resources.

The resources supported by the architecture could include:

1. Bibliographic databases that point to both paper and digital materials.
2. Indexing and finding tools.
3. Collection of pointers to Internet resources.
4. Directories.
5. Primary material in various digital formats.
6. Photographs.
7. Numerical data sets.
8. Electronic journals.
9. Though these resources may reside on different systems and in different databases, they would appear as though there were one single system to the users of a particular community. The problem however , is that across multiple digital libraries, there is a wide

diversity of different data structure, search engines, interfaces, controlled vocabularies, document formats, and so on. Because of this diversity, federating all digital libraries nationally or internationally would an impossible effort.

PRESERVATION

In the preservation of digital materials, the real issue is technical obsolescence. Technical obsolescence in the digital age is like the deterioration of paper in the paper age. Libraries in the pre-digital era had to worry about climate control and the de-acidification of books, but the preservation of digital information will mean constantly coming up with new technical solutions.

There are three types of preservations :

1. The preservation of storage medium.
2. The preservation of access to content
3. The preservation of fixed-media materials through digital technology.

PRESERVATION OF THE STORAGE MEDIA

Storage media such as tapes, hard discs, and floppy discs have a very short life span when considered in terms of obsolescence. The data on them can be refreshed; keeping the bits valid, but refreshing is only effective as long as the media are still current. The media used to store digital materials become obsolete in anywhere from two to five years before they are replaced by better technology. Over the long term, material stored on older media could be lost because there will no longer have the hardware or software to read them. Thus, libraries will have to keep moving digital information from one storage medium to other storage medium.

PRESERVATION OF ACCES TO CONTENT

This form of preservation involves preserving access to the content of documents, regardless of their format. While files can be moved from on physical storage medium to another, what happens when the formats (eg. PDF,Abode Acrobat) containing the information become obsolete? This is a problem perhaps bigger than that of obsolete storage technologies. One solution is to do data migration that is, translate data from one format to an other preserving the ability of users to retrieve and display the information content. However, there are difficulties here too -data migration is costly, there are as yet no standards for data migrating and distortion or information loss is inevitably introduced every time data is migrated format to format.

PRESERVATION OF FIXED MEDIA MATERIALS THROUGH DIGITAL TECHNOLOGY

This involves the use of digital technology as a replacement for current preservation media, such as microforms. Again there are as yet, no common standards for the use of digital media as a preservation medium and it is unclear whether digital media are as yet up to the task of long term preservation. Digital preservation standards will be required to consistently store and share material is preserved digitally.

STEPS INVOLVED IN COLLECTION DEVELOPMENT

Collection Development includes : User analysis; selection policies; acquisition policies; resource sharing; weeding and collection evaluation.

Collection Development Process

Collection development process differs from library to library. The kind of the library, the size, the number of users, their requirement, existing holding on particular subject areas, and the amount allocated for acquisition and such other factors are to be considered. Collection development process is a complex process.

Collection development should be based on the needs and requirements of present users as well as anticipated requirements of the future users. The library collection should be adequate, balanced, relevant and up-to-date. The process of collection development includes selection of current as well as retrospective materials, weeding out of absolute, irrelevant, unused and not to be used materials. Evaluation of existing holding should be made for identification of adequacy and gaps. Collection development is a continuous activity. It involves the users, the library staff and the subject experts. It is a need based, up to date and balanced collection fit to meet the document and information needs of the users. It involves a numbers of activities by which a library acquires material of all types by implementing the selection policy.

Steps Involved in the Digital Collection Development

1. The resource center should create bibliographic database of print and non print materials and such database to be made available via LAN and WAN.
2. Acquisition of need based digital resources in the form of CD-ROM, optical disk etc.
3. High bandwidth Internet connectivity.
4. Subscription to various related areas subjects e-journals.
5. Facility to access commercial database via online in the related areas and
6. Creation of local digital contents available within the resource center.

A major responsibility of a library is to build a collection of documents and other reading material such as non-print reading materials, in order to meet the information needs of the users. In order to provide effective services the reading material should be carefully selected. The reading material may be printed or digital form.

Creation of digital libraries is advocated not only to preserve and conserve materials, but also to increase their customer's base by making older and rarer or heavily used documents available to a much wider audience.

The development of digital library mainly includes methods such as:

1. Direct purchase of electronic version of the documents and
2. Downloading from the web.

Purchase cost of the electronic version is much lower than their printed version. Online access is priced 15% below than the printed version.

In building digital library, the first step is to establish the infrastructure of computing and networking .A Local Area Network (LAN) should be established to connect the various networked information resources. For remote access services beyond the capability of the LAN, the library will need to connect with the Internet. For physical storage of digital formatted materials, the computer server must be equipped with hard disks of several gigabyte capacities. It is also be pointed out that the size of the network server will depend upon the number of users that the electronic library will be serving. The computer will also need specialized software that can efficiently regulate the accessibility of networked information and should be able to provide a user interface through which users can interact with the networked information.

Building digital libraries consists of following steps:

- Creation
- Acquisition.

- Cataloguing/identification
- Preservation and
- Access.

Creation

Building digital library began with creating digital content and collations. Creation is the act of producing the information product. The crater may be an author originator, or a piece of equipment such as a sensing device, satellite or laboratory instrument.

Digital contents may be

1. **Born digital** : These materials are form the beginning in electronic format as an organizing source.
2. **Digitized** : It means materials are converted to digital format from an initial analog form.

Digitization

Digitization is the process of creating digital files by scanning or converting analog materials. The technology used for digitization of analog object is called scanning and the equipments is called scanner. Scanner is imaging technology or the OCR technology for digitizing.

Imaging process creates photo image of the proper document and the later on may be converted to PDF format or can be saved as Jpeg or bit map image as per policy of standard adopted for digitization. The image can be read only and can not be edited.

The OCR technology allows converting the scanned image to the electronic format able to format either in the form of plan text or word processor document format, ready for editing.

Content Selection And Acquisition

A fully developed digital library environment involves the following elements:

1. Digital documents (both digital or by conversion of contents of digital form;
2. The extraction or creation of metadata or indexing information describing the contents to facilitate searching as well as administrative and structural metadata to assist in object viewing, management and preservation;
3. Storage of digital content and metadata in an appropriate multimedia repository. This will meet the requirement of Intellectual Property Rights.

Client services for the browser, including repository querying and workflow.

Content delivery via file transfer or streaming media.

User access through a browser or dedicated client; and a private or public computer network.

DIGITAL COLLECTION BUILDING TOOLS

The following tools are required for building the digital collection:

1. Tools for viewing directory structure.
2. Tools for converting formats.
3. Checking screen layout consistencies.
4. Quickly viewing the objects.
5. Encrypting the data.
6. Interface simulation.
7. Database tools for property rights..
8. File naming histories.
9. Links.
10. Metadata definition.
11. Maintenance tools for automatically checking links.
12. Automatic transaction logs analysis.
13. Maintaining security.

The concept of what constitutes a collection in the networked environment of digital libraries is undergoing a transformation from the age-old concept of library collection signified by ownership. A new concept of a digital collection is developing incorporation adaptations of many old features and standards, and creation of many brand new ones.

22

Sharing of Resources in Digital Environment

INTRODUCTION

The resources have been shared since the beginning of the writing on documents that were portable. Much of this sharing has been informal. The concept of resource sharing in libraries is as old as the librarianship itself. This has been used in different forms in different context. Library cooperation, inter library loan, consortia, library networks, etc. are the terms used in resource sharing. During the older days it was called library cooperation and it mainly existed in the form of Inter-Library-Loan. After the 1960's the term resource sharing has been widely used and practiced. Resource sharing in the context of library and information centers includes all types and forms of resources and services, personnel, equipment, facilities, etc.

The rapid growth of publications, decreasing ability of libraries to go for comprehensive acquisition of document, escalation of prices, regular increasing of foreign currency value with reference to Indian currency, growing demands of increasing number of users and multifaceted user requirements are a few challenges presently facing the library and information professionals. To overcome these problems, sharing of resources through networks assumes greater importance these days. The library management has no other way out but to seek the cooperation of other libraries to meet the requirements of the clientele.

The use of information technology has added new dimensions to the concept of resource sharing and networking in the libraries. During the past two decades, things have drastically changed due to more and more libraries, automated their catalogues, acquiring resources in electronic form, and getting connected to one or the other network. This has resulted in easy accessing of resources from the remote nodes adding a new dimension to the nature of library services.

With the development of application of information technology tools, the sharing has become much easier. It is converting the dream of nationwide resource sharing into a reality. To keep pace with all these problems, we need to get together to formulate policies for sharing resources and build up network among related libraries for rendering effectives and efficient services to the library users, save money and time.

Digital libraries are revolutionizing the information dissemination with respect to access, speed and availability. The information technology is dynamic in nature. The success of libraries depends on the strength of their ability to connect electronically with one another to share their resources.

The basic concept behind the digital library is the sharing of resources globally.

WHAT IS RESOURCE SHARING?

Definitions

The term "resource" applies to anything, person, or

action to which one turns for aid in time of need. The term "sharing" connotes apportioning, allotting, or contributing something that is own to benefit others. Resource sharing in its most positive aspect entails reciprocity, implying in which each is willing and is able to make available the materials when needed (Encyclopedia of Library Science, 1983).

"Resource sharing implies transaction by which a library makes its materials or copies of its materials available to the clientele of an other library upon request".

According to the Allen Kent "Resource sharing is made of operations whereby functions are shared in common by a number of libraries.

Resource sharing is a way of library cooperation. Cooperation means, working together with some effort to achieve the objectives i.e. common work for common goal.

"Resource Sharing is a sort of implied agreement amongst participating libraries where in each participant is willing to share its resources with other members and in turn is privileged to share the resources of its partners".

The various facets of co-operation are:

i. Grouping of individual having common interest.

ii. Action by a group of pursuing certain aims and targets.

iii. Setting up of permanent organization as an operational unit.

Thus, we can say that resource sharing is nothing but sharing of resources such as books, periodicals and other materials among the participating libraries on the bases of cooperation.

Also, due to limited funds and limited staff, it is impossible for any library to acquire this unlimited and endless knowledge. The alternatives is resource sharing.

The term "Library Corporation" allows one to achieve the objectives better by working together, where as the resource sharing assumes a range of physical, intellectual, and conceptual resources on the one hand and a body of people with library and information needs on the other hand covering the activities involved in organizing the one into a set of optimum relationships to meet the needs of the other.

Resource sharing is basically sharing of resources of participating libraries on the basis of agreement of cooperation for the purpose of sharing the resources of each other's materials. This entails not only to share the document resources but also facilities, services, equipments and even the manpower among the participating libraries.

COMPONENTS OF RESOURCE SHARING

Resource sharing is a system for making requests and providing delivery of information, chiefly through the Inter Library Loan (ILL) process. ILL handles both returnable (items that must be returned to the lender) and nonreturnable (photocopies or digital transmissions). ILL may be strengthened by agreements among members of a consortium to provide services to members and permit on site use of collections by clientele of member libraries (Fig. 18).

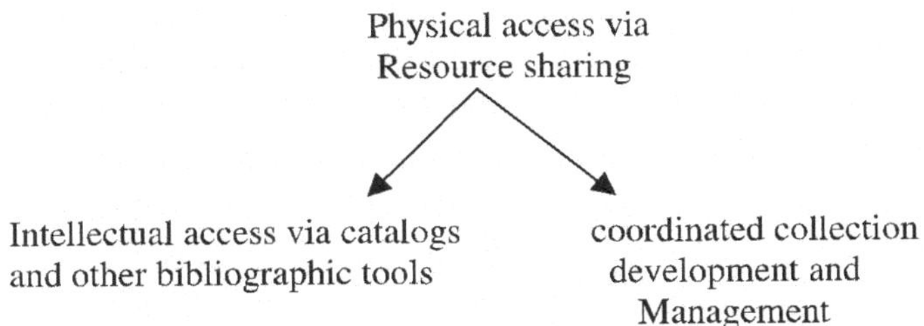

Fig. 18. Three components of successful cooperation

The second component in cooperative collection development is bibliographic access or knowing what is available from other sites through printed or microform catalogs, a shared or union catalog, or a regional, national, or international bibliographic utility. The third component, coordinated collection development and management, is, in its ideal manifestation, a coordinated scheme of purchasing and maintaining collections.

Cooperative collection development's aim is the building of complementary collections on which the cooperating libraries can draw. In recent years, cooperative collection development has expanded to include consortia agreements to purchase group access to electronic resources at discounted price.

Why we need resource sharing?

The cost of reading material like books, journal and other allied material is increasing day-by-day but with the shrinking library budget, libraries are facing difficulties to acquire requisite collections in the field of their interest. This is one side. Another side is information explosion due to research work carried out in various research institutes and universities. The emphasis is now shifting from hard copy of document to soft copy to provide information immediately. It is impossible for any library to acquire this unlimited and endless knowledge. The only alternate is recourse sharing and networking. Today libraries have been acquiring digital media such as CD-ROMs, DVDs and multimedia packages. In the coming years the quality of digital material is likely to increase substantially. It is not possible to one library to acquire all the databases in digital format. It is very expensive also. Now days sharing and exchange of electronic information is badly needed. Resource sharing can be enhanced through the appropriate use of new information technology.

Now it has become enormously difficult for libraries to procure the required reading materials and extend their services especially when one considers the phenomenal increase in the price of the publications and paucity of funds. The answer to the above problem is to go for resource sharing. The resource sharing can be achieved by inter library cooperation by following certain norms. This type of effort could be achieved through library networks also.

In the electronic information age resource sharing is easier. A little investment in computerization and co-operation for sharing and exchange, a library can fulfill the majority of information needs of users. Use of computer and communication technology plays a vital role in the sharing and exchange of resources. Sharing can takes place in acquisition, technical processing of materials, inter library loan, etc.

Sharing and exchange of electronic information is one of the very important activities of the modern library because of:

- Increase is the reading community and information seekers.
- Demand of pinpointed, exhaustive and expeditious information services.
- Increased access to information and services at existing cost.
- Proliferations of literature in each and every field of knowledge. Growth of publications in every discipline.
- Multiplicity of documents in different subjects, languages and formats.
- Developments of new subjects and specializations.
- Decline for library budget every year and rapid increase in the prices of books and journals year after year.

At present these are more than 235 university level institutions in India. In these, there is every likelihood of more than 50% of the library collection being duplicated, which involves a huge dumping of money unnecessarily. On an average, each university library is spending around Rs. 40

lakh on books and periodicals and cumulatively it works out to be around Rs 94 crore. Even after spending such a huge amount, the libraries individually are not able to meet even the minimum information requirements of their users. It is not possible for a standalone library to meet all the information needs of its end users. Resource sharing via networking is only alternative. There is trend towards library and information networks. LANs, WANs, MANs, Intranets, and Extranets are manifestation of this trend. The internet is a major development of our time. It is a vast store house of knowledge. Moreover, it has dramatically changed the whole process of scholarly communication. Conceptual access to tacit knowledge has been improved significantly. The traditional pattern of authorship is also changing. Moreover many people contribute to discussions via virtual conferences, seminars, discussion list, newsgroups, and bulletin boards. As such the traditional competencies are falling short to manage access to the web based digital resources.

So we are to:

- Meet their information needs effectively.
- Avoid duplication of costly resources.
- Reduce the expenditure considerably.
- Enable users easier and wider access to the rich collection of documents and information; they must resorts to resource sharing by forming a network.

Needs for resource sharing in electronic environment:

In the electronic information age resource sharing is much easier. There is no need for a library to purchase all the journals published. A little investment in computerization and cooperation for sharing and exchanges, a participating library can fulfill a majority of demands of its users.

Use of computer and communication technology plays a vital role in sharing and exchange of resources.

Although today's scholars learned their craft in the world of print publications, print indexes, and card catalogs, most are taking full advantages of new information technologies that have emerged in course of their career. They are retrieving, reading, and writing electronic publications and sharing their research results via distributed networking information system. In the future, researcher will have yet more facilities to share data, more means to utilize tools from distributed sources to analyze those data and more opportunities to collaborate across national and disciplinary boundaries

The impact of information technology revolution has made a tremendous change in the routine of libraries. Apart from the print collections of electronic and digital documents which are very useful to researchers and academic faculties. Due to the financial scrounges the libraries of homogeneous in character, run by the same organizations will gather together and organize the digital resource sharing and inter library loan among the member libraries.

Electronic resources mean the publication and dissemination of information by electronic means, especially by the use of optical disc formats (CD-ROM in particular) and networking. Other options can include the use of electronic databases, videotext, e-mail and electronic newsletters.

Electronic journals or E-journals are a major component of electronic recourse. Electronic journal means a journal for which the full end product is available on optical disc, over a network or in any other electronic form. Strictly, a journal in which all aspects of preparation, referring, assembling and distribution are carried out electronically.

The continuous request from the users forced the libraries to borrow the digital resources by resource sharing and inter library loan. The Internet, World Wide Web, E-mail, Electronic Data Interchange (EDI) and the Online Data Access

(ODA) are very much useful for these processes and the digital resources are transmitted by the File Transfer Protocol (FTP) and Z39.50 interfaces from other libraries involved in the cooperative basis of action.

Due to resource crunch in the libraries the library management has no other way out, but to seek cooperation with other libraries to meet the information requirement of its users.

From the above we can say that resource sharing is a method of overcoming the limitations of the individual libraries in respect of their resources by way of cooperation and co-ordination among participating libraries.

Objectives of Resource Sharing

The objectives of resource sharing are more or less the same weather it is traditional library or digital library.

The main objectives of resource sharing are to :

1. Facilitates sharing of resources timely and efficiently
2. Facilitates the maximum utilization of resource to enhance the readers ability to meet the information requirements.
3. Facilitates the users, the range of services available from the participating libraries.
4. Provide communication among the libraries.
5. Avoids duplication in resources.
6. Making overall improvement in the library services.
7. Extending the resources and services to the vast categories of users.
8. Availability of materials and services is possible at the minimum expenses.

Areas of Resource Sharing

There are number of areas that could be considered for sharing of resources. Some of the prominent are:

1. Union Catalogue : A union catalogue has been defined as "a catalogue listing in one sequence, the holding or part of the holdings of two or more libraries" (Knud, Larsen). However, another definition given by William Katz as, 'an inventory common to several libraries and listing some or all of their publications maintained in one or more orders of arrangement. The prime objective of union catalogue is to inform the users of a library who has what, which library has material. Compilation of union catalogues of periodicals. Case collections, reference materials, microforms, audio-visual materials, dissertations, thesis and other such materials held by the participating libraries. This makes resource sharing easy.

The term Union Catalogue is different from Library Catalogue and is associated with the national catalogue. The importance of a union catalogue lies in promoting inter-library cooperation on local, regional, and international levels. The preparation of a union catalogue is the first step in resource sharing when two or more libraries agree to cooperate. They generally begin with the preparation of union catalogue of their holdings.

Union catalogues are the backbone of an effective resource sharing programme. There are certain priorities regarding the type of materials based on which the union catalogues is to be prepared. These union catalogues help the participating libraries to have access to the collection available from other libraries and to have resource sharing depending on the requirement. The development of union catalogue is a tedious job requiring lot of support from the participating libraries.

A few examples of union catalogues are: The US Library of Congress the National Union Catalogue ; the British Union Catalogue of periodicals; the National Union Catalogue of Scientific Serials in India (NUCSSI-INSDOC), the union catalogue Social Scientific Serials in India (NASSDOC), the union catalogue of Books, Serials, thesis, Experts, Projects by INFLIBNET.

2. Collection Development

The political and economic circumstances in which the libraries operate have drastically changed in the last two decades. The explosion in the number and variety of publications, and the increase in the cost of books and serials in particular, compel the libraries to share their resources to improve coverage of the universe of titles. The variety and range of resources demanded by the scholars is growing at a rate beyond capacity and are adding to the library's economic problems.

The libraries' prime task is to guarantee the availability of relevant and representative collections in various fields. The collection development at the higher level is essential for developing core collection that serves the immediate needs of their users. In this situation it is necessary that libraries co-operate in developing their collections.

The starting point for coordinated collection development is collection intensification. It aims at improving the quality of library service by broadening and deepening the range of research materials collectively made available to users.

Librarians are skeptical about the realization of the general aim of coordinated collection development: broadening and deepening the range of titles by reducing overlap because in the last ten years librarians have tried their best to reduce the overlap as far as possible. Many serials even unique and core titles have been cancelled and at many libraries the general policy is to cancel a few titles every year. In this situation, cooperative collection development can better be described as, shared poverty. In spite of this skepticism, librarians are positive about the benefits of making library profiles. The collection of profiles win is very useful for negotiations with faculty, publishers, in contacts with partners of a consortium, to inform others, etc. These collection profiles can be used as a collection management instrument to develop collections more efficiently and effectively.

The objective of collection development is to help the libraries to identify and select the publications which are worthwhile for acquisition. This can be based on the data available at various levels such as circulation, inter-library loan statistics, SDI user profiles etc. After examining the strength and weaknesses in document collections in libraries as well as duplication, a cooperative acquisition system will gradually evolve.

3. Consortia Approach

Introduction

The aim of the consortia is to achieve what members of group cannot achieve individually. Consortium means "group of libraries come together with common interest to form a consortium". One of the libraries or agencies will work as the coordinator on behalf of all libraries to negotiate with publishers, take care of legal issues, etc. The consortium facilitates the libraries to wider access of electronic resources at affordable cost. A consortium develops with the collective strength of resources of various institutions available openly access for all member institutions.

Definitions: Consortium is a Latin word, meaning partnership, association or society' and derives from censors 'partner', itself from con- 'together' and sors 'fate', meaning owner of means or comrade. We define a consortium in simple words as 'consortium is resource sharing organization formed by libraries.

According to US Federal Communications Commission "A library consortium is any local , regional, or national cooperative association of libraries that provides for the systematic and effective coordination of the resources of schools, public, academic, and special libraries and information centers, for improving services to the clientele of such libraries."

It is equally true, as well as applicable, for all types of libraries/information centers not to hold the full stock of information resources or to procure all information, which may be demand by the users. Even not a single library / information center can meet the thrust of knowledge of all the users from its stock of information up to fullest extent. To solve this problem library cooperation started long ago, such as library networks, ILL, document delivery, library consortia etc.

Objectives of Consortia

The main objectives of consortia are:

- Increasing the cost benefit per subscription
- Promote the rational use of funds.
- Ensure continuous subscription to the periodicals subscribed.
- Guarantee local storage of the information acquired for continuous use by present and future users
- Develop technical capabilities of the staff in operating and using electronic publication databases
- Strategic alliance with institutions that have a common interest, resulting in reduced information cost
- Improved resource sharing.

Technological developments, electronic publishing of scholarly journals, the emergence of consortia and the pricing models of the publishers give new opportunities for libraries to provide instant access to information. Through consortia, every member of the consortium gets electronic access not only to the journals currently subscribed to but also to all the journals published by the publisher in most of the cases. Many libraries currently subscribe only to those journals that they can afford. Though interested in other journals they cannot afford to provide access to them. This approach helps them to provide access to journals they cannot afford. Such a consortium agreement will give the library and also the user extended access that is better service - and reduce the costs.

Cooperative Purchase

Cooperative purchasing of e-resources is one of the key activities of a library consortium. The concept of consortium itself has evolved from the idea of cooperation, coordination and collaboration. Collaborative arrangement for acquisition and management of electronic information resources can result in lower prices and shelving in terms of actual cost, time and staff. Moreover, access to resources is now considered more important than collection building itself especially if the access is perpetual in nature.

Major issues of the consortia approach:

- Selecting a coordinating agency to deal on behalf of the entire group of participants and executing and monitoring the work.
- Identification of libraries interested in participating and agreeing to common terms and conditions.
- Identification of potential publishers to provide access under consortia purchase.
- Negotiating with publishers to get a commonly acceptable and affordable price.
- Source of funding to meet the subscription cost.
- Legal issues involved in contracts and usage of material within-the consortia.
- Informing of the usefulness/ importance of the consortia to the heads of the institutions, faculty, etc.,

to act upon the issue.

- Identifying the necessary infrastructure for electronic access to resources.
- Issues relating to backup of databases
- Identification and selection of databases to be acquired and hosted at one place (i.e. coordinating agency).
- Documentation and training to staff.
- Access rights whether to provide direct access from publisher site or mount databases at coordinating agency.

In forming a consortium of libraries a way of life to maximize the resource base to meet the genuine needs of users; the participating libraries need to take an active part.

Major publishers are willing to come forward in the fast changing society, coming together and serving better.

ROLE OF CONSORTIA IN DIGITAL ENVIRONMENT

The consortium facilitates the libraries to wider access of electronic resources at affordable cost. The web based electronic resources fulfill the expectations of users. The information needs of the users have changed with the changing environment. They need right information at right time in a minimum time.

The role of the concept has significantly increased in digital environment. For many years, libraries have been working together in myriad reasons- for example, document delivery, printed books and journal acquisition, and shared storage. However, development in technology have opened up a whole range of other collaborative activities and enabled libraries to band together to acquire enhance bargaining power with supplier , provide shared services and develop new services which are only possible in a wired world.

ADVANTAGES OF CONSORTIA

It helps the professionals to give the effective services to the specified users on time with right information to enrich the knowledge to the maximum extent.

Some of the advantages are:

- Reduce the manpower by avoiding duplication of work.
- Reduce maintenance cost on storage.
- Introduce the new innovative library services.
- Discharge the effective services on time.
- Increase the quality standards of library services.
- Enhance the online search facilities.
- Improve electronic document delivery services.
- Save money on the allocation of budget by perfect planning.
- Multifunctional services will be rendered by the technical staff.
- It boosts the standards of library services.
- Sharing of information with improved resource sharing.
- Wider range of electronic journals available.
- OPAC services.
- Knowledge sharing leads to create new knowledge in the process of exchanging technical information among scientific community.
- Avoid duplication in the field of research.
- Reduce the expenditure in the field of research.
- High discount due to collective subscription.
- Increase the efficiency in the profession.
- Staff development and interaction enhance the quality of service.
- Promotes the rational use of funds.

- Ensure continuous and long term subscription to the subscribed information resources.
- Help in developing local expertise in operation and handling of electronic resources.
- Improve resource sharing amongst member institution.
- Better terms of agreement for use, archival access and preservation of subscribed electronic resources.
- Effective document delivery services will be provided to its users.
- Scope for enhanced facilities by introducing new services.
- Scope to develop the best relationship with develops standards in the present information age.
- Consortia based services helps library networks.
- Provides each institution with the ability to share resources without sacrificing their individuality.
- Collections of the consortium libraries enable each member library support scholarly research for its users.

TYPES OF CONSORTIA

There are many types of consortia worldwide such as;

1. National consortia for example JISC collection in UK.
2. Regional consortia such as Viva in US and
3. Subject based consortia such as medical, engineering, law libraries etc

By clubbing together, groups of libraries can do one single negotiation for all members and make significant cost savings. There is also the added advantage of being in a stronger position to negotiate favorable and standard license terms. Many consortia worldwide also belong to International Coalition of Library Consortia (ICOCLC) which has over 200 consortia members listed on its website.

NATIONAL AND INTERNATIONAL CONSORTIA

Some of the national and international level consortia are given below:

International

Ohio LINK: *http://www.ohiolink.edu.*

Cooperative Storage Control

Several big libraries would like some of their less used materials to be weeded out, and kept at a place where from it can be recalled when needed. Also, in these libraries the rarely used materials of all libraries are stocked in an economical way by making use of compact storage methods of various kinds such as rolling stocks, etc.

Cooperation in Inter-Library Loans (ILL)

Inter-library loans are an age old concept that our libraries have been practicing. In this era of networking and use of Internet, this process has become easier, more reliable and time saving. Most of the ILL transactions take place at very informal level, i.e., understanding between individuals rather than institutions. An ILL policy and an ILL code are essential to achieve optimum results.

Some important factors are:

- Flexibility and choice to meet varied user needs;
- Clearly defined and unambiguous service standards, for example, for turnaround time and delivery method;
- A specified turnaround time for a core level of service;
- Greater predictability and consistency; and
- Increased incentives for libraries to improve their ILL supplying operations

The current manual ILL system is laborious, time-consuming, error-prone and inefficient. Much time is spent on searching, documentation and updating of data.

Duplication of effort is required to complete the ILL loan form since the requester completes a separate form when requesting an ILL. Time is spent in contacting requesters when urgent requests are not fulfilled, filing ILL forms, carrying out manual periodic changes of overdue items and collecting ILL statistics.

The manual system is manageable if the requests are few but leads to a proportionate increase in administrative problems and overloads when ILL demand increases. Such reasons coupled with the rapid advancement of Internet technology, the availability of on-line library systems and OPAC have provided the impetus to provide a new computerized ILL system to manage the complete ILL process.

Impact of electronic technology on traditional inter-library services

Several articles have been written about Electronic Document Delivery Services and their effect on traditional delivery of material by ILL. Crawford and White (1997) address many of the issues associated with electronic information resources and the implications for libraries and librarians. The authors undertook a study to research the effects that the addition of a full text database had on traditional methods of information delivery. Including the financial implications, and have included an analysis of the results, Cornish (1997) looked at the changing role of the library brought about by the widespread use of electronic technology. These issues raised are, what is available? Who should request? and who should supply? and, possibly even more controversial who should pay? The author concludes that individual researchers will eventually realize that they are faced with an information overload and will prefer to rely once again on the expertise of the skilled librarian. Traditional inter-library activity will continue but with the use of modern technology.

However there are certain disadvantages listed below:

First, there is the need for each participating library to use the same system or software in order to carry out the ILL process.

Second the difference in library policies among participating libraries makes it difficult to develop a generic system that would be acceptable to all.

Third as the number of ILL requests traditionally low compared to normal borrowing, few resources have been allocated to administer or computerize the ILL service.

Finally, different systems, even if they exist, suffer from interoperability problems owing to the absence of standards.

Thus, two different ILL systems will not be able to exchange information or data. This problem will only be solved over time when ILL systems become more commonplace.

Document Delivery Service

Despite rising costs, shrinking budget and the information explosion, the role of libraries remains to provide access to recorded information required by their users. To continue to provide users with access to as wide an array of information as possible, libraries have had to shift away from the acquisition of materials for local collections to cooperating with other libraries to provide access to them.

The general components involved in the process of document delivery are:

Requestors	Who request to the document, the end users of the library.
Document Types	Wide variety of document types acquired stored and supplied by the library for use.
Document sources	The library, National and International document supply centers, commercial document supply services, publishers, etc.
Document selection	Finding out the bibliographic references, online searching, searching through CD-ROM's, locally mounted databases network accessible catalogues, etc.
Request management	Verification of user request, compliance with copyright restrictions, and location of a potential document sources(s) followed by request submission, request tracking, as well as a number of other possible transactions
Document retrieval	Physical retrieval of document by library staff, numerous clerical activities, viz. photocopying, packing, posting or shipping, etc. Retrieval of documents from electronic databases is a new concept.
Document transfer	Final delivery of document, forwarding the document to the requestor by fax, post or other modes.

Development in the storage and communication technology has made the process of document delivery more efficient through electronic document delivery.

Pre-Requisites for Resource Sharing

1. Infrastructure : The essential infrastructure for resource sharing includes installation of hardware and software to create the bibliographical, content pages, abstracts and full text databases and networking. The infrastructure will help to build union catalogues and software to handle the user queries, etc. A library desiring to be a part of a resource sharing network should have computers, printers, scanners, databases, and networking software's with specified standards, network connectivity, photocopying machines, fax, scanner, document delivery software, etc

2. Staff Training : Skilled manpower is one of the pre-requisites for the success of any programme. The library, being a man-intensive and service oriented organization, needs a trained and motivated workforce essential for the success of cooperative programmes like resource sharing and networking. The organization of resource sharing cannot be possible without competent, trained and dedicated manpower. Library professionals must get ready with adequate skills and the right attitude. A library resource-sharing programme needs to design and conduct various programmes for the development of staff of the participating libraries. Proper education and training of the user in IT tools and techniques, exchange of library professionals among the libraries, participation in various professional meetings, seminars, workshops, conferences, etc., are some ways to develop the manpower in libraries.

3. Retrospective Conversions : The retrospective conversion of library collections is one of the pre-requisite for resource sharing. Though, it is time consuming and expensive, it is necessary to convert the data in standard bibliographic format. A variety of sources and methods are available for retrospective conversion of library materials.

"Retrospective conversion is the conversion of existing bibliographic records in library is from manual to machine readable format according to specified policies and standards" The primary objective of retrospective conversion is to increase access as widely as possible to the collections already catalogued in the library. The process of retrospective conversion of library catalogue is a pre-requisite for creating a union list or a union catalogue of bibliographic data at local, regional, national and international levels. The converted data may further be useful for sharing bibliographic resources facilitate collection rationalization allowing cooperative acquisition of library materials. Retrospective conversion of the bibliographic data should be created using the set standards which helps sharing of records between libraries.

4. Document Delivery and Inter-library Loan : The success of resource sharing is mainly dependent on the delivery of the right material to the right reader at the right time. Effective document delivery on demand to the end user is one of the pre requisites of resource sharing. Another pre-requisite of sharing of resources from one library to another is through the way of inter-library loan. Information dissemination services by themselves are of no value unless they are backed up by actual provision of copy of such documents. The user is invariably interested in going through the original source document of his interest. The document delivery service is one of the pre-requisite for the success of any resource sharing programme.

The inter-library loan service enables a library to request another library through the network of one or more books on an inter-library loan basis for meeting demands of its users. This may include the facility for reserving a book, if it is-on loan in the lending library. An efficient and effective mechanism for physical delivery / electronic delivery of materials needs to be developed. This success of this service depends on the cooperative spirit of participating libraries. An Inter-library loan code needs to be generated and adopted by all libraries.

5. Internet and the Role of Librarian : The Internet and the facilities of World Wide Web (WWW) provide easy means for information communication not available earlier. One can access information and communicate with an individual throughout the world. The development of the Internet is leading to formation of information super highway, where rapid access to information resources is possible irrespective of the place of initiation of search.

Computer networks help the people to tap into variety of information services. These information services include research, publication of journals, books, reports etc. data sharing, email and other such facilities. Internet and WWW are networking systems that support these information services. Scientific community use Internet as a tool to share their research findings. The concept of universal database that is not only accessible to people around the world but information that links to other pieces of information in other forms as well-data archives, electronic library, electronic journals, video conferencing etc. have become common place. The communication technology and networks are transforming the way we live and work. The future of the world looks to be a single source of information and the enormous expansion of communication facilities will open up new ways of learning, thinking and of sharing. The development in these technologies and the need for sharing resources lead for evolving networks.

Sharing of resources from one network to another network or from one computer to another computer has become possible irrespective of the network they are connected to. Perhaps no other recent innovation has impacted the library profession to such a great extent as Internet. It has created profound impact on Library and Information Science by offering new modes of information delivery and a vast information sources. Innovative use of Internet technologies enables us to reach both local and distant users much more easily and effectively.

Technologies such as email and web provide tremendous opportunities for Library and Information Scientists to deliver the information to the desktops of users. Web offers significant advantage by integrating different library and information services with a common user interface offered by Web browsers. Realizing the potentials, many libraries are rushing to get the connectivity. The internet facilities can be used by the librarians for most of the library activities viz. collection development, cataloguing, circulation, classification, services, preservation, etc.

Barriers to Resource Sharing

In developing countries like India digital resource sharing is in the early stage. In India there is lack of awareness of resources, deficit of resources, inadequate library budget, resources are scattered, heavy demand of users and hence resource sharing is essential.

- Libraries even in the present situation prefer to own the materials, rather than accessing them from other libraries or a network. They do not think of increasing their information base by adding the item that is not available with other libraries.
- The fear of losing an identity is another aspect. The libraries who participate in a network or consortium feel that they are losing autonomy. They will have to follow the guidelines set for a group of libraries.
- Centralization of activities and services under a network is still not preferred or accepted by many libraries.
- Benefits gained through participation in consortia are hard to explain or convince the authorities, particularly in the beginning stage.
- Resource sharing is done for marginal benefits in the peripheral areas as no one likes core areas or collection to be covered for resource sharing, resulting in little saving.
- Lack of institutional support might affect successful resource sharing. Availability of infrastructural facilities, support from authority and users is most essential for the success of a resource sharing programme.

- Lack of a well-tested mechanism of transfer of document or information to build confidence in the end users, which requires timely delivery of required information in an efficient manner.
- There are several other barriers such as geographical, legal, administrative, etc, which also pose certain problems in resource sharing.
- Computerized library requires regular up gradation of hardware, software, training of staff, etc.
- Adequate arrangements for monitoring of services and feedback information.
- Ensuring good transport, courier and communication facilities.
- Resource sharing needs to be treated as a routine job and not to be considered as a burden.
- Proper planning on the part of each individual participating library, and also the group of libraries as a whole, is a must. This plan should take into consideration both long range and short range factors.
- Compatibility, when it comes to sharing resources through the networks following standards, etc., needs to be studied and adopted by all.
- There need to be mechanism to monitor the whole process and collect the feedback from time to time
- Treat with equal importance with other functions, and one should take into confidence all participating libraries, when the major decisions are taken at consortium level and with staff members at the individual library level.
- Resource sharing costs money and does not bring benefits immediately. Benefits are likely to occur in the medium and long range. As far as possible one should avoid looking at the immediate benefit of consortia.

- Improving the document provision it an acceptable speed is necessary.
- Frequent meetings with participating libraries, reviewing various issues involved can make the programme more successful.

Resource Sharing vs. Networking

Resource Sharing is nothing but sharing of resources by the participating libraries among themselves on the basis of the principle of cooperation. In such a cooperative venture, it becomes possible for a user not only to use the resources of one library but also the resources of other libraries. Thus, through a resource sharing consortium, libraries can improve the total collection of reading material, consolidate their technological capabilities improve their dissemination tools and extend their information services to a larger user community (Sujatha, 1997).

Resource Sharing is the methods of sharing library resources like books, periodicals and other materials among the participating libraries on the basis of cooperation. The distant library can be across the city or around the world. Information is thus no more confined within the four walls of any library at one place but due to electronic connectivity every user has accessibility to all sources of information available anywhere.

Library network is a specialized type of library cooperation for centralized development of cooperative programme and services, including use of computer and telecommunication.

Networking can provide a powerful communication media among widely separated people in the world. A network is a collection of computers and communication hardware and software linked together to allow sharing of resources and providing facilities among the participating libraries.

Factors influencing the Resource Sharing

The effectiveness of library services depends on the ability of librarians to provide quick delivery of documents requested by customers either from physical stock or through networks. The electronic resource sharing is often mentioned, as an effective way for meeting user's information needs.

- Financial stringencies or lack of institutional funding makes libraries to look at alternatives way of improving and extending library resources.
- How to make the existing library resources readily accessible to the members and other interested users.
- High journal rates
- Publisher's restrictions on electronic disseminations.

The success of resources sharing essentially depends on:

- Agreement among participating library administration.
- Availability of union catalogue.
- Formation of consortia among the libraries.
- Formation of computer communication network among the libraries.

The Areas of Resources sharing:

What to share?

A fundamental step towards resource sharing in libraries is to understand a basic principle that a library has to share material. Before considering what can be shared, however it way is instructive to consider what cannot be shared. A book acquired by a library that is needed frequently by the users of that library is not a fair game of sharing. It is only those materials that are not needed frequently that can be considered for sharing.

The following are some of the areas in which resources sharing can be done:

- Inter library loan
- Cooperative procurement
- Co-operative technical operation
- Preparation of union catalogue
- Co-operative storage
- Browsing privilege of cooperative members
- Cooperative in documentation
- Exchange of experts

How to do Resource Sharing?

A fundamental step towards resources sharing in libraries is to understand a basic principle that a library has to share materials. Members of participating libraries in a resource sharing system must have Personal Computer (PC) with CD-drive and with E-mail facilities to support library automation requirements. On the other hand, high speed and large storage capacity computers may be installed to support consortium requirements, with cost shared among the members. Today, the technological advances have made resource sharing more effective and efficient. But, some careful planning and analysis is needed to ensure these requirements. Successful sharing requires willingness to cooperate by all institutions involved. The collaborative spirit should take full advantage of electronic networking.

The major factors that are important for resource sharing are:

- The electronic online catalogue and indexes of print resources should be made accessible over Internet to the internal users to check the speed, performance, and integrity and data security.
- Identification of players who are willing to participate

in the venture. The willingness of institutions / members to participate.

- Agreement on standard and formats.
- Creation of infrastructure for joining the network.
- Capability of hardware and software.
- Availability of communication technologies.
- Availabilities of financial resources.
- Trained manpower.

1. Planning

- Discussion with collaborative institutes for the type of resources to be shared. Seminars of participating libraries to formalize the process.
- Identify the overlap of periodical holdings to decide index coverage.
- Determine the availability of core collection of full text periodicals to identify hardware and software requirements for electronic library.
- Archiving of holdings on standard platform would allow libraries to share information though network.
- Identification of specific needs of Internet access of member libraries and network configuration for bibliographic files to online catalogues.
- Gateway (Internet) (that organizes and integrates access to library) information services available from the central system and individual participating libraries.
- Analysis of commercial databases available in the field. This could reduce the effort of indexing.
- Training of staff members and end users.
- The participating library should recognize that other libraries should develop an external programms to meet their requirements effectively and efficient

mechanism will have to be developed to respond to their request or materials.

- Every participating library must have a core collection to meet the requirements of its own user.
- The participating library should recognize its challenging role as member of the network by participating continuously in cooperating programmes, which may strengthen the resources of the nation's libraries collectively.
- The participants will build up their resources on cooperative basis so as to ensure participation by each member of the library to share available resources.
- Every participating library will have mandate from its own authority to participate in the resource sharing programme.
- The participating libraries in the network will maintain the spirit of "give and take" policy.
- A patron is one library may use the books, periodicals and other materials from other library. The distant library can be across the city or around the world. A professional entry has to be developed among the librarians that strongly support the inter-library concept.

2. Basic requirements for Resource Sharing

The following are some of the basic requirements for effective resource sharing:

- There is need for electronic catalogues and indexes for print resources available in the library
- The technology or equipment to link libraries and to make users aware of collections of own library and other libraries
- Standardized software, hardware and databases.
- Operating policies on the type of information and

achieves, which users can access (books, journals, reports, catalogues, indexes, publications, etc.)

- Operating manuals or documentation for consistency in operations

WEB BASED RESOURCE SHARING

Thus, Resource sharing can take in various forms such as inter library loan, cooperative acquisition and processing, preparation of union catalogue, on-line catalogue, bibliographical searches both retrospective and current, SDI, CAS, work in progress or annual reports, e-mail, online or offline search, bulletin board, fax, etc. Modern libraries do all the above works, but some modifications have been adopted for effective and efficient services.

Some of the objectives of web based Resource sharing are:

- To improve the sharing of resources among the member libraries;
- Centralize the information processing system and;
- Reduce the communication gap among the libraries;
- Improved ILL productivity: with fewer blind requests, automated creation and tracking of requests, and faster turnaround.

Thus, web resource sharing is very important for bibliographic control of explosion of literature and knowledge. It also avoid duplication in purchase of costly documents.

2. Infrastructure Requirements

The following computer peripherals and software may be required to build up a network:

- Computer to act as server (P III, or P IV, minimum speed 450 MZ) (Pentium / equivalent processor)
- Memory minimum 16MB expandable up to 128MB

- Operating system software
- Hard disk 20GB or more
- Server network interface card
- Network-compatible applications programs
- Usage monitoring software
- E-mail/desktop software
- Virus protection software
- Uninterrupted Power Supply (UPS)
- CD-ROM Drive
- Network cards for workstation that will be attached the LAN
- Cable and connectors
- Wiring hubs, signal boosters and other units required to complete the cabling.
- Workstations
- Printers: laser, dot matrix, inkjet as per requirement.

For the web based recourse sharing we need

- Web server (Pentium / equivalent processor)
- Hard disk capacity 20 GB(depending upon the data capacity)
- Multimedia kit
- At least 64 MB RAM
- Modems
- Scanner/printer/copier(this special purpose printer has the capacity to scan, print and copy the document and also enables to take color Xerox of the document which is used to send the color output of the data such as tables, charts, maps and other diagrams to the requesting person/institution.

Software

- Operating system UNIX/ Window 2000/ Linux

- Web browsing tool- any web browsing software (popular internet explorer and net scape communicator)
- Network connectively with latest fiber optic cable
- OCR software

Others

- Holding and catalogue
- Separate e-mail ID

Problems during the Process of Resource Sharing

Several constrains seriously hinder our efforts to resource sharing and networking attempts, such as:

- Increased cost of resource sharing components.
- Lack of technical trained staff.
- Lack of financial support by the government and concerned authorities.
- Lack of regular and comprehensive training programme in the area of library automation.
- Absence of overall system control.
- Improper physical facilities in the libraries.
- Lack of communication and cooperation among the various institutions engaged in automation.

SCOPE OF RESOURCE SHARING

Resource sharing can and must extend to include the sharing of staff resources, especially the specialized one, sharing of knowledge and expertise among the libraries. To be fully realized, such efforts must involve combining staff on cataloging at the regional or national level, integrating collection development and sharing equipments and facilities, such as processing areas, storage facilities, bookmobiles, etc.

In short, resource sharing should encompass

information, personals, equipments, facilities and expertise. Part of this sharing of resources can be accomplished without automated support. For resource sharing to be truly effective, however, automation and data communication are essential. Never the less, considerable improvement in resources sharing and thus in the cost of operation in libraries can be achieved through stronger cooperation among the libraries. In the electronic environment these services are delivered through data communication networks provided by the libraries/information centers.

If the information is in electronic form, it can easily be accessed, retrieved and delivered quickly which is more reliable and cost effective. The great success of WWW as a medium of transfer of documents lies in the freedom of access, wealth of information, etc. Not only it is useful and simple, but also web pages look attractive and the area in public domain where anyone can use the information, graphics and data supplied by the pages.

Now the following questions arise

- How to share information/ resources through networking?
- What other resources that can be shared?
- What is the need of networking?

To provide all these service properly an efficient network system is required. New communication media like Internet, e-mail, voice mail, fax, video conferencing make it much easier for researchers and scholars, librarians and libraries as well to exchange ideas and information.

RESOURCE SHARING AND INFORMATION SERVICE

The next logical step in resource sharing, after having created various tools to identify the location of the required materials, so that inter lending of different types of documents can take place. The initiative in this direction is being taken up involving libraries to evolve a mutually acceptable ILL procedure to handle the ILL transactions. Development of suitable and flexible software is being taken up, so that this activity can be started at the earliest.

RESOURCE SHARING AND DEVELOPMENT OF DIGITAL LIBRARIES

Resource sharing is important for creating digital libraries because of high cost of conversion of print material into digital. Collectively, though, libraries and other institutions can work towards converting collections that represent a wide range of topics. By working together, libraries can avoid needless redundancies and enable participants to take advantage of each other's expertise and strong collections owned by one institution but lacked at another.

What we can share for developing digital libraries ?

We can share;

- Expertise
- Information about rich collection
- Preservation programme
- Digitization of government documents
- Joint licensing arrangement etc.

Never before has collaboration been so essential for libraries-essential to the successful introduction, development, and widespread utilization of digital libraries. But collaboration means something far more demanding than the cooperative endeavors we have relied upon for so many years.

It will mean the development of:

- A common new mission and goals;
- Projects undertaken for longer terms results;
- New organizational structures;
- More comprehensive planning;

- Measures that assess user impact;
- Additional level of communication;
- New kinds of authority structures with dispersed leadership;
- Shared and mutual control;
- Pooled or jointly secured resources; and
- Shared products.

HOW WE CAN DEVELOP CO-OPERATION AMONG DIGITAL LIBRARIES

First, we must participate in the discussion about the development of digital library locally, statewide, nationally, and internationally. Continuous education is essential to success. Library schools must incorporate digital libraries into their curriculum.

Second we must work together to promote the concept of digital libraries and get support for collaborative digital library programmes. At the state level, we can seek grant from the state government and other related sources. We must expand our joint licensing efforts. We must work with our state associations, our state libraries regional and other library organizations, archives associations, local and state governments, museums, educational institutions, and others interested in digitizing materials. We must involve every type of library in the effort, recognizing that "the rising tide raises all the boats" and that all have something to gain. We must build strong partnerships with private and non-profit groups concern with learning, technology, culture, economic development, and the like. We must launch pilot projects that demonstrate the value of digital libraries, specially the college age students; digitized collection that relates to improving learning; and caters to the interests of the key policy makers.

The unique strengths that libraries bring to both venues

is our ability to apply our invaluable expertise and rich resources to the digital sphere, similar to the way we have done in the print environment. This is the special role libraries must play if our extraordinary skills, resources, and tools are contributed to the economy, health, and welfare of our citizens. Being digital will not negate the importance of our more traditional resources and services. Rather, it will elevate their value as well as the role of all types of library services in the 21st century information society.

We must find ways to make our collections and services even more relevant in the digital age. And the way we can do that is by "becoming digital".

As a result, collaboration to create digital libraries will need:

- New organizational frameworks;
- Serious comments by library leaders and their organizations;
- Equal risk taking across all organizations;
- Continuous evaluation and assessment of progress ;
- Brokering of relationships and entrepreneurial activities;
- A flexible, creative, responsive learning environment.

Creating true digital libraries, not just digital collection, will require librarians to work closely together to create an open, distributed, publicity accessible resource that documents crucial information for users; establish a collaborative structure to coordinate and guide the implementation of the digital library;

Develop criteria and standard to guide the selection of materials for inclusion in the digital library; Add value to the digital recourses; Assist libraries, museums, archives, schools, govt. and non govt. organizations, and other institutions in digitizing materials and managing digital library projects; and showcase content and the rich resources held by our libraries and other repositories worldwide.

It is critical that digital libraries provide access to valuable, interesting content and assist users in selecting, evaluating, and utilizing resources, no matter what their format. Collection and expertise are the two invaluable additions we offer to the networked world. We must collaborate to optimize the technological opportunities before us.

It no longer matter where digital content resides. But all kind of libraries and other institutions such as archives, colleges, museums, and others will need to work together to create and convert important resources to digital format, index; catalog; archive and preserve them; and make them universally accessible. All libraries must be equipped to provide access to and assist with these emerging digital resources. We must carefully coordinate our efforts to ensure that each participant's contributions complement and not duplicate other initiatives. And no single institution, not even the Library of Congress, has all the collections or resources necessary to respond to the needs of every community of users around the world.

Some efforts can be made which can force the participants to think more seriously about user communities and the need to work closely with them to increase the value and impact of digital libraries. These efforts are allowing participants to become more familiar with the formidable technical challenges facing them.

They also prompt them to work together across lines, institutions, and profession to:

- Create mutual vision for a common future.
- Share expertise and rich collections;
- Build upon earlier models of cooperative activities such

as preservation, interlibrary loan, and collection development;

- Reduce redundancy and the waste of acquiring or converting materials more than ones;
- Leverage scare financial resources;
- Allow the development of selection criteria which focus on coordinated digital collection building:
- Encourage coordinated preservation strategies;
- Ensure equitable access to information from anyplace/ anytime.
- Reduce barrier of distance and time;
- Permit users to leap to actual information;
- Develop value added components to the information contained in the digital library;
- Assists librarians and other institutions in digitizing materials and managing library projects;
- Build the library of the future;
- Create a new service paradigm for the 21st century.

PROBLEMS TO RESOUCE SHARING IN DIGITAL ENVIRONMENT

Yet we must also be aware of the pitfall we face when collaborating. First, plan and good intention are a good start, but without permanent funding and a home, they are unlikely to become a reality.

1. One of the biggest problems that most of the libraries are facing shortage of funding. The libraries are not only geographically dispersed, but also employ a wide diverse of different data structures, search engines, interfaces, controlled vocabularies, document formats, etc.
2. Many libraries and consortia are already heavily invested in their own developments and may be

reluctant to adjust their course in order to accommodate other's effort.

3. There is a wide diversity across libraries of different digital data structures.
4. Many organizations will need major retooling to contribute efficiently and effectively. Indeed, the barriers to collaboration are awesome and must be overcome if libraries are to work together toward a common digital future.

Another problem is administrative problem. Collaborative statewide efforts require many meetings, taking people away from production. They also require extensive planning; the speed of technological change is often faster than a shared planning effort. Cooperative collection development has never been a major success for the libraries, making it work in the digital environment is equally difficult. Providing access to external material is problematic when local control of collections is lacking and long term access and preservation require constant vigilance. In short, a successful collaborative digital library effort needs champions who are willing and eager to promote their cause in the face of great promise along with serious pitfall.

Consequently, federating all digital libraries locally, statewide, nationally or internationally will be virtually impossible.

NETWORKING AND RESOURCE SHARING

Introduction

It is needless to emphasize that in higher education, especially for colleges and universities, libraries play a vital role to activate a free flow of information. They facilitate utilization of information more precisely, exhaustively and pin pointedly in shortest possible time. All this could effectively be achieved by resource sharing through networks.

In the age of digital education and escalating price of electronic information, resource sharing is important for effective functioning of libraries. Increased availability of information in digital format and high cost of journal subscription compels the libraries to work together. Technical advancements provide a platform for digital resource sharing and offer many opportunities for librarians to become more technical and professional.

Libraries have shared their resources for many decades through formal and informal agreement using traditional means. During the last two decades things have drastically changed due to more and more libraries automating their library catalogues, acquiring resources in electronic form (e.g. e-journals) and getting connected to one or the other networks. This has resulted in easy accessing of the resources from the remote nodes adding new dimensions to the nature of the library service. In a resources constrained environment, sharing of library resources among the libraries and providing services through the resource sharing practices is gaining considerable importance. With the development and the application of information technology tools the sharing has become much easy.

What is networking?

Library network may be defined as "a distribution system composed of two or more libraries and /or other organizations engaged in a common pattern of information exchange, through communications for some functional purpose."

The term "network" has been defined by Greenberger and Arnofsky as "Mode for sharing resources and linking otherwise incomparable procedures and formats of different systems and organizations". Millar has defined it as "a cooperative system established by libraries and information centers which are brought together by common subject, geographic proximity to share information resources, human and all other elements essential for providing effective information service."

According to United National Information System for Science and Technology (UNISIST)," Networking is a set of Inter- related information systems associated with communication facilities, which are co-operating through more or less formal agreements and institutional agreements in order to jointly implement information handling operations with a view to pooling their resources and better serving the users. They generally follow identified or compatible rules and procedures."

Thus, from the above definitions it is clear that a network is a cooperative system of sharing resources among two or move libraries through a formal institutional agreement. The networks are often called information networks, electronic networks, library network etc. The exchange of information takes plane among participating libraries by the help of communications system. Computer and telecommunication technology are playing a vital role in the design and operation of resource sharing systems networks. These are required for working of large systems on national and international levels also.

Resource sharing through library networks helps the member libraries in avoiding duplication of document procurement and in inter-library lending.

When a library is computerized, it requires regular up gradations of hardware, maintenance and up gradation of software, but it will take time and frustration increases. In the initial stages the library network faced the problem of creating database is in getting inputs from different participating libraries. There is an emphasis towards computerization, database creation, networking and resource sharing but we are now in the beginning stage. We are behind the advanced technology.

Why networking?

The literature growth in various disciplines is being noticed at an alarming rate and the rising prices of publication too have but great financial stress on the libraries. Even with the increased financial resources, libraries have not been able to meet all the information needs of the readers. Efforts can be made to achieve this by creating viable library networks for better and economical use of library resources.

There is a need to create an environment for effective use of resources at the individual level by automating library facilities like acquisition etc. Besides this, the library networks suppose to:

- Increase resource operations by producing in individual libraries direct approach to databases like bulletins, CAS, SDI, union catalogue, etc.
- To inter exchange duplicate publications if any.
- To provide efficient and meaningful resource sharing in activities such as inter library user seminars, manpower training and access to national and international databases.
- To standardize techniques, methods, procedures, hardware, software services and advocate for their adoption by all participating libraries so that optimum use could be obtains through networking.
- Networks allow more efficient management of resources.

Objectives of Networking

The main objectives of Networking are:

- Facilitating users to have better access to library holdings or services.

- Positive effect on library budget in terms of cost or more services at lesser cost than can be undertaken individually.
- Exchanging of library resources and information to benefit users.
- Enabling the users to be more aware regarding the resources not available in their own library
- Advocate and support creative use of library/ information resources.
- Develop shared policies for ILL, borrowing and reciprocal agreements for special collections and non-circulating materials.

Benefits of Networking

The purpose of library networks is to ensure an easy access to relevant information and its objectives is to make the better use of existing resources available among the participating libraries.

Some of the benefits of the Networking are as follows:

- Utilization of library holdings within the limited budget
- Improve user services
- Reduce investment in multiple subscription
- Effective SDI and CAS services
- Inter library document transfer facility
- Avoiding unnecessary duplication
- Generate appropriate skills to handle information etc.
- High reliability
- Saving money
- Access to remote information
- Person to person communication
- Interactive transfer of information

What is essential for Library Networking?

Some of the basic essentials of library networking are:

- Library networking is meant to promote and facilities sharing of resources available within a group of libraries in order to provide maximum information to user, to lower operational costs and also to make optimum use of national resources.
- In order to do it is necessary to create bibliographic tools like union catalogues and union list based on the resources available in the participating libraries and these tools have in turn to be used for resource sharing and reference purposes.
- Rationalization of acquisitions needs to be undertaken.
- Inter- library loan services should grow and may be interlinked with the search of the union catalogues. Delivery of documents should be fast, either electronically through e- mail fax or through courier.
- The libraries selected to join a networking should be willing partners, ready to buy hardware etc, and should be willing to send professional staff for professional staff training. They should be willing to pool bibliographic records to the central host of the networks besides adhering to other network obligations.
- In-house functions like acquisition, cataloguing, classification, serial control, circulation, Selective Dissemination of Information (SDI), Current Awareness Service (CAS) etc. should be undertaken by the individual libraries. The network software may or may not support this operation of the libraries in the beginning but eventually the network software should not be able to create union catalogues or full text databases, etc. but also be integrated with the in - house operations.

- The network should be able to recommend to participating libraries the type of hardware they need for their in house functions and for networking purpose. Hardware should be selected considering the number of entries the participating libraries can generate within the next 3-5 years. The hardware at the control host will have to be updated regularly depending upon the speed with which participating libraries generate records and the network pools them into the Central Host.
- All the libraries should follow a standard format, cataloging code, thesaurus, etc. uniformly.
- Electronic mail and Internet facilities should be established between libraries and they should be able to access international databases preferably individually or thought the network host to begin with.
- Although effort should be made to have one classification scheme in all participating libraries but use of different class numbers should not become a hurdle as search request are mostly by authors, titles, editors and subject descriptors

Advantages of Networks

Computer networks provide several important advantages to computerization/Institution/Business and individuals in general and for libraries in particular.

- Modern organizations today are widely dispersed with office located in diver's parts of country and the world. Many of the computers and terminals located the sites need to exchange information and data, often on a daily basis. A network prides the means to exchange data among these computers and to make programme and data available to the people of the organization.
- The networking of computers permits the sharing of resources of the machines. For instance, if a computer

becomes saturated with too much work at one site, the work can be loaded through the network path into another computer in the network. Such load sharing permits a more even and better utilization of resources.

- Networking also provides the critical function of back up. In the event that one computer fails, its counterpart can assume its functions and workload. Backup traffic control in the event important in systems such as air traffic control. In the event a computer malfunctions, back-up computers rapidly take over and assume control of operations without endangering air travelers.

Types of Networks

Network can be divided into following types

1) Local Area Network—LAN
2) Metropolitan Area Network—MAN
3) Wide Area Network—WAN
4) Wireless Networks
5) Intranet

1. Local Area Network (LAN) : A Local Area network (LAN) is two or more computers and other items of compute[illegible] equipments such as printers, modems etc. which are direct[illegible] linked within a small well defined area such as ro[illegible] building, or a campus. The main benefit of a LAN i[illegible] reduction of hardware and software costs because us[illegible] share several computers, peripheral devices such [illegible] printers, color-printers, scanners, software. Anothe[illegible] is that the users can share the same data.

According to IEEE (Institute of Ele[illegible] Electronics Engineers) "A local Area Network is[illegible] from other types of data networks in that co[illegible] usually confined to a moderate geograph[illegible] single office building, a warehouse, or a campus, and can depend on a physical communications channel of moderate to high data rate which has a consistently low error rate."

A LAN could be said to be a set of data processing devices interconnected through cable. It sends and receives data transmitted over relatively short distances. The types of data transmitted are LAN may include mail (Messages and notes) manuscripts, reports, computer files and software.

Any network that exists within a single building, or even a group of adjacent buildings, is considered as LAN. A LAN is a geographically small network of computers and supporting components used by a group or department to share related software and hardware resources. Some LANs specifically require all the computers to be of a certain brand, while other allows a variety of brands to be connected. The numbers of computers in LAN varies widely from small LANs that connected two to twenty five computers, to large LANs those more than 10,000 computers.

LAN must get the data to its destination, transmit the data correctly, and prevent unauthorized users from gaining access to that data. The length of the cable connecting to ...mputer through a LAN also varies. Most of the LANs permit ...s of about one thousand feet, but some permit cables ...l miles to be used. The speed of data transfer ranges ...l thousand bits/second to 10 million bits/second.

...nerally consists of the following:

...computers.

...trol the operation of the computers.

...uch as modems, printers, plotters.

...able is usually used to connect ...devices.

...g computer.

CHARACTERSTICS OF LAN

Some of the main characteristics of LAN are:

- High speed (1 to 10 Mbps)
- Short distance (0.1 to 10 Km)
- Low cost
- Low error rate.
- Flexibility.
- Security.
- Centralized management.

Application of LAN

- Sharing expensive peripherals such as printers, etc.
- Sharing expensive softwares.
- Exchange of messages between users connected to LAN.
- Sharing files between users.

2. Metropolitan Area Network (MAN) : A Metropolitan Area Network (MAN) is a network that is larger than a LAN. It is called metropolitan since it normally covers the area of a city. Different hardware and transmission media are often used in MANs because they must efficiently cover these distances or because they don't require complete access to location between the network sites.

3. Wide Area Network (WAN) : Wide-Area Network (WAN) is two or more geographically dispersed computers, linked by communication facilities such as telecommunication or microwave relay. In other words, one of the most significant aspects of a wide area network while comparing it with the freedom of a local-area network is the involvement of a public telecommunications authority. WAN is usually limited to use by the large organizations and government agencies due to high costs involved in building and maintaining them. A special designation has also been given to two specific WAN categories.

Computer Networks

Computer networks provide many services besides travel reservations and financial transactions, but these applications show two important features of computer networks.

1. They provide shared access to information, such as airline flight status or account balances.
2. They permit the movement of data, such as fight status updates, or financial transfers.

A networked computer can be many things which a stand-alone computer cannot do:

1. Share a single copy of a file among all the users, even simultaneously.
2. Share application over the entire network, thus reducing the cost of purchasing the multiple copies. A mult-user license costs much less than buying a stand-alone license for each user.
3. Share resources like printers, hard disks, CD-ROM drives, modems, fax machines, etc.
4. Use e-mail for interest communications, inter office notes etc., creating an almost paper less office.

Components of Computer Network

A Network is a combination of different components. The most essential components of a simple network are:

1) Server
2) Nodes
3) LAN Cables
4) Network Operating System software (NOS)
5) Network Interface Card

1. Server : Servers are the faster computer to run various software stores and process information and to provide a human interface for the user to be able to use the networked computers. The workstation works only for the person sitting in front of it, whereas a server all the people on the network to share its resources. A workstation usually has an inexpensive, small hard disk to carry out local tasks. Some workstations, called diskless workstation, have no disk drive of their own. Such workstation also called dumb terminals; rely completely on the LAN for their access. The network operating system lets the nodes work as if all the resources at the server belong to the node itself.

2. **Nodes** : Nodes are the computer on the network which is provided to the user carry out their tasks using the network. A node which is more powerful and can handle local information processing or graphics processing is called a workstation.

3. **LAN Cables** : This is the medium over which the information travels from computer to computer, from the computer onto the medium (cable) and to take up the information from the medium and make it available to them computer in the from it can read.

4. **Network Operating System Software (NOSS)** : To control the movement of information on the network, networks which are more complex require components like Hubs, Switches and Router to carry out different network functions. On the network, each computer is called a node or a workstation unless there are certain computers designed as servers. Each computer contains a network interface card. LAN cables connect all the nodes and serves together to from the network. In addition to its local disk operating system, each node requires network software that enables the nodes to communication with the nodes.

5. **Network Interface Card** : This is a card used to connect the cables to the computers. These cards help the computer to transfer the data at a faster rate and in the form of packets. These cards are plugged into the computer

mother board. These cards are generally called as earthnet card.

Advantages of Computer Networks

- Networks allow more efficient management of resources.
- Network help keep information reliable and up-to-date.
- Networks help speed up data sharing.

Library and Information Networks

Introduction: The world is in the information age. It is commonly recognized that information and its associated technologies are playing more and more important roles in socio-economic development, and that a nation that doesn't keep pace with the latest advance in information and communication technologies will be left behind in world development. Like most countries in the world, India is drawing up its own information super-highway programme, trying to make it part of the international super-highway system and has greatly promoted the computerization and networking of library and information services.

The activities concerning library automation, inter-library cooperation, generation of new services naturally demand time and energy of the participating libraries. However it is unlikely that, the libraries would get additional manpower for such activities. One way to handle the situation would be to relieve the librarian of some of the activities such as book processing, cataloguing and classification through the shared efforts, so that they could attend to new services.

The term "Network" is used in the present times in place of "Resource Sharing" or "Cooperative systems". Networking and Modernization are becoming very important in all types of libraries as the user have access to the resources of many other libraries in addition to their own one.

The benefits of networking include :

Preparation of union catalogues, retrospective conversion, provision of bibliographies, optimum use of resource sharing, time saving, and minimizing cost of the library services.

Objectives of Library and Information Networks

- Provide reliable access to document collection of libraries, i.e., Union Catalogues etc.
- To promote sharing of resources among the libraries by developing a network of libraries, by collecting, storing and disseminating information and by offering computerized services to the users ;
- To undertake scientific research in the area of Information Science and Technology, create new systems in the field, apply the results of research and publish them ;
- To offer technical guidance to the member-libraries on collecting, storing, sharing and disseminating information;
- To coordinate efforts for suitable collection development and reduce unnecessary duplication wherever possible;
- To establish /facilitate the establishment of referral and /or research centers, and maintain a central online union catalogue of books, serials and non-book materials of all the participating libraries;
- To facilitate and promote delivery of documents manually or mechanically;
- To develop specialized bibliographic database of books, serials and non-book materials;

- To develop databases of projects, specialists and institutions;
- To possess and maintain electronic and mechanical equipmently for speedy communication of information and delivery of electronic mail.
- To coordinate with other regional, national and international networks and libraries for exchange of information and documents.
- Provide access to world wide bibliographical information.
- Provide document delivery service.
- Optimize information resources through resource sharing mechanisms.
- Facilities computerization of all the libraries.
- Facilitate communication among teachers, students, scientists and others.
- Provide effective access to library resources.
- Encourage resource sharing.

Evolve standards, uniform guidelines, methods, and procedures, both for data capturing as well as hardware and software.

Network Topology

The network topology is the arrangement of nodes on a network. This includes the physical arrangement or the geographic pattern by which the nodes are connected. It also includes the logical arrangement; the possible destinations to which each can route data. The interconnection of system can be achieved in many ways but basically there are three most important methods, via, point to point, multipoint/ multi drop and broadcasting. The design of hardware components is called nodes. These nodes when linked form pattern that are classified as star like topology, tree like topology, ring topology and mashed topology.

1. Star Topology : Star network derives its name from the fact that there is one central controller (usually a computer) which has communication channels radiating outward. Each one is connected to a separate device such as a terminal or another computer. These networks are typically found in cases where a large scale central computer is connected to many terminals. The reliability of central control becomes the main issue in star networks, because when it goes down, the entire network fails (Fig. 19).

The star network is a network in which one member of network holds majority of the resources while at the same time all other network member use the same resources. The Fig. 19 illustrates such a network with members. A possessing virtually all the other resources which the other network members B, C, D make use of resources.

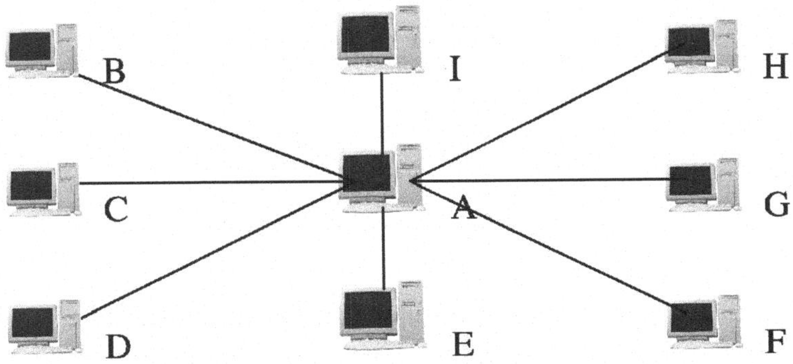

Fig. 19. Star Topology

2. Hierarchical Network or Tree Network Topology : Hierarchical network also known as tree networks, consist of control computer to which several other computers or nodes are connected. Each node is in turn, has devices, such as terminals connected compute centrally. Each node acts as a star network. So a hierarchical network is essentially a multi-level star network. Nationwide organizations with divisional and regional stations are hierarchical networks.

The tree network topology is suitable for an environment where network members share resources locally. In this topology nodes are connected hieratically. Here mini computers are used as intermediately nodes and micro computers as end nodes. It makes for reduced communication costs as several terminals can be connected to a single communication line. This type of topology is illustrated in Fig. 20.

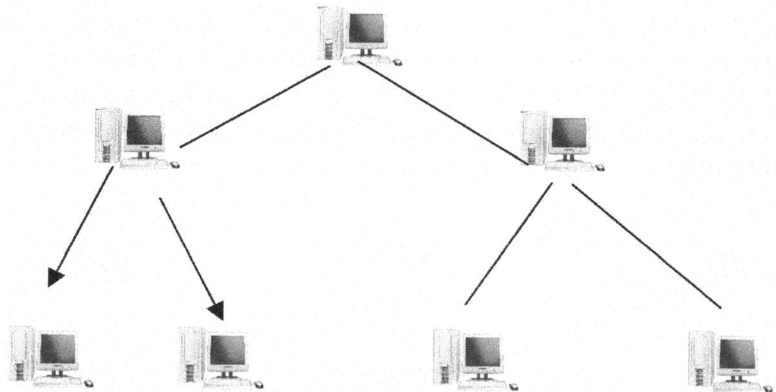

Fig. 20. Hierarchical Topology

3. Ring Network

A ring network is a completely closed loop. A single communication channel with devices connected to it, run through a building office unto the end of the channel connects bulk to the beginning.

In this topology each network member is connected with other members like a ring. This topology generally suits a network in a building, a small campus with well defined but limited operations (Fig. 21).

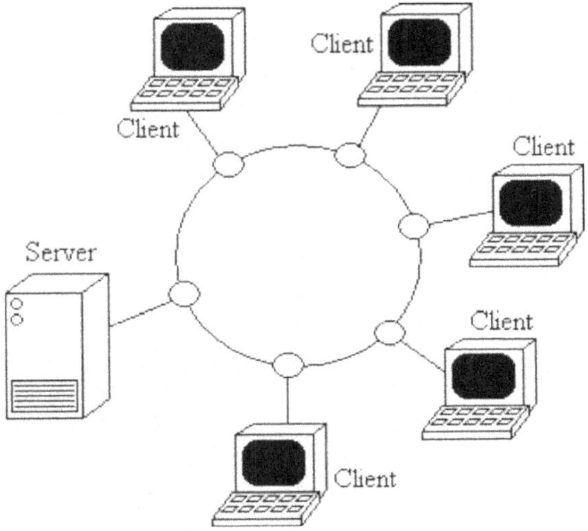

Fig21. Ring Topology

4. Bus Network

A bus network is a single communication channel routed along a path in which various devices can be attached. In this networking adding or taking off one computer from the bus does not disturb the system operation or the rest of the network.

It consist of number of nodes linked to a central communication "highway" or bus in such a way that every node has a single bi-directional connection to a shared cable which enables each node to be directly connected to each of the node over this shared cable(Fig. 22).

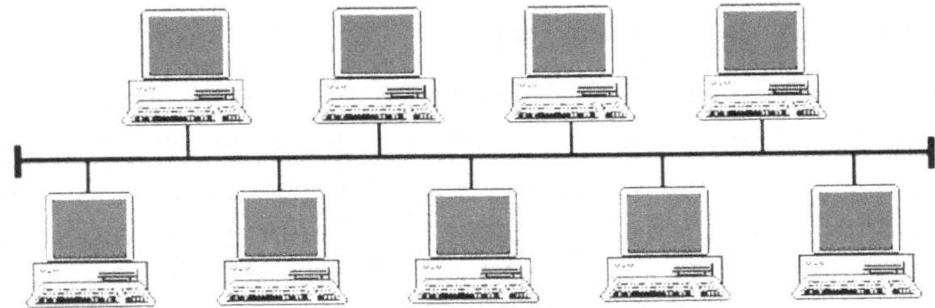

Fig. 22. Bus Topology

Mesh Network

It consists of a number of nodes linked together in such a way that sometimes data from one node has to pass the third party to reach the destination (Fig. 23).

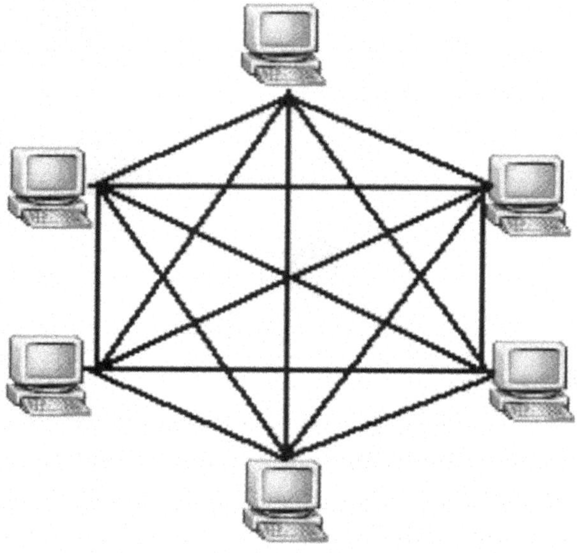

Fig. 23. Mesh Topology

Communication networks can broadly be grouped into the following categories based on the geographical locations of its computer terminals:

TYPES OF NETWORKS

Wide Area Network (WAN)

Wide Area Networks (WAN) is used to interconnect a number of widely disperse computers in various cities of country or different countries. WAN use communication media maintained by telegraph or telephone companies. These networks usually have land telephone lines, underground coaxial cables, and microwave communication and satellite communication. The main objective of such interconnection is to allow users of the networks to access specialized library programs, databases etc, available at any of the computers in the networks. Two big networks of this type are ARPANET and TYMNET in USA.

Metropolitan Area Network (MAN)

Metropolitan Area Network (MAN) refers to the interconnection within geographical limits of a city or town. Usually referred as "last Mile" Problem, the MANs shares problems associated with poor telephone network infrastructure of local telephone authority. While the satellite based MAN provide excellent communication between remote points irrespective of distance, reliability of intra-city communication in case of MAN are doubtful.

Special Interst Network (SPIN)

SPINs are usually within the same city, state or region and are tied together via telephone lines. There are many kinds of SPINs. Local community conferencing systems and electronic bulletin systems are the examples.

GATEWAYS

Gateways consist of software and hardware that are required to interconnect network among themselves. Gateways contend with any differences in packet sizes, protocols and addressing methods between the two networks it connect. Two similar LANs are connected by a type of gateway called a bridge. In such cases since the protocols used are same, there is no need to modify the contents or the format of the packets as they pass from one network to the other. A bridge combines two similar LANs to make one larger network while retaining their individuality of each network in terms of performance reliability and security. Gateways are also used to connect LANs to WANs, in turn, can be linked through gateways to create national and international data communication networks.

DATA COMMUNICATION NETWORKS IN INDIA

The progress in networking in India has been rather slow due to the poor extension of telecommunication networks and overwhelming use of resources and expertise that are available. However, the scene is changing fast. The department of telecommunication is setting up a Public Data Network (PDN) and has plans to expand and revamp the existing telephone system. The potential of data network in India has already been recognized and few networks have already come into operation.

Networks that are already in operation or in various stages of development may be classified into the following two categories depending upon their scope and objectives:

1. General Networks

   Examples

   NICNET, INDONET AND VIKRAM

2. Special Networks

   Examples

   CALIBNET, DELNET, BONET, ERNET, INFLIBNET, BTISNET etc.

1. GENRANAL NETWORKS

The general network namely the National Informatics Center Network (NICNET), the INDONET and the VIKRAM are briefly described below:

National Informatics Center Network (NICNET)

The satellite based National Informatics Networks (NICNET) was set up to provide informatics services to the Central and Stale Government Departments and its organizations. The NICNET provide computing and two-way data communications infrastructure to aid planning and monitoring of schemes and decision-making activities is the Government. The networks consist of Master Earth Station,

Remote Micro Earth Stations and a Geosynchronous Satellite. The master earth station is located at CGO complex, New Delhi. It comprises of 13 meters antenna, network control center and packet switch. Micro earth station connects remotely located district computer with the state computer, which in turn, are connected to the regional headquarters. Specialized services such as computer-added and design and computer-aided management are also offered over NICNET. The network supports X.25 switch and operates at 12000bps transmission speed and 190. Kbps receives speed. The present configuration handles300 packets (128 bytes each) per second. The host computers are connected to this packet switch.

Various facilities and services of NICNET include:

- Gateway to internet by providing internet connectivity
- E-mail service
- USENET bulletin board service.
- Telnet facility to login to remote host
- File Transfer Protocol facility.
- Resources and Educational Network of NIC (RENNIC) service to research, education and medical institutions.
- Bibliographic information service.
- Geographical information systems.
- General Information Service Terminates (GIST NIC) form common public.
- Training facilities.

VIKRAM

Vikram is the packet switched public data network under development by the Department of Telecommunications. This networks will initially have 8 switching nodes is Delhi, Bombay, Calcutta Madras,

Bangalore, Hyderabad, Ahmedabad and Pune and 12 remote areas nodes with its network management center located at Delhi. It will support packet switching interface to CCITTs X.25, X.26, X. 29 and X.75 recommendations.

SPECIALIZED NETWORKS

1. CALIBNET (Calcutta Library Network)

CALIBNET is a Government of India project. CALIBNET is envisaged as a metropolitan network linking some 38 libraries in Calcutta in a phased manner under the financial support of NISSA T. In the first phase, 7 major libraries are being linked. The participating institutions will collect process and held information on local computers which collect. Process and hold information on local computers which will be interconnected through a star X.25 packet switched network. One of the participating libraries would do to the network control. . The software for entire network operation is being developed by the CMC Ltd. The applications to be supported are:

Electronic mail, file transfer, remote log-on database development and document' access. Within individual libraries, the functions to be automated are cataloguing, serials control, acquisition and fund accounting, circulation and local user services. The networking provides for global use of Current Awareness Services, SDI, Union catalogues, partial databases and access to national and international databases.

CALIBNET aims to provide individual libraries and their reading members with cost effective solutions to their information problems.

Services: The network is intended to provide Current Awareness Service (CAS), SDI union catalogue, area to national and international network, etc.

Service also includes:

- Access to CD- ROM databases
- LCMARC
- Biblio file
- Inside information
- E-mail service

2. DELNET

DELNET is a major resource sharing library network in South Asia. It networks more than 900 libraries in India and six other countries and offer access to about fifty lack records of books, journals articles, and other documents. DELNET also provides inter library loan for books and Document Delivery Service for journal articles to the member libraries within and outside India. The facilities have been developed for students, researchers and faculty members of universities.

DELNET is conceived for networking of about 30 libraries in Delhi in its first phase. NISSAT took the initiative for the development of these networks to ensure better utilization for the development of these networks to ensure better utilization of science and technology information to resources through sharing, to moderate functional load of information center management and to take care of motivational factors to a large extent by better means of communications. In order to network the libraries in Delhi, a feasibility study was conducted by the Computer Maintenance Corporation (CMC) Ltd. A number of selected libraries have already been networked electronically.

The DELNET has been actively engaged in the compilation of various union catalogues of the resources available in member's libraries

DELNET Provides

- Union catalogue of 87777 2 bibliographic records.

- Union catalogue of books: MARC format has presently 27231 records
- Union list of current periodical with 16,497 periodicals and is regularly updated.
- Databases of periodical articles have around 200410 records.
- Referral services to participating libraries.

3. INFLIBNET (Information and Library Network Center)

The information and Library Network (INFLIBNET) is an autonomous inter university center established by UGC with its headquarters at Ahemadabad in 1991 with an objective to automate and Network Libraries in Academic and R & D system to facilitates resource sharing at different levels and promotes scholarly communication among academicians and researchers in the country. There was no attempt for formal networking among university libraries in India until INFLBINET was established involving the use of computers and communication technology. Information and Library Network (INFLIBNET) is a major programme of the UGC initiated in 1991. It was initially launched in order to provide effective and efficient library services through library network.

The INFLIBNET is a major national effort to improve capability in information transfer and access as support to scholarship, learning research and academic pursuits. It would link up institutions of higher learning covering all disciplines, about 150 University Libraries, R&D institutions and national organizations like CSIR, ICAR, DRDO, ICMR, ICSSR, etc. The network has been Computerized; as a hybrid of satellite based a terrestrial communication system. The network has been designed to offer a plethora of odd services including online catalogue, database service, electronic document supply, collection development, etc. A national node has been set up at Ahmedabad to coordinate the network activities. The central node would be connected to four regional nodes which will hold union catalogues and databases.

Objectives of INFLIBNET

The main objectives of INFLIBNET are as under:

- To evolve a national network of libraries and information centers in the country and to improve information handling capability;
- To provide reliable access to document collection through online union catalogue;
- To provide better access to bibliographic information sources with citation and abstract through online accessing of international database held by international information networks and centers;
- To provide document services by establishing resources centers around libraries having a rich collection of documents;
- To promote information resource utilization through shared cataloguing inter-library loan service.
- To computerize operations of libraries and information centers in the country following uniform standard;
- To facilitate communication among scientists, engineers, researchers, social-scientist, academics faculties and students through electronic mail.
- To provide speedy and efficient services to the end users.
- To provide required training for manpower development to the personals of the participating libraries.
- To enable users regardless of location and distance to access Information;
- To create online information service and

- To encourage cooperation among libraries

As one of the steps towards achieving the laudable objectives mentioned above, the INFLIBNET has initiated the automation by funding 54 University libraries. It appears that only 17 of these libraries which received financial assistance from INFLIBNET have so far acquired the hardware to commence the automation activity. Even the progress in respect of resources sharing during the period is stated to be rather slow.

INFLIBNET has also taken a number of other measures, which facilitate the realization of its objectives. Some of the significant steps on this direction are: I) for the purpose of promoting resource sharing activity it has already created a union catalogue of about 50,000 records. It may mentioned here that union catalogue is one of the important tools which facilitates the resource identification, location and sharing aspects of resources sharing activity as a whole among members of the network; ii) INFLIBNET has also took great initiative the creation of databases containing 65,000 records of thesis/dissertation and also a periodicals database having 30,000 records. These are some of pioneering efforts undertaken by INFLIBNET to realize its basic objectives. It is making some efforts in software development and also for the creation of suitable manpower necessary for the purpose.

If we critically examine the achievements of INFLIBNET as given in the Review Committee Report, 1996 and try to compare these with the original targets contained in original report of 1988, prepared by the Inter-agency Working Group, we notice that the achievements fall short of expectations of Inter-agency Working Groups.

For instance, some of the targets mentioned in the INFLIBNET report were:

- Compilation of union catalogue of 9 million unique

records of retrospective collections of 179 university libraries as against 50,000 records as mentioned above

- At least 200 research and development(R & D) organizations were to be linked to INFLIBNET. (Even this target does not seem to be realized till now).
- Support would be given to 170 universities and 500 college libraries for library automation (this also remains to be achieved).

It may be stated here that UGC has drafted a new Memorandum of Association and Rules and registered the INFLIBNET Society in the year 1996. The objectives included in this Memorandum of Association are different from those recommended in the working Groups report of 1988. However, it may be noted here that the INFLIBNET Review Committee under chairmanship of Dr. S.Venkatashwaraswamy in its report submitted in 1996, also recommended revision of the objectives for INFLIBNET. INFLIBNET is also engaged in the manpower development activity by undertaking some short-term training programmes and workshops. These are very meager efforts. The network must attempt to develop some standardized software, which it appears; it has not yet succeeded in achieving. Much is expected of this network. It must however be mentioned that the human resources presently engaged in this work appears to be rather inadequate if INFLIBNET is to realize its stated objectives in the near future.

Main INFLIBNET Activities

Some of the activities of INFLIBNET are as follows:

1. Creation of national union database.
2. Development of integrated library management software.
3. Human resource development on site training.
4. Bibliographic information service.

5. Technical help and guidance in automation and networking.
6. E-journal consortium of UGC.
7. UGC is serious efforts to bring computer networking and internet access to University and colleges campuses.

It is expected that UGC infonet would enable below mentioned applications a reality:

- E-access to journals.
- Computer aided learning.
- Distance education.
- E-governance.

1. Automation and financial support

Providing financial support of Rs.6.5 lacks each to about 142 university libraries for the purpose of automation and networking.

An automated library management system is a basic requirement for library automation and networking. To meet this need, the center developed Integrated Library Management Software (ILMS) for library housekeeping activities, such as acquisition, circulation and cataloguing. It was distributed to participated libraries almost free of cost. Recently the center has developed windows based management software 'SOUL' which provides total solution for library automation especially to the university libraries. It is a user-friendly software and has been developed to work in a networked environment based on client-server architecture. Modules of the software are acquisition, cataloguing, circulation, serial control, OPAC and administration. The center is providing this software to all the university libraries under its programme at a nominal cost.

2. Manpower development

Providing training to the staff members working in these libraries, conducted 20 such courses to help the operational staff of these libraries to implement the IT in their libraries outside training has been provided at more than 35 places. INFLIBNET has started providing a regional level training to help the libraries from college libraries and provides necessary support. Emphasis is given on practices including E-mail, remote access, CD-ROM, multimedia, etc.

The center also organizes a national convention every year. Each convention is held in different region of the country focusing on a particular theme. These conventions provide a common plateform to the libraries to interact with each other, access the progress made in computerization activities and plan for the future.

3. Conversion of library records in Machines Readable From

As the conversion of all the records of each participating library in machine readable form is a must for effective resources sharing, the center has advised all the participating libraries to give top priority to creating records of their collection in machines readable form.

4. OCLC'S first search service through INFLIBNET

Providing various kinds of information services such as CD-ROM based services, access to OCLC first search, Contents page service. The center has recently started helping universities by subscribing to OCLC'S first search service. This service enable the center to provide the first search service to all its funded universities, to begin with, in an off line mode. The user of the library will have to send the request for literature search along with keyboard etc, to the center. The center with access the databases, conduct the search and download the records and send it to the requesting libraries. Only request through the libraries are accepted. Initially, charges are born by the center and only bibliographic information is provided under the service. Some of the abstracts are: BIOSIS, Education Abstract, INSPEC, Library Literature etc.

5. E-mail Access to INFLIBNET Database

The center has developed a software tools called 'SEWAK" which automatically process queries received through e-mail and send back replies.

INFLIBNET'S NEW INITIATIVES

1. Electronic Document Delivery Service (EDDS)

This service was started in July 2000. Six universities viz, BHU, Indian Institute of Science, Bangalore, JNU, Punjab University, and Tata Institute of Social Science, Mumbai have been identified to serve as Document Delivery Centers (DDDS). These libraries have fairly large collection of serials.

Under this service, the DDCS will provide the copies of research papers appeared in learned journals, conference proceedings, etc, from the collection available with them to academic and research community at affordable cost. This service will preferably be delivered using the Internet.

2. Retro conversion of library holding

INFLIBNET has also initiated two major projects, viz, Retro conversion of collection of five major libraries and six document delivery service centers. The Retro conversion of five major libraries i.e., B.H.U, IISc, JNU, University of Mumbai and University of Madras has recently been launched under the INFLIBNET programme. The primary objective of this programme is to minimize the effort and cost involved in retro- conversion work of its member libraries. Under this project, the above five libraries, which have the largest and unique collections, will create qualitative databases of their library books holding in a span of two years. The data will be provided to all other universities on CD-ROM for directly downloading these records, thus avoiding the need for entry. INFLIBNET proposes to use this data for retro conversion and shared cataloguing of its member libraries, thereby minimizing the laborious effort and cost involved in Retro conversion. All the five libraries are provided with extra grant for caring out this mammoth task.

3. V-SAT based network for University libraries

To strength online access to union databases, transfer of data between the libraries and the center and Internet access to information, the center proposes to set up its own independent VSAT based captive network covering more than 170 universities. This will indeed prove very beneficial for university libraries to optimize resources and access the information at a minimal cost.

Functioning of INFLIBNET

INFLIBNET in a veritable integrated library and information system, yet, it operates at different levels, national, regional, sectoral and local.

The catalogue of libraries will be aggregated bottom up words i.e.; from catalogue / department to university library and to regional center. Secondary information / databases maintenance and services will be taken care of by sectoral information centers.

End users will be served mainly at local level such as college, department, university and R & D institutions.

National center is located at Ahemedabad overseeing and co-operating the affairs of the network.

There will be four regional centers (North, East, West and South) for the four regions of the Indian union which will maintain union catalogue of holding of libraries in the regions and databases of projects, institutions and specialists.

Sectoral centers

Some institutions will be identified as sectoral

information centers where large collection on a specific subject are already available to center to cater the needs of subject specialists, humanities, etc. These centers will be discipline wise such as science and technology, humanities, etc.

Services Provided by INFLIBNET

The INFLIBNET is intended to disseminate Indian information wealth worldwide by generating appropriate databases through a suitable network linked to internet. It also intend to organized specialized training programmes on networking, internet use, quality control in designing database management and user education.

INFLIBNET offers following services:

i. database service

ii. document supply services

iii. collection development

iv. Communication based services.

PROBLEMS IN THE IMPLIMENTATION

Some of the problems which are coming in the way of the successful implementation of INFLIBNET are:

i. Lack of clear cut policy in the financial assistance.

ii. In-correct identification of nature of expenditure involved in implementation.

iii. Transfer of allocated amount from one head to an other.

iv. The role of librarian is kept aside by the university/ institution authorizes while passing the amount to library.

v. In-sufficient allocation in certain cases.

vi. Procurement of hardware and software by the professionals who do not have adequate knowledge in the field.

vii. No check and monitoring for the requirements and expenditure by competent authorities.

viii. Mismanagement in creation and maintenance of databases created.

ix. And non-availability of professionally qualified computer personals for which UGC has sanctioned the post of 'information Scientists' but the universities are not filling up this position on one pretext or the other,

x. Lack of co-ordination between the authorities of the recipient university/institution and the authorities of INFLIBNET.

- It should be possible through such a system to search for books, no matter where it exists in the country and ask for an inter-library loan-irrespective of whether you belong to a newly set up university or laboratory and irrespective of your location.
- It should be ask to search and get copies of the abstracts of the latest paper published in any major journal through INFLIBNET fascinate service.
- Similarly, you should be also to get synopsis of any of the ten thousand thesis written in the country every year. You should be able to reach and get information from specialized data bank but together by different.
- If are make specific arrangement, it should also be possible to reach foreign data banks from anywhere in the country.
- Beside all these library services, one should be able to Interact with like-minded academic independent of distance and work together on common scientific problems.

- One can have a country wide bulletin board announcing special meeting and conferences and of course, special happening in academic, scientific and technical world.

The INFLIBNET is major national effort to improve information access in academic research and development institutions and other organizations of national importance. In the emerging Indian information society, INFLIBNET is not just a programme or a system, it is actually a kind of IT movement related to library and information systems in India. The scope of the INFLIBNET activities are very vast and challenging. Therefore, it is imperative that there must be a open support from all corners especially from the University sector with an active participation in order to make it a success. It is, now a wellestablished fact that the libraries in India especially the academic one are facing the crucial problems such as lack of adequate funds and manpower for automation and networking, the role of INFLIBNET to come across these problems is undisputedly recognized and accepted. It is hoped that in future the programme will achieve all goals and objectives successfully.

3. ERNET

The ERNET (Education and Research in Computer Network) was initiated by the Department of Electronics (DoE) during the seventh plan (1985-90). It is a computer network for academic and research community in India. Starting with 8 leading institutes the Indian Institute of Technology at Delhi, Bombay, and Madras, Kharagpur, The Indian Institute of Science, Bangalore and the National Centre for Software Technology, Bombay and the Department of Electronics, ERNET has already reached hundreds of academic/research institutions covering a number of scientific and engineering disciplines.

ERNET is the largest nationwide terrestrial and satellite

network with a presence in the premier educational and resource Institutions in major cities in country. The focus of ERNET is providing network connectivity and meeting the entire needs of educational and research institutions by hosting and providing relevant information to their users. Research and development and training are integral parts of ERNET activities.

ERNET has made a significant contribution to the emergence of networking in the country. It has built up national capabilities in the area of networking, especially in protocol software engineering. It has over the years become a trendsetter in the field of networking.

Objectives

The objectives of ERNET are to enhance national capabilities in the area of Design, Development, Research and training of state of art concepts of computer working and related emerging technologies. Immediate objectives are to set up a nation wide network for academic and research community starting with eight participating premier Institutions. Its services include electronic mail; file transfer, news remote log on, data base access, and conferencing and directory services. Multi vendor compiling environment is supported with an internetworking architecture with a variety of underlying sub- network via, campus LANs, WANs and packet radio based Metropolitan Area Network (MAN). ERNET proposes a massive training program to generate critical manpower needed by industry and users in the field. **Address**: Project Director (ERNET), Dept of Electronic, A-Block, 3rd floor, CGO Complex, New Delhi - 3.

The main objectives of ERNET can be submitted as follow:

- Research and Development
- Training and consultancy
- Content Development

Providing state of the art communication infrastructure and services to academic and research institutions, Government organizations, NGOs, private sector R & D organizations, and various other non-commercial organizations.

4. BONET

The Bombay Library Networks (BONET), sponsored by the NISSAT, aims at promoting cooperation among libraries in Bombay. The National Center for Software Technology (NCST) one of the first eight participating institution of ERNET, function as the central node of BONET. The NCST had made available an HP 827 mini computer (NOVA) with one gigabits disk and RDBMS software for inter library activities. The BONET will use local dial up PSTN communication facilities for linking the libraries, the member libraries are however urged to use leased lines to fully benefit from the online services. The BONET will offer training related to computerization and networking to the participating libraries.

23

Standards, Protocols and Formats for Digital Libraries

INTRODUCTION

Standards, formats and protocols are the rules by which objects are described, their data is stored and the systems communicate.

For sharing the digital library efforts at various places it is must that the digital library creation from the beginning itself follows some standards.

Standards within the context of digital library research encompass all protocols and conventions that have been set for digital library architectures, collections metadata formats, interoperability and so forth. This is a major challenge concerned with the development of a digital library. The following are some of the standards which have been the focus of research.

The evolving standards for creating, structuring and disseminating digital contents has allowed libraries to make shift from proprietary methods of information access and management that characterized the early days of electronic information.

Distributed computing and the emergence of standards was a critical step towards achieving a more unified information environment and interoperability among distributed collections and content providers.

These standards have offered libraries new opportunities for handling content (e.g., to add functionality, deliver content differently from different audience, or to sustain digital collections over time) and for enhancing the library's classic role in information access and preservation.

There are various categories of standards.

STANDARDS FOR DIGITAL PRESERVATION

Standards are essential for digital preservation. Though they were not developed for digital longevity, standards facilitate communication and acceptance and are useful to delay the ageing process. They should be merged together according to their identified categories. These standards and strategy have ensured the slowdown of ageing process of the digital materials. Long term preservation of the contents and its access for indefinite period of time has a lot of requirements concerning contents, law, organization and techniques etc.

Like rapid growth of digital objects, standards and formats are also proliferating. It creates a messy situation to choose standards for digital preservation. Therefore, in order to facilitate digital preservation in standardized way it is necessary to merge groups of standards into specific standards 'domain' and this will provide domain communication, acceptance and use of such groups of standards(Lorist; 2002).

Such domain standards would facilitates inter-operability among the desecrate storehouses of digital information.

For preservation of digital documents/information over time, the following types of standards are mentioned:

Standards for Architecture

In a distributed digital environment the management of digital collection cannot be responsibility of just one central organization. In such environment it is important to agree on concepts, definitions and procedures. For this there are several standards for record management architecture.

- ISO/DIS 15489
- AS 4390
- DoD 5015.2-STD
- OAIS (Open Archival Information System)

Standards for Preservation Contents

Standards for preservation contents should be depending upon aging process of the semantic and physical recoverability of document that is being preserved. A standard can only provide such longevity when the standard it self does not change and backward compatibility is provided. Therefore, for future preservation standard should be selected depending upon the technical obsolescence. More often XML and PDF are put forward as two rivals to preserve a document for long term preservation (Hagg; 2002.)

- PDF (Portable Document Format)
- XML (Extensible Markup Language)

Standards for Preservation Access

Preservation of the bit-stream of the document is in some standard format is not enough to preserve a digital document over an infinite period of time. So, it is necessary for the description of the digital, object or various parts into one object means file/formats stored in different physical places in the information system, and by linked by cross references. Such types of description are called metadata, which included the contextual information to manage, retrieve and interpret the electronic information over time (Dempsey; 1998)

Metadata for preservation and access carried out in different projects such as CEDEARS or PANDORA or NEDLIB or by RLG. The information involved in long term preservation metadata gives information about both preserved documents and information about the data processes of the digital objectives that are to be preserved by informing about format name , structure, application etc.(Lupvici and Masanes;2000). There are several existing metadata schemes that have been standardized, each having some specific goal.

- Dublin Core
- MARC
- ISAD (G)
- Z39.50

Standard for Interoperability

Interoperability is the ability of multiple systems with different hardware/software platform, data structure, and interface to exchange data with minimum loss of contents and functionality (understanding Metadata). Therefore, interoperability is a critical problem in the network environment with increase diverse computer systems software applications, file formats, information and users. But, it is important for digital preservation in digital library and archives. In fact digital conversion of traditional print based resources is important and standards pertaining to interoperability are so important.

- ODMA (Open Document APIO)
- DMA (Document Management Alliance)
- Web DAV (World Wide Web Distributed Authoring and Versioning)

Standards for Digitization

There are various types of standards required in the process of digitization:

1. Digital collection development standards.
2. Archiving and preservation standards.
3. Metadata formats such as Dublin Core, MARC etc.
4. Cataloging content and indexing standards.
5. Electronic publishing standards for books, journals and other media, OAI and Z39.50.

Some standards are international standards set by bodies like NISO (National Information Standard Organization) in US or BSA (British Standard Authority) in the U.K. Some of the standards are international standards set by bodies like ISO (International Standards Organization).

Standard may be bibliographic such as MARC, Dublin Core.

BIBLIOGRAPHIC STANDARD

These are concerned with the description of the material, both as to its content and to its physical and descriptive attributes. They are generally very complex (MARC has some 700 field definitions) and cover the most difficult, intellectual part of the object definition. These definitions are necessary for processing the material and also for searching for it.

1. Metadata and Dublin Core

Metadata: Traditional library cataloguing for digital resources is a kind of metadata creation. The identifying information the cataloger creates is metadata. So, far, digital materials follow the same procedures as books, videos, or, other materials. Metadata offers easier way to search and discover material, and being generated automatically from the databases, websites, images, or other electronic materials being transmitted. Metadata catalogers can also create Metadata manually, a process that is easier than traditional cataloguing. Once entered into the catalog system, metadata include links to the material

This is neither a standard nor a description. It is a currently very popular word, which correctly describes the class to which all the above descriptions belongs. It is literally 'data about data'. And thus is the description of the structure of the record, which actually holds the data. An item of metadata may describe an individual data item or a collection of data items. Metadata is used to facilitate the understanding, use and management of data. The metadata required for this will vary with the type of data and context of use. So in the context of a library, where the data is the content of the titles stocked, metadata about a title might typically include a description of the content, the author, the publication date and the physical location. Metadata about a collection of data items, a computer file, might typically include the name of the file, the type of the file and the name of the data administrator. Metadata about an individual data item might typically include the name of the field and its length.

Metadata are higher-level content pointers to original digitized data. Standards of metadata pose a challenge to libraries to ensure interoperability across digital libraries. In some cases only metadata are made available digitally. In such cases users search through pointers and must acquire the primary information physically or through a different medium.

When librarians think of metadata what comes most naturally to mind is descriptive metadata, such as author, title, or subject. Yet in addition to descriptive metadata, two additional types play essential roles. Administrative metadata facilitates rights management, preservation and documentation of software requirement. Without descriptive metadata, the maintenance of long term digital archives would be impossible. In addition, digital assets frequently require structural metadata that express relationships between individual digital files. Structural metadata can be used, for example, to create complex digital object that combine multiple digital files and associated metadata. Obvious use of structural metadata includes binding together separate page images into a virtual monograph or pairing a page image and its textual transcription.

A number of metadata standards are particularly important for repository development:

- **XML**: Provides the universal syntax used by DAM systems. XML is a subject of the SGML markup language that is used extensively by web applications to encode, manage and transmit data.
- **MARCXML**: developed and maintained by the Library of Congress, provides a framework for expressing full MARC records in XML. Because the protocol is capable of rendering completely the highly structured MARC record format, there are many possible use of MARCXML in library environment.
- **MODS (Metadata Object Description Scheme)**: is simplified version of the MARC standard expressed in XML. Because MODS is derived from MARC and provides a contains for hierarchical, structured metadata, in contrast to the flat Dublin Core framework, it is more compatible with library applications. A number of repository software applications are developing MODS support.
- **The Dublin Core**: One of the most frequently used metadata is also one of the least complicated. Dublin Core does not specify how the data should be entered.

  The Dublin Core Metadata Element Standards having

the "ISO-8859-1" is maintained for preparing metadata, a standard character encoding of the Latin alphabet.

Providing access to the internally created digital resources is very important. Therefore, a suitable software and format has to be chosen and adopted in order to access the resources using various data elements. It is necessary to catalog these digital resources using suitable software which support. Dublin core standard that is being adopted internationally to create metadata of digital resources. Metadata is data about the data and objects. This may be cataloged records, or web page or digital resource. Metadata record consists of a set of attributes, which are necessary to describe a resource. It is used to describe the digital and non-digital resources located in a distributed system, in a networked environment.

Dublin Core is another standard for record content and descriptive data. Much simpler than MARC (only 15 elements) and devised for use across the Internet to allow a common description for professionally cataloged material in libraries and for 'amateur' material at other web site. The Dublin Core Metadata is comprised of 15 elements that can be applied to a broad range of resources and shared across many disciplines and organizations. Dublin Core is the most frequently used descriptive metadata standard supported by DAM system and is a requirement of resource sharing via the OAI metadata harvesting protocol.

MARC and Dublin Core and data elements can be interchanged according to a prescribed scheme for user display purposes.

MARC VS Dublin Core

The MARC is difficult for non librarian to use. Librarian, especially catalogers, may see resemblance to MARC, in this type of data encoding. Unlike MARC, which also has protocols to identify data elements, Dublin Core does not specify how the data should be entered. A metadata cataloger can select any title to put into the title field. In contrast, MARC conforms to AACR2 and other library tools(LCSH, Dewey Decimal Classification, Library of Congress Classification etc. which have numerous rules governing how to select and enter data for every element. This makes MARC difficult for non librarian to use. On the other hand Dublin Core is easy to apply for librarians and non librarians alike, but it allows for confusion when different metadata catalogers enter different title(cover title, spine title etc) for the same material or use multiple terms for the same subject. Dublin Core is general metadata element set, but is not the only one used in the library community.

The Dublin Core Metadata elements set is a vocabulary of fifteen properties for use in resource discipline like:

1. Title
2. Creator
3. Subject or keyword
4. Description
5. Publisher
6. Contributor
7. Data of publication
8. Document type
9. Format
10. Identifier
11. Source
12. Language
13. Relation
14. Coverage
15. Rights

The following tags/elements are also used:

1. Copyright data

2. Scanning center
3. Scanning number
4. Digital republishes and
5. Digital publication date.

The Dublin core metadata standards have been developed during the past few years with two main purposes. One has been support "simple resource discovery" for digital collections. The second has been to provide a kind of "lingua franca", with the potential to integrate access to the digital services of libraries with those of institutions such as museums and archives, and with access to the wider universe of web based resources.

Each stored document (in folder) contains five sub-folders namely HTML, OTIFF, PTIFF, RTF, TXT, and Metadata Tag.

HTML: It contains the link among the pages.

OTIFF: It contains original scanned image.

PTIFF: It contains processed image (i.e. after the OCR)

RTF: Rich Text File.

TXT: It contains text file.

Some of the existing worldwide meta-data standards are as follows:

- The international Standard Organization's (ISO) metadata Working Group has a related standard, ISO 11179, specification and standardization of data elements. It may also be available to private sector, civil societies and citizens.
- The American National Standards Institute (ANSI) has established the NCITS L8 (formally X3L8), the National Committee on Information Technology Standards. The committee covers naming, identification, definitions, classification, and registration of metadata.

- The World Wide Web Consortium (W3C), a major governing body of the web has developed de facto standards including RDF (Resource Description Framework) and the platform for Internet Content Selection (PICS) specifications. PICS was originally intended to aid adult in continuing children's access to the internet. However, its standard is usually at a very general level over which meta standards can be imposed.
- The National Special Data Infrastructure (NSDI) has developed an NSDI metadata standard for special data.

Some of the selected projects implementing the following metadata standards:

1. Cooperative Online Research Catalog (OCLC)
2. Medical Metadata Project (Oregon Health Sciences University etal)
3. Gateway to Educational Materials(U.S. Department of Education)

3. MARC

MARC is a standard for recording bibliographic data in the logical level. It contains elements for both contents and physical and process description. This is not a single standard, but rather a framework. Within which each country has developed an individual standard. USMARC is the only closet thing to a universal standard generally maintained by an office within the relevant National Library. The USMARC office within the Library of Congress maintains USMARC.

EAD: (Encoded Archival Description) : Is designed for encoding archival findings aids , inventories and other record types created by archives, museums and libraries. EAD provides collection-level description of archival materials. It is defined with a minimum number of descriptive elements, but in an extensible fashion. It is designed to create descriptive records, which will assists in searching for the original material in a number of ways.

Z39.50 STANDARD

There are several technologies available to implement real time search , like Z39.50.These are basically kinds of protocol on which application services can be developed. The 'http' is the protocol of the www that is most widely used for hosting different services including various web transactions and mail. The Z39.50 standard specifies a client /server based protocol for searching and retrieving information from databases. In other words Z39.50 is a protocol which specifies data structures and interchange rules that allows a client machine (called "origin" in the standard)to search databases on a server machine (called "target" in the standard) and to retrieve records that are identified as a result of such a search. This specification describes the application service definition and the protocol specification for real time searching." Z 39.50" refers to the international standard, ISO 23950: information retrieval (Z39.50): Application Service Definition and Protocol Specification)" and to ANSI/NISO Z39.50—1995.It is maintained by International Standards and Maintenance Agency, Library of Congress.

Basically, Z39.50 is designed to enable communication by specifying both a general framework for transmitting and managing quarries between computers, typically those containing huge bibliographic data, like library catalog.

Apprehension about Z39.50

It is still under development for different extensions as well as for basic element mapping

1. Not widely used
2. It is too complex to implement.
3. It is often deemed that is not required anymore as we have web.

4. It sometimes does not work due to complications in implementation.

But,

1. It is fairly matured standard.
2. Fairly widely implemented for LIS.
3. Organization like museums, art galleries, archives have started using it. Latest version supports non - bibliographic information.
4. It is still useful in web environment. In fact, web provides access to more than one Z39.50 enabled backend databases.
5. It promises interoperability across databases.
6. Supports maintenance of centralized union catalogs.

Glossary

ANALOG: Representations of information or data by some physically measurable quantity. Computers cannot process analog data unless they are first translated into digital format.

ARCHIVE: Collections with related system and services, organized to emphasize the long-term preservation of information.

ARTIFACT: A physical object in a library, archive, or museum.

AUTHORIZATION: Given permission to a user or client computer to access specific information and carry out approved actions.

BOOK SCANNING: is a process of converting physical or print books into digital images, electronic text, or electronic books by using image scanners etc. It may be manual or automated.

BORN DIGITAL: digital materials which are not intended to have an analogue equivalent, either as the organizing source or as a result of conversion to analog form. This term has been used in the hand book to differentiate them from:

1. Digital materials, which have been created as a result of converting analog originals and
2. Digital materials which may have originated from a

digital source but have been printed to paper e.g. some electronic resources.

BROWSER: A general-purpose user interface used with the web and other online information services. Also known as web browser. The basic function of a browser is to retrieve a remote file from a web server and render it on the user's computer.

CHAT: One of the services available to users of the Internet and some online services. Using special chat software or web based chatting tools, users can exchange massages with one another in real time.

CLIENT: A computer that acts on behalf of a user, including a user's personnel computer, or another computer that appears to a server to have that function.

COLLECTION: A group of materials assembled by a library or a previous owner. A collection consists of both physical items held by the library and digital resources currently selected and organized by the library and accessed by library users.

COMPESSION: Reduction in the size of digital materials by removing redundancy or by approximation; loss less compression can be reversed; lossy compression can not be reversed since information is lost by approximation.

CONSERVATION: Physical or chemical methods employed to ensure the survival of manuscripts, books, and other documents.

CONSORTIUM: Two or more libraries that have formally agreed to coordinate, cooperate in, or consolidate certain functions. Consortia may be formed on a geographic, function, type, format, or subject basis.

COPYRIGHT: A set of exclusive rights to permits or forbid particular use of a work for a specified period of time. Copyrights gives the author, the author's employer, or anyone to whom the author transfer his or her right the legal ability to control who may copy, adapt, distribute, publicly perform, or publicly display his or her work, subject to certain legal expectations.

CORE: A project from 1991 to 1995 by Bllcore, Cornell University, OCLC, and the American Chemical Society to convert chemistry journals to digital form.

DATA: Raw facts, numbers, letters, or symbols that the computer processes into meaningful information.

DATABASE: In computer usage, a collection of electronic records, such as computerized index of journal articles, which can usually be searched. In computer usage, an collection of electronic records, such as computerized index of journal articles, which can usually be selected. A large storage of digitized information, consisting of records of uniform format organized for ease and speed of search and retrieval and managed by a database management system.

DATA COMPRESSION: The process of reducing data volume and increasing data transfer rates by using mathematical algorithms to analyses groups of bits and encode repeating sequences of data.

DATATYPE: Structural metadata associated with digital data that indicates the digital format or the application used to process the data.

DESKTOP COMPUTER: A full size personal computer whose system unit is designed to sit on top of desk or table; such computers are not considered to be portable. One variation of the desktop model is the tower model, whose system unit can stand upright on the floor.

DIGITAL: The use of numerals 1 and 0 (digits) to express data in a computer. The computer recognizes the numeral 1 as an “on” state of a transistor, whereas a 0 represents “off” state.

DIGITAL ACCESS: Defined as continued ongoing usability of a digital resource, retaining all qualities of authenticity, accuracy and functionality deemed to be essential for the purpose the digital material.

DIGITAL ARCHIVING: this term is used very differently within sectors. The library and archiving communities often used it interchangeably with digital preservation. Computing professionals tend to use digital archiving to mean the process of backup and ongoing maintenance as opposed to strategies for long term digital preservation.

DIGITAL ARCHEOLOGY: The process of retrieving information from damaged, fragmentary, and archaic data sources.

DIGITAL CAMERA: A camera that converts light intensities into digital data. Digital cameras are used to record images that can be viewed and edited on a computer.

DIGITAL LIBRARY: is a collection of multimedia and other types of resources. A managed collection of information with associated services where the information is stored in digital format and accessible over a network.

DIGITAL LIBRARIES: digital libraries basically store material in electronic format and manipulate large collections of those materials effectively.

DIGITAL LIBRARY FEDERATION: The federation is comprised of leaders of 15 of the nation's largest research libraries and archives and the commission on Preservation and Access (CPA). A primary goal of the Federation is the implementation of a distributed, open digital library accessible across the global Internet.

DIGITAL LIBRARY RESOURCES: The resources of digital library are those, which the computer can store, organized, transmit and display without any intervening conversion process. Examples e-journals, e-books, etc.

DIGITAL LIGHT PROCESSING: A technology used in some types of digital projectors to project bright, crisp images. DLP devices use a special microchip, called a digital micro mirror device, which uses mirrors to control the image display. DLP projectors can display clear images in normal lightning condition.

DIGITAL MATERIALS: A broad term encompassing digital surrogates created as a result of converting analog materials to digital form (digitization), and "born digital" for which there has been never been and is never intended to be an analogue equivalent and digital record. Both digital surrogates created by converting analog materials to digital format and "born digital" materials for which there is no analog equivalent.

DIGITAL OBJECT: An item as stored in a digital library, consisting of data, metadata, and an identifier.

DIGITAL PRESERVATION: Digital preservation or digital archiving means taking steps to ensure the longevity of digital documents. It applies to the documents that are either "born digital" and stored on-line. A process by which data is preserved in digital form in order to ensure usability, durability and intellectual integrity of the information contained therein is called digital preservation. Digital preservation refers to the series of managed activities necessary to ensure continued access to digital materials for as long as necessary. Digital preservation is a long term; error free storage of digital information, with means for retrieval and interpretation, for entire time span, the information is required.

Preservation may be:

Long Term Preservation: continued access to digital materials, or at least to the information contained in them, indefinately

Medium Term Preservation: continued access to digital materials beyond changes in technology for a defined period of time but not indefinately.

Short Term Ppreservation: Access to digital materials

either for a defined period of while use is predicted but which does not extended beyond the foreseable future and/ or until it becomes inaccessible because of changes in technology.

DIGITIZATION: Is the process to convert an image or a sound into a series of binary numbers (1s and 0s) that can be stored in a computer. Is the process of converting analog materials to digital. The process of creating digital files by scanning or otherwise converting analog materials. The resulting digital copy, or digital surrogates, would then be classed as digital material and then subject to the same broad challenges involved in preserving access to it, as "born digital" material.

DIGITAL IMMAGE: digital images are digital snapshots taken of scene or scanned from documents, such as books, photographs, manuscripts, artwork etc.

DIGITAL PUBLICATIONS: "born digital" objects which have been released for public access and either made available or distributed free of charge or for a fee. They may consist of networked publications, available over a communications network or physical format publications, which are distributed on formats such as floppy or optical discs. They may also be either static or dynamic.

DOCUMENT: An object that comprises intellectual or artistic contents or both and is conceived, produced, and issued as an entity.

DPI: (Dot Per Inch): A measure of resolution commonly applied to printers, scanners, and other devices that input or output text or images. The more dots per inch, the higher the resolution. For example, if a printer has resolution of 600 dpi, it can print 600 dots across and 600 down in a one-inch square, for a total of 360,000 dots in one squire inch.

D-LIB MAGAZINE: A monthly, online publication about digital libraries research and innovation.

DOMAIN NAME: The name of a computer on the Internet; the Domain Name Service (DNS) convert domain names to IP address

DUBLIN CORE: A simple set of 15 metadata elements (title, subject etc.) used in digital libraries, primarily to describe digital objects and for collections management, and for exchange of metadata. Dublin core now used also for describing physical and digital collection in archives, museums, libraries, and other repositories.

ELECTRONIC BOOK OR E-BOOK: A book created in digital format, or converted from print to digital format, for electronic distribution.

ELECTRONIC JOURNAL OR E-JOURNAL: A serial publication available in digital format. An online publication that is organized like a traditional printed journal, either an online version of a printed journal or a journal that has only an online existence. These are available via computer rather in paper form. Scholarly periodicals, which are available via computer rather than in, paper format.

ELECTRONIC RECORD or DIGITAL RECORD: Records created digitally in the day-to-day business of the organization and assigned formal status by the organization. They may include for example: word processing documents, emails, databases or Internet web pages.

E-MAIL ADDRESS : An address that identifies an individual user of an electronic mail system, enabling the person to send and receive e-mail messages. The e-mail address

EMULATION : A means of overcoming technological obsolescence of hardware and software by developing techniques for imitating obsolete system on future generation of computer. Techniques for initiating obsolete computer systems on future generations of computers and thus providing continued access to digital contents.

EUROPEON DIGITAL LIBRARY CONSORTIUM (ERCIM): The European Research Consortium for Informatics aims to foster collaborative work within the European research community and to increase cooperation with European industry. Leading research establishments from 14 European countries are members of ERCIM.

FEDERATED DIGITAL LIBRARY: A group of digital libraries that support common standards and services, thus providing interoperability and a coherent service to users.

FLAT BED SCANNER: A type of optical scanner that consists of a flat surface on which we can lay documents to be scanned. Flat bedded scanners are particularly effective for bound documents.

FTP: (File Transfer Protocol): A set of rules that dictate the format in which data is sent from one computer to another. In computerized database, the complete article rather than just a citation or abstract.

GENRE: The class or category of an object when considered as an intellectual work.

HTML: (Hyper Text Markup Language): The document format used on the World Wide Web.HTML files is small, making them easy to store, transmit and download. Browser allow the end user to select the typeface and font size for displaying HTML, so that it is user friendly and accessible. HTML which includes graphics is sometimes called illustrated HTML. A simple markup and formatting language for text, with links to other objects, used with the web. HTML is the central protocol of the web, but browsers also support other protocols.

HTTP: (Hyper -Text Transport Protocols): The basic protocols of the web, used for communication between browsers and web site.

J-STORE: A subscription service, initiated by the Andrew W. Mellon Foundation, to convert back runs of important journals and make them available to academic libraries.

IMMAGE SCANNER: An input device that digitizes printed images. Sensors determine the intensity of light reflected from the page, and the light intensities are converted to digital data that can be viewed and manipulated by the computer. Sometimes called simply a scanner.

INHOUSE RESOURCES: Any resource developed by and for a local archive, library, or other repository, and generally used by that library.

INTERNET: A worldwide network of millions of computers connected to share information and communication, also known as the "information highway".

KEYWORD SEARCH: A search of an online library catalog or other database in word or words are used, rather than only specified subject headings.

LINUX: A freely available version of the UNIX operating system. Developed by a worldwide cooperative of programmers in the 1990s, Linux is a feature-rich, 32bit, multi-user, multiprocessor operating system that runs on virtually any hardware platform.

MARC: (Machine Readable Cataloguing): A format used by libraries to store and exchange catalog records.

METADATA: Data about data. Includes information describing aspects of actual data items, such as name, format, content, and the control of or over data. Commonly divided into descriptive metadata such as bibliographic information, structural metadata about formats and structures, and administrative metadata, which is used to manage information.

MPEG: A family of formats for compressing and storing digitized video and sound.

MULTIMEDIA: A combination of several media types in a single digital object or collection, e.g. images, audio, video.

OCR: (Optical Character Recognition): Automatic conversion of text from a digitized image to computer text. After a page of text has been scanned, OCR software examines the resulting dots, converts the dots to letters and so recreates the text. A technique of converting scanned images of characters to their equivalent characters, which then can be edited.

OCLC: (Online Computer Library System): An organization that provides, among other services, a bibliographic utility for libraries to share catalogue records.

ONLINE: Available via a connection between two computers.

OUTSOURCING: outsourcing is contracting with other company or person or organization to do a particular function. It is service provided that might otherwise be performed by in-house employees.

PDF: (Portable Document Format): A format that allows documents created on one platform to be displayed and printed exactly the same on other. Adobe Acrobat Reader is free software used to read and display PDF files.

PORTALS: Windows on a zooming work surface which can be used to bring distant regions close, to give simultaneous views at multiple scales, or, when given special active functionality, to create magic lenses. A website offering a wide variety of resources, services and links, especially one offering services within a particular field or services to a particular user.

PRESERVATION: preservation is an activity concerned with maintaining or restoring documents etc. for protecting from loss or decay. See also Digital Preservation.

RDF : (Resource Description Framework): A method of specifying the syntax of metadata, used to exchange metadata.

REFERENCE SOURCES: Material in the library, which are usually consulted for specific information rather than read from cover to cover. Example of reference sources includes encyclopedias, dictionaries, handbooks, directories etc.

REFERESHING: copying information contents from one storage media to the same storage media.

REFORMATING: Copying information contents from one storage medium to a different storage medium (media reformatting) or converting from one file format to a different file format (file reformatting)

REPLICATION: Make copies of digital material for backup, performance, reliability, or preservation.

REPOSITORIES: A repository is any computer system whose primary function is to store digital material for use in library. They can be huge or tiny, storing millions of digital objects or just a single object.

SCANNER: scanner a device that captures images from documents and similar sources. There are various types of scanners such as handheld, feed-in, flat bed type etc. It may be black and white or colored. Scanners are generally attached to personnel computers.

SCANNING: Scanning is the process, which involves conversion of paper document into electronic image using image scanner, digital camera and other such devices. Method of conversion in which a physical object, e.g., a printed page, is represented by a digital grid of pixels.

SEARCH ENGINE: On the Internet, indexing tool developed to allow user to search for information by entering a subject. On the internet, indexing tool developed to allow users to search for information by entering a subject.

SERVER: Any computer on a network, other than a client, that stores collections or provides services.

STEMMING: In information retrieval, reduction of morphological variants of a word to a common stem.

STORAGE MEDIA : Storage of the scanned image from hard disk of scanning workstations to external storage devices such as CD-ROM, DVD. etc.

TEI: (Text Encoding Initiative): A project to represents texts in digital form, emphasizing the needs of humanities scholars. Also the DTD used by the programme.

TIFF: Tagged Image File Format is a file format for storing images, including photographs, manuscripts etc.

URL: Uniform Resource Locator, the unique address which identifies a resource on the Internet for routing purposes.

UNICODE: A 16 bit code to represents the characters used in most of the world's scripts. UTF-8 is an alternative encoding in which one or more 8-bit bytes represent each Unicode character.

WEBCRAWLER: A web-indexing programme that builds an index by following hyperlinks continuously from web page to web page. It builds an ever-increasing index of web pages by repeating a few basic steps.

WEB SEARCH SERVICES: Commercial services that provide searching of the web, including: yahoo, AltaVista, Lycos etc.

WEBSITE: A website is a collection of information that the user perceives to be a single unit. Often a web site corresponds to a single web server; however, a large site may be physically held on several servers, and one server may host many websites. A collection of information on the web; usually stored on a web server.

WWW (World Wide Web) : An interlinked set of

information sources on the Internet, and the technology they use, including HTML, HTTP, URLs, and MIME.

Z39.50: A protocol that allows computer to search collections of information on a remote system, create set of results for further manipulation, and retrieve information; mainly used for bibliographic information.

Bibliography

1. ALDRICH (DM) and STEFANELLI (G). Library services for the digital future. Education Quarterly (*http: //www. ifla. org*)
2. ALI (Amjad). Internet and the university Libraries. University News. 39, 17; 6-10.
3. AMUDHAVLLI (A). Impact of electronic Publishing on collection development. DESIDOC Bull of Inf. Tech. 17, 1; 1997; 7-10.
4. ANANDAN (C). and GANGATHARAN (M), eds. Digital libraries : from technology to culture. Delhi; Kanishka; 2006.
5. ARORA (Jagdish). Building digital Libraries: an overview. DESIDOC Bull of Inf. Tech. 21, 6; 2001; 3-11.
6. ARORA (Jagdish). Web based digital resources and services: trends and innovation, CALIBER 2001, 15-16 March 2001, Pune; 185-212.
7. ASHOK BABU (T) and others. Vision of future Library and Information Systems. Viva Books; New Delhi; 2000.
8. ASHOOR (MS). Planning the electronic Library - Suggested guidelines for the Arabian Gulf region. The Electronic Library. 18, 1; 2000; 29-39
9. ALURI (Rao). Electronic publishing : Imfolding of an information. DESIDOC Bull of Inf. Technology. 16, N1; 1996; 3-8.

10. BALDO NA DO (M) and others. The Stanford Digital Library Metadata architecture. International J of Digital Libraries. 1, 2; 1997; 108-121.

11. BANERJEE (Swapna) and CHAKRABORTHY(Biplap). Digital Libraries: some issues and perspectives. ILA Bull. 34, 3-4; 1998-99-; 60-63.

12. BANSODE(SY) and PUJAR(SM). Use of internet by research scholars at Shivaji University Kolhapur. Annals of Library and Information Studies. 53, . 123-126; 2008

13. BARKER (PG). Electronic books and Libraries of 'The future. The Electronic Library. 10, N3; 1992; 139-149.

14. BARKER (PG). Electronic Libraries: vision of the future. The Electronic Library. 12, N4; 1994; 221-230.

15. BARKER (PG). Living books and dynamic Electronic Libraries. The Electronic Library. 14, 6; 1996; 491-501.

16. BANERJEE (SK). Electronic journals: A new era. IASLIC Bull. 44, 2; 1999; 61-8

17. BAWDEN, (D) and VILLAR (P). Digital libraries: to meet or manage user expectations. ASLIB Proceedings, 58, 4, 2006.

18. BHASIN (S) and Arora (A). Internet in present scenario. IASLIC Bull. 48, 3; 2003; 178-179.

19. BONHAM (Mariam). Library services through electronic mail. College and Research Libraries News. 48, 9; 1987; 537-38

20. BORSE (TR). Information and information Technology. IASLIC Bull. 46, 2; 2001; 81-89.

21. BROERING (NC). Changing forms: Tomorrow's virtual Library. The Serial Librarian. 23, 3-4; 1994; 73-94.

22. BROWN (DJ). Electronic publishing and Libraries. London Bowker-Sur, 1996.

23. BURTONC (PF) and MOORE (C), Eds. CD-ROM : a

practical guide for information professionals. 2nd ed. London, UK; OLUG and LITC, 1994.

24. CHANDRA (Ravi S) and SHARMA (RK). Are we ready for digital Library? Herald of Lib. Sc. 39; 2000; 11-17.
25. CHOWDHURY (CG). Text retrieval Systems in information management. New Delhi; New Age Publication; 1996.
26. CHOWDHURY (CG) and CHOWDHURY (Sujata). Introduction to digital Libraries. London; Facet Publishing. 2003; p. 285-286.
27. CHOPRA (HS). Library Information technology in modern era. New Delhi; Common Wealth Pub. ; 1999.
28. CONWAY (Paul). Digital preservation: Paper and microfilm go electronic. Library Journal. 119, 1; 1994; 42-45.
29. CRAWFORD (W). The danger of digital Library. The Electronic Library; 16, 1, 1998; 28-30.
30. CYRIAC (JIJI) and others. Digitization of Libraries: in modern Era. ILA Bull. 38, 3; 2002; 68-73.
31. DALAL (BK). Libraries in the context of Electronic era. Paper presented at 44th ILA Conference held at Hyderabad during Feb. 25-28, 1999; p138-143.
32. DAS (S) . Access to Internet in R & D Libraries and Information Centers. Library Progress (International). 19, 1-2, 13-14, 1999.
33. DEEGAN (M) and TANNER (S). Digital Futures: strategies for information age. London Library Association; 2002; 72.
34. DEMPSEY (D). Prospects for the global Internet: new techniques for delivering Rich digital collection to user worldwide. The Electronic Library. 16, 4; 2000; 253-265.

35. DHAKA (RPS) and ARORA (K). Electronic Library: a myth or a reality. Annals of Lib. Sc. and DOC. 42, 2; 1995; 152-159.

36. DHIMAN (AK). Modern technology in resource sharing for information handling. Library Progress. 16, 2; 1998; 19-21.

37. DURRELL (William R) . Data administration: a practical guide to data administration. London; McGraw - Hill; 1985.

38. FALK (Howard) . Developing digital Libraries. The Electronic Library. 21, 3; 2003; 256-261.

39. FOSTER (Janet B) . Web reference: a virtual Reality. Public Libraries. 38, 2; 1994; 94-95.

40. FOX (EA) and LUMIN (L). Introduction and overview to perspective on Digital Libraries. JASIS. 44, 8; 1993; 441 - 443.

41. GOPAL KRISHAN. Intellectual Freedom in Digital Libraries. Delhi, Authors Press; 2001; 15-16.

42. GOVERNMENT OF INDIA. The Copyright Act 1957 as amended by the Copyright (Amendment) Act 1994.

43. GRAHAM (P Cornish). Copyright. 2nd ed. London; Library Association. 1997; pp. 131.

44. GREENSTEIN (D). Digital Libraries and their challenges. Library Trends. 49, 2; 2000; 290-303.

45. GUPTA (RC). Digital Libraries : an amazing reality, vision of future Library and information systems. Viva Books; New Delhi, 2000 : pp. 225-229.

46. GULATI (Anjali). Implications of electronic Publishing on Library and Information Centers. Annal of Lib. Sc. And DOC. 46, 4; 1999; 121 -125.

47. HARTER (Stephen P) . Scholarly Communication and the digital Library : problems and issues. J of Digital Inf. 1; 1997; 4-14.

48. HARVEY (C Ross). Preservation in Libraries : principals, strategies and practices for Librarians. London: Bowker - Saur, 1993.

49. HULSER (Richard P). Digital library content presentation in a digital world. DESIDOC Bull. of Inf. Technology. 17, 6; 1997.

50. HUMAYYOON KABIR (S). Towards Digital Libraries. ILA Conference Volume. 1996; p. 445-453.

51. IRELAND (Lee). The web and resource sharing. The Electronic Library. 17, 2; 1999; 63 -65.

52. IYER (VK). Library automation and networking in India. New Delhi. 1999.

53. IYER(VK). Networking and future of libraries. Rajat Publications; Delhi, 1999.

54. JAGTAR SINGH and KALRA (HPS). Digital Libraries: new mechanism for Horizontal and vertical integration of Information. In N. M. Malwad etc. eds. Digital Libraries. Bangalore; New Age, 1996.

55. JEEVAN (VKJ). Electronic information services: are we turning away users or are they by passing Libraries ?. Herald of Library Science. 41; 2002; 16 -25.

56. JENG (J). Usability assessment of academic digital libraries: effectiveness, efficiency satisfaction, and learnability. LIBRI, 55, 2005; 96-121.

57. JONSON (Arthur W). The Practical guide to book repair and conservation. London; Thomes and Hudson. 1988.

58. KAPILA (Nandita) and RASTOGI (SP). Digital Libraries: The social implication. Proceeding of XVII IASLIC National Seminar, Calcutta, 1996; pp. 13-19.

59. KELLER (MA) . Libraries in the digital future. Science. 1998; 1461-1462.

60. KENNEY (AR) and CHAPMAN (S). Digital imaging for Libraries and Archives. New York; Cornel University.

1996; p. 198.

61. KRISHAN KUMAR. Library management in electronic environment. Delhi; Har-Anand, 2001.
62. KUNNY (T) and CLEVELAND (G). The Digital Library; with and challenges. IFLA Journal. 24, 2; 1998; 107 - 13.
63. LANKES (RD) and others. Digital Reference Service in the new millennium: planning Management and evaluation. London; Near-Schcman; 2002.
64. LAWRENCE (S) and GILES (CL). Searching the World Wide Web. Science. 280, 5360; 98-100.
65. LESK (M). Practical digital Libraries: Books bytes and bucks. San Francisco; Morgan Kaufman. 1997.
66. LEST (M). Going digital. Scientific American. 1996; 58 -60.
67. LILI (L) Leveraging quality web based library user services in the digital age. Library Management. 27, 6/ 7/; 390-400; 2006.
68. LIPOW (Anne Grodzins) . Reference service in Digital age. Reference and User Services Q. 38, 51 (1); 1998.
69. LOMBARDI (JV). Academic Libraries in a digital age. D-Lib. Magazine. 6, 10-18.
70. LUKASIEWICZ(A). Exploring the role of digital academic libraries. Library Review. 56, 9; 2007; 821-827.
71. MAHAPATRA (PK) and CHAKRABRATI (B). Preservation in Libraries : perspective 'Principal and practice. New Delhi; Ess Ess Publication; 2008-2009.
72. MAHESSWARAPPA (BS) and TADASAD (PG) Collection development in context of electronic Publishing and networking : problems and prospect. DESIDOC Bull of Inf. Tech. 17, 1; 1997; 25 -31
73. MALIN CONICO (SM) and WARTH (JC). Electronic

Libraries : how soon. Program. 30, 2; 1996; 133 -148.

74. MALWAD (NM) and other. Digital Libraries. New Delhi; New Age. 1996.

75. MALWAD (NM) and other. Digital Libraries. : dynamic store house of Digitized information. New Delhi; New Age International. 1996.

76. MARCHIONINI (G). Information seeking In electronic environments. Cambridge University Press. New York. 1995.

77. MARCHIONINI (G). Reserch and Development in digital Libraries in Encyclopedia of Library and Information Science. Mercel Decker; New York. 1988. vol. 63; pp. 259-280.

78. MARCHIONINI(G). Evaluating digital libraries: a longitudinal and multifaceted view. Library Trends. 49, 2, 2000; 304-333.

79. MARCUM (Deawa B). Digital Libraries; For whom ? Journal of Academic Librarianship. 23, 2; 1997; 81-84.

80. McKNIGHT (C) Electronic journals past and future. ASLIB Proceedings, 45, 1, 1993; 7-10.

81. MINCHEW (Tessa LH). Collection development for an electronic library. Missicippi Libraries, 66, 4, 110-112.

82. MING (Ding Choo). Access to digital Information : some break through And obstacles. J of Librarianship and Inf. Science. 32, 1; 2000; 26-32.

83. MISRA(J). and SATYANARAYANA (NR). Users of internet in a university library : a case study. ILA Bulletin. 37, 4; 132-134; 2001.

84. NATRAJAN (M) and PERUMAL (R). Impact of new information Technology; ILA Bull. 4, 2; 1979; 189-205.

85. NEELAMEGHAM (A). Information and Communication Technology (ICTS) and Developing Countries. IASLIC Bull. 41, 1; 1996; 12-13.

86. NOERC (Peter) . The digital Library Tool Kits. California : 1998.
87. PANDIAN (Paul M) and JAMDHEKAR(Ashok). Internet for library and information centers. Delhi: Tata Mcgraw-Hill; 2001.
88. PARKERS (M). A review of the preservation Issues associated with digital documents. Australian Library Journal. 48, 4; Nov; 1999; 358-377.
89. PATEL (DR) and SHARMA (RS). DigitalLibrary: a need of tomorrow in planner - 2003. ed by T. A. V. Murthy. Ahemdabad, INFLIBNET Center. 2003; p. 365-370.
90. RAITTC (D). Digital Libraries Conference Report on NIT 99. The Electronic Library. 17, 5; 1999; 287-288.
91. RAJASHEKHAR (TB). Digital Libraries: Attributes and architectures. Digital Libraries: Dynamic store house of digital information. Ed. MN. Malwad and others. 1996; 192-206.
92. RAMIAH (CK). Electronic publishing trends in India. Serials. 19, (2) July; 2006; 142-154.
93. RAMESH (LSRCU). Need for preparing Information professionals for a digital era. Indian J of Inf. Library and Socity. 14, 1-2; 2001; 43-45.
94. RATHORE (RS). Digital Libraries: A boon for resource sharing and Networking. Viva Books; New Delhi; 2000; pp195-199.
95. RAVI CHANDERA RAO (IK). Impact of Recent advance in IT on collection Development. DESIDOC Bull of Inf. Tech. 17, 1; 1997; 3-6.
96. ROTHENBERG (J). Ensuring the longevity of digital document. Scientific American 40, 3; 1995; 72-115.
97. ROWLEY (Jennifer). The Electronic Library. 4th ed. London; Library Association; 1998; pp390.

98. ROWLEY (JE). And HARTLEY (R) . Organizing knowledge: an introduction to managing access to information, 2009.

99. SALTON (G). Automatic information Organization retrieval. New York: McGraw- Hill 1968.

100. SARACEVIC (T). Digital library evaluation; towards an evaluation of concepts. Library Trends, 49, 3, 350-369; 2000.

101. SATIJA (MP). Digital Information System and services. IASLIC Bull. 48, 1; 2003; 10-15.

102. SCHATZC (Bruce R). Information Retrieval in digital Libraries: bringing Search to the net. Science. 275; 1997; 327-33.

103. SCHWEINSBURG (Jame D). Research and development in digital Libraries. Encyclopedia of Library and Information Science. New York, Marcel Dekkar. 1998; 63; pp. 259-278.

104. SHARMA (PC) and ARORA (IP). Building a digital Library: a need of present Environment. Herald of Library Science. 44; 2005; 39-44.

105. SHARMA (RK) and VISHWANATHAN (KR). Digital Libraries: development and challenges. *Library Review.* 50, 1; 2001; 10-16.

106. SHARMA (Sumati) and others. Digital Reference Service. DESIDOC Bull. of Inf. Tech. 24, 6; 2004; 11-18.

107. SHERBINI (Magada EL). Metadata and the future cataloguing. Library Review. 50, 1; 2001; 18-27.

108. SHREEVES (E). is there a future for Co-operative collection development in Digital age? Library Trend. 4, 3; 1997; 379-390.

109. SIDDIQUE (Jamal Ahmad) and RANA (M). Electronic emergence in modern Libraries. Library Progress (International). 21, 1; 2001.

110. SINGH (NEENA) . Internet: importance and usage for library and information Professionals. DESIDOC Bull of Inf. Technology. 23, 3; 2001; 17-28.

111. SINGH (SONAL)and SINGH (Surendra) . Role of Librarians in electronic information era. New Delhi; ESS ESS, 2002; 212-216.

112. SINGH (Prem) and KHANNA (JK). Information technology in Libraries. Pragrati Publication, New Delhi. 1994.

113. SIRURMATH (S Sangayya) and others, ed. Electronic Libraries. P. Sadasiva Murthy Festschrift, Mumbai; Allied, 2002.

114. SIVASUBRA MANIAN (V). Virtual information centers : vision of information aid. IASLIC Bull. 47; 2002; 107-109.

115. SMITH (TR). Meta information in digital Libraries Information. J of DigitalLibraries. 1; 1997; 105-107.

116. STEWART (Grainger). Emulation at a Digital preservation strategy. D Lib. Magazine. 6, 10; 2000.

117. TENNANT (R). Skills for a new Millennium. Library Journal. 124; 1999; 139.

118. TENOPIR (Carol). Online scholarly journals. How many? Library Journals. 2, 1, 2004.

119. VARALAKSHMI(RSR). Collection management in digital environment : policy statement for university libraries in India. SRELS Journal of Information Mnagement. 41, 1, March 2004; 77-90.

120. VEERANJANEYULA (K) and RAMESH (LSRCV). Digital libraries : the pillars of quality Assurance. Paper presented at ILA National Seminar held during Jan. 2001 at Ahamdabad; 355-357.

121. WAKHARE (AS) and ABDULJALEEL (T). Collection development in electronic Era. DESIDOC Bull of Inf.

Tech. 17, 1; 1997; 221-223.

122. WAN ABDUL KADIR WAN DOL. Determining the effectiveness of digital reference service in selected academic libraries in Malaysia. PhD Thesis, University of Malaysia, 2008.

123. WHITAKERC (Becki). Electronic mail in Library: a perspective. Library Trends. 37, 3; 1989; 357-65.

124. WITTEN (I. H) and BAI NBRIDGE (D). How to build a digital library? San Francisco : Morgan Kaufman, 2003.

125. WOODS (LB). Networking: . Resource sharing and Information Networks Yesterday, Today and tomorrow. 6, 1; 1990.

126. YUMBA (B). INTERNET in the Library: Potentials. African J of lib and Inf. Sc. 7, 2; 1997; 163-167.

127. WILSON(R). Digitizing a Readable E-book. Information Today and Tomorrow. 20, 3; 2001; 7-8.

128. XIE (HI). Evaluation of digital libraries: criteria and problems from user's perspective. Library and Information Research. 28; 2006; 433-452.

Index

F

G

I